ARTHURIAN STUDIES XXXVII

A COMPANION TO MALORY

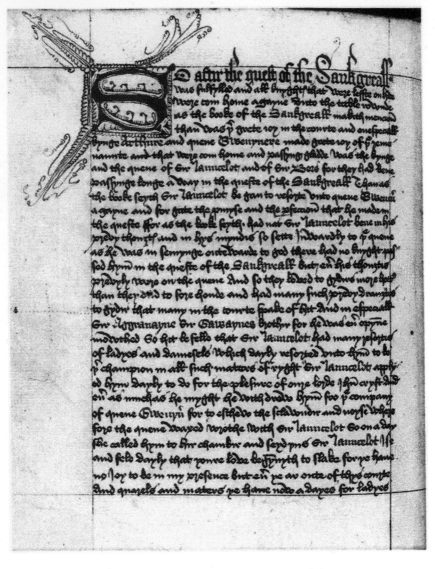

A page from the Winchester manuscript.
British Library, Additional MS 59678, fol. 409v
(Vinaver p. 611, Caxton Book XVIII; the
beginning of *The Book of Sir Lancelot and Queen Guinevere*)

A COMPANION TO
MALORY

EDITED BY

**Elizabeth Archibald and
A. S. G. Edwards**

D. S. BREWER

First published 1996
D. S. Brewer, Cambridge
Reprinted in paperback 1997, 2000

ISBN 085991 443 7 hardback
ISBN 085991 520 4 paperback

D. S. Brewer is an imprint of Boydell & Brewer Ltd
PO Box 9, Woodbridge, Suffolk IP12 3DF, UK
and of Boydell & Brewer Inc.
PO Box 41026, Rochester, NY 14604–4126, USA
website: http://www.boydell.co.uk

Arthurian Studies ISSN 0261–9814
Previously published volumes in the series
are listed at the back of this book

A catalogue record for this book is available
from the British Library

Library of Congress Catalog Card Number: 95-37294

This publication is printed on acid-free paper

Printed in Great Britain by
Athenæum Press Ltd, Gateshead, Tyne & Wear

Contents

Acknowledgements   ix

The Contributors   x

A Note on Malory's Text   xi

Introduction   *by Elizabeth Archibald and A. S. G. Edwards*   xiii

PART I.   MALORY IN CONTEXT

1. 'The Hoole Book': Editing and the Creation of Meaning in
   Malory's Text   3
   CAROL M. MEALE

2. Chivalry and the *Morte Darthur*   19
   RICHARD BARBER

3. The Place of Women in the *Morte Darthur*   37
   ELIZABETH EDWARDS

4. Contextualizing *Le Morte Darthur*: Empire and Civil War   55
   FELICITY RIDDY

5. Malory and His Sources   75
   TERENCE McCARTHY

6. Language and Style in Malory   97
   JEREMY SMITH

7. The Malory Life-Records   115
   P. J. C. FIELD

PART II.   THE ART OF THE *MORTE DARTHUR*

8. Beginnings: *The Tale of King Arthur* and *King Arthur and the
   Emperor Lucius*   133
   ELIZABETH ARCHIBALD

9. *The Tale of Sir Gareth* and *The Tale of Sir Lancelot*   153
   BARBARA NOLAN

10. *The Book of Sir Tristram de Lyones*   183
    HELEN COOPER

11. Malory and the Grail Legend   203
    JILL MANN

12. The Ending of the *Morte Darthur*   221
      C. DAVID BENSON

PART III.   POSTERITY

13. The Reception of Malory's *Morte Darthur*   241
      A. S. G. EDWARDS

14. A Selective Bibliography of Malory Studies   253
      ELIZABETH ARCHIBALD and A. S. G. EDWARDS

Index   256

We dedicate this volume to
DEREK BREWER
with affection and gratitude and
in acknowledgement of his many contributions
to Malory studies over the past forty years.

Acknowledgements

We are particularly grateful to all our contributors for the promptness and efficiency with which they have completed their chapters and to Diana Rutherford of the English Department at the University of Victoria for vital assistance in the final preparation of this volume. Thanks are due to the University of Victoria for a research grant to assist Dr Edwards in work on this volume.

The Contributors

ELIZABETH ARCHIBALD   Associate Professor of English, University of Victoria, British Columbia

RICHARD BARBER

C. DAVID BENSON   Professor of English, University of Connecticut

HELEN COOPER   Fellow of University College, Oxford

A. S. G. EDWARDS   Professor of English, University of Victoria, British Columbia

ELIZABETH EDWARDS   Lecturer in the Humanities, University of King's College, Halifax, Nova Scotia

P. J. C. FIELD   Professor of English, Department of English, University College of North Wales

JILL MANN   Professor of Medieval and Renaissance Literature, Cambridge University

TERENCE McCARTHY   Section d'anglais, Faculté de Langues, Université de Dijon

CAROL MEALE   Reader, Department of English, University of Bristol

BARBARA NOLAN   Professor of English, University of Virginia

FELICITY RIDDY   Professor of English, University of York

JEREMY SMITH   Lecturer, Department of English Language, University of Glasgow

A Note on Malory's Text

The standard edition of Malory is *The Works of Sir Thomas Malory*, ed. Eugène Vinaver, 3rd ed., rev. P. J. C. Field, 3 vols (Oxford, 1990). This great edition is beyond the means of most students. We have therefore cited throughout the one volume Oxford Standard Authors edition by Vinaver, 2nd ed. (Oxford, 1971). Citations from this edition are given parenthetically by page and line. We have, in addition, given after such citations references to Caxton's edition, cited by book and chapter. We refer to the Penguin edition, *Le Morte D'Arthur*, ed. Janet Cowen, 2 vols (Harmondsworth, 1969).

Readers should be aware that the text in Field's revision of Vinaver differs in some particulars from the Oxford Standard Authors edition. We have attempted to ensure that any quotations from the latter edition incorporate Field's revisions. They should also note that Caxton's edition varies in a number of important respects from the version of Malory in the Winchester manuscript. The Penguin edition of Caxton also modernizes the spelling and punctuation.

Some mention is appropriate here of the various ways of talking about sections of Malory's text. Vinaver's edition calls the work we generally refer to in this book as *Le Morte Darthur* (or 'the *Morte Darthur*') *The Works of Sir Thomas Malory*, which he defines as eight separate narratives variously described as either 'book' or 'tale' (for example, *The Book of Sir Launcelot and Queen Guinevere* and *The Most Piteous Tale of the Morte Arthur Saunz Guerdon*). He states in his edition that he has 'given each work the title which Malory himself assigned to it in his colophon' (p. ccxxv). This claim is not altogether correct. In the first place, it is not absolutely certain that all these titles were assigned by Malory himself. Secondly, the forms of title given in the colophons of the manuscript are not invariably those Vinaver employs. For example, the title of the first of Vinaver's divisions *The Tale of King Arthur* (I, 1–180) does not have any manuscript authority. The second, *The Tale of the Noble Kynge Arthure*, is also called in the colophon *The Noble Tale betwyxt Kynge Arthure and Lucius the Emperour of Rome*. (Vinaver confuses the matter further by using the first form as his title, but a version of the second as his running-title.) *The Book of Sir Tristram de Lyones* is actually divided in the manuscript into two separate books (Vinaver, p. 343). But Vinaver's forms of titles are generally used to identify the divisions of Malory's work. The reader should, however, be aware that other forms of citation are also used by scholars. For example, the concluding sections of the work are sometimes referred to as Parts 7 and 8.

In talking about individual parts of the work (Vinaver's 'book' or 'tale') we have generally followed the forms of title in Vinaver's edition. These titles have been capitalized according to modern usage and italicized. These section titles have generally been differentiated from the titles for particular episodes within parts, which are capitalized according to modern usage and printed in Roman type; for example: The Red City, The Great Tournament, The Day of Destiny.

While we have tried to impose a general level of uniformity on such references to the various divisions of Malory's work, we are conscious that there is no completely standard way of referring to them. We have not sought to achieve an absolute consistency where the circumstances of a particular discussion seemed to warrant some alternative way of talking about sections of the text. If this seems confusing and/or inconsistent it is at least a reflection of the general situation in this aspect of Malory studies.

Introduction

ELIZABETH ARCHIBALD
A. S. G. EDWARDS

The popularity of Thomas Malory's *Morte Darthur* has proved astonishingly enduring. For over five hundred years it has retained an appeal that, with the exception of Chaucer's works, no other work of medieval English literature has sustained. This volume is by its nature an acknowledgement of both the continuing power of that appeal and the distance that separates us, as modern readers, from Malory's book. It is primarily an attempt to bridge that distance by offering a series of inter-related studies that will explore important aspects of Malory's work and offer new critical evaluations of its various parts.

Any account of the *Morte Darthur* must begin with Caxton. He was its first publisher in 1485, and for nearly four hundred and fifty years Malory's work was synonymous with Caxton's edition. The discovery of a manuscript in Winchester College Library in 1934 (it is now in the British Library) revealed the extent to which Caxton had altered the shape, and sometimes the style and content, of Malory's text. The evidence of the manuscript establishes him as the earliest editor of the work. Caxton never approached the publication of the *Morte* merely as a printer. It is clear that he took particular care to reshape his source text into a form that emphasized the narrative coherence of the work as a whole while simultaneously seeking to make it as accessible as possible to his readers.

Comparison of manuscript and printed text has introduced a complex of new issues into Malory scholarship, issues that have become even more complicated with the subsequent discovery that Caxton actually had the Winchester manuscript in his shop at the time he was preparing his edition. Chief among these has been the question of the unity of the work. Eugène Vinaver, who produced the first edition based on the manuscript in 1947, elected to call it not *Le Morte Darthur* but *The Works of Sir Thomas Malory*. He argues that Caxton's editorial interventions were an effort to present the appearance of a single seamless narrative for a text that, in fact, comprises separate narratives. The issue of whether the work is really a single unified narrative, what Malory terms 'the hoole book' or a collection of separate tales, as Vinaver has urged, has been central to modern criticism of the *Morte*.

Modern scholarship has shed new light on other aspects of Malory's undertaking. In his Preface Caxton affirmed the comprehensiveness of the vision of noble conduct in the *Morte*:

> [it] treateth of the noble acts, feats of arms and chivalry, prowess, hardines, humanity, love, courtesy, and very gentleness, with many wonderful histories and adventures.

'Noble' is the adjective that echoes most insistently through his account of the work. The insistence on noble conduct here and in the actual narrative has become a paradox of Malory scholarship. For, as research has made clear, Sir Thomas Malory of Newbold Revell, now established as the author, is identified in contemporary records as thief, rapist, would-be murderer and oft-imprisoned felon: he tells us himself that he was writing *Le Morte Darthur* while in prison. Much of his recorded criminal activity can be linked to the Wars of the Roses, the divisive internal conflict that racked England in the latter part of the fifteenth century.

Malory's involvement in this civil war was typical of his class. He belonged to a growing class of provincial gentry, one distinct from the nobility, but bound to it by ties of personal loyalty and the possibility of advancement. The final pages of the *Morte* draw a number of insistent parallels between the collapse of the Round Table and the situation 'nowadays' in ways that feelingly suggest personal experience. Such experience was not untypical among the gentry who had been exposed most directly to the shifting fortunes and loyalties of the Wars of the Roses in which Malory fought and as a consequence of which he was imprisoned. Malory's creation of an imagined chivalric past in the *Morte Darthur* speaks to a general sense of the gap between such a past and contemporary English political reality. And the Englishness of Malory's narrative may have seemed particularly relevant in 1485, the year of Caxton's first publication of the *Morte* and also the year of the battle of Bosworth Field that signalled the end of the Wars of the Roses and the establishing of the Tudor dynasty with the accession of Henry VII. It is perhaps this sense of contemporary relevance that governs Caxton's insistence on the conception of the *Morte Darthur* as a work of historical writing. In his Preface Caxton talks at length about the historicity of Arthur and his knights, and cites both written and archaeological evidence. The contemporary interest in an Arthurian past reflected in Malory's undertaking can be plausibly related to the cultural, political and social situations in which he lived and wrote.

Malory's choice of form for his subject signifies a new direction for Middle English prose. *Le Morte Darthur* is the first major work of secular prose fiction in English. The decision to write in English prose can be seen, in its deliberateness, as a decision comparable with Chaucer's to write in English verse a century earlier. Just as before Chaucer there were only attenuated traditions of English verse writing, so before Malory there was little in the tradition of English prose fiction that leads on to prose romance.

There are, admittedly, a few earlier fifteenth-century prose works which literary history has sometimes rather uncomfortably categorized as romances: the unique manuscripts of the *Life of Alexander*, copied in the north of England c. 1440, the mid-fifteenth century *King Ponthus* and *Ipomedon C*, the translation of Merlin (extant in two manuscripts), *The Siege of Jerusalem*. But Malory does not seem to have been aware of these precursors. His vernacular debts are most clearly to Middle English Arthurian narratives in verse, the Stanzaic *Morte Arthur* and Alliterative *Morte Arthure*. He also was familiar with the verse account of Arthur in the *Chronicle* of John Hardyng. With his *Morte Darthur* English prose became for the first time a medium for extended fictional writing, offering a precedent, if not a model, that was to remain in circulation throughout the sixteenth and early seventeenth centuries, during the period when English prose came to establish itself as a significant form of imaginative literature.

The chief inspiration for this decision was, however, primarily French in source and genre. The materials from which Malory constructed his work were, in Caxton's words 'taken oute of certeyn bookes of Frensshe and . . . reduced into Englysshe.' Although, as we have noted, Malory did draw significantly on some Middle English Arthurian verse narratives in the *Morte*, his main source was the influential Vulgate Cycle, the series of French prose romances composed in the early part of the thirteenth century (in particular the *Lancelot*, the *Queste del Saint Graal* and the *Mort Artu*). He also used the slightly later *Suite du Merlin*, and the enormous – and enormously popular – prose *Tristan*. The effect of the reworking of these various source materials was to create an English prose Arthuriad that was to influence the writing of historical fiction, in prose and verse, from the sixteenth century to the present.

The aim of this Companion is to render Malory's achievement more accessible to modern readers. The plan is quite straightforward. The opening section offers a series of contexts for our understanding of Malory's work, including discussion of such historical questions as the nature of chivalry and the relationship between Malory's account of Arthurian history and those of earlier writers. There are, in addition, examinations of particularly important aspects of Malory: his biography, his treatment of women and chivalry, his sources, his style and the issues raised by the various forms of the work as we now have it, manuscript, printed book and critical edition. The middle section is a series of new readings of each of the major sections of the *Morte Darthur*. The final section consists of a brief account of the reception and influence of the *Morte* and a selective guide to further reading.

PART I

MALORY IN CONTEXT

1

'The Hoole Book': Editing and the Creation of Meaning in Malory's Text

CAROL M. MEALE

In 1934 the phrase which Malory used to describe his Arthurian compendium – 'the hoole book of kyng Arthur & of his noble knyghtes of the rounde table' (726; XXI.13) – took on a new resonance. For in this year Walter Oakeshott identified a manuscript lacking its opening leaves in a safe in the Warden's bedroom at Winchester College as a manuscript copy of Malory's text, and as a result of this discovery, the book known for four and a half centuries to scholars and general readers alike only from versions deriving from William Caxton's print of 1485 was now understood by a modern audience to have existed in two, very different, states.[1]

The finding was of significance in several respects. To begin with, the text as preserved in the manuscript offered additional autobiographical information about the author of the book, known after Caxton's appellation as the *Morte Darthur*, in the colophons which concluded many of the constituent tales. The writer's envoy, as printed by Caxton,[2] had included a request for prayers by the 'Jentyl men and Jantyl wymmen' who read the book 'of Arthur and his knyghtes,' 'that god sende' him 'good delyueraunce' while he was alive (sig. ee vi). The hint here that 'syr Thomas Maleore knyght' was restrained in some way was confirmed by authorial statements such as that on fol. 70^v of the manuscript, where the writer referred to himself as 'a knyght presoner,' whilst elsewhere he requested prayers for 'good delyueraunce sone and hastely' and invoked the name of

---

[1] W. F. Oakeshott, 'The Finding of the Manuscript,' in *Essays on Malory*, ed. J. A.W. Bennett (Oxford, 1963), pp. 1–6. For the respective versions of the text see *The Winchester Malory: A Facsimile*, with an Introduction by N. R. Ker, EETS Supplementary Series 4 (1976); and the facsimile of the only complete extant copy of the earliest print, *Sir Thomas Malory: Le Morte D'Arthur, Printed by William Caxton in 1485* . . . with an introduction by Paul Needham (London, 1976).

[2] Despite the fact that Malory's text is now known in manuscript as well as printed form it is still necessary to rely on Caxton for Malory's conclusion, since the last gathering of the codex is missing, as well as the first. For details on the quiring see Ker, intro. to *The Winchester Malory*, pp. ix, x–xi.

Jesus in prayers for aid (fols 148, 409, 449). But the importance of the
Winchester codex for Malory studies was not confined to the new
biographical details it offered. Reading its pages, the lineaments of another
form of the text became clear, one in which the narrative structure was of a
different order to that now seen to have been imposed by Caxton in his
printshop. The finding, therefore, apparently brought modern readers closer
to the author of the Arthuriad and to the text which he wrote, even though,
as the work of two scribes, it was immediately evident that it was not a
holograph copy.[3] The critical furore initiated by the identification is one which
continues to fuel discussions of Malory as a creative writer. The questions
which have most frequently been addressed in the course of extensive and
often heated debate concern Malory's procedures as a translator of French
– and to a lesser extent, as an adaptor of English – romance, and the theories
and practices of narrative composition in the late medieval period.[4]

The initiatory move in this debate was made by Eugène Vinaver in his
first edition of Malory, published in 1947.[5] Readers of Caxton were
accustomed to a text mediated in such a way as to create little difficulty of
interpretation for those familiar with the various structures adopted later
by the writers of novels: the organization of the narrative into chapters lent
an internal logic and momentum to events which, if presented differently,
would appear merely episodic. Vinaver's designation of the text as
preserved in the codex as the *Works*, on the other hand, called into question
the notion of narrative unities. His decision as to how to entitle his edition
carried the implication that new interpretative strategies on the part of critics
were required: he believed that Malory's methods of approaching the task
of translating a variety of earlier Arthurian romances varied over time; he
also felt that Malory's attitude towards the individual tales, as this could be
reconstructed from authorial remarks at their conclusions, demonstrated
that he viewed them as separate entities.[6] The framework which he

[3] For discussion of the apportioning of work between the two scribes (one of whom was
     clearly more experienced than the other in the copying of books, as opposed to other
     kinds of documents, and who seems to have acted as an instructor) see Ker, *The
     Winchester Malory*, pp. xiii–xiv. And for an account of scribal errors in the manuscript,
     which indicate this copy's distance from Malory's original text, see, e.g., Ker, p. xvii and,
     more recently, Tomomi Kato, 'Some Scribal Differences in Malory,' in *Arthurian and
     Other Studies presented to Shunichi Noguchi*, ed. Takashi Suzuki and Tsuyoshi Mukai
     (Cambridge, 1993), pp. 189–99.
[4] For bibliography on Malory see Page West Life, *Sir Thomas Malory and the Morte Darthur,
     A Survey of Scholarship and Annotated Bibliography* (Charlottesville, 1980); Toshiyuki
     Takamiya, 'A Bibliography to Aspects of Malory,' in *Aspects of Malory*, ed. Toshiyuki
     Takamiya and Derek Brewer, rev. ed. (Cambridge, 1986), pp. 179–93; N. F. Blake, *William
     Caxton: A Bibliographical Guide* (New York, 1985). These guides constitute an invaluable
     supplement to the literary/critical discussion which follows, which is, of necessity,
     highly selective.
[5] *The Works of Sir Thomas Malory*, ed. Eugène Vinaver, 3 vols (Oxford, 1947).
[6] *The Works of Sir Thomas Malory*, ed. Eugène Vinaver, 3rd ed. rev. P. J. C. Field (Oxford,

constructed for reading Malory was one based on his extensive knowledge of French Arthurian texts, themselves of disparate origin and date, but which collectively offered a 'history' of the Round Table and its founder.[7] His disquiet with the idea that 'the hoole book' was anything other than a publisher's construction even extended to suggesting that Caxton's copy-text was not *physically* whole, in that he may have worked from a series of separate volumes.[8]

The most influential critique offered in response to the position adopted by Vinaver was formulated by Derek Brewer in his essay on 'the hoole book' published in 1963. Whilst acknowledging the essential difference of the manuscript text from that of Caxton he argued that, nevertheless, there was a thematic 'connectedness' between the constituent 'works' that gave evidence of a 'sense of continuity' based on 'the unity of atmosphere and the continuous moral concern' and 'the chronological continuity of the main events and characters,' a continuity emphasized 'by significant references back and forward to important characters and events' and 'by links between the various tales.'[9] Brewer's essentially liberal, generous interpretation of the idea, as opposed to the material substance, of 'the hoole book' continues to command respect, as Andrea Clough's essay demonstrates; here, the connotations of 'hoole' are expanded to include the metaphorical, as she explores the images 'of physical health, spiritual well-being, and the political unity of the fellowship of the Round Table' employed by Malory throughout his writing.[10]

The most controversial response to Vinaver's theories, though, came in a volume of essays edited in 1964 by the American critic, R. M. Lumiansky, the informing principle of which was that Malory did, *contra* Vinaver, write 'a single unified book.' The premise underlying the collection was that, irrespective of how he may have set about achieving it, the creation of unity was Malory's 'final intention.'[11] The viability of this interpretation necessitated a complex exposition by individual contributors of the process

---

1990), pp. xxxvi–xxxvii; the colophons were mostly excised by Caxton, as observed by Vinaver. It may be noted here that Vinaver's editorial process was not confined to attempting to establish the existence of a number of separate 'works,' but extended to the imposition of further divisions within the text for which there is little or no authority within the manuscript: see below, pp. 15–17.

7 *The Works of Sir Thomas Malory*, 3rd ed., I, chapter III of the introduction; see also Vinaver's discussion of Malory in *The Rise of Romance* (Oxford, 1971), esp. pp. 123–39.

8 *The Works of Sir Thomas Malory*, 3rd ed., I, p. xxxvi.

9 D. S. Brewer, ' "the hoole book," ' in *Essays in Malory*, ed. Bennett, pp. 41–63 (pp. 59, 61).

10 Andrea Clough, 'Malory's *Morte Darthur*: The "Hoole Book," ' *Medievalia et Humanistica*, n.s. 14 (1986), 139–56 (p. 139).

11 *Malory's Originality: A Critical Study of Le Morte Darthur*, ed. R. M. Lumiansky (Baltimore, 1964); the quotation is taken from the introduction, p. 4. See also the rebuttal of the approach adopted by the contributors to that volume included first of all in Vinaver's second edition of Malory (1967) and reprinted in *The Works of Sir Thomas Malory*, 3rd ed., I, pp. xli–li.

of composition, including the notion of 'retrospective narratives' to account for the incompatibility of various aspects of chronology and incident within the tales. The remaining inconsistencies within the text, such as the resurrection of knights whose deaths are recorded earlier in the book, however, resist analysis in this way, suggesting either that Vinaver was correct in his assumption of there being a number of separate works, or that Malory himself never carried out a final revision of his completed text which would have eliminated such contradictions.[12]

The centrality of critical notions of narrative coherence has in recent years been displaced, to some extent, as a consequence of the combined influence of developments within the fields of literary theory and manuscript studies. Felicity Riddy's study, for example, in which she seeks to locate Malory culturally, recognizes the inherent 'instability' of the text in respect of both local detail and overall design, and offers readings of its constituent parts by analogy with the diverse contents of manuscript miscellanies contemporary with the author: just as English romances, when they are included in such miscellanies, take on additional meanings from the texts with which they are juxtaposed – whether these are saints' lives, courtesy books, or historical pieces – so diverse interests and genres are invoked, and in part incorporated, by Malory within his re-writing of the Arthurian story.[13]

This process of historicization is one which can only be enriched by a closer examination of the manuscript and the early print. Oakeshott's discovery, or recovery, of the former has enabled scholars to explore how the text was presented to and received by Malory's earliest readers. That is, as a preliminary, it has become possible to document the changes between manuscript and print, and to examine these changes in relation to manuscript production, and subsequent publishing policy and print-shop practice. But by looking at the text's presentation from the point of view of its potential audience(s), it also becomes possible to offer a partial reconstruction of the cultural framework in which the work was embedded, and of the expectations and reading practices which it embodies. Analysis of lay-out and decoration, of the *mise-en-page*, for instance, not only describes scribal and print-shop habits, but also provides insights into the multiplicity of ways in which the text could, and can, be read, at the same time establishing a context in which to place more recent editorial theory and convention.

Caxton's edition of Malory, issued by him on 31 July 1485, was one of the printer/publisher's most substantial productions, running to 432 folios, or

---

[12] Ellyn Olefsky, 'Chronology, Factual Consistency, and the Problem of Unity in Malory,' *Journal of English and Germanic Philology*, 68 (1969), 57–73, remains the most perceptive account of the contradictions within the narrative.

[13] Felicity Riddy, *Sir Thomas Malory* (Leiden, 1987); the reference to instability is taken from p. 28.

863 printed pages. In his preface, which acted in no small measure as a publisher's advertisement in which the virtues of the book were proclaimed,[14] Caxton stated that he had 'deuyded' the text 'in to xxj bookes and euery book chapytred as here after shal by goddes grace folowe,' and he takes the opportunity in the table of contents which follows to list the subject-matter of each division and sub-division within the book. There are five hundred and six chapters altogether, but these are not distributed with any regularity between the twenty-one books: Book Fifteen, for instance, which details Lancelot's early adventures in his search for the Holy Grail, contains only six, whereas Book Ten, which concentrates on the exploits of Tristram, has eighty-eight. These are, though, the outside limits; the majority of the books (fourteen out of twenty-one) comprise between ten and twenty-five chapters. There is, similarly, some variation in length between these sub-divisions but most of the chapters (as a rough calculation will indicate) are short, extending from only one to three pages.

The assumption that this narrative structure was the one adopted by Malory in the drawing-out of his sources into English prose (the descriptive phrase is Malory's own, employed in his colophons), in the absence of any other version, was not questioned prior to 1934, despite Caxton's affirmation that he was responsible for the division of the text; criticism of the *Morte Darthur* was accordingly predicated on the evidence offered by the earliest printed edition. The identification of the manuscript, however, turned much of this criticism on its head, for the differences between the two texts were so great that it became clear that the object of this earlier critical discourse had been Caxton's actions as editor rather than Malory's as translator and adaptor.

The manuscript, now British Library MS Additional 59678, is as substantial as the Caxton print. It comprises 473 folios or 946 pages although, as noted above, there are two gatherings lost, one from the beginning and one from the end of the volume, and in addition there are three folios missing from the body of the codex. A precise date for the compilation of the manuscript is impossible to determine. The evidence offered by analysis of palaeographical features and the watermarks of the paper alone is insufficient;[15] but, given the statement in the final colophon that Malory completed his writing in 'the ix yere of the reygne of kyng edward the fourth,' the book clearly cannot pre-date 1470 (Edward's ninth regnal year ran from 4 March 1469 to 3 March 1470), whilst it was certainly in existence by the time that Caxton had finished preparing his edition, since Lotte Hellinga has proved through forensic examination of offsets of type on its pages that it was in Caxton's printing shop between 1480 and 1483.[16]

---

[14] N. F. Blake, 'Caxton Prepares His Edition of the *Morte Darthur*,' *Journal of Librarianship*, 8 (1976), 272–85.

[15] Ker, *The Winchester Malory*, p. xiv.

[16] Lotte Hellinga, 'The Malory Manuscript and Caxton,' in *Aspects of Malory*, ed. Takamiya

Unlike the printed version, the manuscript contains no chapter headings as such (although there are some marginal glosses, an aspect of the lay-out which I shall refer to in more detail in due course). As a consequence, the volume perhaps appears at first glance to be decidedly user-unfriendly to a modern eye. There is, though, an extensive decorative programme consisting of various types and sizes of embellished initials, and this hierarchy of decoration acts as a formal scheme of division within the narrative. There are, for example, three major breaks marked, which divide the text into four sections. These occur at folios 71, 349, and 409^v (marking the beginnings of Vinaver's 'tales' of The Noble King Arthur, p. 113; the Sankgreal, p. 515; and Sir Launcelot and Queen Guinevere, p. 611). The initials here are respectively five, three, and five-line lombards, embellished with filigree penwork.[17] That on fol. 349 is of blue ink flourished with red; those on fols 71 and 409^v of a slightly dull scarlet. It is probable that the same hand was responsible for executing these initials, but it is not possible to identify the rubricator with either of the scribes; it may well be that the work was carried out by an independent book-artist once copying of the text was finished.

Other breaks within the work are marked with less emphasis. There are, for example, one hundred and eight two- or three-line lombard initials coloured in red distributed throughout the book. Nine of these divisions, including the three marked with the most extensively decorated initials, receive additional emphasis through the use of red ink and a more formal anglicana or textura 'display' script in the copying of surrounding portions of text. Each of these visual breaks is, furthermore, linked with a hiatus of some sort within the text itself. In four (fols 70^v, 346^v, 409^v, 449) the author names himself (on fol. 70^v, as mentioned above, as 'a knyght presoner Sir Thomas Malleorr') and prays for God's help and deliverance. Elsewhere there is a simple explicit to whichever tale has just concluded, sometimes followed by an incipit to the following one. Folio 34, copied by the scribe designated as A by Neil Ker, for instance, contains the lines 'Thus endith the tale of Balyn + Balan ij brethirne that were borne in Northumbirlonde that were ij passynge good knyghts as euer were in þo dayes,' followed by 'Explicit' written in red ink (Vinaver, 59/8–11). The next section begins with no preamble, although the opening five words are highlighted by being copied in a formal script, again in red: 'In the begynnyng of Arthure aftir he was chosyn kynge . . .'. Folio 113, on the other hand, the work of scribe B, contains both explicit and incipit: 'Explicit a noble tale of Sir launcelot du lake Here folowyth Sir Gareth is tale of Orkeney þat was callyd Bewmaynes By Sir kay' (Vinaver, 173/9–177/1–2). The story of Gareth begins directly

and Brewer, pp. 127–41 (revised version of the article in The British Library Journal, 3 [1977], 91–101).

[17] For some of the terminology used here see Lucia N. Valentine, Ornament in Medieval Manuscripts: A Glossary (London, 1965).

after, at the head of the following page but, unlike the example I have just cited, it is not distinguished by the use of different script or ink. Too much weight should not, though, be attached to the difference in treatment accorded these, and other, divisions within the book, reflecting as they in all probability do, differences in scribal training and practice: scribe A, for instance, routinely signals breaks in the text through a change to red ink, whereas scribe B does not. In total there are one hundred and eleven breaks marked within the manuscript, and one hundred and seven of these coincide with Caxton's chapter divisions, nineteen of them occurring at the beginning of his constituent books.

Other forms of what may be called reading apparatus are also supplied in the surviving manuscript. Marginal glosses, for example, written in red and sometimes framed within roughly-drawn shields or other geometric shapes are to be found scattered throughout the volume. The glosses not infrequently coincide approximately with other of the chapter divisions to be found in Caxton's version. In twenty-eight instances the correlation between manuscript side-note and printed chapters is sufficiently close to appear significant (this total includes two occasions on which glosses coincide with the occurrence of lombard initials, and in addition another nine instances may be cited where a gloss is written either just above, or just below, breaks in the narrative which are signalled by similar capitals). The occurrence of glosses is more frequent in the earlier sections of the manuscript – twenty-one of the total of eighty appear on the first forty-two folios – and a greater number are found on the pages copied by scribe A: forty-six, as opposed to the thirty-four added by scribe B. Neil Ker suggests that the glosses derive from the scribes' exemplar,[18] but his observation may be amplified. The clustering of side-notes in certain passages of text, and the differing rates of their appearance in the work of the two scribes, for instance, imply either that scribe B was less conscientious than A in the exactness of his copying (and perhaps also that A himself became less careful as copying proceeded); or that the exemplar itself lacked consistency in its employment of such aids to reading. A later user of the manuscript (though how late it is difficult to determine) added her or his own marginal annotations, which in general take the form of hands which point to the text; there are six instances of this form of glossing altogether, and it seems that this reader soon lost the impetus to add any kind of apparatus, since all occur within the opening twenty-nine folios.[19]

---

[18] Ker, *The Winchester Malory*, p. xvii.

[19] The marginal additions on fol. 23 are interesting, in that a pointing hand occurs in conjunction with a gloss written in a hand later than that of either of the text's two scribes. On the basis of palaeographical features I would tentatively date this gloss to c.1500: it may be that the same person was responsible for this note (which, curiously, coincides with the beginning of Caxton's Book II chapter 2) and all the pointing hands in the manuscript.

Another important system of visual organization of the text is the high-lighting of proper names within the narrative by the use of red ink. The standard facsimile of the manuscript, necessarily predominantly in black-and-white, cannot adequately convey the importance of this feature of the book's production.[20] Although the Additional manuscript is not unusual amongst fifteenth-century hand-produced books in receiving this kind of detailing,[21] the care which was taken in its execution in the Malory book is: for it would seem that, rather than the names being filled in after copying was completed, which would have been more economical in terms of both labour and expenditure on ink, the scribes changed pens and ink on each occasion when names were required to be distinguished.[22] The effect of the changes in ink is considerable. In conjunction with the glosses, this form of highlighting enables a reader to find her or his way around the text more readily. It constitutes a form of signposting within the text which is formalized by the introduction of chapter breaks in Caxton's edition.[23]

The exact nature of the relationship between the manuscript and Caxton's print remains open to debate. Eugène Vinaver early ruled out any possibility of a connection between the two, designating them 'collateral versions of a common original,'[24] but Dr Hellinga's findings, establishing beyond any reasonable doubt that the manuscript was, indeed, in Caxton's hands at some stage whilst he was actively engaged in editing the work for the press, re-opened the debate. The recent argument, advanced by Peter Field, that Caxton may well have used the only surviving codex as a supplementary copy-text to that which he employed as his primary source, is convincing in relation to the similarities and differences between the two texts, and plausible with regard to Caxton's editorial procedures as these may be reconstructed generally.[25] Yet, as modern readers, we remain at a

---

[20] Pages containing roll-calls of knights associated with Arthur's court are particularly striking; see, e.g., fols 14[v], 15, 411, 446[r–v], 447, 454, 457[v], 469[v].

[21] See, e.g., amongst other romance manuscripts, the copy of *Generides* in New York, Pierpont Morgan Library MS M 876.

[22] Proof that the names were written in contemporaneously with the copying of the text is given by scribal errors: e.g. in line 7 of fol. 113 scribe B has mistakenly written out 'launcelot' and corrected it to 'kay' before carrying on with the narrative; cf. fols 152[v], 239, 242, 318, 333, 343, 465[v].

[23] De Worde carried this process of 'signposting' further in his 1498 edition of the *Morte*, in his introduction of illustrations and in the changes he instituted in the format of the text: e.g. by introducing double columns of text, by using a larger typeface for chapter headings, and by spacing these headings and the colophons to create an effect of separation. Little work has hitherto been carried out on the visual aspects of de Worde's Malory, but see Edward Hodnett, *English Woodcuts 1480–1535*, rev. ed. (Oxford, 1973), pp. 14, 16, 17 and pp. 303, 309–12 (nos 1265–84, 1224), and figs 84–5; also Muriel Whitaker, 'Illustrating Caxton's Malory,' in *Studies in Malory*, ed. James W. Spisak (Kalamazoo, 1985), pp. 297–319 (pp. 298–302).

[24] *The Works of Sir Thomas Malory*, ed. Vinaver, 3rd ed., I, p. ciii.

[25] P. J. C. Field, 'The Earliest Texts of Malory's *Morte Darthur*,' *Poetica*, 38 (1993), 18–31; cf. Sally Shaw, 'Caxton and Malory,' in *Essays in Malory*, ed. Bennett, pp. 114–45. On the

remove from what Malory actually wrote. There are sufficient scribal errors within the manuscript itself, and a sufficient number of instances where the Caxton print clearly retains better readings, to cast doubt on the closeness of the codex to Malory's holograph.[26] The consequent impossibility of attributing greater authority to one or the other of the versions confuses the issue of the authorship of certain passages or stories, such as that of the Roman War, where the stylistic and linguistic changes between the two imply wholesale revision.[27] In spite of these difficulties of interpretation, comparison of the arrangement of the text in the manuscript and the print, and the high level of coincidence between the divisions marked within each, suggests that it may be possible to attribute those elements of narrative structure common to both to authorial intention.

Alive though Caxton may have been to the desirability of making texts more accessible to his potential readers in terms of their presentation, the process of creating a more obviously episodic narrative structure may also have been dictated by commercial considerations. As I have already observed, he added a preface to the book which acted as a form of summary and endorsement of its contents – the 'noble actes feates of armes of chyualrye prowesse hardynesse humanyte loue curtosye and veray gentylnesse wyth many wonderful hystoryes and aduentures'; as he exhorts his readers to 'Doo after the good and leue the euyl' (Preface, sig A iii^{r-v}; Vinaver, p. xv) the effect of this introduction is to underline the work's status as both an exemplary and an entertaining text. But Caxton also took care to situate the work in relation to contemporary debates over the historical veracity of Arthur. Through the device of recounting a (presumably fictional) discussion in his printshop with 'many noble and dyuers gentylmen,'[28] he is able to refer to current scepticism regarding the existence of the British king, entering into the dialogue by citing the survival within Britain of various Arthurian relics (including that of

more general issue of the rationale underlying Caxton's editorial practices see, e.g., N. F. Blake, *Caxton and His World* (London, 1969) and *Caxton: England's First Publisher* (London, 1976); George D. Painter, *William Caxton: A Quincentenary Biography of England's First Printer* (London, 1976); and Lotte Hellinga, *Caxton in Focus: the Beginning of Printing in England* (London, 1982).

[26] The most authoritative account of the relationship is that of Field, 'The Earliest Texts of Malory's *Morte Darthur*,' and cf. Toshiyuki Takamiya, 'Editor/Compositor at Work: the Case of Caxton's Malory,' in *Arthurian and Other Studies*, ed. Suzuki and Mukai, pp. 143–51.

[27] On the relationship between the texts of the heavily alliterative verse romance of the *Morte Arthure*, Malory, and Caxton, see John Withrington, 'Caxton, Malory, and The Roman War in *The Morte Darthur*,' *Studies in Philology*, 89 (1992), 350–66. The conclusion reached here is that Caxton's 'candidacy' for the textual revisions 'must remain the stronger' (p. 366).

[28] Blake, 'Caxton Prepares His Edition of the *Morte Darthur*,' p. 273, but cf. Lotte Hellinga, 'Manuscripts in the Hands of Printers,' *Manuscripts in the Fifty Years after the Invention of Printing*, ed. J. B. Trapp (London, 1983), pp. 6–7, on Caxton's revised edition of *The Canterbury Tales* for a possible modification of this view.

Gawain's skull, said to be preserved at Dover castle), and then appealing to an emergent sense of patriotism by stating the case for the publication of a book of Arthurian feats in English on the basis that accounts of Arthur could be found – and by implication, purchased – in nearly every other European language. Prefaces were certainly not unknown in manuscript culture, but it took the advent of printing in England to institutionalize them, as it were, to exploit them for their marketing potential.[29]

The other changes which Caxton introduced to the text may also have had their genesis in continental practice, and his importation of ideas from other countries regarding the organization and presentation of literary texts emphasizes the extent to which England continued to participate in a European culture in the late Middle Ages. Chapter divisions, for example, often additionally signalled by illustrations, had been a feature of copies of the French Arthurian cycle from its inception.[30] The taste for prose romance as a genre, too, may have owed much to continental precedent. Caxton himself had a number of substantial prose romances in his publications list: indeed, the history of Troy by the Burgundian writer, Raoul Le Fèvre, had been his first publication in Bruges, in 1473–4.[31] It has frequently been suggested that Caxton was influenced in his choice of texts to print by his desire to emulate the fashionable reading-matter of the Burgundian ducal court, and England's ties with Burgundy were certainly close at this period: not only was there intermarrying between members of the English and Burgundian nobility which led to sustained (if not always easy) political ties, but Burgundy was also an important trading partner. Caxton himself, whilst pursuing his career as a Merchant Adventurer, lived in Bruges for many years as Governor of the English Nation.[32] But it would be a mistake to overestimate the importance of this one continental connection to the exclusion of others; the so-called Hundred Years War with France was only recently concluded when Caxton set up business in Westminster in 1476, and there is ample evidence amongst surviving manuscripts to suggest that French books, and amongst them many lengthy prose romances, were brought back to England with other kinds of cultural booty by returning

---

[29] See A. S. G. Edwards and Carol M. Meale, 'The Marketing of Printed Books in Late Medieval England,' *The Library*, 6th ser. 15 (1993), 95–124.

[30] See, e.g., Cedric E. Pickford, 'An Arthurian Manuscript in the John Rylands Library,' *Bulletin of the John Rylands Library*, 31 (1948), 318–44.

[31] For the most complete listing of his publications, including the romances, see Paul Needham, *The Printer and the Pardoner: an unrecorded indulgence printed by William Caxton for the hospital of St Mary Rounceval, Charing Cross* (Washington, 1986), pp. 83–91.

[32] See, e.g., Diane Bornstein, 'William Caxton's Chivalric Romances and the Burgundian Renaissance in England,' *English Studies*, 57 (1976), 1–10, on the case for influence extending from the Burgundian ducal court; but for a qualified interpretation, which stresses the importance of considering the possibility of the influence of other, contemporary, book collections cf. Lotte Hellinga, 'Caxton and the Bibliophiles,' *Actes du XIe Congrès International de Bibliophilie* (Brussels, 1981), 11–38. For accounts of Caxton's career see, e.g., Blake, *Caxton and His World*, and Painter, *William Caxton*.

English soldiers and statesmen. In other words, there would appear to have been an established taste in England for the kind of romance texts which Caxton published long before he set up his press. By issuing romances such as the *Morte Darthur* he could be seen to have been catering for this taste, and at the same time maximizing his market potential by providing English translations.[33] French may have retained its status as the language of international culture well into the sixteenth century, but English had a greater appeal to the native book-buying public, with its broader social base.

The attempt to reconstruct the cultural context within which Malory himself worked is more problematic. There was little tradition of composing English prose romance prior to his period of activity as a translator,[34] and there was virtually no precedent amongst copies of secular works which could have suggested ways of organizing a narrative and presenting it in material form, in a manuscript.[35] And it is not even certain, as observed, what relation the sole extant copy of his compendium bore to the text as he originally wrote it. But what is certain is that the influence exerted upon later generations of readers by Caxton's version – itself the result of the combined pressures of the transference of a work from manuscript into print, and the operation of particular cultural and commercial circumstances – has served to suppress readings of the text which were available to fifteenth-century audiences and which may be recovered in part by a study of MS Additional 59678.

Perhaps the most significant of these readings – and the most startling, to those of us now most accustomed to the appearance of the text as established by Vinaver – is the division of the work into four major sections, the subject-matter of each of which corresponds with a particular phase in the Arthurian history.[36] These sections are of unequal length, as I have implied in my discussion of the hierarchy of decoration within the

---

[33] See Carol M. Meale, 'Caxton, de Worde and the Publication of Romance in Late-Medieval England,' *The Library*, 6th ser. 14 (1992), 283–98.

[34] See Derek Pearsall, 'The English Romance in the Fifteenth Century,' *Essays and Studies*, n.s. 29 (1976), 56–83; George R. Keiser, 'The Romances,' in *Middle English Prose: A Critical Guide to Major Authors and Genres*, ed. A. S. G. Edwards (New Brunswick, 1984), pp. 271–89.

[35] It might, perhaps, be worth looking at manuscript copies of the Middle English *Brut*, the most popular and widely-circulating of non-religious prose texts in fifteenth-century England, to see whether any comparisons may be drawn between the lay-out adopted here by the various scribes, and that followed by the scribes of the Additional MS. For a survey of fifteenth-century prose texts in general see *Middle English Prose*, ed. Edwards.

[36] This interpretation of the manuscript evidence as it affects the issue of narrative structure differs from that of Murray J. Evans in his articles 'The Explicits and Narrative Division in the Winchester MS: A Critique of Vinaver's Malory,' *Philological Quarterly*, 58 (1979), 263–81; 'The Two Scribes in the Winchester MS: The Ninth Explicit and Malory's "Hoole Book,"' *Manuscripta*, 27 (1983), 38–44; and 'Ordinatio and Narrative Links: The Impact of Malory's Tales as a "hoole book",' in *Studies in Malory*, ed. Spisak, pp. 29–52. Evans proposes a manuscript division into five sections. We disagree on the nature of the evidence offered by scribal practice.

manuscript. The first consists of fols 9–70 (the first gathering, as noted, having been lost); the second of fols 71–346; the third of fols 349–409; and the last of fols 409ᵛ–484 (originally this would have extended to fol. 492). The work opens with an account of the establishing of the Arthurian kingdom, from the conception of Arthur to his marriage with Guinevere and the associated foundation of the Round Table, the source material here being the thirteenth-century French prose romance *La Suite du Merlin*. The second phase, or movement, details the exploits of individual knights including Arthur, Lancelot, Gareth and Tristram de Lyones; these are drawn from a variety of sources, in both French and English. The third section is constituted by 'þe tale of the Sankgreal,' the story of the Arthurian quest for the Holy Grail, based on the French *Queste del Saint Graal*; and the fourth by the recounting of the decline and end of the Arthurian kingdom, known in earlier versions in both French and English as the death of Arthur.

From the textual evidence offered by explicits, and through analysis of certain features of scribal practice, it would seem that the first section has a further significant division, creating two sub-sections (from the conception of Arthur to the ending of the tale of Balin and Balan, fols 9–34; 3–59; I.1–II.19, and the episodes designated by Vinaver as 'Torre and Pellinor,' 'The War with the Five Kings,' 'Arthur and Accolon' and 'Gawain, Ywain and Marhalt,' fols 35–70ᵛ; 59–110; III.1–IV.29); whilst the second is sub-divided into five parts (encompassing the adventures of Arthur in his war against the Emperor Lucius, fols 71–96; Lancelot's early exploits, fols 96–113; and the stories of Gareth of Orkney, fols 113ᵛ–148, and of Tristram, with a break being introduced within the latter at the beginning of the account of La Cote Male Tayle, fols 148ᵛ–187, 187–346ᵛ; 113ᵛ–511; V.1–XII.14); and the fourth into two, corresponding with Vinaver's last two 'works,' *The Book of Sir Launcelot and Queen Guinevere* and *The Most Piteous Tale of the Morte Arthur Saunz Guerdon* (fols 409ᵛ–449, 449–484; 609–726; XVIII.1–XXI.13). The third book, concerning the Grail, contains no sub-divisions (fols 349–409; 515–608; XIII. 1–XVII.23).

The narrative scheme which emerges from this examination of the manuscript, whilst it entails a recognition of inconsistency of detail, has both coherence and consistency, charting as it does the history of Arthur's England from its beginnings, through its heyday, to its inevitable decline. Although each of the sections forms a discrete unit within the whole, they function together to create a work framed and informed by notions of an historical process and political contingency. Given the absence of a holograph copy of the text, and the varying textual corruptions within the manuscript and Caxton's print, it is not, of course, possible to equate this scheme with authorial intention – and it must be borne in mind that various inconsistencies and contradictions remain within the story, suggesting that either Malory never completed a final revision of the text, or that his ideas on how to organize his material evolved as he wrote.[37] But this reading of

---

[37] See, e.g., Terence McCarthy, 'The Sequence of Malory's Tales,' in *Aspects of Malory*, ed. Takamiya and Brewer, pp. 107–24.

the work, lent authority by the fact of the manuscript being such an early witness of the translation's reception, differs radically from that put forward by Vinaver which, in the very title he chose, dispenses with any idea of there being a necessary relation between, or textual or thematic continuity within, the constituent parts of the narrative.[38]

By way of illustrating the extent to which editorial intervention has served to shape perceptions of the text locally, as well as with regard to the overall structure of the Arthuriad, I should like to look at two episodes from the final stages of the work, those entitled by Vinaver 'The Maid of Astolat' and 'The Knight of the Cart' (621–42; XVIII.8–21; 648–63; XVIII.25–XIX.9). The appearance of these two stories within Vinaver's edition is that of narrative elements which, whilst self-contained, draw meaning from their positioning within the larger framework of the account of the fragmentation of the Arthurian kingdom. Each documents a significant event in the relationship between Lancelot and Guinevere, a relationship which, with the inevitable tensions in loyalties which it produces, contributes to political disintegration. But their force as discrete episodes derives from the imposition of editorial judgement, and not from the evidence offered by the manuscript.

Vinaver chooses to begin his 'The Fair Maid of Astolat,' for instance, immediately after Malory's explanation of the outcome of the murder of 'Patryse of Irelonde' by 'Sir Pynell le Saveaige,' and the story of Elaine of Astolat therefore commences with Arthur's announcement that there should be a tournament at Camelot on the day of Our Lady's Assumption, this being the tournament at which Lancelot, to avoid recognition by the King and court, adopts Elaine's sleeve as a favour. It ends, after Elaine's death, with praise of the performance of her brother, Lavayne, and his election to the Round Table. It is therefore characterized by a pleasing symmetry. In MS Additional 59678, however, the story is integrated within a sub-section of text which extends from fols 414^v–431^v, beginning with Lancelot's arrival in disguise to defend Guinevere against the charge of treason made against her in the killing of Sir Patryse (fol. 414^v; 619/9ff; XVIII.7) and concluding after the account of Lancelot's wounding prior to the Candlemass joust and the arrival of the combatants at Westminster, itself a portion of the narrative which Vinaver chose to initiate the section he entitled 'The Great Tournament' (644/37ff; XVIII.23). (It may be noted, too, that Vinaver could not claim the authority of Caxton's edition for the breaks which he imposed here: the openings of his 'The Fair Maid of Astolat' and 'The Great Tournament' occur respectively half-way through chapter 8 of Caxton's Book XVIII, and nine lines into chapter 21 of the same

---

[38] It may be noted here that, despite Vinaver's apparent reliance on the manuscript evidence for the textual divisions which he adopted, he was not consistent in the way in which he interpreted it; he ignored, for instance, the first two explicits within the codex (those on fols 34 and 44^v, at the end of the stories of Balin and Balan, and of 'the weddyng of kyng Arthur'), subsuming these episodes within his larger narrative units.

book.) The result of Vinaver's decision is therefore to emphasize the chronology of events, to highlight cause and effect, to separate off what may be interpreted as significant events in Lancelot's career which, when seen in the sequence which he, as editor, establishes, document the knight's increasingly tenuous control of his relationships with both the king and the queen. The manuscript, on the other hand, offers a reading of this portion of the narrative which is less judgemental, in that it encompasses both Lancelot's triumphal reinstatement of Guinevere's reputation after the episode of the poisoned apple, and his misery at being injured, which calls into question his participation in the planned tournament. The framing of the story of Elaine of Astolat in this way shifts the narrative emphasis onto Lancelot's role as knight, rather than as lover.

A similar change of focus can be observed where Vinaver's episode of 'The Knight of the Cart' is concerned. In his edition the tale of Guinevere's abduction by Meleagant is prefaced by the lyrical passage in which the author reflects on the nature of true love between men and women, which ends with his justification of the queen that, 'whyle she lyved she was a trew lover and there for she had a goode ende' (fol. 435v; 648/36–649/35). In Caxton's version this passage constitutes a chapter in itself (XVIII.25). In the manuscript, though, this rare intrusion of the authorial voice is included within a section of text which encompasses the final stages of the episode entitled by Vinaver 'The Great Tournament': a lombard initial indicates the break within the account of the tournament, at the bottom of fol. 431^v, and this sub-section continues without any further hiatus until fol. 435^v, separated off by Caxton as Book XIX. Neither of these divisions on fol. 431^v or 435^v, Caxton's chapters 23 and 25 of Book XVIII, is acknowledged in Vinaver's edition. But the arrangement of the text within the manuscript makes sense, in that the tournament is taken by the court as an occasion on which to celebrate the chivalric ethos, its finale being a speech by Arthur in which he extols the virtues of a code formulated by a social and military élite, a speech which is followed by the narrator's comment that 'he that was curteyse // trew and faythefull to hys frynde was þat tyme cherysshed.' This leads naturally into the more reflective passage on love, and to read the section unbroken is to gain a sense of the relation between the secular and the military, between love and loyalty and physical prowess and achievement, which the ideology of chivalry sought, if failed, to enact. By placing the passage where he does, Vinaver renders the succeeding story of Lancelot's rescuing of Guinevere more problematic; the increasing casuistry of Lancelot's defence of her against the accusation of adultery is set in a context which is made to seem deliberately ambivalent. And again, the fact that in the manuscript this whole episode is undifferentiated from its surrounding narrative, and hence larger and more complex than Vinaver's editing implies – the section extends to include the recounting of the healing of Sir Urry by Lancelot (fol. 449; 663–69; XIX.10–13) – suggests a reading of the text in which attention is focused on Lancelot's prowess rather than on his moral equivocation. (That Malory himself envisaged no disjunction in his work between what Vinaver distinguishes as two distinct episodes is indicated by the explicit in the codex at the conclusion of the tale of Sir Urry, which runs 'And by cause I haue loste the very mater of shevalere de Charyot I departe frome the tale of sir launcelot and here I go vnto þe morte Arthur and that caused sir Aggravayne' fol. 449).

Malory's 'hoole book,' it is clear, has undergone major revisions at the hands of successive generations of editors. And, given the lack of an authoritative copy of the work, it is necessary to conclude that the exemplar which lay behind the sole surviving manuscript may be as much the product of editorial intervention as Caxton's or Vinaver's versions. But to acknowledge the differences in the interpretations which these various texts generate, and the extent to which the process of editing itself determines critical judgements, is to alert us to the open-ended nature of the act of reading, and to its shaping by historical and ideological circumstance.[39] And as readers of Malory today, in choosing which version we privilege above the others, we should recognize that we actively participate in the creation of meaning.

[39] For a discussion of de Worde's text in this light see Tsuyoshi Mukai, 'De Worde's Displacement of Malory's Secularisation,' in Arthurian and Other Studies, ed. Suzuki and Mukai, pp. 179–87; also the moralizing passage on the mutability of earthly glory inserted into de Worde's edition of the text at the point where Lancelot lies 'grovelyng' on the tomb of Arthur and Guinevere (XXI.12), reprinted in Malory: The Critical Heritage, ed. Marylyn Jackson Parins (London, 1988), pp. 51–2.

1) chivalry
 - where came from
 - history
 - word derivatives

2) worldly view

3) Malory view
 - Lancelot e Guenevere
 - transcendental love
 - instability
 - Malory's views
    e acceptance

4) final big ideas
 - Grail quest
 - Vinaver quote

2

Chivalry and the Morte Darthur

RICHARD BARBER

Le Morte Darthur is, first and foremost, a chivalric romance. Chivalry permeates its pages, and shapes the actions and attitudes of the protagonists. Heroes are assessed on a scale of chivalric prowess, and the climactic moments of the work, whether erotic, spiritual or tragic, all invoke this overriding ideal. Lancelot's love for Guinevere, Galahad's achievement of the Grail, the 'dolorous departing' of the Round Table are the triumphs and disaster of chivalry. To understand Malory, we must first understand chivalry.

Historically, chivalry is inextricably bound up with the dominance of the knight in medieval society.[1] The concept of the three orders of society, interdependent and each with a special function, saw mankind as divided into warriors, priests and tillers of the soil: the priest prayed for all, the farmer provided for all, the warrior defended all. The idea of a distinct warrior-class was to be found in Teutonic and Roman society equally; the German war-bands described in Tacitus,[2] looking to their leader for reward and to each other for comradeship, are forerunners of the Round Table. The ethos of mutual dependence is a central feature of the Round Table which can be traced from Germanic society down to the so-called fraternal orders of knighthood in the late Middle Ages, spontaneous alliances of independent knights (or even freebooters). Furthermore, in the pre-feudal centuries after the fall of the Roman Empire, the members of the war-band acquired a particular social and economic status. Instead of merely being part of their leader's household, they became landholders, whose estates were intended to support them and enable them to maintain the necessary equipment for war. This equipment in turn grew more elaborate and expensive: the Romans had largely marched and fought on foot, but the barbarian invaders had used horses for both transport and combat. Their medieval successors were primarily armed horsemen, reluctant to

---

[1] For a general view of chivalry see Maurice Keen, *Chivalry* (New Haven, 1984) and Richard Barber, *The Knight and Chivalry* (Woodbridge, rev. ed., 1995).

[2] Tacitus, *On Britain and Germany*, tr. H. Mattingly (Harmondsworth, 1948), pp. 111ff.

dismount; and each knight was expected to provide his own warhorse as well as horses for his attendants. So the warrior became the lord's servant, owing him war-duty for his estate: our English word 'knight' comes from the same root as 'Knecht' – servant, in German. Chivalry, on the other hand, derives from the French 'chevalier', a horseman. Knighthood and chivalry imply at once service and superior social status.

The culture of the war-band is celebrated in the old German epics and in *Beowulf* in Anglo-Saxon England: it is close-knit, centred on the lord's hall, a male society where loyalty is the supreme virtue. This same ethos holds true in the first centuries of knighthood: the *Song of Roland* envisages chivalry as an entirely war-like virtue, and Roland's betrothed, 'la belle Aude,' appears in the story only to die of grief at the news of his death. The *chansons de geste* of the twelfth century reflect a male-centred society whose chief occupation is warfare and whose chief preoccupation is power. The *chansons de geste* centred on Charlemagne explore the ideals of kingship and conquest, while the stories about Guillaume d'Orange portray the consequences of betrayal of a vassal by his lord. Treachery is the greatest of all crimes, loyalty the greatest of all virtues. Although they usually deal with the heroic figures of earlier centuries, they do not disappear into the mists of antiquity, whether classical or Celtic, and there is always a strongly historical element, even if it is history reshaped in the image of contemporary society. These epic poems tell us about knighthood: they only hint at the emerging ideals of chivalry.

The development of chivalry in the course of the twelfth century was the result of deep-seated changes in society and in the circumstances of the knightly class. The tenth and eleventh centuries, the formative period for knighthood, had been a time of almost continuous warfare in western Europe, whether against Moslems, Vikings or fellow-Christians, and the *chansons de geste* echoed the triumphs and disasters of earlier heroes in the same kind of struggle. The twelfth century brought relative peace and substantial prosperity to much of the west, particularly France and England. Germany and Italy also prospered under Frederick Barbarossa. The arts of leisure, unknown since Roman times, re-emerged and flourished. In southern France a highly sophisticated literary culture developed, drawing not only on half-remembered classical tradition but also on popular Latin songs and the verses of Arab poets in Spain. The work of the troubadours centred on their peaceful social world, where minor lords and their ladies engaged in sophisticated debates about love, or picaresque minstrels delighted in earthy descriptions of the same topic. War, although an ever-present concern, took a back seat, in literary terms, for the first time since the silver age of Latin literature.

However, neither the troubadour world nor that of the *chansons de geste* is the world of chivalry. Chivalry derives from both, and combines the two into a new ethos. This came about in northern France from the 1150s onwards, under the patronage of the magnates of the French kingdom. The unprecedented periods of peace in the second half of the century, made possible by the growth of the central mechanisms of administration, led to the development of a society similar to that of the south in earlier decades. The south, however, had never been as highly organized in feudal terms, and the stricter hierarchy in northern France gave a more stable ambience.

It was in this ambience that military training, which had once been largely a matter for the individual or of firsthand experience on the battle-field, became an activity in its own right, and the links between knightly prowess and love were first forged. The exact process by which the two fundamental concepts of chivalry, courtly love and tournaments, evolved is obscure. We can point to a growing sophistication in social and intellectual life from the beginning of the twelfth century – the so-called 'twelfth-century renaissance' – and both concepts are part of this sophistication. Tournaments are not real war; courtly love is not real love. Both are idealized versions of the actual world, in that they do not carry the consequences of real love and real war: a hostile view might be that matters of life and death have become mere games for an idle moment. In a more favourable light, chivalry is a kind of Platonic ideal of knightly life; and as an ideal it was to be the inspiration of much medieval literature.

The concept which links courtly love to knightly activity is the idea that love for a lady can inspire a knight to nobler and braver deeds. This first appears in the *History of the Kings of Britain* by Geoffrey of Monmouth, completed about 1135. When the nobles gather at Arthur's court

> every knight in the country who was in any way famed for his bravery wore livery and arms showing his own distinctive colour; ladies of fashion often displayed the same colours. They scorned to give their love to any man who had not proved himself three times in battle. In this way the womenfolk and women became chaste and more virtuous and for their love the knights were ever more daring.[3]

This embryonic version of chivalry is developed further in the romances of Chrétien de Troyes, in the latter part of the twelfth century, and is reflected, on such evidence as we have, in contemporary tournaments. In *Erec et Enide*, written in the 1170s, we learn that at the tournament held at Tenebroc 'many a pennon flew there, vermilion, blue, white, and many a wimple and sleeve that had been given as love-tokens.'[4] Without the tournament, the conjunction of love and war is difficult. A real battle was no place for spectators, though there are occasional examples, as at Stirling in 1304, when ladies did watch warfare from a safe distance. Tournaments were almost from the beginning spectator sports: to such occasions we owe

---

[3] Geoffrey of Monmouth, *The History of the Kings of Britain*, tr. Lewis Thorpe (Harmondsworth, 1966), pp. 229.

[4] Chrétien de Troyes, *Arthurian Romances*, tr. D. D. R. Owen (London, 1987), pp. 28–29.

the development of heraldry. Heralds identified knights, provided a commentary for the onlookers, and gradually came to regulate such occasions. A tournament usually had a clear result, unlike warfare; by the late twelfth century, one knight would be adjudged the winner, and the motif of the lady whose hand is to be given to the victor in a tournament appears in Chrétien's *Erec et Enide*.

However, tournaments and courtly love alone are not the sum total of chivalry. Knights were powerful and potentially anarchic figures in society, physically able to dominate their neighbours. It was in the interest of both secular and spiritual rulers to ensure that their power was channelled and regulated. At the same time as the first chivalric romances, we begin to find manuals of knighthood, usually written with a secular audience in mind, but with strong religious overtones. Knighthood has become more than a mere rank: like kingship or priesthood, it has become something ordained by God when he created the different conditions of men, and it entails duties and responsibilities as well as privileges.

This view of knighthood as a distinctive institution was symbolized by the ritual attached to the making of a knight.[5] This ceremony was the distant descendant of such formalities as may have attended the acceptance of a new warrior into the following of a lord. It was quite distinct from the ceremony of homage by which a knight took possession of his lands, a ceremony which any free man could undertake. Initially, it took the form of girding on a sword, and marked the coming-of-age of a young prince or lord: it was simply an acknowledgement that the recipient was of an age to bear arms, and the arms were usually presented by the young man's father, as when, in 1086, William I 'dubbed his son Henry a knight,' according to the *Anglo-Saxon Chronicle*.[6] This presentation of arms remained the basic form of knighting until relatively late in the Middle Ages, when we find the more familiar modern form of a light blow on the shoulder with the flat of a sword and the words 'Be thou a knight.' This brief ritual may have evolved on the battlefield; to 'win one's spurs' in battle was regarded as the most honourable way of attaining knighthood, and for an impoverished squire might be the only way. Grants 'to maintain the estate of knighthood' which had been won in battle (or sometimes in tournaments) are frequent in the English records of the fourteenth and fifteenth century.

Knighthood therefore functioned at two levels. The first was practical and economic, the payment of a warrior by his lord, and worked at a political level. The second was idealistic, the chivalric aspect of the institution. The secular ideal of a knight as brave, generous, and courteous (quite apart from his success with ladies or in the lists) is what we might call the chivalric aspect of knighthood. There was a further stage in the

---

[5] Jean Flori, *L'essor de la chevalerie* (Geneva, 1986), pp. 43–118.
[6] *The Peterborough Chronicle, 1076–1154*, ed. Cecily Clark (Oxford, 1958), p. 9.

development of chivalric knighthood in the mid-fourteenth century, with the foundation of the secular orders of knighthood.[7] These appear at much the same time in Hungary, Spain, England and France, and are essentially creations of medieval monarchs, trying to bind together in mutual harmony the often faction-ridden members of their court. Their model seems to have been the Arthurian order of the Round Table, as portrayed in the romances of the thirteenth century. The Arthurian order was the imaginative creation of writers, most of whom came from a clerical background, and their ideals were drawn from the Church's teachings on knighthood.

The church had seen the potential of the newly-emerging institution at an early stage, and from the eleventh century onwards, attempts were made to divert the energies of knights away from the self-seeking use of force into the service of idealistic ends. Religious knighthood is the third factor, beside heroic and courtly knighthood, in chivalry. The church engaged with knighthood in three very different ways. Firstly, it drew the existing secular order into its orbit, defining its function as part of God's pre-ordained structure of society. Secondly, it extended its own institution of monasticism to embrace a form of knighthood. Thirdly, it enlisted knights to wage secular war for spiritual reasons.

The Church's efforts to harness the concept of knighthood for its own purposes first appear in the tenth and eleventh centuries, in liturgical books which include prayers and rites for the blessing, first, of the sword, and later of the newly made knight.[8] It is part of a general movement by the church to involve itself with the everyday life of its congregation, and in some ways the prayers are parallel to those used for blessing the tools of a man's trade, the farmer's plough or the fisherman's nets. But because the knighting ceremony involved men of the highest rank, it came to be part of the great church festivals: Whitsuntide was especially popular as a time for the making of knights. The ideas put forward in the liturgy gradually gained a wider circulation, and religious writers astutely saw the possibility of promoting their ideas about knighthood through the romances.

The greatest exposition of knighthood as an institution on the borders of the sacred and profane is in the speech in *Le Livre de Lancelot du Lac* from the Vulgate Cycle, which the Lady of the Lake makes when giving Lancelot the arms which she has kept for him since he was entrusted to her care.[9] The Lady of the Lake begins by warning Lancelot that even the boldest man will tremble when he hears what a knight is required to be. Lancelot replies that although a man may lack bodily graces, he can acquire the qualities of the heart by perseverance, and so may learn chivalry. She answers by

---

[7] D'A. J. D. Boulton, *The Knights of the Crown: the Monarchical Orders of Knighthood in Later Medieval Europe 1325–1520* (Woodbridge, 1987).

[8] Jean Flori, *L'essor de la chevalerie* (n. 5 above), pp. 84ff.

[9] *Lancelot-Grail: The Old French Arthurian Vulgate and Post-Vulgate in Translation*, ed. Norris J. Lacy (New York,1992–) II, 59.

explaining how at first all men were equal, but when the sins of envy and greed appeared, some men had to defend the weak against the strong: they were called knights. They were chosen for their goodness of heart and prowess, and their particular calling was to defend Holy Church, which could not take up arms or render evil for evil.

The Lady of the Lake goes on to describe the symbolism of the armour and weapons of the knight. The shield denotes that the knight should protect the church from robbers and infidels; the hauberk reminds him that he must defend the church as closely as the hauberk protects his body; the helm is a symbol of the way in which the knight must be at the head of the defenders of the church. As to the knight's relationship with the common people, this is mirrored in his sword and in his horse. The two edges of the sword show that he must serve both God and the people, while the point of the sword is a reminder of the obedience which the people owe to the knight. In the same way that the horse carries the knight, so, in return for his protection, the people must provide the knight with everything he needs in order to lead an honourable life. The knight guides his horse, and must also guide the people. Equally, the church must give the knight spiritual support.

This elaborate allegory is based on a kind of reasoning which we find difficult to follow, which assumes that everything in God's creation has not only a physical function, but also a spiritual meaning, just as the creatures of the Bestiary are seen as examples provided by God to convey a moral message to mankind. But it was nevertheless a very real part of medieval attitudes to chivalry, and the idea that knights are both more privileged and more bound by duty is inherent in Malory's view of the Round Table.

The other aspects of religious chivalry are the crusades and the monastic orders. The idea that warriors could be enlisted in the Church's service to fight wars in pursuance of its spiritual ends first emerges in the late eleventh century, about the same time that the church embodies the making of knights into the liturgy. Its first clear expression was in the First Crusade, when Urban II's eagerness to see Jerusalem back in Christian hands led him to appeal for an international volunteer army of knights to effect its recovery. The enthusiasm which he aroused extended to the common people as well, but it was the knightly army rather than the disorganized footsoldiers of Peter the Hermit which succeeded in recapturing the Holy City. The Church's hold over its warriors was far from perfect: the moment of triumph was marred by a massacre of innocent civilians. But the principle of holy war had been established, and the Crusades were to loom large on the chivalric agenda for the next four hundred years, despite the disasters which befell the Frankish kingdom in Palestine. Chaucer's Knight in *The Canterbury Tales* – a paragon, not a parody as some modern critics believe – had crusaded in Palestine, Egypt, Poland and elsewhere, and it was his crowning chivalric adventure.[10] Even though in Malory's day the crusade was little more than a dream, the unattainable ambition of a Philip of Burgundy or of a Pope Pius II, he nonetheless felt the attraction of the crusading ideal sufficiently to invoke it on the very last page of his work:

> And somme Englysshe bookes maken mencyon that they wente never oute of Englond after the deth of syr Launcelot – but that was but favour of makers. For the Frensshe book maketh mencyon – and is auctorysed – that syr Bors, syr Ector, syr Blamour and syr Bleoberis wente into the Holy Lande, thereas Jesu Cryst was quycke and deed. And anone as they had stablysshed theyr londes, for, the book saith, so syr Launcelot commaunded them for to do or ever he passyd oute of thys world, there these foure knyghtes dyd many bat<a>ylles upon the myscreantes, or Turkes. And there they dyed upon a Good Fryday for Goddes sake. (725/44–6/19; II.531)

The church quickly converted the idea of the occasional secular crusade into a more permanent institution, the religious orders of knighthood. These began in the twelfth century as fraternities of knights devoted to the protection of pilgrims, and quickly became a kind of standing army for the defence of Palestine. Those who could not go to the Holy Land gave lands and money to the orders, and they soon abandoned their original vows of strict poverty and abstinence. Nonetheless, they were a formidable fighting force, if prone to rashness and over-confidence. The Templars, wealthiest and most powerful of the orders, lost their sense of purpose once Palestine was lost in the early fourteenth century, and succumbed to the greed of the French king, who dissolved the order on largely trumped-up charges: but the Teutonic Knights and the Hospitallers continued to prove their worth in Poland and in Rhodes. These powerful institutions were seen as distinct from and yet related to the world of chivalry: many noble families had relatives within the orders, and the custom of making a journey to Prussia for the relatively brief summer campaigning season was a major experience for many young knights. They also served as models for the secular orders of knighthood, in a distant way, and are therefore another element in the origins of the Round Table. (Their closest analogy in literature is however the company of Grail Knights in Wolfram von Eschenbach's *Parzival*, who have no parallel in Malory.)

Chivalry in real life and chivalry in literature, although closely linked, were by no means identical. One of the great problems for the historian of chivalry is the extent to which our knowledge of the subject relies on literary evidence, which is often very difficult to translate convincingly into reality. Literature continued to inspire real chivalric events, such as

---

10 Maurice Keen, 'Chaucer's Knight, the English Aristocracy and the Crusade,' in *English Court Culture in the Later Middle Ages*, ed. V. J. Scattergood and J. W. Sherborne (London, 1983), pp. 45–62

tournaments where knights adopted Arthurian names and guises. But there was also a distinct literary tradition of chivalry, an idealization of knightly life, which was to some extent independent of historical chivalry. We can distinguish three strands: military chivalry, courtly love, and spiritual chivalry, and each of these is important for our understanding of Malory. The concept of military chivalry centred round the heroic exploits of Arthur, Alexander and the Trojan heroes on the battlefield. It evolved largely from the *chansons de geste* and in English literature is best represented by the great alliterative masterpiece, the *Morte Arthure*. Here chivalry is only one step removed from the traditions of the warrior-band, and the chief loyalty is that of knight to knight, and of knight to lord. Its ideals are nobly summed up in Mordred's lament over the dead Gawain:

'This was Sir Gawain the good, the greatest of all
Of men who go under God, the most gracious knight,
Hardiest of hand-stroke, highest-fortuned in war,
Most courteous in court under the kingdom of heaven,
And the lordliest leader as long as he lived.
In many lands his lion-like lustre was praised
Had you encountered him in the country he came from, sir King,
And known his knighthood, his noble acts and wisdom,
His manners, his might, and his marvellous deeds in war,
You would deeply mourn his death all the days of your life.'

(3875–84)[11]

This vein of warrior-chivalry is to be found also in the chivalric bio-graphies of Bertrand du Guesclin, the fourteenth-century constable of France, and above all in the pages of Jean Froissart, whose avowed object as a historian was to record the noble feats of arms which had taken place in the wars between France and England. Among Malory's near-contemporaries, Jacques de Lalaing and Don Pero Niño of Castile were made into chivalric heroes by their biographers, and the idea of an outstanding knight who has made his way by prowess in arms is a recurrent theme in chivalric literature, from William Marshal in the twelfth century to Malory's own *Tale of Sir Gareth*.

If the concept of prowess is one of the major strands in chivalric literature, the development of the love-theme is obviously the next. The romances centred on Tristan best illustrate this aspect of chivalry. The origins of the Tristan story are obscure; on the evidence of Chrétien de Troyes, the story was regarded with suspicion by the purists of courtly love, and in its final form it does breach many of the conventions, social, political and chivalric. Tristan is shown as a paragon in the peaceful accomplish-ments of knighthood, a hunter so skilled in venery that he was said to have

---

[11] *King Arthur's Death [Morte Arthure]*, tr. Brian Stone (Harmondsworth, 1988), p. 154.

first brought the words and customs of the art into order, and a musician of rare talent. He is also a notable warrior, but this is perhaps the least memorable aspect of his character. French poets in the twelfth century and, in the following century, Gottfried von Strassburg, made the story of his love for Iseult into something that went far beyond the bounds of courtly rituals of dalliance.[12] The archetypal situation in courtly love is that of a young knight enamoured of the lady of the castle in a remote relationship, at most an *amitié amoureuse*. Reality, at least in the literary depictions of this kind of chivalry, is scarcely allowed to intrude. The story of Tristan and Iseult is quite different: it is about the harsh confrontation between the love of a woman and a man and their respective obligations to society. As Gottfried puts it, at the core there is only

> A man, a woman; a woman, a man:
> Tristan, Isolde; Isolde, Tristan.[13]

Each writer in turn has to find excuses for their behaviour: the magic potion, drunk by the lovers by mistake, is the first line of defence, the second that their passion puts them outside the normal rules of society. But magic and passion consorted ill with chivalric ideals, particularly since Isolde was the wife of Tristan's lord, King Mark, and the adultery and treachery implicit in much of courtly love here becomes explicit and blatant. Yet it was a famous story, and its fame ensured it a place in the romances of chivalry. In the thirteenth and fourteenth centuries, when writers turned from verse to prose, the romances grew immensely long; Tristan was to dominate one series of versions of Arthurian romance, but in so doing he and Iseult are diminished, and become just another pair of lovers, their adultery excused by the portrayal of Mark as evil and treacherous, unworthy of loyalty.

> 'That ys hard for to do,' seyde sir Launcelot, 'for by sir Trystram I may have a warnynge: for whan by meanys of tretyse sir Trystram brought agayne La Beall Isode unto kynge Marke from Joyous Garde, loke ye now what felle on the ende, how shamefully that false traytour kyng Marke slew hym as he sate harpynge afore hys lady, La Beall Isode. Wyth a grounden glayve he threste hym in behynde to the harte, whych grevyth sore me,' seyde sir Launcelot, 'to speke of his dethe, for all the worlde may nat fynde such another knyght.' (681/21–8; XV.6)

The tragedy of divided loyalties is simplified into a question of black and white, and lacks the force of the earlier versions. The process of adaptation tells us much about the limits of tolerance within the literary ideals of

---

[12] Gottfried von Strassburg, *Tristan*, tr. A. T. Hatto (Harmondsworth, 1960).
[13] *Tristan*, p. 43.

chivalry. Lancelot, whose situation with regard to Guinevere is exactly parallel to that of Tristan and Iseult (as he himself tacitly acknowledges), and whose history may in part derive from theirs, stays within the bounds of convention until the closing pages of the Arthurian tragedy.

The third strand in literary chivalry is perhaps the most original of all. This is the theme of religious chivalry, which finds its highest expression in the romances centred on the Holy Grail. This is not the place to explore the much-debated origins of the Grail. Suffice it to say that it was the subject of Chrétien de Troyes' last, unfinished romance, and that other hands took up the theme and made it a religious relic, the cup used by our Lord at the Last Supper, preserved with the lance with which Longinus struck him at the Crucifixion in the Grail Castle. Some decades later, a writer (or writers) with a strong interest in turning chivalric romance into a didactic weapon in the hands of the church, perhaps a Cistercian monk, fashioned a version of the Grail story which ran from the time of Christ to Arthur's death. The quest of the Holy Grail becomes the epitome of all knightly quests. Beside it, the adventures of a knight in pursuit of a white brachet or even a questing beast pale into triviality. In the hands of a great writer, it mirrored the combination of chivalry and devotion which we find in many lay magnates of the period, men such as Henry Duke of Lancaster, author of *The Book of Holy Remedies*. Even when lesser writers overloaded the story of the quest with elaborate symbolism and endless hermits whose function was to expound the symbolism, it continued to strike a chord with a wide audience. It is not a clarion call to arms in the manner of the Crusades, nor a demand for total surrender to the religious life, as with the monastic orders. The Grail story is about the individual's journey towards the realms of the spirit, and reinforces the chivalric insistence on the knight's duty to seek for achievement, whether in arms, love or the salvation of his soul. In its later versions it reflects the supreme self-confidence of chivalry: the knight is the representative of all that is highest in human society, and as such has pre-eminence in religious matters as well. The priests and hermits in the romance are there only to serve and assist the knights on their way, if need be by admonishing them. There is no sense of the claims made by the church in the real world to dominion over secular matters by virtue of its spiritual authority. Here, secular prowess leads to religious perfection.

The Grail Quest, for all its powerful imagery, can seem austere and even perverse: for a warmer view of chivalry in relation to spiritual perfection, we can turn to the German version of part of the same story, Wolfram von Eschenbach's *Parzival*.[14] Although this poem had no direct influence on or connection with Malory's work, it offers a picture of chivalric achievement touched with humanity which Malory would have found entirely sympathetic. Interestingly, Wolfram, like Malory, had little formal education:

---

[14] Wolfram von Eschenbach, *Parzival*, tr. A. T. Hatto (Harmondsworth, 1980).

most of the more sophisticated chivalric romances were written by men who were clerks, in the sense of having either taken minor orders or having some professional reason for acquiring the skill of writing. Wolfram declares that 'he does not know a single letter,' though this is probably a dig at his all too learned rivals; he certainly came from a knightly family, whose social status was similar to that of Malory. In his poem, Parzival woos and wins Condwiramurs at the end of his first set of adventures, and the love that Wolfram celebrates is therefore married love. For the essence of chivalry, and the bond on which the whole of society rests, is *triuwe*: men and women should be true to each other, and to themselves. It encompasses the idea of loyalty, steadfast love, and just reward: the lord should reward his vassal for his loyalty, the lady should reward the lover for his devotion. Wolfram extends and humanizes the basic concept of chivalry until it can be applied to all sorts and conditions of men: but his tale deals exclusively with noble heroes – he records their heraldry meticulously – and there is no doubt in his mind that noble birth is a prerequisite if chivalry is to come into play.

We have looked briefly at the two great German chivalric poets, Gottfried and Wolfram, to explore the nature of chivalry. Malory, however, worked only from the Anglo-French chivalric tradition. If chivalry was a unifying factor among the knights of Europe, the Anglo-French knights were even more closely linked, sharing a common language and a common culture up to Malory's own time. Malory's attitude to chivalry was undoubtedly coloured by the recent history of England and France. Although he is unlikely to have known men who could remember Edward III and the Black Prince, he was only a generation away from the heady days of the great English victories at Crécy and Poitiers; his initial vision of Arthur as a military leader is very much in the image of Edward III.[15] But as the work progresses, the increasing nostalgia for a golden age of chivalry reflects his own troubled times, and it is tempting to read him as a chronicler of the decline of a high ideal, setting the past above the present.

However, this would be a serious misconception: European chivalry was experiencing a considerable revival in the fifteenth century. But it was not in the traditional centres: France, victim of the devastations of the Anglo-French wars and with a court preoccupied by the larger concerns of politics, no longer maintained its pre-eminence. Instead, the new enthusiasm for chivalry came from Spain, together with the new style of tournaments involving an arena divided by a barrier to separate the combatants. The magnificence of Spanish chivalry under Juan II of Castile and his favourite Alvaro de Luna in the 1420s and 1430s was imitated by the Burgundians, who brought one particular form of chivalric festival, the *pas d'armes*, to its

---

[15] On Edwardian attitudes to chivalry, see Juliet Vale, *Edward III and Chivalry* (Woodbridge, 1982).

apogee. These events were modelled closely on romances, and often had a
complex literary programme, acted out by the protagonists using disguises
and even scenery. Malory's *Tale of Sir Gareth*, with its ritual succession of
knights guarding the right of passage (*pas*) is a series of such encounters, as
if Gareth was moving from one such festival to another, but with a more
serious purpose in mind.

> And on the morne the damesell toke hir leve and thanked the knyght,
> and so departed and rode on hir way untyll they come to a grete
> foreste. And there was a grete ryver and but one passage, and there
> were redy two knyghtes on the farther syde to lette the passage.
>
> 'What seyst thou?' seyde the damesell. 'Woll ye macche yondir two
> knyghtis other ellys turne agayne?'
>
> 'Nay,' seyde sir Bewmaynes, 'I woll nat turne ayen, and they were
> six mo!'
>
> And therewithall he russhed unto the watir, and in myddys of the
> watir eythir brake her sperys uppon other to their hondys. And than
> they drewe their swerdis and smote egirly at othir. (183/10–21;
> VII.6)

The *pas d'armes* usually centred on a knight's vow to wear a piece of
armour or a fetter until he had encountered a certain number of opponents,
and the vows could often be extravagant. Suero de Quiñoñes, the prime
mover in the *Passo Honroso* on the road to Santiago de Compostela in 1434,
had great difficulty in finding sufficient opponents.[16] The challenge was
genuinely applied to all passers-by, since knights on their way to the shrine
of St James complained at being forced to fight while on pilgrimage; this
confirms the impression that the enthusiasts who declared a *pas d'armes*
were trying to copy the romances as closely as possible. We find knights
pursuing quests as well, usually in search of an opponent willing to meet
them in single combat: a number of Burgundian and Spanish knights
travelled across Europe on such missions in the middle years of the
fifteenth century. But the real knight-errantry of the romances was
impossible to imitate: the sole example recorded was at Sandricourt in
northern France in 1493, where ten defenders were stationed in the 'forest
without tracks' to await the challengers, who rode in search of adventures
'like knights errant, just as the Knights of the Round Table used to do in
former days.'[17]

This chivalric revival spread to England in the 1460s, by way of
Burgundy, with the accession of Edward IV. I have argued elsewhere that
Le Morte Darthur belongs in the context of the renewed interest in
tournaments shown by Edward and his circle: in particular, the Woodville

---

[16] Pero Rodriguez de Lena, *El Passo Honroso de Suero de Quiñones*, ed. Amancio Labandeira
Fernandez (Madrid, 1977).

[17] A. Vayssière, *Le pas d'armes de Sandricourt* (Paris, 1874), p. 13.

family were enthusiastic jousters. Anthony Woodville, Lord Scales, was only imitating his father's chivalric exploits on a grander scale in his famous encounter with Antoine, Bastard of Burgundy in 1467. Tournaments had been virtually unknown in England for half a century, and it is hard to see how the procession of tournaments in *Le Morte Darthur* could have much meaning if they were written for an audience which had never seen them. Malory even adds tournaments in the last books, and gives details which correspond to jousting practice at Edward's court,[18] and just before the final tragedy begins, he inserts 'The Great Tournament' as a last apotheosis of the Round Table:

> So at afftir Crystemas kynge Arthure lete calle unto hym many knyghtes and there they avysed togydirs to make a party and a grete turnemente and justis. And the kynge of North Galys seyde to kyng Arthure he wolde have on hys party kyng Angwysh of Irelonde and the Kynge wyth the Hondred Knyghtes and the kynge of Northhumbirlonde and sir Galahalt the Haute Prynce. So thes four kynges and this myghty deuke toke party ayenste kynge Arthure and the knyghtes of the Rounde Table.
>
> And the cry was made that the day off justys shulde be besydes Westemynster, uppon Candylmasse day, whereof many knyghtes were glad and made them redy to be at that justys in the freysshyste maner. (642/23–33; XVIII.21)

So when Malory talks about chivalry, he is invoking a newly-revived but flourishing ideal, not an echo of past traditions.[19] Like many medieval writers, he believes that the past is better than the present: hence his allusions to a chivalric past in which men were more loyal and steadfast, both in their allegiances and in their love. But this is a *topos* common in medieval literature; it is implicit in the whole of romance literature, which is invariably set in a remote and golden age. It in no way detracts from the present relevance and vigour of chivalry as an inspiration.

What then does Malory make of the chivalric ideal? It is, in his view, primarily a secular institution. His story is the story of the Round Table, a fellowship bound by a common loyalty to Arthur, and oaths of friendship and mutual support. Its purpose is set out in the oath administered to the knights by Arthur at the end of the description of his wedding to Guinevere and acquisition of the Round Table:

> the kyng stablysshed all the knyghtes and gaff them rychesse and londys; and charged them never to do outerage nothir mourthir, and allwayes to fle treson, and to gyff mercy unto hym that askith mercy,

---

[18] Richard Barber, 'Malory's *Le Morte Darthur* and Court Culture under Edward IV,' *Arthurian Literature XII*, ed. James P. Carley and Felicity Riddy (Cambridge, 1993), pp. 133–56.

[19] See Larry D. Benson, *Malory's Morte Darthur* (Cambridge, Mass., 1976), pp. 137–204.

uppon payne of forfiture of their worship and lordship of kynge
Arthure for evirmore; and allwayes to do ladyes, damesels and
jantilwomen and wydowes socour: strengthe hem in hir ryghtes, and
never to enforce them, uppon payne of dethe. Also, that no man take no
batayles in a wrongefull quarell for no love ne for no worldis goodis.
So unto thys were all knyghtis sworne of the Table Rounde, both
olde and younge, and every yere so were they sworne at the hyghe
feste of Pentecoste. (75/36–76/2; III.15)

We can find parallels for this oath in contemporary accounts of the making
of knights of the Order of the Bath, and in the oaths sworn by members of
tournament societies in Germany at about this time. There is a common
theme of justice and the upholding of right which is the accepted basis of
chivalry. To this we must add the concept of mutual loyalty and defence,
which prevents knights of the Round Table from fighting each other in
earnest: even to take different sides in a tournament is not quite the
done thing.

Beyond this practical knighthood lie the more exotic realms of heroic
chivalry. For Malory, Lancelot is the paragon, the hero *par excellence*. The
adventures which he selects from his French romances tend to be those
with a high moral tone, where the distinction between right and wrong is
unambiguous. He draws his villains more sharply, so that the wickedness
of a Breunys Sans Pyté or a Tarquyn offers a better contrast to his champions'
virtue. In so doing, he tends to reject the magic and enchantments which
were once so popular with the French writers and their audience. On this
plane, his choice of Lancelot as a central figure offers no problems: he is a
match for all his opponents as a fighter, and his reputation for courtesy and
nobility of heart is immaculate. Lancelot's apotheosis in 'The Healing of Sir
Urry,' where, through his ability to heal the sick knight, he is once again
confirmed as 'the best knight in the world,' extends the concept of chivalric
prowess as far as Malory dares: secular achievements confer powers
usually held to belong to the spiritual world.

Malory is less at ease with the emotional and religious aspects of chivalry.
He is ambivalent about courtly love: it is both Lancelot's glory and his
Achilles' heel to love and be loved by Guinevere. The problem arises early
in *The Noble Tale of Sir Launcelot du Lake*; Lancelot encounters a number of
ladies who accuse him of loving Guinevere and refusing to pay homage to
any other lady. His actions confirm this, in that he sends the knights whom
he vanquished to yield to Guinevere; and he never actually denies the
rumours. Malory is neither confirming nor denying what most of his
readers know to be the case, that Lancelot is indeed Guinevere's servant in
love. Lancelot is challenged by one damsel to 'love som mayden other
jentylwoman,' hinting that he is in love with Guinevere. Lancelot's reply is
remarkable in chivalrous terms:

'Fayre damesell,' seyde sir Launcelot, 'I may nat warne peple to speke of me what hit pleasyth hem. But for to be a weddyd man, I thynke hit nat, for than I muste couche with hir and leve armys and turnamentis, batellys and adventures. And as for to sey to take my pleasaunce with peramours, that woll I refuse: in prencipall for drede of God, for knyghtes that bene adventures sholde nat be advoutrers nothir lecherous, for than they be nat happy nother fortunate unto the werrys; for other they shall be overcom with a sympler knyght than they be hemself, other ellys they shall sle by unhappe and hir cursednesse bettir men than they be hemself. And so who that usyth peramours shall be unhappy, and all thynge unhappy that is aboute them.' (161/1–11; VI.10)

Constant love, whether married or not, is hostile to the practice of chivalry, in Malory's view. Tristram, when he refuses to go to Arthur's court because Iseult cannot accompany him, is told that other knights will say: 'A! se how Sir Trystram huntyth and hawkyth and cowryth wythin a castell wyth hys lady, and forsakyth us. Alas . . . hyt ys pyté that ever he was knyght, or ever he shulde have the love of a lady' (507/2–5; XII.11).

Yet the convention that knights should fight for the sake of a lady and wear love-tokens in a tournament is perfectly acceptable to Malory. It is the formalities of courtly love that he dislikes, as we learn in *The Book of Sir Launcelot and Queen Guinevere*, where Malory launches into his most extensive diatribe in the whole of *Le Morte Darthur* on the subject of love, à propos of Queen Guinevere's traditional maying expedition. The passage in which Malory deplores the unstability of love in his own time has often been quoted, but the paragraph which precedes it has received less attention:

Therefore, lyke as May moneth flowryth and floryshyth in every mannes gardyne, so in lyke wyse lat every man of worshyp florysh hys herte in thys worlde: firste unto God, and nexte unto the joy of them that he promysed hys feythe unto; for there was never worshypfull man nor worshypfull woman but they loved one bettir than another; and worshyp in armys may never be foyled. But firste reserve the honoure to God, and secundely thy quarell muste com of thy lady. And such love I call vertuouse love. (649/14–29; XVIII.25)

The logic of Malory's argument is not entirely clear, but the picture he paints, of an ideal where skill in arms both deserves and stems from the relationship between knight and lady, is notable for the way in which he places this love outside marriage or courtship, and sees it as set apart from morality or contracts. And before he resumes his story, he makes another telling comment:

And therefore all ye that be lovers, calle unto your remembrance the monethe of May, lyke as did quene Gwenyver, for whom I make here a

lytyll mencion, that whyle she lyved she was a trew lover, and therefor
she had a good ende. (649/32-5; XVIII.25)

The final tragedy coincides with the consummation of Lancelot's love for
Guinevere; the rumours become truth, and, like Tristan and Iseult before
them, they retreat to Joyous Gard. The knightly deeds and high purpose of
the Round Table are abandoned: personal feelings take precedence over
fellowship and loyalty. Chivalry gives way to civil war in the closing pages
of *Le Morte Darthur*, and Arthur's lament over the lost ideals for which he
has striven once again puts love at a lower level: 'quenys I myght have
inow, but such a felyship of good knyghtes shall never be togydirs in no
company' (685/31-2; XV.9).

The third element of chivalry, the quest for spiritual fulfilment, presents
Malory with similar problems. Although the knights of the Round Table
take up the Grail Quest with enthusiasm, and the Grail appears at the
Round Table itself, the two ideals pull in different directions. In response to
Gawain's rash vow to seek the Grail after it has departed from the hall at
Camelot, Arthur says that 'ye have nygh slayne me for the avow that ye
have made, for thorow you ye have berauffte me the fayryst and the
trewyst of knyghthode that ever was sene togydir in ony realme of the
worlde. For whan they departe frome hense I am sure they all shall never
mete more togydir in thys worlde . . .' (522/23-7; XIII.7).

Malory's attitude to the Grail Quest is in any case ambiguous, largely
because he is anxious to maintain Lancelot's heroic status. As Eugène
Vinaver says, he regards the quest 'not as a means of contrasting earthly
and divine chivalry and condemning the former . . . but as an opportunity
offered to the knights of the Round Table to achieve still greater glory in
this world.'[20] (For 'condemning the former' it might be fairer to say
'praising the latter': the French original does not regard earthly chivalry as
intrinsically sinful, but as an institution easily corrupted by human frailty.)
In the original, Lancelot is ready to repent, and the essence of his role in the
story is that he fails, where his more perfect son and successor, Galahad,
achieves the adventure. Malory emphasizes Lancelot's partial triumph:
apart from the three chosen knights, he comes closer than any other knight
to the vision of the Grail, and gains at least a glimpse of the holy vessel,
albeit at great cost. In a sense, this reading of the Grail story restores it to a
logical place within the framework of Arthurian chivalry; it is part of the
story of the Round Table, but not its ultimate objective. It is more than just
another adventure; it is the greatest of all the quests undertaken by
Arthur's knights, but it still remains an adventure, and not an integral part
of the Table's purpose. And this tells us a great deal about Malory's attitude
to chivalry. It is essentially human in scale and scope. Not for him the

---

[20] *The Works of Sir Thomas Malory*, 3rd ed., rev. P. J. C. Field (Oxford, 1990), III, 1535.

transcendental love of Tristan and Iseult or the ecstasy of Galahad before the Grail, noble though his account of the closing pages of the history of the Grail may be. His story is about chivalry in the real world, where human weakness tragically undermines the greatest and most ambitious of its achievements. But it is equally human endeavour and human emotion, the quest for a better way in this world through justice, valour and courtesy (in its highest sense) that is Malory's vision of chivalry.

3

The Place of Women in the Morte Darthur

ELIZABETH EDWARDS

I

The 'place of women' is a phrase commonly used to mean the social or textual position of women, but my title is also meant to suggest that, in relation to gender roles, I consider physical location important in the *Morte Darthur*: where you are has a lot to do with what you are. The queens in their castles seem to have a different ontological status than the damsels who inhabit the forests of adventure. Geography is important to gender, as I shall argue in the first part of this essay; the second part deals with the more abstract senses of positioning – the geometrical rather than the geographical. One of the geometrical figures I have in mind is, for example, the love triangle.

The opening of the section Vinaver entitles 'Torre and Pellinor' establishes the paradigms for the place of women in establishing the chivalric ethos of the the Round Table. The story begins with Arthur's courtship, by which he obtains both Guinevere and the Round Table. Indeed, the end of this tale reads 'Explicit the Wedding of King Arthur' which arguably provides a better title. The wedding feast is interrupted by the arrival at the newly established court of a deer, a dog, and a damsel in that order. We are told that Arthur is rather unchivalrously glad when the lady is carried off 'for she made such a noyse' (63/40–4; III.4). But Merlin will not allow such laxity; he explains the duties of the future Arthurian court thus: 'Nay . . . ye may nat leve hit so, thys adventure, so lyghtly, for thes adventures muste be brought to an ende, other ellis hit woll be disworshyp to you and to youre feste' (63/42–44; III.4).

This beginning is, then, the initiation of both the political stability constituted by the institution of the Round Table which comes with the queen and with marriage, and the forest or wilderness realm of quest and adventure, which is articulated as the project of that (male) political entity.[1]

---

[1] War is another such project of the Round Table knights, and occurs frequently in the early books as Arthur tries to consolidate his realm. 'The War with the Five Kings'

Merlin is informing Arthur of the rules of this second sphere of action. Put another way, these two locations represent the centripetal force of the attraction of a centralized court (which we might call civilization) and the centrifugal force of adventure (which usually takes place in a wilderness). The implication of women in the knightly quest is made explicit when Arthur dictates the oath of the Round Table to his knights at the end of this quest: 'allwayes to do ladyes, damesels, and jantilwomen and wydowes socour: strengthe hem in hir ryghtes, and never to enforce them, uppon payne of dethe' (75/41–43; III.15).

The queens, and landed women, are immobile, castle-bound, while the damsels roam about in the forest of adventure apparently at will. In *Sir Gareth of Orkney*, for example, Lyones is confined by a siege to her castle, while her sister Lynet freely crosses the enemy lines. Tellingly, Lynet is not only a damsel but a sorceress; magic is in the outside world of adventure. The contrast is, then, between what Catherine La Farge calls 'the inner and the utterly outside,' the queens guarded inside strong walls, and those women associated with a world which is outside even the laws of nature, which is 'beyond the known and the social.'[2] When queens leave their castles, it seems they become damsels, subject to the perils of quests, to the wagers of strange knights, to abduction and danger. So Tristram ventures Isolde in a beheading beauty contest with Sir Brunor (259/13–14; VIII.25); Guinevere, out Maying, is kidnapped by Sir Meleagant (650/ 42–651.3; XIX.2).

There is a difficulty which arises when the decree of the Round Table, to succour damsels, comes into conflict with the half-suppressed anxiety about women as the source of baleful magic. So, when some forest damsels malign Marhalt as a woman hater, he clarifies his position thus:

> 'Sir . . . they name me wrongfully, for hit be the damesels of the turret that so name me and other suche as they be. Now shall I telle you for what cause I hate them: for they be sorsseres and inchaunters many of them . . . And this is the pryncipall cause that I hate them. And all good ladyes and jantyllwomen, I owghe them my servyse as a knyght ought to do.' (96/39–97/2; IV.18)

Obviously, there is some knightly discretion involved in deciding who the real women are.

The women who roam the landscape are not usually the object of the quest, but the means to the achievement of it. 'We be here,' say the damsels

---

follows the establishment of the Round Table society in 'Torre and Pellinor,' for example. War, with its ethic of the male collective, excludes women almost entirely; and occurs contrapuntally with quest adventures.

[2]   'The Hand of the Huntress: Repetition and Malory's *Morte Darthur*,' *New Feminist Discourses*, ed. Isabel Armstrong (London, 1991), p. 264. This is the best recent work on gender in Malory, and what follows is indebted to La Farge's work.

of 'Gawain, Ywain, and Marhalt,' 'for this cause: if we may se ony of arraunte knyghtes to teche hem unto strong aventures' (97/35–36; IV.19). Because it is the site of male desires, the forest of strong adventures has frequently seemed to me to have some feminine quality; that is, the scene of male activity is gendered as female. This is a symbolic femininity, a gendering detached from biological bodies and grounded in the signifying capacity of gender, which acts as a polarity which draws signs into gender affinities. The wilderness, the magical and the unexplained thus fall in line with the mystery that is woman, from the male perspective. This view is at least partially supported by the work of Patricia Parker. She argues that the romance world typified by the forest or wasteland of the quest is the arena of dilation, delay, pendency and deferral; it is the dilatory space of errancy, with an etymological pun on errancy meaning both 'wandering' and 'erring.' The knight errant wanders in a potentially limitless divagation between beginning and end, which is also a realm of potential error – delusion, lostness, enchantment. Parker writes: '"romance" is that mode or tendency which remains on the threshold before the promised end, still in the wilderness of wandering, "error" or "trial".'[3] Parker comes increasingly to see this liminal space as equated with, or watched over by, a lady, who is often a figure of mediation.[4] This forest is also the space of the inherited or appropriated remainders of Celtic myth (though Malory may not have recognized it as such), which delineated a terrain imbued with marvels and to some extent free from morality – according to Auerbach, free from history and political reality.[5] The mood of otherness, enigma and danger which characterizes the forest of adventures generates physical damsels who populate it, perhaps representing the male projection of otherness as female. The damsels of 'Gawain, Ywain and Marhalt' speak as guides and the mediators of the trials the knights must face, and therefore assist in the errancy, but the ambivalence of the errancy/error pun is amply evident, especially in the early books, in the malevolence and deceptiveness of many women: the Lady Lyle of Avalon, and her sinister handmaiden in 'The Knight with Two Swords;' the second Lady of the Lake, Nineve, who deludes and enchants Merlin after learning everything he knows; the necrophiliac sorceress Hallewes in Lancelot du Lake; the damsel with the falcon in the same tale, and Morgan le Fay – all are associated with deception and error. Morgan particularly is the cause of anxiety and suspicion. In 'Arthur and Accolon' she replaces Arthur's sword, and almost succeeds in destroying him. Morgan's message to Arthur is:

---

3 *Inescapable Romance* (Princeton, 1979), p. 4.
4 *Literary Fat Ladies* (London, 1987), pp. 8–35.
5 Erich Auerbach, *Mimesis* (Princeton, 1953), pp. 131–3. The attempt to reclaim the terrain of romance for mainstream theology is demonstated in the *Queste del Saint Graal* and in part by Malory's translation of that work.

'tell hym I feare hym nat whyle I can make me and myne in lyknesse of
stonys, and lette hym wete I can do much more whan I*se my tyme.'
(93/7–9; IV.15)

The particular fear here is of shape-shifting, a fear that things may not be as
they appear to be – that Arthur's sword may look the same yet have no
virtue. Later this anxiety about the ability of women to change reality will
express itself in the potion by which Elaine seduces Lancelot, not once but
twice. In this context we find the dream-like and faintly sinister repetitions
typical of romance, where there are two Isoldes, two Elaines, two love
potions, and so on. This is a kind of condensation that is like the psychic
thrift in symbolism documented by Freud; the names of all women are the
same, and thus you may absent-mindedly marry a woman other than the
one you love, as Tristram marries Isolde Blaunche Maynes.

The sense of menace in female sexuality is most clearly found in the *Tale
of Sir Lancelot du Lake*. Lancelot is set upon by various kinds of lethal
femininity, beginning with the queens who find him asleep and vulnerable
and imprison him with the aim of forcing him to choose one of them, and
continuing through a series of deceptive and manipulative women. Felicity
Riddy sums up the logic of *Sir Lancelot* thus:

> Women are able to tap sources of malignant power: they put spells on
> him, imprison him, dissemble and tell lies to him and seek his death,
> calling it love. The final episode . . . also seems to express this painful
> ambivalence about women: by virtue of their sex they should be
> protected, but by virtue of their sexuality they deserve to die.[6]

The source of the male anxiety here is the desirous female; the desired
female is elsewhere, safely immured. Lancelot in particular is the object of
female desires throughout the *Morte*, the most gruesome of which is the
desire of Hallewes to settle for even his embalmed body (168/34–6;VI.15),
but other knights have similar experiences. Morgan le Fay wants not only
Lancelot, but Accolon and Alisaunder the Orphan. Arthur's sister comes 'to
aspye the courte' and leaves pregnant with Mordred by him. Lynet in *The
Tale of Sir Gareth* is the comic type of the threatening woman; she wanted
another kind of knight than Gareth, and her revenge is not to imprison or
torment him, but only to nag at him, and to point out his inadequacies at
every possible juncture. In all these cases the threatened psyche, or subject
position, is male, but, as Riddy suggests, the body count of those who die
as a hazard of the quest includes many women: in the first tale alone,
Columbe, Sir Garnish's lady, Pellinor's daughter, the lady killed by
Gawain.

Part of the menace is the result of a dichotomy between love and

---

[6] *Sir Thomas Malory* (Leiden, 1987), p. 58.

adventure. These are two separate poles of experience for the knights, and, in the paradigms of romance, they are often contradictory. In Chrétien de Troyes' *Yvain*, for example, to stay with the beloved is to risk censure for sloth, and to go on adventures is to risk alienation from the beloved. Malory prefers adventure, for the most part, and tries to suppress the difficulties of love, but love as a problem for adventure nonetheless occurs frequently. One arena seems to cancel the other, so that the two knightly activities cannot even come to consciousness at the same time. Palomides is in a trance when Tristram finds him besieging Isolde: 'sir Palomides sate at the gate and sawe where sir Trystrames cam, and he sate as he had slepe, and his horse pastured afore hym' (266/20–22; VIII.31). He does not respond to a challenge, and convinces Governal that 'he slepe or ellys he was madde.' Later, Palomides, like Yvain, simply forgets all about his beloved, and Tristram, too, forgets about La Belle Isolde. Alisaunder the Orphan is so dazzled by his love for Alis that he nearly allows himself to be tricked into breaking a vow (398/1–7; X.39). The depth of these trances is like the fugue state of a disassociated personality; similarly, though love is often proposed as a motive for chivalric being, and even though both love and adventure are key elements, the two remain eerily disassociated and contribute to an uncanny or dream-like atmosphere.

But such disassociation is never complete, and there is no clear designation of the court as the site of 'courtly love' and the forest as the arena of action. The forest space is not simply a wilderness but is articulated as the 'forest of adventure,' organized by something beyond nature; part of this organizing force is the enchantments and part is the motivating love of the knight for his lady. When an unbearable crisis of love occurs, the result is madness and flight to the forest. This is what happens to Tristram when he fears that Isolde has come to love Keyhydyns, and to Lancelot when he finds he has been tricked into sleeping with Elaine for the second time. In both cases, the heroes run 'woode wylde,' *wode* in Middle English meaning both 'wild' and 'mad' as well as 'a forest'; naked and battered, they live in the same forest they had quested in, but without memory or identity. This is the most radical form of disassociation for the protagonists, the low ebb of chivalric identity, the purposelessness of the knight without the lady. In these episodes, both Lancelot and Tristram conform to the medieval typology of the wild man, as described by Bernheimer, or more precisely, to a related figure, the wild knight.[7] The wild knight has certain innate qualities which cause him to perform chivalrous deeds: 'whan sir Launcelot saw that, yet as woode as he was he was sory for hys lorde, sir Blyaunte . . . and so sir Launcelot ran oute at a posterne, and there he mette wyth tho two knyghtes that chaced syr Blyaunte' (497/20–25; XII.2). The very sight of a

---

[7] See the discussion of the semiotic function of wild men in Richard Bernheimer, *Wild Men in the Middle Ages* (Cambridge, 1952), and of wild knights in Louise O. Fradenburg, *City, Marriage, Tournament* (Madison, 1991), p. 326.

sword can inspire this wild chivalry. But in the absence of an organizing love, when the knight has only his martial prowess, he has no culture, no memory, and no sense of himself. It is interesting that in the absence of love, the forest of adventure itself seems to disappear. The heroes run into classes of people hardly encountered elsewhere in the *Morte*. Tristram falls in with 'herdemen and shyperdis' who, 'whan he ded ony shrewde dede they wolde beate hym with roddis. And so they clypped hym with sherys and made hym like a foole' (305/11–15; IX.18). Lancelot meets the 'yonge men of that cité' who 'threwe turvis at hym and gaff hym many sad strokys' (499/2; XII.3). The forest that is merely the scene of the 'wild' rather than of the adventure is contaminated by a kind of leakage from a far more mundane world, that of pastoral economy and civic organization, which might appear to us to be more realistic than the romance world, but which here occurs only in a parodic, debased form, in conjunction with madness.[8]

On the Grail quest, the anxieties about the female reach the point of demonization. The turret of sorceresses commented on by Marhalt returns in an even more malevolent form, as a turret of demons from which Bors narrowly escapes (571/10–29; XVI.12). There are no women questers except Perceval's sister, who bleeds to death in accord with the demand of a wicked chatelaine. Other females encountered on the quest are chiefly symbolic or allegorical, though a few, such as Perceval's aunt, are recluses. Somewhat surprisingly given that chastity is the spiritual quality which is rewarded on the Grail quest, no real women are present as temptation. Sexual experience or the lack of it are simply givens at the beginning of the quest, which does not test chastity but rewards or punishes knights on the basis of past life experience. Rather, other more spiritual temptations are represented allegorically as seductive women. For example, mainstream medieval iconography provides Malory with the form of the female allegorical figures of Church and Synagogue.[9] Perceval, on his quest, first kills a snake who is attacking a lion, then dreams of a young lady riding a lion and an old lady riding a snake, the latter of whom tells him he will become her man. An old man then arrives who explains that the young lady 'betokenyth the new law of Holy Chirche' – that is, the New Testament – while the older one 'signifieth the old law, and that serpente betokenyth a fynde' (547/31–42; XIV.7). The sense then is not literal, but allegorical, not worldly ('terrestrial' is Malory's word) but spiritual. But in narrative, such allegorical figures will act *like women*; they will try and seduce the knight in question. To Perceval, the woman turns out to be not only the old woman of his dream, but 'the mayster fyende of helle' (551/8; XIV.10). The spiritual

---

8   This 'world' of towns, townsfolk, and ordinary people does not reappear until after the battle of Salisbury and the final dissolution of the Arthurian kingdom, and there mainly in the guise of grave-robbers.
9   An example is found on the portal of the south transept of Strasbourg cathedral; see George Zarnecki, *Art of the Medieval World* (Englewood Cliffs, 1975), plates 372, 373.

message is that fornication is a metaphor for abandoning one's baptism and Christ for the devil, but such is the power of misogyny that this diabolic power might simply be attributed to woman herself, rather than woman as symbol. That is, chastity is a virtue in itself, and a metaphor or allegory of other virtues; women are a vice in themselves and an allegory for other vices. On the Grail quest, women are utterly without an objective existence, even that of the shadowy and sinister women of adventure; they exist only as part of a theological signifying system, which for the most part assimilates the female with the diabolical.

Ambivalence, then, characterizes the feminine in the sphere of Arthurian adventure. Women are divided into an aspect of malevolence and ill-will characterized by a threatening sexual voracity most associated with Morgan, and another aspect of mediation and guiding, and sometimes of healing. It is this last aspect that apparently prevails among the ladies on the barge, surprisingly including Morgan le Fay herself, who mysteriously arrive to take away the grievously wounded Arthur. 'Evyn faste by the banke hoved a lytyll barge wyth many fayre ladyes in hit, and amonge hem all was a quene, and all they had blak hoodis' (716/8–10; XX.5). Malory departs from his sources in naming these ladies, and in his suggestion that the ladies were successful and that Arthur will return again. Avalon had been named in 'The Knight with Two Swords' as the source of adventure; it is traditionally associated with the supernatural Celtic realm, a marginal reality which abuts that of Logres – Arthur is reabsorbed into the source of the marvellous, now conceived as a place of healing. The arts of medicine and healing have been female activities all along: Elaine of Astolat nurses and heals the wounded Lancelot; both Isoldes are first sought out by Tristram because of their ability to heal; and Elaine (Galahad's mother) is responsible for the healing of Lancelot by the Grail. This is the obverse side of the love potions and poisoned weapons that ladies, sometimes the same ladies, wield. Femininity is equated with a drug, in its benevolent and malevolent aspects; with the potion's compulsion to love, the cankering wounds inflicted by Hallewes and Isolde's mother, the loss of identity in madness and trance, and finally the possibility of healing, of returning to wholeness, if only in Avalon.

II

In contrast to the feminine domain of the forest, the queens in their castles are associated with the forms of courtly love, marriage, culture, the social order – and with tighter plotting. They are also so strongly associated with adultery that I will argue that adultery is the central or sustaining contradiction of the Arthurian chivalric world, and that the plot of Malory's last books concerns the exposure of that contradiction whereby allegiance to the king is also adultery with the queen. The ideological structures of chivalry and love which sustain the court are matched by a shadow structure of adultery which, when made explicit and brought into the open, destroys it.

'Torre and Pellinor' gives an account not only of the initiation of the errant questing world of the knights of the Round Table, but, by implication, of Guinevere's part in that male fellowship.[10] Arthur tells Merlin 'I love Gwenyvere, the kynges doughtir of Lodegrean . . . the whyche holdyth in his house the Table Rounde that ye tolde me he had hit of my fadir Uther' (59/25–27; III.1). The queen and the Table are constantly linked:

> And so kyng Lodgreaunce delyverd hys doughtir Gwenyver unto Merlion, and the Table Rounde with the hondred knyghtes . . . Whan kynge Arthure herde of the commynge of quene Gwenyver and the hondred knyghtes with the Table Rounde, than kynge Arthure made grete joy for hir commyng and that ryche present . . . (60/15–21; III.1–2)

The reason Arthur wishes to marry is because 'My barownes woll let me have no reste but nedis I muste take a wyff'(59/20–1; III.1). The usual reason barons demand the marriage of their lord is so that he will get heirs and be followed by a secure succession, but the issue of issue here seems to involve not Arthur's children, but Uther's. The barons are turbulent because 'the moste party of the barowns knew nat he was Uther Pendragon son . . . many kyngis and lordis hylde hym grete werre for that cause' (59/14–16; III.1). Discord among the barons will be settled by the Round Table, apparently by means of a symbolic metonymy: the acquisition of an artefact indubitably once the property of Uther, as Arthur is not. Arthur has his patrimony and his bride at the same time. Once he acquires the Table and his bride, his mother comes too, to testify to his legitimacy. The institution of a chivalric and non-hierarchical social order among men, which will solve the destructive strife caused by Arthur's insecure filiation, is curiously dependent on the marriage. And that marriage is undertaken with a warning from Merlin of the future adultery (59/36–39; III.1). I mean to suggest a kind of symbolic equivalence between Guinevere and the Round Table – she has a profound and ambivalent role in the fellowship which holds the knightly order together. The warning about adultery is something Malory has added, with the effect of putting the entire marriage, from its inception, under suspicion. Curiously, the Merlin of his source in the *Suite de Merlin* hints at the adultery but gives an entirely positive message about Guinevere's political function; Merlin praises the marriage because, through her beauty and her liaison with Lancelot, Prince Galehot will be brought to peace with Arthur.[11] Thus the benefits of adultery are made strikingly clear.

[10] On fellowship, see Elizabeth Archibald, 'Malory's Ideal of Fellowship,' *Review of English Studies*, n.s. 43 (1992), 311–28.

[11] *Merlin*, ed. Gaston Paris and Jacob Ulrich (Paris, 1883) II, 61.

The paradoxes of adultery which are expressed symbolically in the early books are worked out in all their complexity in the later books. One poignant expression of the adulterous paradox is in the 'Poisoned Apple' episode where, while Guinevere is without Lancelot, she is also considered by the court to be 'a destroyer of good knyghtes' (617/13–14; XVIII.5) and is scolded by her own husband for not being able to control her lover:

> 'What aylith you,' seyde the kynge, 'that ye can nat kepe sir Launcelot uppon youre syde? For wyte you well . . . who that hath sir Launcelot uppon hys party hath the moste man of worship in thys worlde uppon hys syde.' (615/35–38; XVIII.4)

The grammatical shift to the generic 'hys syde' shows what the queen's role is supposed to be here, a role which is also defined in Bors' many accusations: 'Now, fye on youre wepynge . . . for now have ye loste the beste knyght of oure blood, and he that was all oure leder and oure succoure' (489/6–10; XI.9); or 'Therefore, madame, I mervayle how ye dare for shame to requyre me to do onythynge for you, insomuche ye have enchaced oute of your courte by whom we were up borne and honoured' (616/6–8; XVIII.5). Guinevere, like the Round Table that was her marriage portion, holds the knights at court and is culpable if she drives them away. Guinevere's role is not to uphold the court, but to uphold the 'homosocial' bonds between men who uphold the court.

'Homosocial' is the term used by Eve Kosofsky Sedgwick to explain non-sexual bonds between men.[12] She elaborates the work of René Girard, who has explained triangular relations in terms of the mediation of desire. The object of desire, here Guinevere, is produced as desirable by being valued or desired by another, here the king himself. Guinevere's value is that she is married to Arthur. In the triangles of male homosocial desire, the woman is the focus which enables the men who desire her to bond, to make social contracts, and, importantly, to enact their rivalries. Indeed, it is one of the more interesting features of Sedgwick's work that both hostility and fellow-ship are included in her model; when one thinks of the many quasi-ritual combats in the *Morte Darthur*, it is plain that most of these are within a group bound by common aims and interests, while only a few are with

---

[12] See Eve Kosofsky Sedgwick's *Between Men: English Literature and Male Homosocial Desire* (New York, 1985). The *Mort Artu*'s statement of Guinevere's 'homosocial' role is strikingly clear. Bors tells the queen: 'My lady, you can maintain all these virtues in my lord so perfectly that none are lost, because you know he is the most handsome man in the world, and the noblest, and the boldest . . . But just as he is now clothed and covered in all good virtues, in the same way you would strip and deprive him of them . . . You can see quite clearly, my lady, that you would be damaging this kingdom and many others much more than one lady ever did through one knight. That is the great power for good we expect from your love' (*The Death of King Arthur*, trans. James Cable [Harmondsworth, 1971]), p. 78.

enemies genuinely outside the familiar court milieu (Sir Tarquin and Sir Breunis Sans Pité stand as examples of the latter).

It is the condition of the Queens Isolde and Guinevere to be *always* in a triangular relation, though the points of the triangle often shift. In 'The Knight of the Cart,' for example, the triangle is composed of Lancelot, Meleagant and Guinevere. Isolde is even more plainly the stable focus of a flux of desirous males: Tristram, Palomides, Mark, Keyhydyns, and even Sir Brewnor, all of whom change in relation to each other during the course of the narrative largely as a result of how they see themselves in terms of Isolde. During the time Palomides forgets Isolde, he is Tristram's liegeman, for example. It is worth noting in passing that those women who are not the object of desire, such as Elaine of Astolat or Isolde Blaunche Maynes, perform their ·homosocial function by a process of substitution; in both cases, the desired knight, Lancelot or Tristram, takes the lady's brother when he leaves her.

The way in which love of the lady animates homosocial bonds is seen in exactly those almost ritual combats which occur so frequently in the *Morte Darthur*. Much of *The Book of Sir Tristram* is a restless repetition of events which illustrate courtly love questions, many of them of an at least apparent simplicity which defies credibility. The issue of whether different knights might love different ladies becomes a life and death issue to be jousted over in forest encounters. It is partly in this way that love organizes the adventurous realm. For example, Meleagant and Lamorak fight over whether Guinevere or Morgause of Orkeney is 'fayrest'; Lamorak is obliged to explain, in order to prevent Lancelot joining the fray:

> 'I am lothe to have ado with you in thys quarell, for every man thynkith hys owne lady fayryste, and thoughe I prayse the lady that I love moste, ye sholde nat be wrothe. For thoughe my lady quene Gwenyver be fayryst in youre eye, wyte you well quene Morgause of Orkeney ys fayryst in myne eye, and so every knyght thynkith hys owne lady fayryste.' (298/32–37; IX.14)

While this paradox seems to have come from the kindergarten of love school, at a deeper level the problem here is the confusion of objective and subjective categories, that is, whether the fairness of the lady is the source of love, or love the source of fairness, a quality of the beloved or of the loving gaze; that is to say, it is a problem central to the discourse of courtly love. Because beauty has some objective existence, Lamorak's subjective answer can never entirely prevail. One result of this failure is that the problem will recur (as it does). Lancelot attempts to trump Lamorak by conflating beauty with rank, another common trope from the courtly love tradition: 'Hyt is nat thy parte to disprayse thy prynces that thou arte undir obeysaunce and we all' (298/27–9; IX.14). An amorous question has been elided into a matter of feudal and social hierarchy.

The feud over the subjectivity of beauty is a trivial example of thought about love – in part because such themes are worked out elsewhere, in other texts, in much more interesting ways; Malory's work is not one of the monuments of courtly love. Such love is nonetheless dangerous, potentially lethal; how much more dangerous then will be issues that approach the central dilemma of adultery more closely. Other writers on the subject of adultery and narrative stress the transgressive nature of adultery. Tony Tanner writes, in *Adultery and the Novel*, that in the bourgeois novel marriage 'is a means by which society attempts to bring into harmonious alignment patterns of passion and patterns of property . . . It is the structure which maintains structure';[13] adultery, then, is the paradigm of transgression itself. While the medieval romance reveals a set of aristocratic values quite different from those found in the novel, social structures are nonetheless maintained by marriage there too; but the structure of literature, especially of plot, is that of adultery. I am suggesting that for the Arthurian cycle, adultery is the structure of structure. It is what sustains the court, and what drives the plot towards its ending on Salisbury Plain. I do not mean to suggest that adultery is morally sanctioned by the characters in, or authors of, these works (though at places in the *Book of Sir Tristram* it seems that it is). On the contrary, adultery is the great danger to the society which houses it. That adultery is transgressive, that the peril to the Arthurian kingdom consists in the private room of love being broken open and exposed to the world is hardly surprising. What is more surprising is that the socially beneficial effects of that adultery are barely repressed, and sometimes openly acknowledged. The hidden conflicts of the Arthurian court are often produced overtly and even parodically in the court of Mark. Though Mark has definitive proof that Tristram and Isolde are lovers early on, his attempts to bring them to justice, or at least to revenge himself on them, are reduced to farce. The barons, with the exception of Andret, oppose Mark and side with Tristram, refusing to allow the queen to be burnt (270/29–31; VIII.34), or Tristram to be executed (309/32–37; IX.22). Mark is despised not because he is a cuckold, but because he is a bad knight. Lamorak speaks for a legion of accusers when he says of Mark:

> 'there dwellyth the shamfullist knyght of a kynge that is now lyvynge, for he is a grete enemy to all good knyghtes. And that prevyth well, for he hath chased oute of that contrey sir Trystram that is the worshypfullyst knyght that now is lyvynge, . . . and for the jeleousnes of his quene he hath chaced hym oute of his contrey.' (355/1–6; X.8)

In other words, Mark's jealousy about a woman prevents him from achieving the male-bonded fellowship of Arthur's court. In terms of the homosocial triangle, his problem is exactly that he has not effaced the position of the woman to get to the man.

---

[13] *Adultery and the Novel* (Baltimore, 1979), p. 15.

In the Arthurian court, however, adultery remains a painful and largely repressed subject; it is the scene of open rivalry between Arthur and Lancelot for only a few pages before the king is again reconciled with the queen, and conflict displaced onto the kinship vendetta of Gawain. What, then, makes adultery the structure of structure? Some oddities are of interest here; chiefly that not only are adulterous queens barren, but the problem of illegitimate children is not even raised as a possibility. Marriage, in Malory, has nothing to do with succession, possibly because the Arthurian world is known to be coming to annihilation. The adultery of the queen with the knight is a breach of feudal allegiance to the king; in fact, because it is the queens who are adulterous, adultery is represented not as breach of contract, or as domestic betrayal, but as high treason, punishable by burning. Thus, in its hidden state, adultery sustains the lateral political ties of fellowship; exposed, it causes a swift reversion to hierarchical feudal relations.[14]

Terence McCarthy has argued persuasively that the final conflict in the last books of the *Morte Darthur* is the result of a conflict between public life, involving fealty to the king and bonds of fellowship with the other knights of the Round Table, and private life, involving a clandestine love affair.[15] But this analysis supposes 'private' and 'public' to be trans-historical categories; I would suggest that the great romances of adultery are a stage in the development of the space of privacy, which is both physically the bedroom of the lady and the private emotion in the psyche of the lover.

The relation between public, and hence political, conduct and the private sphere of love is not contingent, nor are they mutually exclusive. John Stevens, for example, stresses the social necessities which lie behind the medieval conceptions of romantic love and romance as a genre; he describes the 'essential paradox of courtly love, that an intensely private experience is made the ground of social well-being.'[16] The unresolvable tension between public life and private love is also that between realms of experience that are, respectively, masculinized and feminized, as Catherine La Farge argues.[17] The contradiction of adultery, whereby stability is maintained by the most disruptive force of all, comes about because public life is sustained and nurtured by something other than itself, that is by a sphere of action which is not public and political but magical, subjective, private. The public aspect of love is chivalry, and the private aspect of love is adultery.

---

[14] On the subject of lateral and hierarchical ties in the *Morte Darthur* see Riddy, p. 106.
[15] See Terence McCarthy on the conflict between what is publicly acceptable and what is privately known in '*Le Morte Darthur* and Romance,' *Studies in Medieval English Romance*, ed. Derek Brewer (Cambridge, 1988), pp. 148–75.
[16] *Medieval Romance* (London, 1973), p. 40.
[17] La Farge, p. 265.

One reason for the necessity of adulterous relationships is in their implication in narrative itself; adultery is the condition for the possibility of narrative after the Grail questers have put an end to the marvels which were the objects of quests. The world of spiritual perfection suffers from a poverty of plot, and so Malory's work, after that quest, immediately returns to the love affair: 'Than, as the booke seyth, sir Launcelot began to resorte unto quene Gwenivere agayne and forgate the promyse and the perfeccion that he made in the queste . . . and so they loved togydirs more hotter than they dud toforehonde' (611/10–17; XVIII.1). The continuation of the story is not only about the resumption of adultery, but the attempt to hide it; Lancelot takes up the causes of damsels in an attempt to camouflage his love for the queen. He says:

> 'And wyte you well, madam, the boldenesse of you and me woll brynge us to shame and sclaundir, and that were me lothe to se you dishonoured. And that is the cause I take uppon me more for to do for damesels and maydyns than ever y ded toforne, that men sholde undirstonde my joy and my delite ys my plesure to have ado for damesels and maydyns.' (612/9–14; XVIII.1)

The immediate context of this speech puts the two spheres of the feminine that I have discussed in direct opposition. To have ado for damsels and maidens is the 'woman as quest' function, a reason to go forth, a project moralized as duty, while the renewed adultery is both a turning inward, and the mechanism of the fatality of plot. The scene of this fatality is represented in the final books as the inner room of love experience, as, for example, the barred room which Lancelot breaks into in the 'Knight of the Cart' and the room he attempts to defend from the incursions of Agravain and Mordred when he is taken with the queen. The similarity of these rooms to the various prisons he is incarcerated in, often as the result of sexual demands by women, aligns the joy of love with the penal servitude which often represents female sexual desire. Guinevere's jealousy stands for the notion that knightly honour is now in direct conflict with courtly love, and that the central contradiction is unsustainable.

I have suggested, then, that adultery is necessarily implicated in both the paradigmatic and syntagmatic drives of the *Morte Darthur*; as what sustains the court (the paradigm of knightly fellowship), and what destroys it (the syntagm of revelation in plotting). Mordred completes the logic of the plot; by attempting to appropriate the queen for himself he reduplicates what Arthur himself had done. The Arthurian kingdom is not won by filial succession (the queen's children) but by seizing the queen who is the key to a stable court.

The account I have given of gender in the *Morte Darthur* concentrates on its function in the plot and the symbolic order of the work, rather than on character. This tactic seems appropriate, especially in the earlier books where narrative function is far more important than the representation of a unified psyche underlying actions, which is what is usually meant in discussions of literary 'character.' The contradictory traits of many characters in the book reveal the ascendency of plot function over consistency; Gawain is a prominent example – he is a lady killer in 'Torre and Pellinor' (66/7–8; III.7) and a great champion of ladies in 'The Day of Destiny' (711/34–44; XXI.3). Similarly, the Lady of the Lake seems benevolent when she gives Arthur his sword (35/20–21; I.24), yet malevolent when she demands Balin's head (40/40–41; II.3). But, increasingly toward the end of the work, character comes to be important in Malory, and Guinevere emerges as his most striking character.

Guinevere is imperious, impulsive, and sometimes witty. She exercises her power by exiling Lancelot on several occasions, usually when she is in a jealous rage. Her power is that absolute power of the beloved in the courtly love tradition, which is revealed as merely the power to reject; the exercise of that power labels her as capricious, cruel and arbitrary in the view of her husband and other knights. Faced with such hostility, she easily regrets what she has done – she spends twenty thousand pounds on the search for the mad Lancelot, for example (505/17–19; XII.9). Though she has accused Lancelot in very severe terms of betraying her with Elaine of Astolat, when the corpse of the Fair Maid floats down to Westminster the queen is moved to pity, and to Lancelot's exasperation suggests: 'ye myght have shewed hir som bownté and jantilnes whych myght have preserved hir lyff' (641/29–30; XVIII.20).

These features – jealousy, anger, and pity – are the subjective internal emotions of a character; they are also all the result of the adulterous plot situation, as are other features which are signs of both character and plot, such as secret motivations, scheming and deceit, which cause the final tragedy of the *Morte*. The adulterous situation, I would argue, has a great deal to do with the creation of 'character.' The equation seems to be between the closed-in private space which is the room of secret love, and the metaphorical inner-chamber of the mind, the repository of those private intentions, desires, and most importantly, deceits, which emerge when the public persona contradicts the private, when the adulterous motivation is different than the stated motive. In 'The Poisoned Apple' for example, Guinevere turns Lancelot out, then, in order to disguise her inward thought, arranges a dinner party 'for to shew outwarde that she had as grete joy in all other knyghtes of the Rounde Table as she had in sir Launcelot' (613/15–17; XVIII.3). The public act results in the accusation of murder, the concealed crime par excellence; her 'crime of the heart,' an internal mental act, is registered in the actions of the narrative as murder.

III

Much of what happens in Malory is a matter of inherited forms. While some items found in his sources are present in his text only as faint ghosts, others are more apparent, or, in some cases, structurally more essential. An example of the former is the lover's trance (a prominent feature of the *Lancelot en prose*); of the latter, the adultery which is itself an essential part of the structure of the narrative and of the society represented by the narrative. But, given that Malory had decided to re-tell the story which is the epitome of adulterous love, it is nonetheless true that his narrative seems to proceed with reluctance. Malory shows an ambivalence about the sexuality of his protagonists, evidenced particularly by the excision of the kind of language and sentiment considered to be appropriate to 'courtly love' (to use the modern critical term) or *fine amor* (the medieval term). He has deleted a very great deal of the eroticism of his sources. In the *Lancelot en prose* for example, when Lancelot sees the queen at the Queen's Ford, he falls into a trance so deep that he rides into the river without noticing it, and is captured by Dagonet, a wholly inadequate adversary; when he approaches the queen, in his confusion he stumbles in such a way that his lance tears her dress. His incapacitation and abstraction – his very weakness – heighten the mood of languorous desire, the picture of a lover ravished by longing. Malory's contrasting coyness or prudery in matters of sexuality have caused certain critics to claim that Malory means to suggest, unlike his sources, that love relations do not necessarily include sexual relations. While this extreme position is in my view untenable, many passages demonstrate Malory's reluctance to speak of sexuality, such as the celebrated passage which asserts that love then was not as love is nowadays (649/25–32; XVIII.25). Perceval suggests to King Mark that Tristram 'may love youre quene synles' and Malory draws a curtain over the question of what Lancelot and Guinevere did in bed (657/35–6; XIX.6). P. E. Tucker has provided a comprehensive account of the evidence. Tucker suggests that Malory is at first 'irritated' by the French sources' emphasis on the subject, which does not match his own, and only late in his book does he arrive at a conception of chivalry which could include Lancelot's love for Guinevere.[18] Indeed, in the later books, Malory comes to write quite a lot about love, and much of that is from the woman's perspective.

Malory has, then, chosen to write, or re-write, a story which obliges him to confront love and adultery on many levels, yet he seems unwilling to do so. Catherine La Farge sees Malory's treatment of, or, more properly, his failure to treat the feminine, as a form of repression, which, as in psycho-

---

[18] P. E. Tucker, 'Chivalry in the *Morte*,' *Essays on Malory*, ed. J. A. W. Bennett (Oxford, 1963), p. 72.

analysis, is partially defeated by an eery leakage of the repressed material, taking such shapes as the 'lady hunteresse' who appears from nowhere to shoot Lancelot. La Farge writes: 'the disregarded problem of gender, particularly the role of the feminine, comes back to haunt the progress of the narrative, as Elayne's own corpse floats back down the Thames.'[19]

This repression of the 'feminine' content of his sources would be widely conceded by Malory's critics, and it is often formulated as a stylistic feature – the deletion of rhetoric. Tucker writes: 'Malory's distaste is not so much for the physical part of love as for a sophisticated account of it.'[20] Derek Brewer has suggested that Malory writes in the 'style of a gentleman,'[21] and his claim finds support in the recent work of Terence McCarthy: 'the speech of Malory's characters is dignified, terse, to the point, and not expansive or articulate after French models of eloquence. Malory's knights are not great talkers and the economy of their speech gives it at times a proverbial ring. They are restrained and manly, in a word, knightly.'[22] This discussion of the speech of characters slides easily into the assumption that the characters are male, and the speech is somehow male too. This is a style, it appears, particularly suited to knights; but what makes this style masculine? Terseness, economy and restraint, it would seem; but these features are less in evidence in the final books where speeches are often long-winded, extravagant, and accompanied by floods of unrestrained tears. Nor do the female characters speak in a different style than the male characters, even when they speak about love, though one of the assumptions underlying accounts of what Malory has done is that the rhetoric of love is a 'feminine' way of speaking. I do not wish to deny that this is a 'masculinist' work, and that this is not a result of a mere style preference. Rather, as Mark Lambert has claimed, Malory's is a 'unitive' style,[23] and the unity it styles is that of the male fellowship of the Round Table. As La Farge writes, 'Malory's text may represent something of a rearguard action in defence of . . . wholeness, the public, the masculine.'[24]

Given his apparent aversion to 'feminized' discourse, it is all the more striking that in the last two books he gives many more long speeches than do his sources, and many more are in the mouths of women. The effect of this is to give what seems to be a more individualistic subject position to such women. This is most evident when the rejected lovers of Lancelot express their regret, and, in a simple way, assert their own desires in the face of an inexorable plot. Such speeches in fact first occur in 'Lancelot and Elaine,' a section which seems to veer schizophrenically between an Elaine

[19] La Farge, p. 265.
[20] Tucker, 'Chivalry,' p. 78.
[21] 'Introduction,' *The Morte Darthur: Parts Seven and Eight* (London, 1968), p. 12.
[22] *An Introduction to Malory* (Cambridge, 1988), p. 131.
[23] *Malory's Morte Darthur* (New Haven, 1975), p. 122.
[24] La Farge, p. 274.

who is heavily determined by the rules of magic – Lancelot meets her by rescuing her, 'nakid as a nedyll' (478/18; XI.1), from a scalding bath enchanted by Morgan le Fay – and a courtly domestic Elaine who seems to belong to the more realist mood of the final books. When Lancelot goes to the forest to escape the tension of the competition between Elaine and Guinevere, Elaine rebukes Guinevere for monopolizing Lancelot:

> 'And therefore, alas! madame, ye have done grete synne and youreselff grete dyshonoure, for ye have a lorde royall of youre owne, and therefore hit were youre parte for to love hym; for there ys no quene in this worlde that hath suche another kynge as ye have. And yf ye were nat, I myght have getyn the love of my lorde sir Launcelot; and a grete cause I have to love hym, for he hadde my maydynhode and by hym I have borne a fayre sonne . . .' (488/1–7; XI.9)

This Elaine does get a few years in the company of Lancelot at Joyous Isle after healing him of his madness; this is more than Elaine of Astolat gets, though she too heals him of serious wounds. She delivers a plaint very much like the first Elaine's, in speaking out for the validity of her own experience. As she is dying, she responds to her confessor:

> 'Why sholde I leve such thoughtes? Am I nat an erthely woman? And all the whyle the brethe ys in my body I may complayne me, for my belyve ys that I do none offence, though I love an erthely man, unto God, for He fourmed me thereto, and all maner of good love comyth of God. And othir than good love loved I never sir Launcelot du Lake. And I take God to recorde, I loved never none but hym. . .' (639/31–36; XVIII.19)

Indeed, the Fair Maid is arguing for the legitimacy of her love, as the kind of love which is divinely ordained, the kind of love which leads to marriage (though she would settle for having Lancelot as her paramour 'at the leste'). The propriety of such love is, however, no argument that it will be reciprocated. The modesty of the ambitions of both Elaines, in contrast with the titanic passions that are about to destroy the entire Arthurian kingdom, result in a striking pathos which is exactly that of the personal voice, expressing a simple desire, as contrasted with destiny itself. The first Elaine emerged from a supernatural background into a quasi-domestic milieu; the second emerges from the domestic to enter, in death, the semiotics of the supernatural, as she floats downstream in a barge, with a letter in her hand, exactly as Percival's sister had on the Grail quest, accompanied by 'a poure man' whose silent presence is an eery echo of earlier quest figures. Elaine, then, returns to the realm of otherness.

The Maid's suggestion of a legitimate love, one which combines earthly love and godliness, raises the possibility of a synthesis of the terms of the contradiction which Lancelot and Guinevere are sentenced to live, a synthesis which is represented by the bourgeois novel, and not by chivalric romance. This is largely because of the political and social status of the characters, and in the end, both Lancelot and Guinevere come to take their role in history seriously; Guinevere in particular takes responsibility for her actions.

> 'Thorow thys same man and me hath all thys warre be wrought, and the deth of the moste nobelest knyghtes of the worlde; for thorow oure love that we have loved togydir ys my moste noble lorde slayne. Therefore, sir Launcelot, wyte thou well I am sette in suche a plyght to gete my soule hele . . . And therefore, sir Launcelot, I requyre the and beseche the hartily, for all the love that ever was betwyxt us, that thou never se me no more in the visayge.' (720/15–25; XXI.9)

Guinevere's penitence means she can never see Lancelot again, but even as she expresses this resolution, she reaffirms the great contradiction, now apparently fully realized just as it is finally fixed in time, between the nobleness of Arthur, the greatness of his kingdom, and her love for Lancelot. The only solution, for Guinevere, to the horror of this realization is to turn away from the things of this world.

There is a subjectivity for women emerging in these speeches; and this is a decided contrast to the early books where external events often seem to be nothing more than the anxious and desirous projections of a psyche which is always male. Although these women may speak in the same style as their male counterparts, they are not thereby united, or held in any community, but are, rather, isolated and abandoned. Lancelot comes to his religious end by following the queen's example, but only after the queen has rejected his proposal to go into his 'owne royame' (721/9; XXI.10). When Lancelot is cast out of Arthur's court, it transpires that he has a court of his own to go to, fiefs and kingships to distribute in Benwick. Increasingly in the last books, events which affect Lancelot are held to affect his kin and retainers; when he is at odds with the queen, she, and not he, is friendless. Pathos is the condition of the individual isolated from community, and it has also become, for Malory, the new condition of femininity.

4

Contextualizing Le Morte Darthur*:*
Empire and Civil War

FELICITY RIDDY

When Malory wrote *Le Morte Darthur* he was in prison for treason during the worst political crisis England had known since the Norman Conquest. This chapter locates *Le Morte Darthur* in that crisis. It does so in two ways, literary and historical, while attempting to show at the same time that literature and history cannot easily be separated. I begin with the plot, the 'canonical' life-story which structures *Le Morte Darthur*[1] and which, in Walter Benjamin's words, borrows its authority from death;[2] the title of Malory's book, since Caxton's print of 1485, has been 'The Death of Arthur,' not the 'The Life.' The plot can be seen as a narrative of empire and civil war, which Malory inherited and invested with new meanings. This leads me to history, and to another narrative of empire and civil war: of the English withdrawal, complete by 1453, from the territories it had occupied in France, and the internal strife following that withdrawal – the Wars of the Roses – which led to Malory's own final imprisonment and which was not over when he died in 1471. This chapter brings these two narratives together in order to suggest that literary and historical representations of empire and civil war together provide a context for *Le Morte Darthur*.

I

Arthur was not a people's hero in the later Middle Ages; he belonged to a past which was conceived of as the scene of chivalric activity, and was a way of representing the interests of that section of society whose function had been, traditionally, to fight. John of Salisbury, in his *Policraticus* of the mid-twelfth century, defines the role of this estate, the *bellatores*, as being 'to protect the Church, to attack faithlessness, to venerate the priesthood, to

---

[1] Arthur's 'biography,' drawn from a large number of sources, is discussed by Rosemary Morris in *The Character of King Arthur in Medieval Literature* (Cambridge, 1985).

[2] Walter Benjamin, 'The Storyteller,' in *Illuminations*, ed. Hannah Arendt, trans. Harry Zohn (London, 1973), p. 94.

avert injuries to the poor, to pacify provinces, to shed blood . . . for their
brothers, and to give up their lives if it is necessary.'[3] This, by and large, is
the function that Arthur's knights have, even in *Le Morte Darthur*, despite
the fact that by Malory's day the theory of the three estates – the division of
society into those who pray, those who fight and those who labour – was an
anachronistic fantasy.[4] The fifteenth-century gentry, of whom he was
himself a member, included knights, esquires and gentlemen, who were
increasingly distinguished from the nobility and divided among themselves, and who acted as agents of the king's justice in the shires, as estate
managers, lawyers and bureaucrats of various kinds, and not simply as
warriors. The society of Arthurian narrative is imagined as a community of
knights, unleashed from the interdependence and responsibilities of estates
theory. It is different from Langland's *Piers Plowman*, written a century or so
before *Le Morte Darthur* and from a quite different perspective, in which
Piers creates a temporary community through the ploughing of the half-
acre. The role of the Knight in this community is that of a local peacekeeper,
protecting the other two estates from 'wastores and fro wikked men.' The
Knight's aristocratic pastimes are given a specific social function: he is to
hunt in order to keep down countryside pests; he is to train his hawks to
kill the birds which damage the corn. He is not to exploit his tenants, or
accept gifts from them, or mistreat his serfs.[5] Langland invokes estates
theory as a way of redefining the values of the knightly class, and of
locating it in a nexus of social responsibilities. In return for the Knight's
protection and justice, Piers, as labouring man, undertakes to 'swinke and
swete and sowe' for the Knight. But, of course, this community does not
work: the social vision of mutuality and complementarity is rapidly undermined by idleness and greed, and Will's search takes new directions.
Arthurian narrative projects an equally temporary society, as I shall argue,
but it is not an inclusive one. Peasants do not know their place because they
do not have one: in *Sir Launcelot du Lake* a 'carle' challenges Lancelot with
'a grete club shodde with iron' (161/20–1;VI.10), and in return Lancelot lifts
his sword and gives him a blow that splits open the upper half of his body,
obliterating him from the story. But the aristocratic perspective of
Arthurian narrative is not only a matter of excluding the third estate: by the
fifteenth century Arthur, who had begun as a Celt, was an English king,
and his life provided ways of exploring the upper-class perceptions of
Englishness which had been sharpened by the Hundred Years War. The old

---

[3] John of Salisbury, *Policraticus: Of the Frivolities of Courtiers and the Footprints of
Philosophers*, ed. and trans. Cary J. Nederman (Cambridge, 1990), p. 116.
[4] See Georges Duby, *The Three Orders: Feudal Society Imagined* (London, 1980). The opening
chapter of Maurice Keen's *English Society in the Later Middle Ages 1348–1500*
(Harmondsworth, 1990) is a helpful introduction to the estates in medieval England.
[5] See William Langland, *Piers Plowman: an Edition of the C Text*, ed. Derek Pearsall
(London, 1978), passus VIII, lines 32–53.

story took on new meanings, as it had always done. The process by which Arthur shifted from being one of the conquered to being one of the conquerors is part of that shift of meaning.

II

This leads me to my first context for *Le Morte Darthur*, then: the 'canonical' story of Arthur's life. From the vantage point of the late twentieth century, the English past over the last nine hundred years can seem satisfyingly stable. The various contemporary myths of Englishness include the comforting, if not complacent, image of the sometimes beleaguered but nevertheless unconquered island. In the late Middle Ages, however, people looking back nine hundred years did not see an unconquered island; they saw discontinuities, not continuity. They saw the Norman invasion of the eleventh century, the Danish invasion of the ninth, the Anglo-Saxon invasion of the fifth, which was preceded by a failed attempt by the Picts and the Scots, and the Roman invasion of the first century BC.[6]

The Anglo-Saxons were the only group to achieve a permanent hegemony, in that they gave their name to the country and to its language. When the Anglo-Saxons invaded Britain, the British – that is, the Celtic peoples who had lived under Roman rule for some five hundred years – either capitulated or retreated westwards: to Wales, to Cornwall and to Galloway. Arthur is the product of this discontinuous history. If we put aside the question whether or not Arthur existed, and approach the legend simply as a story, we can say that he – or one version of him[7] – was brought into being by what has been called 'the passage of dominion,'[8] or transfer of rule, by the narratives of the arrival of the Anglo-Saxons and the dispossession of the British, as told by both sides. An account of this invasion was given in the eighth century by Bede, in his *Historia*

---

[6] The early fourteenth-century Chronicle of 'Robert of Gloucester' gives what was by then the received account, when it describes England as having been conquered first by 'þe emperours of Rome,' then by 'Picars and Scottes,' then by 'Engliss and Saxons þat hider were ibro3t,' then by 'þe folc of Denemarch,' and finally by 'þat folc of Normandie, þat among vs wonieþ 3ut and ssulleþ evere mo.' See *The Metrical Chronicle of Robert of Gloucester*, ed. W. A. Wright, Rolls Series, 2 vols. (London, 1887), I, lines 42–58.

[7] For two excellent discussions of the non-existence of Arthur, see David N. Dumville, 'Sub-Roman Britain, History and Legend,' *History*, n.s. 62 (1977), 173–92, and Oliver Padel, 'The Nature of Arthur,' *Cambrian Medieval Celtic Studies*, 27 (1994), pp. 1–32. Padel usefully distinguishes between the 'historical' Arthur (of the *Historia Brittonum*, ch. 56, and the *Annales Cambriae*) and a pan-Brittonic 'folklore' Arthur who is the hero of local wonder-tales. He argues that the folklore Arthur is 'the true one, and the "historical" Arthur [is] the secondary development' (p. 30). I am concerned solely with narratives about the 'historical' Arthur.

[8] See R. William Leckie, Jr, *The Passage of Dominion. Geoffrey of Monmouth and the Periodization of Insular History in the Twelfth Century* (Toronto, 1981).

ecclesiastica.[9] This is the story as seen from the winning side – in Bede's words, the 'history of our nation'[10] – of the establishment of the Anglo-Saxon kingdoms and their conversion to Christianity, conceived of as a divinely-ordained plan. In the course of his narrative, Bede tells the story of a last-ditch stand among the Britons, led by a figure called Ambrosius Aurelianus.[11] According to Bede, he is not a Celt but the last of the Romans, who leads the Celts in a temporarily successful resistance against the Anglo-Saxons, but the larger sweep of history is against him. Bede does not record what happens to him, and he simply drops out of the narrative. The invasion cannot be stayed because it has already happened by the time of writing; any story about the British resistance is bound to be about a last stand, just as narratives about native Americans in the history of the American west inevitably have written into them, implicitly or explicitly, the larger tragic outcome of their story. Bede's Ambrosius Aurelianus is not Arthur, though he occupies the same narrative function as Arthur; the earliest surviving written story of a figure called Arthur comes in a history composed from a different point of view from Bede's. This is the *Historia Brittonum*, compiled by a Welsh author known as pseudo-Nennius in 829–30.[12] In this text the British Arthur fights twelve battles, 'and he was victorious in all his campaigns.' Then the defeated English bring reinforcements from Germany, 'and they brought over their kings from Germany to rule over them in Britain.'[13] After this nothing more is said about the victorious Arthur, but the subsequent history that Nennius tells is the history of the English kingdoms. So there is a hiatus in the text – a curious gap or silence. Arthur seems to be there in the narrative as the site of a heroic militarism that nevertheless does not stop the course of history; he is created by the passage of dominion, in that the advent of the English

[9] See Bede's *Ecclesiastical History of the English People*, ed. Bertram Colgrave and R. A. B Mynors (Oxford, 1969, corr. edn 1991).

[10] 'historia . . . nostrae nationis'; see *Ecclesiastical History*, ed. Colgrave and Mynors, p. 7.

[11] See Bede's *Ecclesiastical History*, ed. Colgrave and Mynors, ch. XVI. Ambrosius Aurelianus is taken by Bede directly from Gildas's *De excidio et conquestu Britanniae* (see Gildas, *The Ruin of Britain and Other Documents*, ed. and trans. Michael Winterbottom [London, 1978], pp. 28 and 98). Gildas was writing in the early sixth or even late fifth century, too early to have a clear sense of the larger narrative of the passage of dominion. Although British himself, Gildas is nevertheless deeply critical of the British who, he says, have brought about their own downfall. For a recent reinterpretation of Gildas, see N. J. Higham, *The English Conquest: Gildas and Britain in the Fifth Century* (Manchester, 1994). In Geoffrey of Monmouth's *Historia regum Britanniae*, a figure called Aurelius Ambrosius, who is king of Britain, is Arthur's grandfather.

[12] See Nennius, *British History and the Welsh Annals*, ed. and trans. John Morris (London, 1980). For the attribution to pseudo-Nennius, see David Dumville, 'Nennius and the *Historia Brittonum*,' *Studia Celtica*, 10–11 (1975-6), 78–95.

[13] See Nennius, *British History*, pp. 36 and 76. There is general agreement among scholars that the list of Arthur's twelve battles, beginning with the battle at the mouth of the river Gelin, and ending with the battle of Badon Hill, probably derives from an Old Welsh battle-catalogue poem.

seems to require resistance. Pseudo-Nennius gives us a paradoxically victorious and yet unsuccessful hero, the man who does not have history on his side.

The coming of the Anglo-Saxons meant the end of Roman-British rule, and for the Britons it meant marginalization and retreat. Inevitably, the unexplained gap that I have referred to in pseudo-Nennius – that is, between Arthur's victories and the arrival of the German kings – comes to be filled by Arthur's death, which is the creation of the larger narrative as seen from the British point of view. If the history of the invasion is written as tragedy, the last resistance fighter has to die. This has to do, of course, not with what 'really' happened, but with the way stories work. The death is created by the tragic tone of the narrative and the horizon of expectations it creates. Moreover, it is of the nature of stories that we ask of them the question we first ask as children: why? Why does Arthur win twelve battles and yet fail to save Britain? And it is of the nature of stories that they adjust themselves to supply answers. The *Annales Cambriae*, written in their present form possibly in the late tenth century, which are another voice of the dispossessed, fill the gap in pseudo-Nennius: after the battle of Badon, which in pseudo-Nennius is the last of the twelve, is the battle of Camlann, 'in which Arthur and Medraut fell.'[14] The larger narrative cannot be changed: the Anglo-Saxons cannot be sent home to Germany, except in prophecy, as in the tenth-century Welsh *Armes Prydein*.[15] Prophecies project history into the future, while the passage of dominion belongs to the past. And in this cryptic annal, which does not even reveal whether Arthur and Medraut were on the same side, we can see new stories about the final battle waiting to be born.[16]

By the late tenth and early eleventh centuries – that is, when the English kingdom was about to be superseded in turn by the Norman – there were a number of other texts of different kinds, not apparently of a tragic cast, circulating among the Welsh in which Arthur is alluded to as a war leader with a regular set of heroic companions, Cai, Bedwyr and Gwalchmai. He has a wife called Gwenhwyfar, who is abducted, sometimes by the figure called Medraut and sometimes by Melwas, king of the summer country.[17]

---

[14] For *Annales Cambriae* see Nennius, *British History*, pp. 45 and 85. For the dating of this annal, see Thomas Charles-Edwards, 'The Arthur of History,' in *The Arthur of the Welsh*, ed. Rachel Bromwich, A. O. H. Jarman and Brynley F. Roberts (Cardiff, 1991), pp. 15–32, at p. 28.

[15] *Armes Prydein: 'The Prophecy of Britain,'* trans. Rachel Bromwich (Dublin, 1982).

[16] The apparently neat chronology of the texts I discuss – first Bede, then pseudo-Nennius, then the *Annales Cambriae* – makes it look as if I am arguing that the 'historical' Arthur developed in precisely these stages. I am not; I am simply putting the three texts alongside one another in order to compare their points of view and their plots.

[17] The abduction of Guinevere by Melwas is related in Caradog of Llancarfan's *Vita Gildae*, which predates Geoffrey of Monmouth. The Welsh triad of the Three Faithless Wives of the Island of Britain ends: 'And one was more faithless than these three: Gwenhyfar,

Hostility to Guinevere is an ancient element in the legend of Arthur, and I shall return to this. All these figures have a fluid and evanescent existence; they must have occurred primarily in oral stories and poems, and were only occasionally fixed in writing.

Arthur was decisively textualized by Geoffrey of Monmouth in his *Historia regum Britanniae* of 1138.[18] Despite his Welsh name, Geoffrey did not live in Wales, and may have been of Cornish or Breton descent. He was a canon of Oxford who dedicated his work to powerful Anglo-Norman lords, offering them the unwritten history of the kingdom they had conquered, that is, the history before Bede. He writes from a similar perspective to that of pseudo-Nennius, but presents a much more complete and coherent chronology than pseudo-Nennius had done (not truer, of course, because Geoffrey's history is a fabrication, but more coherent). Geoffrey develops the founding myth of Britain in the story of Brutus, great-grandson of Aeneas[19] – after whom Britain is called – and an unbroken succession of kings, including Arthur, who is located at the same point as in pseudo-Nennius: at the point of final effective resistance to the Saxon invaders. Geoffrey's regnal sequence memorializes the past as a series of life-spans, as a space in which the living supersede the dead, generation after generation, ever since Troy. He gives Arthur what becomes the standard biography: an ambivalent birth story; accession to the throne at fifteen; defeat of the Saxons at home and abroad; marriage to Guinevere; a great court; the conquest of Europe; a challenge from Rome; a fight with a giant and defeat of the Roman army. As he is about to march to Rome in triumph, he is called back by news of the treachery of his nephew, Mordred, who has taken Guinevere and made himself king. Arthur returns to England and fights three battles against Mordred, who is killed, but he is mortally wounded himself. He is taken to the isle of Avalon and the throne passes to his nephew Constantine.

Geoffrey, who knew pseudo-Nennius's history and probably knew

---

Arthur's wife, since she shamed a better man than any (of the others).' This triad is first found in a fifteenth-century manuscript, National Library of Wales, MS Peniarth 47. It is not in the early version of the Triads of the Island of Britain, and may derive from Geoffrey or from French romance. See *Trioedd Ynys Prydein: The Welsh Triads*, ed. and trans. Rachel Bromwich, 2nd ed. (Cardiff, 1978), pp. 200 and 380–85.

[18] Geoffrey of Monmouth, *The History of the Kings of Britain*, trans. Lewis Thorpe (Harmondsworth, 1966). For the Latin text, see *The Historia regum Britannie of Geoffrey of Monmouth I: Bern, Burgerbibliothek, MS 568*, ed. Neil Wright (Cambridge, 1985). There is an extensive bibliography on Geoffrey of Monmouth. Two important studies, in addition to that of Leckie (see n. 8), are J. S. P. Tatlock, *The Legendary History of Britain* (Berkeley, 1950), and especially Robert Hanning, *The Vision of History in Early Britain* (New York, 1966).

[19] The story of Brutus as founder of Britain was not Geoffrey's invention. It occurs in pseudo-Nennius' *Historia Brittonum*, from where Geoffrey presumably derived it, greatly elaborating it.

other Welsh material as well,[20] fills in the gap in the text to which I have referred: where pseudo-Nennius says Arthur was undefeated, and yet the English invasion took place, Geoffrey rationalizes this. Arthur dies undefeated by the Saxons; he can only be defeated by treachery from within. Civil war, and not just empire, is his undoing. In the reigns after Arthur's death there is further internal strife, plague and famine, and eventually the Britons flee to Brittany, leaving the country open to the transfer of power that Arthur had so heroically withstood. The invasion takes place in part because Arthur dies prematurely, unable to consolidate his victories; that is, Arthur's death now explains the invasion.

Geoffrey of Monmouth's biography of Arthur in the *Historia regum Britanniae* is thus a life written backwards: it is a life constructed to make sense of the death that is required by the larger narrative of the tragic passage of dominion from the Britons to the Anglo-Saxons. Whereas pseudo-Nennius left Arthur's story incomplete, Geoffrey allows him to die and thus to become part of the natural sequence of the generations which structures the *Historia*. This sequence, in which one reign succeeds another, is a continual re-enactment of Freud's 'masterplot for organic life':[21] 'the most universal endeavour of all living substance – namely to return to the quiescence of the inorganic world,' the death-wish.[22] Geoffrey's kind of history – history as a generational series – naturalizes the story of the drive to death. And it is death which makes life narratable, as Walter Benjamin says: 'A man's . . . real life . . . first assumes transmissible form at the moment of his death.'[23] Death gives life shape; the whole narrative of the life presses towards, and yet seeks to defer, the death. Death provides not only narrative closure but also the reader's desire for closure, and provides in addition a point of origin.

Arthur's death, the death that is required by the sweep of history and by the nature of stories, is Geoffrey's starting-point, and the plot of the life is what Peter Brooks calls 'the complicated detour'[24] which leads back to it. Between his birth and his death, the story – the complicated detour – is concerned with Arthur's insatiable desire for possession. Geoffrey's version of his life is what Brooks, writing of nineteenth-century novels, calls a narrative of male ambition:

[20] See Brynley F. Roberts, 'Geoffrey of Monmouth, *Historia regum Britanniae and Brut y Brenhinedd*,' in *The Arthur of the Welsh*, pp. 97–116.

[21] The phrase is from Peter Brooks, *Reading for the Plot. Design and Intention in Narrative* (Cambridge, Mass., 1992), p. 102. Much of my thinking on Arthurian narrative has been stimulated by Brooks's work.

[22] Freud, *Beyond the Pleasure Principle*, in *The Standard Edition of the Complete Psychological Works of Sigmund Freud*, ed. James Strachey (London, 1953–74), vol. 18, p. 62, quoted by Peter Brooks, *Reading for the Plot*, p. 107.

[23] Benjamin, 'The Storyteller,' p. 94.

[24] Brooks, *Reading for the Plot*, p. 107.

Ambition is inherently totalizing, figuring the self's tendency to appropriation and aggrandizement, moving forward through the accomplishment of more, striving to have, to do and to be more . . . The ambitious heroes of the nineteenth-century novel . . . may regularly be conceived as desiring machines whose presence in the text creates and sustains narrative movement through scenarios of desire imagined and then acted upon.[25]

Geoffrey of Monmouth's Arthur is, like these heroes, a desiring machine who moves forward from one scene of conquest to the next. The old grand narrative of British dispossession and marginalization generates in Geoffrey's hands its complete reverse: the imperialist hero who occupies centre stage as he sweeps across Europe; not the dispossessed but the dispossessor. The problem Geoffrey faces, of course, is how to get this character to where the narrative of the passage of dominion requires him to end up. Arthur conquers the Roman army (in an extraordinary trans-formation of the Roman conquest of Britain) but cannot actually install himself as emperor because Roman history has its own narratives in which Arthur does not figure; besides, the overall story – the story of the end of British dominion – is tragic. Somehow Arthur has to be got back home to die. Geoffrey does it by making Arthur's nephew, Mordred, betray him. This conclusion is also the beginning, since Arthur's birth story is a repetition of his death story: Mordred's desire for Guinevere echoes Uther Pendragon's desire for Ygerna, and the plot moves from one to the other via the 'bestial desire'[26] of the giant of Mont St. Michel for Arthur's niece. It is the illegitimacy of all these desires that makes them so energizing for the narrative: they are imperious and amoral movements of the will that power the sequence of events out of which the plot is constructed. Uther, the giant and Mordred are all counterparts to Arthur: Arthur's desire, equally imperious and amoral, is legitimized by being represented as military rather than sexual. In Arthur, conquest is an erotic drive that is satisfied only by death.

In Geoffrey's narrative, Arthur is king of Britain, not of England. The Saxons are the enemy, and the line of kings whose history Geoffrey tells runs into oblivion. The end of his narrative, which is the end of British dominion of the island, signals a hiatus in the transfer of power. The discontinuity is so profound as to be a closure. Other chroniclers after Geoffrey override this closure; they take over his story of the kings of Britain and continue with the narrative of the Saxon kings, then the Danish and then the Normans. By the later Middle Ages the kings of England could construct pedigrees for themselves that traced their ancestors almost uninterruptedly back to Brutus. But the story of the life of Arthur does not

---

[25] Brooks, *Reading for the Plot*, p. 39.
[26] Geoffrey of Monmouth, *History of the Kings of Britain*, trans. Thorpe, p. 239.

only begin with his death: all of it leads to his death. For readers and listeners, Arthur is always already dead. The legend of his return, already old when first recorded in the twelfth century, seems to contradict this, by opening up the possibility of his being alive. But second comings require, not only first comings, but crucifixions; the legend of the return of Arthur is only meaningful when, in narrative terms, he has ceased to be, when he is no longer a desiring machine, a generator of stories. This is why the legend of the return can survive the discovery of Arthur's grave at Glastonbury in 1191:[27] the issue never was whether or not Arthur was 'really' dead; it was about wresting him from the oblivion to which the ambitious hero goes when narrative movement has reached its promised end. His return will not save the English but generate new stories.

III

Between Geoffrey of Monmouth in the middle of the twelfth century and Malory in the late fifteenth, the many narrative accounts written in England of the whole reign of King Arthur, from his accession as a youth till his death in the civil war with Mordred, were embedded in chronicle histories, written in Latin, French and English. There were, of course, numerous verse narratives written before *Le Morte Darthur* about parts of Arthur's reign. One of the earliest of these is *Of Arthour and Merlin*, composed in the late thirteenth century, which deals with Arthur's birth and accession, while the story of his death is told in two fourteenth or early fifteenth-century poems which Malory knew: the Alliterative *Morte Arthure* and the Stanzaic *Le Morte Arthur*. Writing the whole of the reign, though, was the province of chroniclers, most of whom worked within the by now traditional biographical framework established by Geoffrey. The whole reign, and more, had also been included in the thirteenth-century French prose Vulgate and post-Vulgate cycles which were read in England in the fourteenth and fifteenth centuries and formed part of the staple of aristocratic culture. In Malory's *Le Morte Darthur* the material of these French prose cycles is married with the English chroniclers' focus on the reign itself; the pre-history with which the Vulgate *Estoire del Saint Graal* and much of the *Merlin* are concerned has been discarded and Malory begins with Uther's desire for Ygrayne. Almost all of the huge Vulgate *Lancelot* has gone too. It is not the adventures of Lancelot but of Tristram, from the French prose *Tristan*, which occupy much of the central part of *Le Morte Darthur*, allowing the themes of adulterous passion, of jealousy and madness, to be explored, primarily at the expense of the inept King Mark of Cornwall, and not of

---

[27] In this year, in what turned out to be an extremely successful publicity stunt, the monks of Glastonbury Abbey announced that they had discovered the graves of Arthur and Guinevere within the abbey precinct.

Arthur. The differences between Malory's structure and that of the French prose cycles amount to an anglicization of the Arthurian legend. Put briefly, Geoffrey of Monmouth's account of Arthur's reign had embedded him in a sequence of kings of Britain, not of England; the twelfth- and thirteenth-century French romances extracted him from this historical sequence and developed the legend synchronically: French writers were not, by and large, interested in the issues of nationhood that the legend could be made to bear. In the late fifteenth century, however, Malory's *Le Morte Darthur* goes back to the regnal structure; for the first time in English outside a chronicle he writes the whole reign, expanding the traditional biography with material drawn from French and English romances. Malory's Arthur is king of England, not of Britain – or, as Caxton puts it, 'of thys noble royalme thenne callyd Bretaygne' (xv.6) – and the narrative is written from an English point of view. This point of view may be crudely patriotic in the account of the foreign wars in *The Tale of Arthur and Lucius*, or may be much less obtrusively positioned as, for example, in a comment such as: 'Than syr Constantyn that was syr Cadores sone of Cornwayl was chosen kyng of Englond, . . . and worshypfully he rulyd *this royame*' (725/32–4; XXI.13; my italics). Nevertheless, obvious or not, it gives *Le Morte Darthur* a specifically English orientation.

Malory's Englishing of his French sources, then, is not simply a matter of translation but of narrative perspective and, as I shall go on to argue, of ideology. Extracted from the historical sequence of the chronicles, the reign of Arthur no longer lies at the crossing-point from British dominion to English, since what I have called the grand narrative has been eliminated. In *Le Morte Darthur* the reign of Arthur is taken out of Geoffrey's generational sequence to become a signifier of aristocratic crisis, of a failure to project a future. There is no secular aftermath to Arthur's death, no subsequent society outside the monastery, and there are no superseding generations. At the end of the story all the sons – Arthur's, Gawain's, Lancelot's – are dead, all except Constantine, son of King Cador of Cornwall. It is like the closing moments of *King Lear* (also a narrative excerpted from the legendary regnal sequence, and also a scene in which only one of the children is left alive): 'Is this the promised end? Or image of that horror?' To which the only answer is: 'Fall and cease.' The masculine society of *Le Morte Darthur* collapses, and the narrative cannot reimagine the social order as a continuity. The death of Arthur, no longer held in place by the grand narrative or necessitated by the larger sweep of history, is freed to create new meanings. And Arthur, who had originally been part of a narrative of dispossession, is now part of a narrative of empire; in an extraordinary political reversal, which happens only in the mid-fifteenth century, Arthur is now the conqueror of Rome.[28]

---

[28] In the *Chronicle* written and rewritten by John Hardyng between c.1446 and 1463, a

It is worth considering more closely what Malory has done to the received version of Arthur's biography. Whatever the order of its composition, it looks as if Malory must have taken a view of Arthur's death by the time he completed the second book, *The Tale of Arthur and Lucius*, which tells the story of the Roman war. As my earlier discussion of Geoffrey of Monmouth shows, the Roman war usually comes late on, as part of the death story, and traditionally Arthur's ambition to assume the imperial crown in Rome is left unfulfilled. This is what happens in the Alliterative *Morte Arthure*, in which Arthur's triumphant military campaign across Europe and into northern Italy is cut short by the news from home of Mordred's treachery. Here the bloody imperialism which the narrative of ambition sustains is shockingly exposed for what it is by the fact that the final goal of the plot is not empire but death.[29] Malory worked directly from this poem, and presumably already knew when he rewrote the Roman war as an unqualified victory, ending with Arthur's coronation as emperor at the hands of the pope, that he would not need it later. This suggests that he had already chosen between the two versions of the end of the Round Table which were available from previous writings. On the one hand was the version deriving from Geoffrey of Monmouth, which the Alliterative *Morte Arthure* and the chronicles use, in which Lancelot either does not appear at all, or figures simply as one of Arthur's leading knights. In this version Arthur leaves England to fight against Rome. On the other, which derives from the French Vulgate *La Mort le roi Artu* and is used in the Stanzaic *Le Morte Arthur*, Lancelot is Guinevere's lover, and Arthur leaves England in order to fight him in France, urged on by Gawain, after the adultery has been made public. The Mordred plot remains essentially the same: Arthur has to return to England to recover his throne, and Lancelot also returns to support him, but arrives too late. This is the version that Malory chooses. His use of the Roman war in the second book effectively precluded him from using it again, with a different outcome, in the last.

Malory's ending, using the love affair between Lancelot and Guinevere, isolates the civil war which destroys the Round Table from the imperialist version of the Roman War, separating out the scenarios of desire. Empire is exclusively masculine, while the divisions of civil war issue from the intervention of the feminine into the world of homosocial ambition:

version of which Malory may have known, Arthur also reaches Rome and is crowned emperor there. See *The Chronicle of Iohn Hardyng*, ed. Henry Ellis (London, 1812).

[29] Lesley Johnson, 'Arthur at the Crossroads,' in *Noble and Joyous Histories: English Romances, 1375–1650*, ed. E. Ní Cuilleanáin and J. D. Pheifer (Dublin, 1993), pp. 87–112, argues that in the Alliterative *Morte Arthure* 'judgements on the ethics of [Arthur's] campaign become more complicated by the nexus of political, chivalric and Christian values which the participants claim both motivates and determines their action' (p. 95). See also the eloquent study by Lee Patterson, 'The History of Romance and the Alliterative *Morte Arthure*,' in his *Negotiating the Past* (Madison, Wisconsin, 1987), pp. 197–230.

'Thorow thys same man and me hath alle thys warre be wrought, and the deth of the moste nobelest knyghtes of the worlde', claims Guinevere (720/15–16; XXI.9). In the end, Arthurian narrative pays the price of its hostility to Guinevere, since that hostility ensures that royal power will not be transmitted from father to son; as the faithless wife she is not the mother of heirs. But of course this hostility needs to be inspected further and not just treated as a given. The faithless Guinevere can be seen as herself the creation, rather than the cause, of the crisis for patriarchy which the passage of dominion represents. That is, the discontinuous history of rule which I have been discussing is a disruption in the lineal and stable transference of power between men; but if Guinevere is written as adulterous then this disruption can be ascribed to her and not to Arthur's impotence. In Malory's version all this is put under pressure by the decision to allow Guinevere to have 'a good ende' (649/35; XVIII. 25), so that she repudiates her ancient identity as the faithless wife before she dies; and by the fact that although the crown passes to Constantine, there is no transfer of dominion because there is no royal power: almost the last words Arthur speaks are 'Comforte thyselff, . . . and do as well as thou mayste, for in me ys no truste for to truste in' (716/23–4; XXI.5). It is as if once Guinevere's faithlessness ceases to be an issue, after she has been returned through the mediation of the pope, then Arthur's impotence is no longer obscured. From then on, during the war in France, Arthur is unable to assert his authority over his nephew, Gawain. Where in Geoffrey of Monmouth's *Historia regum Britanniae* Arthur's continental war had been driven by ambition, in *Le Morte Darthur* he dwindles into enfeeblement. To read all this as a direct comment on the politics of the 1450s and 60s, and particularly on Henry VI's failed rule, would be too crude.[30] It may be that a larger failure of Englishness is being represented: the loss of empire, not just the civil war.

IV

This leads me to the second context which I proposed at the beginning of this chapter, and the historical narrative of empire and civil war which I undertook to provide. It is the story of the end of the Hundred Years War between England and France. It starts in 1415, the year of the celebrated English victory at Agincourt, in northern France, under Henry V, and

[30] Henry VI, who came to the throne as an infant, was always an ineffectual ruler, temperamentally unfitted for kingship. In the 1450s he had periods of mental instability and Richard, Duke of York, acted as regent. In 1460, York claimed the throne. He was killed a few months later, but his son, Edward IV, was crowned in 1461. Henry VI escaped to the north and remained at liberty for four years before being captured by the Yorkists. In 1470 he was briefly restored by his supporters, but lost the throne to Edward IV again in 1471 and was put to death. His son had been killed in battle three weeks earlier.

possibly the year of Malory's birth.[31] Agincourt was a battle fought by exhausted armies, knee-deep in mud. There were huge French losses; the roll-call of the dead nobility in the pages of French chronicles is like Malory's summoning-up of the Round Table for the healing of Sir Urry. One reason why so many of the French nobility died is that at a crucial stage of the battle, faced with an unexpected cavalry assault, Henry gave the order to kill the prisoners. It was no more *dulce* or *decorum* than the battles of the First World War, fought over much the same ground; in John Keegan's words 'it is . . . a story of slaughter-yard behaviour and outright atrocity.'[32] Henry's chastened demeanour during his triumphal reception back in London – remarked on by contemporaries – suggests that he knew this; but Agincourt was quickly turned into legend by chivalric chroniclers, and it provided a touchstone for a certain kind of Englishman of what it meant to be English. By 1419 Henry had gone on to conquer the duchy of Normandy which England had lost two centuries earlier. Although he was supported by the aristocracy, for whom war held out promise of reward, not all sections of society approved of the enterprise. John Barkefolde, a London wiredrawer, was accused in 1419 of having publicly affirmed that

> taxes and tallages were falsely and unfaithfully levied from the poor and wretched people and that the king had caused liege and faithful men to be hanged and burnt and had crossed to a foreign land and there had destroyed God's people, and that neither he nor any of his race had ever done otherwise.[33]

This is a voice of the third estate: the resentful taxpayer, the Lollard sympathizer,[34] sceptical of nationalism and undeluded by the glamour of chivalry.

In the following year, the treaty of Troyes made Henry V heir to the throne of the ailing Charles VI, king of France. This arrangement was confirmed by Henry's marriage to Charles's daughter, Catherine, later in 1420. Henry granted lands to his followers in occupied Normandy, and it became an English settlement, garrisoned by English troops. Henry's justification was that Normandy was English, but very few French noblemen offered him allegiance. There was continuing French hostility to the terms of the treaty and Henry did not live to inherit the throne; he died in 1422 while leading the siege of Meaux, near Paris, leaving a son who was less than a

---

[31] The summary in this paragraph owes much to Christopher Allmand, *The Hundred Years War: England and France at War c.1300–c.1450* (Cambridge, 1988), pp. 20–32.

[32] John Keegan, *The Face of Battle. A Study of Agincourt, Waterloo and the Somme* (Harmondsworth, 1978), p. 78.

[33] *Calendar of Plea and Memoranda Rolls of the City of London AD 1413–1437*, ed. A. H. Thomas (Cambridge, 1943), p. 82.

[34] Barkefolde's allusion to hanging and burning is probably to Henry V's punishment of the Lollards involved in Sir John Oldcastle's rising in 1414. Oldcastle himself was burnt in 1417. Lollards were frequently critical of warfare against other Christians.

year old. Two months later, Charles VI died, and Henry's son, the infant
Henry VI, now assumed the French throne as well as that of England,
although many parts of France supported Charles's son, the dauphin.
During the 1420s the English, under Henry V's brother John, Duke of
Bedford, who acted as regent on behalf of his young nephew, consolidated
their hold on French territories by pushing southwards into Maine and
Anjou. These years of expansionism until 1429 marked the high point of
England's triumph in France. In that year Joan of Arc raised the siege of
Orléans and the dauphin was crowned king of France at Reims. The
English retaliated by crowning Henry VI at Paris in 1431; Joan of Arc had
already been captured and burned. The next decade or so saw continual but
inconclusive fighting on French soil on behalf of the two kings, interspersed
with periods in which attempts were made to achieve a negotiated peace.
Years later, the Norman chronicler, Thomas Basin, former bishop of Lisieux,
recalled the devastation of his native land in the 1430s:

> I myself have seen the vast fields of Champagne, of Beauce, of Brie, of
> the Gatinais, of the regions round Chartres and Dreux, of Maine, of
> Perche, of the Vexin, French as well as Norman, of the Beauvaisis and
> the region of Caux, from the Seine to Amiens and Abbeville, the region
> round Senlis, the Soissonais and Valois right to Laon, and beyond to
> Hainault, absolutely deserted, uncultivated, abandoned, emptied of
> inhabitants, covered with brambles and briars, or in the places where
> trees will grow, springing into dense forest.[35]

Henry VI was neither a soldier nor a statesman. His council was divided:
opposition to settlement with France was led by his uncle, Humphrey,
Duke of Gloucester, for whom it was a betrayal of all that had been won
since Agincourt. By the mid-1440s Henry had married the French king's
kinswoman, Margaret of Anjou, and was ready to renounce his claim to the
French throne; within a few years the English had surrendered Maine and
Anjou, and in 1450 they were driven out of Normandy. Their remaining
territories in Aquitaine, in the south-west, were lost in 1453. Only Calais
remained English thereafter. For many, it was a period of national shame.

The colonization of Normandy, which was represented as a reassertion
of England's ancient rights (just as Arthur claims that he has ancient
rights over Rome), was a reversal of what had happened to England
when it was colonized by the Normans in 1066. The story of Arthur's
march on Rome and triumphant crowning in *The Tale of the Noble King
Arthur that was Emperor Himself through Dignity of his Hands* (i.e. through
his military prowess) reads like a fictional version of Henry's Norman
conquests, as Vinaver argued in the commentary in his three-volume

---

[35] Thomas Basin, *Histoire de Charles VII*, ed. and trans. Charles Samaran, 2 vols (Paris, 1964),
I, 86.

edition.[36] Nevertheless Vinaver did not go on to suggest, as I wish to, that the tale is an imperialist narrative. The monster of Mont St. Michel, whom Arthur encounters as he leads his army through France to Rome, is now a kind of Caliban, configured by the colonizing mentality which represents the native as a brutish and cannibalistic rapist. English hatred and fear of foreigners is projected on to Arthur's grotesque enemies – 'fyffty gyauntys that were engendirde with fendis,' 'the Emperour with all hys horryble peple' (117/15–6; 19.V.2). Similar figures haunt Basin's chronicle, which describes the brigands who emerged in Normandy under English rule and who are imperialism's Other. These are bands of lawless men who lived deep in the forests like animals, who owed no allegiance, who preyed on both their fellow countrymen and on the hated English whom they butchered ruthlessly whenever they could. In Basin's chronicle these guerilla groups are represented explicitly as the creation of colonization: they are a bestial force, 'leaping out like wolves from their hiding-places,'[37] brought into existence by English rule, and when English power disappears, they revert to civilization as farmers, husbands and fathers:

> For as soon as the English, thrown out of Normandy, were compelled to return to their own land, the country was freed of that terrible human plague . . . They applied themselves to cultivating the land or, if they had learned a trade, they used it to procure the necessities of life for themselves, their wives and their children.[38]

I use the term 'imperialist' in a modern, as well as in a medieval, sense. The idea that 'the king is an emperor in his own kingdom' was a commonplace of late-medieval political thinking,[39] but it has to do with royal sovereignty and jurisdiction, not territorial expansion. It means that the king has the powers of the Roman emperor within his own realm.[40] Henry V's colonization of Normandy can be regarded as 'imperialist' in this medieval sense, in that he was asserting sovereignty over territories which England claimed were English, not French. Nevertheless, to the French who did not recognize Henry's claim, and to many of the Normans who lived for a generation under English rule, the English were imperialists in the modern sense, who held the duchy by terror. Thomas Basin, the chronicler, who did well under the English régime, acknowledges this. He was only a few years older than Malory, and as a child fled with his family from their home in

---

[36] *The Works of Sir Thomas Malory*, ed. Eugène Vinaver, rev. P. J. C. Field, 3rd ed., 3 vols (Oxford, 1990), I, xxxi.

[37] Thomas Basin, *Histoire de Charles VII*, II, 112.

[38] Basin, *Histoire de Charles VII*, I, 110.

[39] In Latin: 'Rex in regno suo est imperator.' See Walter Ullmann, '"This Realm of England is Our Empire,"' *Journal of Ecclesiastical History* 30 (1979), 175–203, and *The Cambridge History of Medieval Political Thought c.350–c.1450*, ed. J. H. Burns (Cambridge, 1988), pp. 464–69.

[40] See Ullmann, '"This Realm of England is Our Empire",' 176.

Caudebec at the mouth of the Seine, when Henry V's armies landed en route to Agincourt. Years later in 1449, as count-bishop of Lisieux in Normandy, he negotiated the surrender of the city, which had been in English hands for twenty-four years, to the French army.[41] Describing the joy which followed the English retreat in 1450, Basin comments: 'The English had conquered Normandy by force, and it was also by force that they had maintained their dominion; the locals had lived under the tyranny of fear.'[42] He wrote his *History of Charles VII* in the 1470s, as an exile in Trier, a few years after Malory wrote *Le Morte Darthur* in prison in London; both works are scarred by the war, and by their authors' ambiguous implication in the history of their times.

V

In the preface he wrote for the 1485 printed edition of *Le Morte Darthur*, which ought to be treated with the scepticism reserved for all publishers' blurbs, William Caxton makes a connection between King Arthur and Englishness, and suggests that Arthur has a special appeal for the upper-class Englishman. One of the reasons he gives for publishing *Le Morte Darthur* is that 'many noble and dyvers gentylmen of thys royame of Englond' (xii; 3) have told him that he ought to print a book about Arthur, rather than the one he had already printed about Godfrey of Boulogne, because Arthur 'was a man borne wythin this royame and kyng and emperour of the same' (xii; 4); that is, in printing the book he is performing a patriotic duty. Reading it is patriotic, too, if not jingoistic: according to the same 'noble and dyvers gentlemen,' 'Kyng Arthur . . . ought moost to be remembred emonge us Englysshemen tofore al other Cristen kynges' (xii; 3), and so Caxton says he has printed it so that 'noble men may see and lerne the noble actes of chyvalrye, the jentyl and vertuous dedes that somme men used in tho dayes' (xiii; 5). The point of this sales pitch seems to be to try and locate *Le Morte Darthur* in a narrow and anachronistic idea of the English gentleman, for whom Arthurian knighthood provides the

---

[41] For details of Basin's life and writings, see Bernard Guenée, *Between Church and State: The Lives of Four French Prelates in the Late Middle Ages*, trans. A. Goldhammer (Chicago, 1991).

[42] Basin, *Histoire de Charles VII*, II, 106. Guenée argues that Basin's choice of words at this point, especially his use of *imperium* (which I translate as 'dominion') is a way of discreetly conveying his view, against that of French chroniclers like Gilles le Bouvier and Mathieu d'Escouchy, that 'the invasion of Normandy was not improper. The sovereignty of the English was perfectly legitimate . . . To be sure, it had been established by force, by right of conquest. It was maintained by fear. But it was perfectly legitimate.' Guenée is alluding here to the doctrine *Rex in regno suo est imperator* (see n. 39): *imperium* is the proper authority of the king who is emperor in his own kingdom. Guenée's biography presents the Norman Basin as a skilful and, in his own terms, principled collaborator with both the English and French authorities.

pattern. The models Caxton proposes are Malory's passionate and ignorant characters, members of a last generation who blindly kill the men they love most; competitive, desiring and violent, they perform their roles in a tragic plot, the larger shape of which they cannot see. At the end of the book Ector can articulate only a private loss in his elegy over Lancelot; he is not granted even Hamlet's partial insight into the carnal, bloody and unnatural acts of which he has been part. Caxton is the salesman of the unexamined life.

The class of men to whom Caxton recommended *Le Morte Darthur* – the knights, esquires and gentlemen who separated themselves off from the yeomen on the one hand and the nobility on the other – was in place in the shires by the end of the fourteenth century. As I have already said, during the fifteenth century these men became administrators rather than warriors; soldiering was a life-cycle phase rather than a vocation. The skills they developed were literacy and toughness, and the ability to find a good lord to protect their interests in violent times. They made prudent and advantageous marriages (which does not mean that they could not also be loving and companionate), and they assiduously extended their properties, creating for themselves fictitious lineages and genealogies which they recorded in their armorial bearings. We can see *Le Morte Darthur* as a post-imperial, or even post-colonial, text, which speaks with the voices of these 'noble and dyvers gentylmen' of Malory's generation, for whom the loss of the French territories in 1453 had been a personal disaster, and who could not accommodate themselves to the diminished view of their country and of their own role and prospects – both financial and social – that that loss brought with it.[43] These are the men whom Colin Richmond, who does not need to flatter them as Caxton did, describes as 'conquistadores.' After being kicked out of France they turned, he says, to internal imperialism, lording it over their fellows: 'what i would term internal colonization therefore dates from 1450 – english gentlemen as conquistadores like cortes and co against those they considered a rabble.'[44] A good deal was at stake for men of this class. During the fifteenth century the material conditions of the peasants improved: they freed themselves from serfdom, they gained access to ownership of land, and they were able to negotiate better terms of employment from their masters, all of which put the structures of society under strain.[45] *Le Morte Darthur* circulated in precisely that period of moral

---

[43] See, for example, William Worcestre, *The Book of Noblesse*, ed. J. G. Nichols (London, 1860). Worcestre was Sir John Fastolfe's secretary, and the text was probably originally composed before Fastolfe's death in 1460, and revised around 1475 to rouse patriotic support for Edward IV's projected invasion of France. Fastolfe had made enormous profits from the English occupation of French territories.

[44] Colin Richmond, 'The fifteenth century: 18 november 1992,' *Journal of Historical Sociology* 6 (1993), 471–85, at p. 477.

[45] See Christopher Dyer, *Standards of Living in the Later Middle Ages: Social Change in England c.1200–1520* (Cambridge, 1989), esp. pp. 274–77.

crisis, that vacuum of aristocratic values in the second half of the fifteenth century, when the governing élites, no longer united against the French and the Scots, first fell upon each other in the Wars of the Roses and then reassembled themselves under the Tudors against their own tenants. The great myth of the fifteenth century is the gentility to which these men all aspire, and Le Morte Darthur is the great repository of that myth. It imagines a world in which the kitchen boy who can handle arms and armour must be a prince in disguise, in which the only kind of man who can pull the sword from the sheath is a 'clene knyght withoute vylony and of jantill strene of fadir syde and of modir syde' (38/37–9; II.1), and in which the goodly terms that distinguish a gentleman from a yeoman and a yeoman from a villein will last till the day of doom. But although Malory's book sustains and is sustained by the ideology of aristocracy, nevertheless it is an aristocracy in crisis.

The crisis is, I am suggesting, one that is figured in Le Morte Darthur as the death-wish of a class. The narrative records the aristocracy's sense that its values are under threat, and locates the source of that threat within. The estates theory on which the Le Morte Darthur rests does not provide any way of analyzing the changing relations between peasants and landlords, and so the aristocracy's predicament can only be represented as the self-generated collapse of its own defining ethos. Brother turns against brother, and in the end the Round Table turns parricidal as well.[46] The last battle, which brings in its train the end of everything, is a symbol of the chivalric world turning its nihilistic energy upon itself, and destroying its own possibility of continuity. The mutual murders of Arthur and Mordred recall the much earlier murders of Balin and Balan, but now these close off history: there are no allusions forward, as there had been in Balin and Balan's story, to other succeeding narratives. The death of Mordred is followed by that apocalyptic moment on the battlefield at night, when the dying Arthur hears people crying in the field and sends Lucan to find what it means:

> and so as he yode he saw and harkened by the moonelyght how the pyllours and robbers were com into the fylde to pylle and to robbe many a full noble knyght of brochys and bees and of many a good rynge and many a ryche juell. (714/23–6; XXI.4)

This is the entry into the narrative of that class which has been excluded from the imagined community of knights; it is a return of the repressed. It is as if the dispossessed inhabitants of the devastated fields of Champagne, of Beauce, of Brie, of the Gatinais, of Chartres and Dreux, those voiceless and unrepresented presences, have finally made their way – vengeful and

---

[46] In Geoffrey of Monmouth's Historia regum Britanniae, Mordred is Arthur's nephew, not his son, so the issue of parricide does not arise.

pitiless – into the chivalric text, to snatch the emblems of the chivalrous class from it in its death throes.

But of course, the aristocracy did not destroy itself, nor was it destroyed, in the second half of the fifteenth century; it merely reconsolidated its wealth and prestige.[47] We can see two of its new men in the painting by Hans Holbein the Younger known as *The Ambassadors*, now in the National Gallery in London, which was painted in 1533.[48] The painting is of two figures, a layman and a priest. The scene is an interior: the two young men stand looking out at the viewer, at either end of a dresser on which each of them rests an elbow in an informal pose; the layman is on the left and the priest on the right. Between them on top of the dresser and on a lower shelf lie, carelessly stacked, books, including a hymn-book, a globe, a lute with a broken string, and various astronomical instruments. A barely visible crucifix, at right angles to the viewer, looks down on them both. Holbein is able to catch the palpable luxury of their clothing. The man on the left is richly dressed in satin, velvet and furs, and his right hand rests on the gold sheath of his dagger. The man on the right is in clerical dress, but his full-length gown is of sleek fur. His priestly status is marked by his dark clothing and his contemplative demeanour, but the implication of the dresser with its paraphernalia of contemporary learning is that the two men share a common intellectual culture. The boundary between the two estates is now blurred; for the purposes of this painting it is no longer the primary means of categorization. More important are the modern humanist attributes that unite them, and the way in which they seem to confront the viewer as if the future were theirs. They are ambassadors from a new world which seems utterly remote from that of the bookless Sir Lancelot and Sir Baldwin of Brittany, the hermit who heals his wounds in 'The Fair Maid of Astolat.' Holbein, though, has a deeply sceptical eye. In the front of the picture, a strange, elongated oval shape extends diagonally from the calf of one young man to the feet of the other, a shape which, if the viewer stands at the right angle, reveals itself as a foreshortened skull: the young men are united by their mortality as well as their culture. And so the painting does not simply celebrate the intellectual sympathies of the two men, or simply accord them the status to which they lay claim by virtue of their class, their gender and their assured contact with the new learning; it is also a *memento mori*. So, too, is *Le Morte Darthur*.

[47] See J. C. K. Cornwall, *Wealth and Society in Early Sixteenth-Century England* (London, 1988).

[48] The ambassadors are French: the layman is Jean de Dinteville who was the French ambassador to England. In 1533 he was visited in London by Georges de Selve, who acted as ambassador to the Holy Roman Emperor, to the Pope and to Venice. Holbein painted the two men in London.

5

Malory and his Sources

TERENCE McCARTHY

Readers who wish to become acquainted with Malory's sources are in a fortunate position today: nearly all the texts are available in convenient editions and even translations. Most of the books Malory used were in French but the influence of a small number of English sources goes well beyond the brief sections of the *Morte Darthur* they gave rise to.

The French volumes Malory used most often were parts of the cycle of prose romances we know as the Vulgate Cycle, and the separate but parallel romance known as the *Prose Tristan*. There are five branches of the Vulgate Cycle, which French scholars refer to more appropriately as the *Lancelot-Graal*. The story of Arthur is here part of a much vaster history, of which the central figure is Lancelot, and the events described go back well beyond Arthur to the origins and exploits of the wizard-counsellor, Merlin, and to the early history of the Grail. Malory dispenses with the first two branches of the cycle entirely, *L'Estoire del Saint Graal* and *Merlin* – if he knew them, that is. There are at least signs that he had read the *Merlin*, but he chose to focus his Arthuriad more closely on Arthur, and began by adapting the *Suite du Merlin*,[1] a later continuation of the *Merlin* proper, which had been expanded to cover the early years of Arthur's life and reign, and to provide a better link with the third branch of the cycle, the *Prose Lancelot*.

The second section of the *Morte Darthur*, what Vinaver calls *The Tale of Arthur and Lucius*, is a rough prosification of the Middle English Alliterative *Morte Arthure* minus its tragic ending.[2] Since Malory places the narrative of Arthur's campaign against the Roman emperor at an early stage in the

---

[1] Only one of the four (incomplete) manuscripts of the *Suite* has been edited. See *Merlin, roman en prose du XIIIe siècle*, ed. G. Paris and J. Ulrich, 2 vols (Paris, 1886). Garland Publishing are in the process of producing a complete translation into English of the French Arthurian romances, but until it appears students will find the translation by Henri de Briel into modern French useful: *Le Roman de Merlin l'enchanteur* (Paris, 1971).

[2] Ed. E. Brock, EETS os, 8 (London, 1871); ed. V. Krishna (New York, 1976); ed. Mary Hamel (New York, 1984); ed. L. D. Benson in *King Arthur's Death* (Indianapolis, 1974). Non-specialists might be tempted to consult the translation by Brian Stone published (with the stanzaic *Le Morte Arthur*) under the title *King Arthur's Death* (Harmondsworth, 1988).

king's career, he cannot give a complete version of the poem, at the end of
which Arthur is killed. Instead, the English king is crowned emperor, a
detail Malory may well have taken from John Hardyng's chronicle, which
was produced in two different versions (and with differing political
sympathies, therefore) during the reigns of Henry VI and Edward IV, when
Malory himself was active.[3] Hardyng's chronicle may have appealed to
Malory because it includes – and therefore gives historical credibility to –
Arthurian material that other chroniclers usually ignored. It may also have
encouraged him to distance himself from the more overtly literary
approach of his French sources, with their concern for amorous intrigue
and private motivation, and may have helped him to focus his own more
historical vision of the Arthurian world.

The Book of Sir Lancelot, the shortest of Malory's tales, is based on a few
brief extracts from the third and largest branch of the Vulgate Cycle, the
Prose Lancelot, although certain episodes at the end are taken from the
Perlesvaus.[4] There is still disagreement as to whether Malory consulted this
romance himself or whether his text of the Lancelot contained interpolations
from the Perlesvaus. There is also disagreement about the origin of The Tale
of Sir Gareth, the only tale for which no extant source is available. It was
long thought to be based on a lost French romance of the 'Fair Unknown'
variety, closely connected to the literary branch of the Prose Tristan, but it
has recently been shown that Malory's source may well have been a verse
romance in English.[5]

The source of the next, and longest, section, The Book of Sir Tristram, is the
first two books of the French Prose Tristan.[6] The third book of this was a
version of the Grail Quest, but Malory preferred to adapt his Tale of the
Sankgreall, the next section of the Morte Darthur, from the fourth branch of
the Vulgate Cycle, La Queste del Saint Graal.[7] For the final stages of his
Arthurian history Malory used a number of different texts. The major
source is the fifth branch of the cycle, La Mort le Roi Artu, but this is

[3] The Chronicle of Iohn Hardyng, ed. Henry Ellis (London, 1812).
[4] A. Micha, ed., Lancelot: roman en prose du XIIIe siècle, 9 vols (Paris, 1978–83). Two volumes
   of selections based on this edition have been translated into modern French by Micha
   (Paris, 1984). W. A. Nitze and T. A. Jenkins, eds, Perlesvaus, 2 vols (Chicago, 1932-7). See
   also Nigel Bryant, The High Book of the Grail: a translation of the Perlesvaus (Cambridge,
   1978). Precise guidance through these vast sources can be found in P. J. C. Field, 'Malory
   and the French Prose Lancelot,' Bulletin of the John Rylands University Library of Manchester,
   75 (1993), 79–102.
[5] E. Vinaver makes the French claim ('A Romance of Gaheret,' Medium Ævum , 1 [1932],
   157–67), and P. J. C. Field the English ('The Source of Malory's 'Tale of Gareth',' Aspects
   of Malory, ed. T. Takamiya and D. S. Brewer [Cambridge, 1981], pp. 57–70).
[6] An edition of the French prose Tristan is in progress under the direction of Philippe
   Ménard. Five volumes have appeared (Geneva, 1987–92). The first volume of a
   translation of the text into modern French appeared in Paris in 1990.
[7] Albert Pauphilet, ed., La Queste del Saint Graal (Paris, 1967); trans. P. Matarasso
   (Harmondsworth, 1969).

supplemented and sometimes replaced by the fifteenth-century stanzaic English poem, *Le Morte Arthur* (itself based on the French text).[8] At least one part of the final section comes from a version of the *Prose Lancelot*, but as yet the precise version has not been identified, and Malory uses recollections of the *Lancelot* to fill out and modify his narrative elsewhere.

These are the main sources, the ones that provide the bulk of Malory's material and the ones that he systematically abridged, adapted, and even at times translated. Since he makes no pretence to be inventing the story he tells, Malory does not hesitate to quote his sources when the occasion arises to corroborate the information he provides. When he tells us that Lancelot 'wende, whan he felte sir Gawaynes double hys strengthe, that he had bene a fyende and none earthely man' there is no reason to believe that he is exaggerating or inventing; 'the Freynshe booke seyth' exactly the same thing (704/21–3; XX.21). On the other hand, when his sources do not provide the necessary information, Malory refuses to commit himself. He is unable to identify the London churchyard in which the sword in the stone was to be found because 'the Frensshe booke maketh no mencyon' (7/28; I.3).

This apparent concern for the reliability of his narrative is such that Malory is in fact guilty of a degree of subterfuge. At times he claims that the French book says what the French book does not say at all.[9] Consequently, when reference is made to sources that have not survived, it is difficult to know what to think. At one point Malory tells us that he is taking up a new source because he has lost the one he had been using until then, the (unidentified) 'Shevalere de Charyot' (669/32–4; XIX.13). P. J. C. Field points out that it is certainly possible that such a source did exist and that Malory knew it, but it may well be that he merely invented it to give authority to the events he was narrating. If he did know the source, his claim to have lost it might well be an excuse for omitting material he did not wish to include.[10] After all, when his French source says what does not suit his purpose, Malory is even ready to withhold information. When Lancelot and Guinevere are trapped together in the queen's chamber Malory refuses to say what in the French text is made clear – whether the lovers were in bed together or not (676/1–4; XX.3).

This mixture of accuracy and dishonesty, of quotation and camouflage, can be confusing to readers unfamiliar with Malory and I begin therefore with some remarks on the role of what it is convenient to call the traditional

---

[8] Jean Frappier, ed., *La Mort Le Roi Artu*, 3rd ed. (Geneva and Paris, 1964); trans. James Cable (Harmondsworth, 1971). The stanzaic *Le Morte Arthur* is edited by J. D. Bruce, EETS es, 88 (London, 1903); ed. P. F. Hissiger (The Hague, 1975); ed. L. D. Benson in *King Arthur's Death*; trans. Brian Stone (Harmondsworth, 1988).

[9] Some – but not many – of these apparent contradictions may well be due to the difference between the manuscripts Malory used and those which have survived. See R. H. Wilson, 'Malory's French Book Again,' *Comparative Literature*, 2 (1950), 172–81.

[10] Sir Thomas Malory, *Le Morte Darthur, The Seventh and Eighth Tales*, ed. P. J. C. Field (London, 1978), p. 264.

author.[11] Most twentieth century readers have literary assumptions that
have been largely influenced by the novel – a name which in many ways
says it all. We expect something new. But the premise that a writer's first
duty is to invent, to create, to be original, must be modified when we deal
with literature of earlier periods. Of course, we soon learn to come to terms
with the fact that Chaucer or Shakespeare borrowed nearly all their story
material, but their borrowings pale into insignificance in the light of their
own considerable contributions.

Malory is much more completely a traditional writer, one for whom
invention, as such, is not the prime concern. Instead, he borrows and
assembles in order to recreate, to give new form to old stories in a way that
does full justice to what he sees as their true significance. Indeed, the
different meanings of the word 'original' are the dividing line between
the traditional writer and the modern novelist. For a traditional writer,
borrowings are not so many skeletons in the cupboard he will seek to
conceal; they are the bare bones of his narrative. If there is anything he
might wish to hide, it is precisely those parts which he has added himself
and which cannot be traced back to an authoritative original. Malory does
this frequently. He affirms the authenticity of his account when in fact he
would have had difficulty producing the necessary documents if
challenged. He claims to be borrowing when he is being original.

This is the first point to remember: as we consult Malory's sources to
examine the process of literary re-creation, as we comment on his skills and
lay bare his shortcomings, we must not make the mistake of thinking that
borrowing and assembling in themselves minimize Malory's achievement
in any way. We must not, above all, seek to strip away what has been
borrowed in order to discover his original contribution. For the real Malory
is not to be found by means of our notions of originality. It is his book as a
whole that we must assess – the parts he translated (sometimes almost
word for word), the parts he borrowed wholesale, the parts he adapted, the
parts he rearranged, and the parts which he added himself. Our critical
assessment must cover 'the hoole book,' as Malory called it, must take into
account the overall impact of a literary re-creation for which he is entirely
responsible, however little he invented himself.[12]

In the hands of a gifted writer like Malory, the re-creative process can
amount to a considerable contribution in itself, and it is unwise to
exaggerate the extent to which he is limited by his borrowed material. The
principal elements remain fixed, but there is ample opportunity for a

[11] D. S. Brewer, 'Malory: The Traditional Writer and the Archaic Mind,' *Arthurian Literature I*,
    ed. Richard Barber (Cambridge, 1981), pp. 94–120.
[12] The somewhat exaggerated importance given to Malory's additions is a criticism which
    could be made, perhaps, of one of the earliest book-length studies of the *Morte Darthur*
    and its sources. It was tellingly entitled *Malory's Originality*, ed. R. M. Lumiansky
    (Baltimore, 1964).

creative response. In part this freedom with source material comes from the fact that fifteenth-century readers must have been in a very different position from us. Stories of Arthur were in circulation, but not many readers would have had the kind of detailed knowledge which would have enabled them to question Malory's interpretation or presentation. His frequent reminders that he was following his sources faithfully would have silenced any doubts. It was not until Caxton's version of Malory was printed that in England one Arthurian text achieved authoritative status.

It is even difficult to know how much of the Arthurian story was known in Malory's day. According to Caxton, far more texts were available in other languages, and Robert Mannyng had said much the same thing a hundred and fifty years earlier.[13] Allusions in non-Arthurian texts in the Middle Ages represent Arthur and his knights in the most stereotyped terms: Arthur is famous for the splendour of his court and Lancelot as a figure of gallantry, but little detailed knowledge is revealed.[14] Indeed, certain major figures and episodes of the legend – Lancelot, Perceval, the Grail Quest, and Tristram – owe their existence in English almost entirely to Malory's book, and the public's lack of prior knowledge inevitably adds to the liberty of the traditional writer.

It is perhaps not even true that the basic elements remain fixed – unless we accept a very loose definition of the word basic. For English readers, because of the impact of Malory, Lancelot's love for Guinevere is a *sine qua non* of the legend, and yet this plays no part at all in one of the very sources Malory used, the fourteenth-century English alliterative poem *Morte Arthure*. The love affair is hardly a minor point and shows that there is clearly room for manoeuvre. As we bear this in mind we can, I think, abandon our concern with inventiveness and originality and focus attention elsewhere. The sources will not merely be a constant reminder that Malory's book is not really his own, and no one should discourage readers from turning to the sources for fear that Malory's reputation might suffer. On the contrary, it is by reading the sources that we can usefully assess that reputation.

There is one condition: we must not be too selective. It might seem regrettable that no one so far has published a parallel text edition of Malory's book (along with the corresponding passages of his sources) or a convenient volume (or more) of 'Malory's Sources.' Most of us have an insufficient knowledge of the vast French romances and a collection of the extracts Malory used would considerably facilitate our task. And yet it must be admitted that an edition of this kind would sadly limit our appreciation of Malory's book in one important direction: it would encourage us to overlook what Malory omits. *Le Morte Darthur* is not a

[13] See Caxton's preface to Malory (p.xiv), and lines 10607–11 of Mannyng's *Chronicle*, ed. F. J. Furnivall, Rolls Series xlvii (London, 1889).
[14] See Christopher Dean, *Arthur of England* (Toronto, 1987).

reproduction of its French sources in miniature; what Malory chose to leave out changes the essential nature of the story as a whole. Students should be encouraged to look at as much (and as many) of the sources as possible and not merely those parts Malory felt able to include. It is in this way that they will realize just how different the French texts are.

Malory has little time for the mysticism and the magic, the religious doctrine and the personal sentiment, the psychological enquiry and the amorous intrigue of French romance. These elements are not entirely absent from his book, but the quantity of them and hence their relative importance are radically reduced. The spirit, the ambience of Malory's Arthurian world is entirely different. In abbreviated and illustrated form *Le Morte Darthur* has often been considered a suitable book for boys; in the sixteenth century the French texts came under attack because they were thought appropriate reading matter only for young girls.[15] One hesitates to use such sexist stereotypes these days, but they are not entirely without significance.

Malory's knowledge of the major sources, the ones he specifically adapted, goes well beyond the extracts he chose to adapt, and we also believe that he had a good general knowledge of them before he began to write. Sometimes this prior knowledge is not always very accurate but it appears that working with a text refreshed Malory's memory. P. J. C. Field points out that a reference by Malory to the *Perlesvaus* in *The Tale of King Arthur*, before he actually took up that source, is incorrect, whereas the references in *The Book of Sir Tristram*, made no doubt after Malory had consulted the *Perlesvaus* directly for *The Tale of Sir Lancelot*, are correct.[16]

The question of the order of composition (and revision) of the tales, however, is very complex. In the first tale, for example, Malory makes a reference to the Grail story (52/1–3; II.13) which is far more precise than anything contained in his direct source, the *Suite du Merlin*, and yet a little later in the same tale he makes another reference to the Grail claiming that Sir Pelleas was one of four who 'encheved the Sankgreall' (109/44–110/1; IV.29), which is outrageously wrong. What conclusions are we to draw? That the first (correct) reference was added in revision? Perhaps. But the reviser worked shoddily if he could allow the second (faulty) reference to stand. In this case we could also ask ourselves whether the Grail story was quite as well known in fifteenth-century England as we suppose. After all, apart from Malory's version (and twenty-four seven-line stanzas of John Hardyng's chronicle), no other account of the story in English has survived.[17]

---

[15] Joachim du Bellay, *Deffence et Illustration de la langue francoyse* (1549), book II, chapter v.

[16] P. J. C. Field, 'Malory and *Perlesvaus*,' *Medium Ævum*, 62 (1993), 159–69.

[17] For Hardyng's rather strange account of the Grail quest see ed. cit. pp. 131–6. An Irish version of the Grail story translated from English but not from Malory's text suggests that another version did exist. See the introduction to *Lorgaireacht ant Soidhigh Naomtha: An Early Modern Irish Translation of the 'Quest of the Holy Grail,'* ed. S. Falconer (Dublin, 1953).

The major sources are not the only Arthurian texts Malory knew. There are signs that he was familiar with Chrétien de Troyes, for example, but most important, there is evidence that he knew a whole host of Arthurian texts in English. He often prefers the English form of proper names, and certain characters he mentions, like Sir Degrevaunt, Sir Ironside, and Sir Gromoresom Erioure, exist only in English texts. It is impossible to say how well Malory knew these other works, and of some it is possible that he had only the slightest knowledge.

With others, it is clear that his acquaintance was more extensive. At one point he takes time off from the description of a battle in which the participants are too numerous to mention (and this is not something which happens often to Malory, who delights in providing exhaustive lists), not only to provide the name of one knight's mother (and there are not many mothers in the *Morte Darthur*), but to tell us that her son was 'begotyn uppon a mountayne' (134/19–21; not in Caxton). This bizarre detail is not present in Malory's direct source, the alliterative *Morte*, but is a distant recollection of another English poem *The Jeste of Sir Gawayne*, in which the phrase 'uppon a mountayne' occurs several times as a sort of refrain. We will never know why Malory made a point of adding information which is so uncharacteristic of his usual method, but it would seem that he knew the poem well enough for one line to be ringing in his head.

The chances are very high that Malory had a good knowledge of some of the texts he merely alludes to, but we cannot know which. It is also likely that he knew works which have left no indubitable traces in his book. Since medieval literature relies heavily on conventional devices and motifs, similarities between Malory and any other text must be extremely detailed and precise before we can assert definite knowledge.

Rather than seek to establish unproveable theories it is important to underline the breadth and (to varying degrees) depth of Malory's knowledge of Arthurian literature. In this way we see him as an expert with his materials, in control of his task of re-creation, and not as a timid translator/abridger/compiler at the mercy of his originals and incapable of doing anything other than follow them slavishly. Paradoxically, it is essential, at the same time, to remember that one of the liberties of the traditional writer (whom the spectre of plagiarism never haunts) is, precisely, to follow his source slavishly if he so chooses. And from time to time, but not often, Malory does just that.

It is in the Grail book that Malory follows his source most faithfully and certain passages can be traced back to the French text word for word, as the following extract shows:

'And whan kynge Hurleine saw thys swerde so kerveyynge, he turned agayne to fecch the scawberd. And so cam into thys shippe and entird, and put up the swerde in the sheethe, and as sone as he had done hit he felle downe dede afore the bedde. Thus was the swerde preved that never man drew hit but he were dede or maymed. So lay he here tyll a maydyn cam into the shippe and caste hym oute, for there was no man so hardy in the worlde to entir in that shippe for the defens.' (581/32–38; XVII.3)

Quant li rois Varlans vit l'espee si trenchant, si pensa qu'il retorneroit por prendre le fuerre. Et lors revint a la nef et entra dedenz et remist l'espee ou fuerre; et si tost come il ot ce fet, si chai morz devant cest lit. Einsi fu esprovee ceste espee, que nus ne la treroit qui ne fust morz ou mehaigniez. Si remest li cors le roi devant cest lit, tant que une pucele l'en gita fors; car il n'avoit ilec home si hardi qui dedenz ceste nef osast entrer, por le deffens que les letres dou bort fesoient. (*La Queste del Saint Graal*, pp. 204–5)

Not all of the Grail book is translated as faithfully as this extract would suggest since Malory abridges his source considerably. But to do this, he tends to rely on straightforward omission rather than summary, and consequently his version remains close to the French: what he retains he translates. And yet the apparent fidelity that a word-for-word comparison with the source reveals is misleading because at the same time Malory displays an independence of mind we should not overlook.

Although he cannot simply ignore Lancelot's sinfulness, for example, the result of his adulterous relationship with Guinevere, Malory changes the emphasis considerably by omitting most of the lengthy condemnations of his favourite knight. More interestingly, he never quite endorses the otherworldliness of the French *Queste*, in which the values of earthly chivalry are systematically undermined and replaced by spiritual ideals embodied by the chaste knight Galahad. While following his source closely, Malory modifies a few words here and there to reassert values he is reluctant to abandon. When Bors tells a man of religion that he has undertaken the quest, he adds that 'he shall have much *erthly worship* that may bryng hit to an ende' (564/8–9; XVI 6, italics mine). Even though nothing could be more alien to the spirit of the French text, Malory's holy man does not throw up his hands in horror. Quite the contrary, he agrees with Bors: 'Sertes . . . that ys sothe withoute fayle, for he shall be the beste knyght of the worlde and the fayryst of the felyship.' In the French text it is truth and purity that ensure success (*Queste*, p. 162; trans. p. 176); 'the fayryst of the felyship' would not stand a chance. But for Malory the values of earthly chivalry are not tarnished. There may indeed be a better world, but his subject is the best of the sinful. In this he is not unchristian, but it is clear that he is no saint – at best something of a doubting Thomas who has faith, above all, in a world he can see and feel.

A few words are sufficient for Malory to bring about a considerable change of emphasis even when he is relying closely on a source, and this is an important aspect of his method. His own reading of his text remains in evidence and all the references, allusions, additions and borrowings are a further sign of an awareness of Arthurian story which goes beyond the scope of his immediate source. Malory frequently interrupts his narrative to add references to later or earlier events in 'the hoole book.' In the first tale there are references ahead, for example, to Gareth, to Tristram, to Lancelot's love for Guinevere, to Mordred's arrival at court, to Galahad's handling of Balin's sword, and to Sir Pelleas's success in the Grail Quest. Similarly the later tales contain references back, and in particular the story of Sir Urry in *The Tale of Lancelot and Guinevere* contains a number of brief reminders of the early careers of knights who take part in the healing. Cross-references of this kind have sometimes been used to establish the order of composition of Malory's tales, but we should perhaps see them above all as allusions within the general body of Arthurian material and evidence of the fact that Malory had an overall view of the history of Arthur. He was not merely a slave to the source open before him.

I have suggested elsewhere that Malory probably used his (perhaps unconscious, perhaps not) recollections of the *demoiselle guérisseuse* episode of the French *Prose Lancelot* when he refashioned the story of the Maid of Astolat in Tale VII.[18] The Maid is in many points unlike her counterpart in the *Mort Artu* and Malory has been credited with the variations. But Malory's Elaine, in the points in which she differs from the demoiselle d'Escalot, is in fact very similar to the forthright damsel of the *Prose Lancelot*, whose story so closely resembles that of the demoiselle d'Escalot that critics have considered the possibility of borrowings between the two French texts. It may well be that what we take to be original contributions to the characterization of Elaine are not. But if Malory dresses his maiden in borrowed robes, his achievement is none the less his own. The traditional writer responds creatively in this magpie fashion; he is less likely to invent than to patch together, and we are not undermining his reputation in any way if we suggest that details hitherto considered original may well have been borrowed after all.

Comparison with the sources is always easiest, of course, where Malory contents himself with almost word for word (abridged) translation, as in Tale VI, the Grail book, or in Tale II, the Roman war episode, where he translates (more or less) from a regional variety of English. In this tale there are times when Malory follows the text of the alliterative poem so closely that he does little more than corrupt the verse into prose – and he does not even do that with regularity. A mere glance at an extract alongside its poetic source is enough to see why *The Tale of Arthur and Lucius* is so unlike the rest of Malory:

> 'And sir Florens in this fyght shall here abyde for to kepe the stale as a knyght noble, for he was chosyn and charged in chambir with the kynge chyfften of this chekke and cheyff of us all. And whethir he woll

---

[18] Terence McCarthy, *An Introduction to Malory* (Cambridge, 1991), pp. 152–4.

fyght other fle we shall folow aftir; for as for me, for all yondir folkys
faare forsake hem shall I never.'

'A, fadir!' seyde Florens, 'full fayre now ye speke, for I am but a
fauntekyn to fraysted men of armys, and yf I ony foly do the faughte
muste be youres.' (139/37–140/1; V.10)

> 'We are with sir Florent,   as to-day falles,
> That is flowr of Fraunce,   for he fled never;
> He was chosen and charged   in chamber of the king,
> Cheftain of the journee,   with chevalry noble;
> Whether he fight or he flee   we shall follow after;
> For all the fere of yon folk   forsake shall I never!'
>
> 'Fader,' says Sir Florent,   'full fair ye it tell!
> But I am but a fauntekin   unfraisted in armes;
> If any folly befall   the faut shall be ours . . .'
>
> (*Morte Arthure* 2729–37)

Not all of the second tale is translated as closely as this, for Malory's
version is much shorter than the *Morte Arthure*. Even so, the poem
influences (or infects) Malory's style throughout. Indeed, Malory sometimes goes even further: he adds to his own version poetic features that the
poem itself does not contain. There are whole alliterative lines that have no
parallel in the *Morte Arthure* and Malory inverts the word order or adds the
kind of conventional tags and weak endings a poet would use to complete
the requirements of the verse.[19] The following are just a few examples; all
of them were removed from the standardized version published by Caxton:
'with his bowerly bronde that bryght semed' (124/19–20); 'dyscover the
woodys, bothe the dalys and the downys' (127/24); 'I am com of olde
barounes of auncetry noble' (127/35); 'sir Bors the brym' (129/18); 'sir
Bedwere the ryche' (132/42); 'he slew a kynge and a deuke that knyghtes
were noble' (133/36); 'many of oure knyghtes good' (133/38); 'Kylle doune
clene for love of sir Kay' (134/12); 'with barounes full bolde' (134/40); 'of
Ethyopé the kyng' (134/41); 'the rubyes that were ryche, he russhed hem in
sundir' (137/15); 'There was none that playned on his parte, ryche nothir
poore' (145/19–20).

Source comparison in Tales II and VI is a fascinating subject, but in many
ways it has had unfortunate results. The Roman War episode is so
obviously unlike the rest of the *Morte Darthur* that it is usually dismissed
overhastily, and I believe that the full depth of the poem's influence (on
Tale II and on the 'hoole book') has been underestimated. And the obvious
debts of Malory to the French Grail text have led to the misleading
impression that this is how Malory always worked. Indeed, Malory's close
reliance on his source was a basic principle for Vinaver when he established

---

[19] Terence McCarthy, 'Malory and the Alliterative Tradition,' *Studies in Malory*, ed. J. W.
Spisak (Kalamazoo, 1985), pp. 53–85.

the actual text of the *Morte Darthur*. If the Winchester and Caxton versions of Malory's book disagree (or fail to make sense) the French source may well be able to arbitrate.[20] Vinaver admits that there is always an element of doubt, but he sometimes gives greater authority to the French text than is justifiable. He works on the assumption that Malory must be trying to say what the French text says, but this would only be true if the *Morte Darthur* throughout were a straightforward translation, which it is not. Medieval translators have a wayward streak at the best of times, and Malory is only too ready to stray from his source.

If we fail to appreciate the freedom with which Malory worked we will, I think, misrepresent the *Morte Darthur*. There are, it is true, passages where he was obviously following his source closely – so closely that examples of narrative confusion can easily be explained by comparison with the French original. Malory's abbreviated version occasionally lacks the narrative links that the sources, fuller and more accomplished in this matter, never fail to provide. Vinaver points out many of these in his commentary. At one point, for example, Merlin addresses a lady who is in fact absent (42/15–6; II.4); Malory, reducing the events, has forgotten to include the passage where, having made an indignant exit, she reappears. There is no need to seek excuses for slips of this kind, although it is possible to suggest that Malory's incompetence has been exaggerated. It is detailed comparison with the sources that draws attention to the errors; the general reader can take them in his stride. P. J. C. Field has suggested, quite rightly I think, that links of this kind can be taken for granted in a much swifter style of narrative like Malory's.[21]

Other 'errors' cannot be dismissed so easily. Is the reader confused or mystified by the fact that the lady who provides Arthur's sword and is granted a reward for her beneficence turns up to ask for the head of the guileless Balin, who lops off hers in reprisal (40/310–41/12; II.3)? The sources show us that there are, in fact, two ladies, one gracious, one perfidious. It would seem that Malory, reducing too radically or unthinkingly, simply failed to differentiate clearly. But this time, although the source can explain the confusion, it does nothing to explain the literary effect of a text which must be allowed an independent existence. Malory's Camelot is a strange place that we can never quite fathom, a world of unexplained and inexplicable significances where characters come together in bewildering combinations.

The beheaded lady is a minor detail, but a similar contradiction, which the sources can explain without explaining away, is at the basis of the

---

[20] *The Works of Sir Thomas Malory*, ed. Eugène Vinaver, 3 vols, 3rd ed. rev. P. J. C. Field (Oxford, 1990), pp. c–cxxvi.

[21] P. J. C. Field, 'Hunting, Hawking, and Textual Criticism in Malory's *Morte Darthur*,' *Arthurian and Other Studies presented to Shunichi Noguchi*, (Cambridge, 1993), pp. 95–105, 98.

portrait of Morgan La Fay. How is it that she who plots to kill Arthur and directs so much malice at him can come at the end and carry him away to be healed, speaking words full of that ambiguous love that earthly brothers and sisters are not meant to share: 'why have ye taryed so longe frome me?' (716/16; XXI.5). C. S. Lewis draws attention to 'the deep suggestiveness of Arthur's relation to that dark family (Morgan, Morgause, and the rest) from whom he emerges, who lie in wait for him, and who mysteriously return in his last hour to take him away.'[22] And yet have we explained anything of the literary impact when we point out that the sisterly Morgan (whose animosity is centred on Guinevere and Lancelot) is a figure from the Vulgate Cycle, while the hateful villainess comes from the pages of the later tradition of the *Suite du Merlin* and the *Prose Tristan*? Malory has failed to reconcile the contradiction inherent in his sources, but would the 'deep suggestiveness' not have disappeared if he had?

Malory's independence from his sources is seen more clearly in his *Tale of Sir Lancelot*, where he merely selects a few brief extracts from his source and dispenses with all the rest. As a result his account of Lancelot's career bears little resemblance to the French *Prose Lancelot* and readers can profitably contrast the two to establish Malory's very different vision of things. The French source gives a full account of the young hero's sentimental development in his relationship with Guenièvre, all against a background of sophisticated infidelity. The Queen is a woman of considerable worldly experience, Arthur is likewise engaged in a career of marital infidelity, while Lancelot is the tongue-tied, blushing youth of exacerbated sensibility. Malory never presents his king and queen in this way, and he reduces Lancelot's role as lover to a mere rumour (160/40; VI.10), to nothing more than the amorous reputation which courtiers give him and which he rejects outright. The mere idea goes against everything he stands for as a knight, he protests (161/1–11; VI.10).

The *Prose Lancelot* is a perfect example of how we can isolate Malory's attitude to Arthurian history not through what he borrows but through his independence of mind in rejecting his source so radically. Scholars sometimes give the impression when they underline his clumsy handling of the carefully wrought narrative of his sources that Malory is, at least at the beginning of his career, not quite up to his task; it is worth pointing out that Malory seems to have thought along parallel lines: his sources were somehow not quite up to *his* standards. He was forced to do a considerable amount of pruning and editing away of excess to bring them in line with his own, more sober, more historical view of Arthurian history.

By the end of his narrative, Malory has achieved considerable independence from his sources. In the final two tales he manipulates

---

[22] C. S. Lewis, 'The English Prose *Morte*,' *Essays on Malory*, ed. J. A. W. Bennett (Oxford, 1963), p. 25.

several texts at once, selecting from them, abandoning first one then the other, and rearranging the chronology to suit his purpose. Events from a (lost) version of the *Lancelot* are incorporated in *The Tale of Lancelot and Guinevere* into a narrative based largely on the *Mort Artu* and the stanzaic English poem *Le Morte Arthur*, and Malory uses his recollections of the *Lancelot* to add new adventures to underline the key significances: 'The Healing of Sir Urry' gives Lancelot a final moment of glory before his reputation is publicly compromised, and a grand tournament is organized to bring Gareth once again to the fore in preparation for his tragic death.

Even when he seems to be following his source in a straightforward manner, Malory makes changes which have a considerable impact. He modifies details at the beginning of the poisoned apple episode to underline the queen's responsibility: the poisoning does not occur during an ordinary meal (as in the sources), but during a meal Guinevere specifically and ostentatiously organizes as a snub to Lancelot (613/9–17; XVIII.2–3). Similarly, slight changes are made to the story of Elaine of Astolat to promote rather than criticize Lancelot. In both the French *Mort Artu* (Section 71) and the English *Le Morte Arthur* (1032–1103), when the body of the Maid is brought to Camelot, a letter is discovered in her hand. The letter is addressed to the whole court and contains an open condemnation of Lancelot's behaviour. After reading the letter, Arthur adds his own condemnation to that of the Maid. In Malory's version (640/25–641/38; XVIII, 20) the Maid's body comes to court and there is again a letter in her hand, but Malory removes all blame from his favourite knight. The letter is addressed to Lancelot alone and exonerates him entirely; he is 'pereles,' not guilty. Even the Maid's own brother will vouch for him. Interestingly, the only one to express any criticism is Guinevere, who declares that Lancelot might have shown the Maid 'som bownté and jantilnes' to save her life. This is a fine piece of characterization (perhaps suggested by a similar reaction on the part of the queen in the *demoiselle guérisseuse* episode of the *Prose Lancelot*). It would not be hard to imagine how Guinevere would have reacted if Lancelot had anticipated her last-minute compassion. And when the only condemnation comes from such an unreasonable woman, this is surely the equivalent of total justification.

Malory's independence in his final tales has long been acknowledged, and those who feel happier assessing his art in terms of originality are more at ease here. Strangely enough, although Vinaver was always ready to credit Malory with these modifications and refused to postulate a lost *Mort Artu* manuscript containing the events as we find them in Malory, t is he who still sows the seeds of doubt. He seems to consider that Malory has misrepresented his sources.

The 'Knight of the Cart' episode, Vinaver points out, really belongs to a much earlier period of Lancelot's career, before the Grail Quest, and is quite out of place at this late stage. Indeed, Vinaver was so reluctant to let the French text be misrepresented in this way, as though its authority must not be questioned, that when he published a volume of selections from Malory's tales, he placed the 'Knight of the Cart' episode where he believed it belonged, back before the Grail.[23] Since it was his opinion that Malory did not write one book but several, there was no reason why the tales could not be rearranged. But in order to correct the chronology and to repair the damage done to the French source, Vinaver is led to damage Malory's book instead. Other episodes from the same Tale VII ('The Poisoned Apple', 'The Maid of Astolat') are left to the end, as Vinaver dissects one of Malory's tales in order to reestablish a chronology which exists only in the Vulgate Cycle. In the *Morte Darthur* it is perfectly clear that the kidnapping of the queen is integrated into a series of three rescues in which the love affair and, therefore, the kingdom are in increasing danger.

This is surely a perfect example of how the critic should not use the sources. Malory has claimed the traditional author's right to rearrange material and to insert episodes into a new context. It may be inappropriate in the Vulgate Cycle to have the 'Knight of the Cart' episode at this point, but the *Morte Darthur* is not a miniature Vulgate Cycle in English. It may be inappropriate in the Vulgate Cycle to reaffirm Lancelot's undiminished moral excellence after the Grail Quest, but in the healing of Sir Urry episode Malory chooses to do just that. It is of no importance that the only parallel to this episode in the French texts comes in the *Prose Lancelot* and constitutes, therefore, one of the hero's achievements *before* his imperfections have been so damningly exposed in the *Queste*, for there is no reason why we should impose the implications of the sources on Malory's design.

How then should we use the sources? If we affirm Malory's right to alter and rearrange, have we removed the right to criticize? Of course not; simply we must be clear about what constitutes an error and what a liberty. We should certainly not be afraid to point out where Malory has dealt hastily and poorly with his original, sacrificing logic and clarity for the sake of brevity. This is part, after all, of his narrative technique and linguistic competence. We will find numerous examples in Tale VI, the Grail Quest, where the pious explanations of the (ubiquitous) men of religion are at times abbreviated to the point of confusion. One hermit, for example, explains to Ector the significance of the fact 'that sir Launcelot felle doune of hys horse' (562/21; XVI.4), but in theory there can be no significance, for Lancelot has not fallen from his horse at all. We are given the meaning of a symbol that does not exist.

Some of the confusion and error in the *Morte Darthur* is no doubt due to the fact that Malory was not always a very good *translator* as such. At times his version is so unclear that it is only when we read the French original that we realize what Malory (presumably) meant to write. Take, for example, the following extract, the interpretation of a dream:

---

[23] Eugène Vinaver, ed., *King Arthur and his Knights* (London, 1968).

'The whyght fowle betokenyth a jantillwoman fayre and ryche whych loved the paramours and hath loved the longe. And if that thou warne hir love she shall dy anone – if thou have no pité on her. That signifieth the grete birde which shall make the to warne hir. Now for no feare that thou haste, ne for no drede that thou hast of God, thou shalt nat warne hir; for thou woldist nat do hit for to be holdyn chaste, for to conquere the loose of the vayneglory of the worlde; for that shall befalle the now, and thou warne hir, that sir Launcelot, the good knyght, thy cousyn, shall dye. And than shall men sey that thou arte a man-sleer, both of thy brothir sir Lyonell and of thy cousyn sir Launcelot, whych thou myght have rescowed easyly, but thou wentist to rescow a mayde which perteyned nothynge to the.' (569/40–570/8; XVI.11).

It is the French text that shows us that the phrase 'thou woldist nat do hit' should not be negative, and that 'whych thou myght have rescowed easyly' does not refer to Lancelot, as Malory's text implies:

Li oisiax qui venoit a toi en guise de cisne senefie une damoisele qui t'amera par amors et t'a amé longuement, et te vendra proier prochainement que tu soies ses amis et ses acointes. Et ce que tu ne li voloies otroier senefie que tu l'en escondiras, et ele s'en ira maintenant et morra de duel s'il ne t'en prent pitié. Li noirs oisiax senefie ton grant pechié qui la te fera escondire. Car por crieme de Dieu ne por bonté que tu aies en toi ne l'escondiras tu pas, ainz le feras por ce que len te tiegne a chaste, por conquierre la loenge et la vaine gloire del monde. Si vendra si grant mal de ceste chastée que Lancelot, tes cosins, en morra, car li parent a la damoisele l'ocirront, et ele morra del duel que ele avra de l'escondit. Et por ce porra len bien dire que tu es homicides de l'une et de l'autre, ausi com tu as esté de ton frere qui le poisses avoir resqueus aiseement se tu vousisses, quant tu le lessas et alas secorre la pucele qui ne t'apartenoit. (*Queste del Saint Graal*, 179.10–26; trans., 191–2)

It may well be that Vinaver is right: quite simply, Malory did not have the mentality of a translator.[24] In that case we can only be glad that he did not translate very often, although these occasional failures with the technique of translation should not make us call into question Malory's command of French. The *Morte Darthur* itself is ample testimony to the fact that Malory was an expert linguist, and we must not imagine that he plodded his way laboriously through the *Lancelot-Graal*. On the contrary, he was in control of his materials and fully equipped to move around freely in the vast folios of Old French finding material suitable for his own vision of Arthurian history. Although there are mistakes, far more often Malory handles his text with considerable success.[25] He has the art of picking out from his source

[24] *The Works of Sir Thomas Malory*, vol. 1, lxxxiii.
[25] The quality of Malory's French is a subject in need of discussion. The only study to date is by M. A. Muir and P. J. C. Field: 'French Words and Phrases in Sir Thomas Malory's

the details that summarize a narrative with greatest effect. This is evident
even at what is probably an early stage in his career. Tale I is not without a
certain muddle, but there are passages – like the arrival and knighting of
Torre, for example (61/3–63/18; III. 3-4) – which remodel the *Suite du
Merlin* with skill and offer different but equally effective versions of the
chosen episodes.

There are so few manuscripts of the *Suite* that it is best to be cautious over
the details we credit Malory with, but in more general matters the sources
are a fruitful way of providing information about Malory's 'intentions, his
achievements and the creative process by which his work came into being'
which the 'shortage of conventional biographical data' keeps from us.[26] It
is to the sources that we must turn for any sort of answer to a number of
intriguing questions: how long did it take Malory to write his book? Did he
write it in chronological order? Where did he find the source material?
Have the manuscripts he used survived?

The answer to this last question would seem to be no: none of the
manuscripts Malory used has come down to us. Collectively the extant
manuscripts can give us a good idea of what Malory's originals must have
been, as long as we are not too dogmatic over small matters of disagreement between the *Morte Darthur* and its sources.

Unfortunately, since we have none of Malory's manuscripts we can
hardly hope to discover where he acquired them. Attempts have been made
to identify the library Malory might have had access to, but before we solve
that problem we really ought to ask how long it took to produce the *Morte
Darthur* and wonder whether there is any *a priori* reason why he should
have found all of his source books in one place.

The composition of the *Morte Darthur* is obviously a question closely
allied to the biography of Malory. We have to fit his literary productions
into a turbulent career. We know that some parts of the book were written
in prison – which makes the availability of sources an all the more
fascinating riddle. The whole book may have been prison therapy for all we
know, but we do not know, nor do we know how long it took to produce.
Two years has been suggested as a minimum,[27] but since Malory's methods
vary considerably, a longer period of composition, a slower process of
literary maturing, might be involved, with more clearly marked prentice
and proficient periods. Certainly the skill Malory displays in manipulating
multiple sources in the books which we assume he wrote last is far greater

---

Le Morte Darthur,' Neuphilologische Mitteilungen, 72 (1971), 483–500. The impression they
give is, I believe, misleading because Malory tends to be judged by notions of
grammatical correctness that did not exist in the fifteenth century. I have not
discouraged readers from using translations of the French sources; I trust they will not
underestimate Malory's linguistic achievement. There were no translations, grammars,
dictionaries or cribs of any kind for him to use.

[26] P. J. C. Field, 'Malory and the French Prose *Lancelot*,' 79.

[27] P. J. C. Field, ed., *Le Morte Darthur*, p. 34.

than that revealed in the first tale with its occasional muddle. But it could equally be argued that the very unadventurous word-for-word translation of the Grail book is also a sign of inexperience when compared with the assured independence of the final tales, and it has been suggested that the Grail book is Malory's literary début.[28] The order of composition is a fascinating but unsolved question. All sorts of theories are possible. Many are enlightening but the last word is far from spoken, and no doubt never will be. In the absence of autobiographical evidence, it is to the book and its sources that those who are interested in pursuing the matter must turn for any sort of answer.

We are on much firmer ground if we turn to the sources to illuminate Malory's achievement by contrast. The essentially military spirit of the *Morte Darthur*, its lack of interest in matters of personal sentiment, its insistence on public loyalties, its notions of virtue – these are features which are visible in Malory's book and which the sources help us to put into perspective. In the French texts we will find long soliloquies and analyses of private feeling (in *Mort Artu*, for instance, Guenièvre is in torment as she wonders whether she should return to Arthur);[29] their absence from the *Morte Darthur* is of vital importance. Similarly, the interest in love and amorous reputations is dispensed with by Malory and the difference is considerable. Imagine, for instance, how the tragic climax of Malory's book would have been modified if he had included the scene where a lady bewails the death of Gawain – much to the annoyance of her cuckolded husband – and declares that her lover will be sorely missed by the female population.[30] There may be a time for such laments in the Vulgate Cycle, but in the *Morte Darthur* that time never comes. On the other hand there is always time for combat and war, and Malory seems not to spare the reader's patience with his long lists of combatants or victims. They are, after all, a measure of the importance of events, and no historical record can afford to leave the names of a nation's heroes unrecorded.

In these matters, Malory's book is quite unlike his sources, but our use of these texts must be submitted to one important condition: the sources can corroborate or enlighten, but we must not let them lead us to inter-pretations that the book itself does not offer. Let me take one example.

At the centre of the *Morte Darthur* is the division of loyalties Lancelot owes to his king and to his lady. It has been suggested that Arthur is to be blamed for this situation for neglecting Guinevere, and E. D. Kennedy, in a very well-documented essay, suggests that Arthur's love for the queen develops in the course of the *Morte Darthur* from that of an affectionate husband, in Tale I, to the indifference of a king who only has time for his

---

[28] Terence McCarthy, 'Order of Composition in the *Morte Darthur*,' *Yearbook of English Studies*, 1 (1971), 18–29.
[29] *La Mort le Roi Artu*, sections 169–70.
[30] *La Mort le Roi Artu*, section 174.

band of knights.[31] Kennedy is not alone in questioning Arthur's love at the end, and the famous lament 'much more I am soryar for my good knyghtes losse than for the losse of my fayre quene' (685/29–30; XX.9) has often been interpreted as a slight on the lady. What constitutes the real problem with his argument however is the method he uses to illustrate the king's growing indifference: Kennedy refers us to the sources as though it were perfectly appropriate to seek their help when Malory fails to provide the proof we need.

In the Alliterative *Morte*, when Arthur goes to war, he leaves Guinevere, racked with grief, in the care of regents, but before leaving he expresses his concern and affection for the queen (*Morte Arthure*, lines 652–9 and 695–716). Malory follows his source half way, but has nothing to say about the king's love for the queen. This is not mere narrative economy on the part of an author who has already described the king's love in no uncertain terms; Kennedy suggests it is a deliberate omission. Arthur's love is on the decline and a glance at the alliterative *Morte* will make Malory's meaning clear.

Later, in the Tristram book (490/5–19; IX.16), Arthur is tempted by the sexual advances of a sorceress and although he refuses the favours of the lady, he does so without making any declaration of love for Guinevere. For Kennedy, such a silence undermines the value of the king's fidelity, and if we look at the Spanish version of the Tristan story we will discover a much more loving king and realize that Malory's Arthur is growing cold. In the Spanish text Arthur rejects his temptress but also sings the praises of his wife.

Kennedy also selects a later incident in the *Tristram*, in which Arthur seems to have an eye for Isolde (460/39–462/15; X.78). What exactly happens in this passage is not entirely clear, and critics have suggested that Malory is reducing the narrative with more speed than skill. Kennedy feels that there is no ambiguity: Malory is showing us an Arthur whose love for Guinevere is on the decline and who is taking an interest in other women. The full episode in the French source makes things clear. But could we not object that if Malory wanted us to interpret his book along these lines, he went about it in a rather perverse way? If, as Kennedy suggests, he wanted to draw our attention to Arthur's faithless love, why did he remove as he does – all examples of the king's infidelity from both the French *Prose Tristan* and *Prose Lancelot*?

My remarks do not do justice to Kennedy's densely argued essay, but the problem seems to me that he is using the sources to provide evidence Malory does not give. I would willingly have believed that Arthur's love was growing cold if Malory had told me, if he had shown us Arthur behaving inconsiderately, refusing Guinevere the attentions due to her

---

[31] E. D. Kennedy, 'The Arthur–Guinevere Relationship in Malory's *Morte Darthur*,' *Studies in the Literary Imagination*, 4 (1971), 29–40.

rank, or scheming to slip away for trysts with paramours. But he does not. Malory concentrates on the public roles his characters play, and tells us nothing about their personal involvement, except in the most formal terms. If we believe that no news is bad news, we are free to force an interpretation from the sources, but I would suggest that we use the sources more profitably if we let them corroborate or invalidate interpretations based on evidence in Malory's book, rather than if we use them to offer inter-pretations based on evidence they alone provide.

Among the changes that comparisons with the French book do bring to light, one of the most important leads me finally to Malory's use of English sources. In another article, Kennedy has drawn attention to the way English romances (not only the major sources, but other texts Malory apparently knew) may have guided his approach.[32] The much simpler narrative structure of the *Morte Darthur*, which reduces the complex *entrelacement* of the French texts, may well have come from his reading of English romance. This is an important point.

Furthermore, English Arthurian literature does not seem to have been a vehicle for amorous investigation. Most of the Arthurian texts concentrate on the military aspects of knighthood, while the dashing behaviour of gallant knights in the presence of ladies is of secondary (if any) importance. Even the two great lovers of Arthurian literature, Lancelot and Tristram, do not seem to have caught the imagination of medieval English writers, and although no one could tax Malory with having an insular cultural attitude, and although he gives Lancelot and Tristram much attention, he too plays down their romantic involvements.

Most strikingly, one of the major sources Malory used, the Alliterative *Morte*, makes no mention of Lancelot's love at all, and consequently offered, at an early and formative stage in Malory's career, a vision of the Arthurian world without an adulterous queen. The enormous prestige of the French sources was such that Malory could not ignore their example entirely, but he brings about a clear Anglo-French compromise: the relationship becomes part of the public clash of loyalties, but Malory washes his hands of the private experiences that the French writers relish.

Malory is not a historian but he deals with the stuff of history – the reigns of kings, wars, and political factions. He has the historian's concern to sift information, to withhold misleading facts, to dispense with unreliable sources, and to expose the prejudices of 'makers' or story-tellers, and this approach is also something we can trace back to the English tradition of Arthurian literature, which shows a historical interest quite unlike the literary turn of mind of the French *romanciers*. Later, when Caxton wrote the

---

[32] E. D. Kennedy, 'Malory and his English Sources,' *Aspects of Malory*, pp. 27–55. See also L. D. Benson, *Malory's Morte Darthur* (Cambridge, Mass., 1976) and R. H. Wilson, 'Malory's Early Knowledge of Arthurian Romance,' *Texas Studies in English*, 32 (1953), 33–50.

preface to launch Malory's text, he was clearly aware of the historical relevance of the book.

Since the vast majority of the *Morte Darthur* is based on French texts, the English sources tend to be studied only for the sections based directly on them and consequently to receive insufficient attention. This is to be regretted because the English influence, the general cultural traditions of English Arthurian literature, has left a much wider mark on Malory. Even the Alliterative *Morte* – in itself an extraordinary choice of source material if Malory were really working under the guidance of the French romances – exerted an influence that is by no means as anomalous as some critics suggest. One might add that even the ability to understand the text shows a rare knowledge, and that it is unlikely that this would be shed as soon as the poem was set aside.[33]

In fact the Alliterative *Morte* remained with Malory well beyond the second tale. Right at the end of his career, as he was bringing his book to a close, Malory found nothing in his French source which could provide a fitting verdict on his finest knight. Instead he turned to the alliterative poem once again, adapting words describing Gawain (*Morte Arthure*, 3872–84) to fit Lancelot (725/16–26; XXI. 13). There are those who believe that Malory fell into bad company when he took up with the alliterative poem and are pleased that Caxton made Tale II 'more like the best and most typical parts of Malory.'[34] But it could be argued that Malory remained faithful to old friends and that the English poem – and others of the same tradition that he might have known – coloured his response to his French sources in a genuine and lasting way.

For frequently Malory's book is heroic in tone in a way which is not true of the French sources. J. A. W. Bennett has drawn attention to 'the specifically English qualities of Malory's code, which in its ethics, its political and social ideals, its very utterances, sometimes reveals affinities with the world of Layamon and even the world of *Beowulf* and *Maldon*.'[35] This is something no one would be tempted to say of the Vulgate Cycle and the difference is not merely due accidentally to Malory's reduction of the amorous elements in his source, for these seem to be rejected deliberately in favour of a military ideal whose inspiration is to be sought elsewhere. After all, Malory's exclusion of the personal biography of his favourite knight would have been a perverse literary decision indeed if he had been genuinely under the domination of his French sources, if his own vision of

---

[33] Even if the Winchester version of Tale II is only a first draft, the fact that Malory did not apparently notice that he had barely standardized the language of the poem suggests a familiarity with the alliterative tradition that very few of his contemporaries would have shared. It is hard to believe such a familiarity could be merely accidental and that having been idiosyncratic enough to integrate a poem from his native tradition into a series of French-based romances he should then merely forget that native tradition altogether.

[34] C. S. Lewis, 'The English Prose *Morte*,' p. 26.

[35] *Essays on Malory*, p. vi.

things had not been coloured by his knowledge and appreciation of a native tradition in which the key virtues are those of 'a military aristocracy whose highest good is the warrior's code,'[36] a world where gracious living and fine loving are less important than courage, endurance, loyalty, generosity, piety, love of fame, truth to one's word, wisdom, and devotion to the realm. Regularly, Malory exhorts us to know what constitutes manly, noble behaviour and he does not hesitate to point it out if need be, in the way the *Beowulf* poet does too.

The *Morte Darthur* is not a miniature Vulgate Cycle and it will be interesting to see how his book appears when it is translated back into French, for the project is at present under way. Malory's plain, unembellished, coordinating sentences with their loose syntax will not be easy to translate into a language which has the rigours of the Latin period behind it and which accommodates verbal and structural repetitions less willingly. No doubt the easy solution to this arduous task will be to use the Vulgate Cycle to provide a number of ready-made stylistic answers. But the complex subordinations of the French will misrepresent Malory's rough-hewn prose and will give a false veneer of elegance. I am speaking of stylistic matters, but then, as the French know, *le style c'est l'homme même*. Like Malory's translators, we would do well to take stock of the fact that his French book is not the solution to everything, and that the English sources have had an effect far and beyond the precise passages which they have inspired.

As we seek to link Malory to these sources, to the English tradition, we may not always be able to trace direct borrowings (though the verdict on Lancelot in the closing pages is particularly significant), but this still remains a vital part of source studies. Borrowings are not the only matter. Malory's originality – if we must think in such terms – may well come from the fact that his romance material has been given a distinctly English spirit.

---

[36] I borrow the phrase from Gwyn Jones, *Kings Beasts and Heroes* (London, 1972), p. 50.

6

Language and Style in Malory

JEREMY SMITH

I

Many critics have commented on the Janus-like quality of fifteenth-century English and Scottish literature. On the one hand, poets such as John Lydgate and William Dunbar look back overtly to the values and methods of the great fourteenth-century medieval English poets, such as Chaucer and Gower. On the other, the characteristic elaborated poetic style of Lydgate, Dunbar and their contemporaries, with its aureate diction and complex sentence-structure, prefigures the 'inkhorn terms' and Ciceronian sentences of the sixteenth-century English Renaissance. As we shall see, something comparable applies to the prose of the period, and it is within this stylistic context that Malory's achievement must be placed. The fifteenth century might not – if we are interested in making such judgements – be one of the great centuries of English letters, whose monuments demand immediate inclusion in the 'canon' established in university-level literature courses. But one of its fascinations is that it is, perhaps even more than usual, an epoch of literary transition, with all the features of experiment and uncertainty which characterize such periods. Such uncertainty reflected the uncertainties of contemporary society, whose upper classes were divided through dynastic wars and whose rising middle classes were beginning to assert their presence in the newly developing towns and cities.

In such a situation it is not surprising that, like contemporary poets, prose writers of the fifteenth century demonstrate a tendency to stylistic experiment, drawing upon two older traditions. On the one hand, there is what may be called the native tradition of prose discourse, deriving ultimately from the Anglo-Saxon period. Old English prose began with an early expository style found in wills and early manuals of practical wisdom. In the ninth century, this style, characterized by an avoidance of complex subordinate clauses and by a two-stress rhythmical unit related to contemporary speech-patterns, appears in an elaborated form in the writings of King Alfred, and in the annalistic *Anglo-Saxon Chronicle* which seems to have originated in his circle. Here, for instance, is a well-known

passage from the *Chronicle* entry for the year 755. (The punctuation is that
of a modern editor, and is designed to help the present-day reader by
indicating grammatical structure; in the original manuscript, punctuation
would have been much more sparing):

> Her Cynewulf benam Sigebryht his rices ond Westseaxna wiotan for
> unryhtum dædum, buton Hamtunscire; ond he hæfde þa oþ he ofslog
> þone aldormon þe him lengest wunode. Ond hiene þa Cynewulf on
> Andred adræfde; ond he þær wunade oþ þæt hiene an swan ofstang æt
> Pryfetes flodan – ond he wræc þone aldormon Cumbran. Ond se
> Cynewulf oft miclum gefeohtum feaht uuiþ Bretwalum; ond ymb XXXI
> wintra þæs þe he rice hæfde, he wolde adræfan anne æþeling se wæs
> Cyneheard haten - ond se Cyneheard wæs þæs Sigebryhtes broþur.[1]

> [In this year Cynewulf and the council of the West Saxons deprived
> Sigebryht of his kingdom because of unrighteous deeds, except for
> Hampshire; and he had that district until he drove him (i.e. Sigebryht)
> into the Weald; and he dwelt there until a swineherd stabbed him to
> death by a stream at Privett – and he avenged the ealdorman Cumbra.
> And that Cynewulf often fought in great battles against the Britons; and
> after 31 years during which he had the kingdom, he wanted to drive
> out a prince who was called Cyneheard – and that Cyneheard was that
> Sigebryht's brother.]

If the present-day editorial punctuation is ignored, it becomes clear that,
despite occasional simple subordinate constructions, the passage quoted
here is basically paratactic rather than hypotactic. In other words, it consists
largely of a string of coordinated rather than subordinated grammatical
structures, linked together by the conjunction *ond*. Moreover, if the stress-
patterns of such passages are examined it will be found that they frequently
fall quite naturally into two-stress units, e.g.:

        x   /   x   x   /
        Her Cynewulf benam
        / x x   x / x
        Sigebryht his rices
        x   /   x x / x
        ond Westseaxna wiotan
        x   x   /   x   /   x
        for unryhtum dædum

---

[1] D. Whitelock, ed., *Sweet's Anglo-Saxon Reader* (Oxford, 1970), pp. 1–2 (henceforth cited as
Sweet's Reader). For an authoritative short history of English prose, see still I. A. Gordon,
The Movement of English Prose (London, 1966); it is my opinion that a more up-to-date
general survey of late medieval prose will not be possible until many more detailed
studies of individual texts have been carried out.

Such patterns reflect the trochaic rhythms of contemporary speech; and, in the early eleventh century, these techniques of rhythmical prose were further elaborated by the great homilists of the period, Ælfric and Wulfstan.

This native tradition of prose survived the Norman Conquest of 1066. Copies of the homilies and other writings of Ælfric and Wulfstan continued to be made until at least the year 1200, and new texts whose technique derives from theirs were composed; good examples of the latter include the *Lambeth Homilies* in London, Lambeth Palace Library MS 487, which date from the end of the twelfth century. And the use of a paratactic prose style based on speech-rhythms, with limited subordination, continued into the later Middle Ages. Here, for instance, is part of a Wycliffite sermon on the nature of the Eucharist, surviving in a late fourteenth-century manuscript, London, British Library MS Royal 18.B.ix. Notable still are the restricted use of subordination and the frequent use of the coordinating *and*. The punctuation is, once more, that of the modern editor.

> And where suche lambren þat weren offrid felde sumtyme to þe prest, þis lomb þat made eende of oþir fel fulli to Goddis hond. And oþir lambren in a maner fordiden þe synne of oo cuntre, but þis lombe propirly fordide þe synne of al þis world. And þus he was eende and figure of lambren of þe oold lawe.[2]

> [And where such lambs who were offered pertained at some time to the priest, this lamb who succeeded others pertained fully to the hand to God. And other lambs in a way took away the sin of one country, but this lamb in his own person took away the sin of all this world. And thus he was purpose and symbol of lambs of the old law.]

This kind of prose was not restricted to religious use; by the fifteenth century it is found in documentary texts, and in the prose of secular writers such as the author(s) of the anonymous prose *Brut* and Sir John Fortescue's *The Governance of England*.

However, at approximately the same date as the *Lambeth Homilies* a new kind of prose begins to appear in English. Between 1168 and 1175, Maurice of Sully, Bishop of Paris, composed a cycle of French homilies on the Gospel lessons for the year, and in the thirteenth century five of these were translated into Middle English. These homilies, in which characteristically French stylistic patterns were transferred into the target language, represent a new departure in the history of English prose. Despite its use in sermons, essentially an oral and aural medium, this style was literary, a product of a culture where the intended audience was constituted of readers rather than hearers. Here is a short passage from the Middle English translation of one of these sermons, on Christ's miracle of turning water into wine:

---

[2] A. Hudson, ed., *Selections from English Wycliffite Writings* (Cambridge, 1978), p. 113.

Þet water bitockned se euele Cristeneman. For also Þet water is
natureliche schald, and akelÞ alle Þo Þet hit drinkeÞ, so is euele
Cristeman chald of Þo luue of Gode, for Þo euele werkes Þet hi doÞ; ase
so is lecherie, spusbreche, roberie, manslechtes, husberners, bakbiteres,
and alle oÞre euele deden, Þurch wyche Þinkes man ofserueth Þet fer of
helle, ase Godes oghe mudh hit seid.[3]

[The water signifies the evil Christian. For as the water is naturally cold,
and cools all those who drink it, so is an evil Christian unwarmed by
the love of God, because of the evil deeds which he does; as is lechery,
adultery, robbery, murders, burners of houses, backbiters, and all other
evil deeds, through which things man earns the fire of hell, as God's
own mouth said it.]

The idiom of this passage is very close to that of the French original, notably
in its use of a trailing subordinate structure marked by link-words ('for as',
'so', 'as is', 'through which,' 'as'). Such trailing structures, based on French
models, became a dominant style of later Middle English prose, both
religious and secular, and were adopted by, for instance, Geoffrey Chaucer
in his prose writings, and, in the fifteenth century, by William Caxton.

II

It is within the context described above that Malory's prose must be placed.
The following may be taken as a characteristic passage:

And aftir that feste was done, within a lytyll whyle aftir, by the assente
of two ladyes that were with the quene they ordayned for hate and
envye for to distroy dame Brangwayne that was mayden and lady unto
La Beale Isode. And she was sente into the foreste for to fecche herbys,
and there she was mette and bounde honde and foote to a tre, and so
she was bounden three dayes. And by fortune sir Palomides founde
dame Brangwayne, and there he delyverde hir from the deth and
brought hir to a nunry there besyde for to be recoverde. (263/12–19;
VIII.29)

Ignoring the (editorial) punctuation, the reader may perceive clearly that
the passage is essentially paratactic in structure, using the coordinating
conjunction 'and' to link together the stages of narrative. A few subordinate
clauses appear, but they are straightforwardly related to single main
clauses; no attempt is made to produce the trailing series of subordinate
clauses in the French manner.

Many such examples could be taken from Malory's work, and it is

---

[3] J. A. W. Bennett and G. V. Smithers, ed., *Early Middle English Verse and Prose* (Oxford,
1974), p. 217.

therefore obvious that his style owes much more to the native than to the French fashion of prose; a choice between available styles has been made. In his outstanding and still invaluable study of Malory's prose style, *Romance and Chronicle*,[4] P. J. C. Field gives a convincing detailed account of this connection, which he considers to derive from chronicles such as the prose *Brut*, and to be paralleled in contemporary letters, such as those of the Pastons and the Celys. Malory's writing may be seen as essentially native, and his sentence-structure as in a direct line of descent from that found in *The Anglo-Saxon Chronicle*. Field sees this as a limitation; in his opinion, Malory was an essentially untutored writer whose stylistic beauties were the result of unconscious narrative skill. Malory's writing, in Field's opinion, is not the product of a sophisticated mind, but has a forcefulness born of essential simplicity – and this alleged simplicity gives Malory's prose 'the . . . strengths of verisimilitude, directness and pathos.'[5] As I hope to demonstrate, this view is somewhat limiting for our proper appreciation of Malory's prose achievement.

It may, for instance, be objected that Field's statement that 'there are no signs that Malory was in any way a conscious stylist'[6] is misleading, and perhaps indicates a limited conception of the notion of style. Style is about choice, and the act of translation from and adaptation of his originals forced Malory to make certain choices; at what level of consciousness he made these choices is really beside the point. The key fact to grasp is that, as a translator and adaptor, Malory chose comparatively few features of style from his largely French sources; as Field points out, his use of the 'figures' of rhetoric is very limited, and he avoids – unlike the translators of some contemporary texts such as the *Prose Merlin* – 'stencil-copying,'[7] whereby the word-order of the original is slavishly retained. Even a usage which may be derived from French, the progressive lengthening of verbal units characteristic of French oratorical style,[8] has been naturalized. Here is a famous and much-quoted instance, the lament of Ector over the body of Lancelot:

> 'And now I dare say,' sayd syr Ector, 'thou sir Launcelot, there thou lyest, that thou were never matched of erthely knyghtes hande. And thou were the curtest knyght that ever bare shelde! And thou were the truest frende to thy lovar that ever bestrade hors, and thou were the trewest lover, of a synful man, that ever loved woman, and thou were the kyndest man that ever strake wyth swerde. And thou were the godelyest persone that ever cam emonge prees of knyghtes, and thou

4 P. J. C. Field, *Romance and Chronicle: A Study of Malory's Prose Style* (London, 1971).
5 Field, *Romance and Chronicle*, p. 45.
6 Field, *Romance and Chronicle*, p. 72.
7 Field, *Romance and Chronicle*, pp. 36–68.
8 E. Vinaver, 'A Note on Malory's Prose,' *Aspects of Malory*, ed. T. Takamiya and D. S. Brewer (Cambridge, 1981), pp. 9–15 (14–15).

was the mekest man and the jentyllest that ever ete in halle emonge
ladyes, and thou were the sternest knyght to thy mortal foo that ever
put spere in the reeste.' (725/17–26; XXI.13)

Although the broad direction of the passage may derive from French, the
grammar is wholly native. In fact, several constructions derived from Old
English syntax but which have disappeared from present-day standard usage
are found here, such as the divided modifier in the noun phrase 'the mekest
man and the jentyllest,' a construction known as 'the splitting of heavy
groups,'[9] and the anacoluthic break of continuity reinforced by repetition of
the pronoun in 'thou sir Launcelot, there thou lyest, that thou were . . . .'.[10]

   These last features are syntactic rather than stylistic, in the sense that they
are native structures which, once understood, have no literary salience.
However, there are usages in Malory's prose, deriving from Old English
patterns, which do seem to be 'marked' in some way. Mark Lambert has
distinguished two characteristic features of Malory's prose style: a shifting
between direct and indirect speech, and the use of collective utterance.[11]
Here is an example of the former:

> Than Elyas sente unto kynge Marke in grete dispyte uppon hede
> whether he wolde fynde a knyght that wolde fyght with hym body for
> body, and yf that he myght sle kynge Markis knyght, he to have the
> trewayge of Cornwayle yerely, 'and yf that his knyght sle myne, I fully
> releace my clayme for ever.' (385/8–13; X.29)

As an example of the latter, the following passage may be cited; in it, no
fewer than 'seven score knyghtes' speak in unison:

> Than they seyde all at onys with one voice:
>   'Sir, us thynkis beste that ye knyghtly rescow the quene. Insomuch as
> she shall be brente, hit ys for youre sake; and hit ys to suppose, and ye
> myght be handeled, ye shulde have the same dethe, othir ellis a more
> shamefuller dethe. And, sir, we say all that ye have rescowed her frome
> her deth many tymys for other mennes quarels; therefore us semyth hit
> ys more youre worshyp that ye rescow the quene from thys quarell,
> insomuch that she hath hit for your sake.' (680/35–42; XX.6)

It is perhaps worth pointing out that neither of these usages is Malory's
invention. Such structures seem to be a characteristic of Germanic prose
designed for oral delivery – they appear, for instance, in the thirteenth-
century Old Icelandic prose sagas – and may be compared with the
following extract from the *Anglo-Saxon Chronicle* annal for 755, which
demonstrates them both:

---

[9] See B. Mitchell, *Old English Syntax* (Oxford, 1985), I, 612–616.
[10] Mitchell, I, 776–7.
[11] M. Lambert, *Malory: Style and Vision in Le Morte Darthur* (New Haven, 1975).

Þa cuædon hie Þæt hie hie Þæs ne onmunden 'Þon ma Þe eowre geferan Þe mid Þam cyninge ofslægene wærun'.[12]

[Then they said that they cared for that 'no more than your companions who were slain with the king'.]

In the *Chronicle* passage, the function of the sudden shift into direct speech, used by a group of men speaking with one voice, is performative, in the same way as the form of words used in such religious rituals as the marriage service; it emphasizes the loyalty of the speakers to their lord by using their own words as evidence. In the passages from Malory, similar performative functions may be distinguished; Elyas' speech is a legalistic declaration, and the speech of the 140 knights (however unrealistic) is a statement of personal solidarity which emphasizes moral commitment rather than individuated character. We shall see further examples of this performative use of language later in this essay.

More generally, Vinaver has shown quite conclusively that Malory reworked the syntax of his French originals so as to replace subordinated with paratactic structures, and this must have been a conscious act of translation.[13] Here is an example, taken from Vinaver, of parallel passages in Malory and his French original, *La Queste del Saint Graal*.[14] Subordinating conjunctions in the French text have been italicized. It will be observed that Malory has replaced the complex subordinated syntax of the French with the coordinated structures characteristic of the native tradition. It will also be remarked – a notable feature of his practice of translation – that Malory has considerably abbreviated his original.

Mes *por ce que* vous m'avez dit *que* je n'ai mie encore tant alé *que* je ne puisse retorner *se* je me vuel garder de renchaoir en pechié mortel creant je premierement a Dieu et a vos aprés *que* je mes a la vie *que* je ai menee si longuement ne retornerai, *ainz* tendrai chasteé et garderai mon cors au plus nettement *que* je porrai.[15]

[But because you have told me that I have not gone so far that I cannot go back if I refrain from deadly sin I swear to God and then to you that I shall never go back to the life I have led but shall observe chastity and keep myself as free from stain as I can. (Vinaver's translation)]

'Sertes,' seyde sir Launcelot, 'all that ye have seyde ys trew and frome henseforwarde I caste me, by the grace of God, never to be so wycked as I have bene but as to sew knyghthode and to do fetys of armys.' (540/10–13; XIII.20)

---

[12] *Sweet's Reader*, p. 3.
[13] Vinaver, 'A Note,' pp. 9–11.
[14] Vinaver, 'A Note,' p. 10.
[15] A. Pauphilet, ed., *La Queste del Saint Graal* (Paris, 1923), pp. 70–71.

This preference for coordinated rather than subordinated structures can make Malory's prose-style seem at first sight unsophisticated to the present-day reader. Field's criticism is typical:

> . . . the chronicle [ie. paratactic] style is a very limited one, unsuitable for reflecting the movement of a sophisticated mind, for organising complicated material, or delivering ironic judgements . . .[16]

and this view of parataxis is one which has been held in the past by a number of linguists as well as critics. Thus the Anglo-Saxonist S. O. Andrew believed that the use of coordination rather than subordination in building up sequences of statements was 'immature and almost childish.'[17] This, however, is an extreme position. Although most modern historical linguists believe that parataxis precedes hypotaxis in linguistic development, it cannot be considered somehow more primitive: languages are all equally efficient for the purposes required of them, and there is no sense in which they 'progress' or 'decay.' And a number of scholars have recently drawn attention to how paratactic structures have their own stylistic strengths – strengths which are not just to do with those homespun virtues of narrative directness commented on by Field, but are to do with the significant juxtaposition of contrasting statements. The paratactic style is intensely audience-centred in that, avoiding making causal relationships overt, it leaves the audience to draw its own conclusions. It is thus a style appropriate to the communal approach to literary creation which dominated medieval culture and which – in these days of 'reader-response' criticism and 'reception-theory' – recent critical theorists may be again more ready to value. By adopting the paratactic style, Malory is claiming for himself the traditional role of the romancer: the enunciator of his audience's ethical ideology.[18]

The subtle effects Malory achieved with the paratactic style can be demonstrated by passages such as the following:

> Than spake sir Gawayn and seyde,
> 'My lorde Arthure, I wolde counceyle you nat to be over hasty, but that ye wolde put hit in respite, thys jougemente of my lady the quene, for many causis. One ys thys, thoughe hyt were so that sir Launcelot were founde in the quenys chambir, yet hit myght be so that he cam thydir for none evyll. For ye know, my lorde,' seyde sir Gawayne, 'that my lady the quene hath oftyntymes ben gretely beholdyn unto sir Launcelot, more than to ony othir knyght; for oftyntymes he hath saved her lyff and done batayle for her whan all the courte refused the quene. And peraventure she sente for hym for goodnes and for none evyll, to

---

[16] Field, *Romance and Chronicle*, p. 35.
[17] S. O. Andrew, *Syntax and Style in Old English* (Cambridge, 1940), p. 87.
[18] See further C. La Farge, 'Conversation in Malory's *Morte Darthur*,' *Medium Ævum*, 56 (1987), 225–238, esp. 227.

rewarde hym for his good dedys that he had done to her in tymes past.
And peraventure my lady the quene sente for hym to that entente, that
sir Launcelot sholde a com prevaly to her wenyng that hyt had be beste
in eschewyng and dredyng of slaundir; for oftyntymys we do many
thynges that we wene for the beste be, and yet peradventure hit turnyth
to the warste. For I dare sey,' seyde sir Gawayne, 'my lady, your quene,
ys to you both good and trew. And as for sir Launcelot, I dare say he
woll make hit good upon ony knyght lyvyng that woll put uppon hym
vylany or shame, and in lyke wyse he woll make good for my lady the
quene.' (682/22–41; XX.7)

This passage is interesting for a number of reasons, not least because of the
'love-problem' with which it presents its fifteenth-century audience.
Gawain is attempting to persuade the king that the relationship between
Lancelot and Guinevere is a pure one – apparently Malory's own opinion,
since not long before this passage he states, in a comparatively rare
authorial comment, that 'love that tyme was nat as love ys nowadayes'
(676/3–4; XX.3). Gawain is given a subtle rhetorical trick to strengthen his
argument; it is surely significant that he shifts from 'my lady the quene'
to 'my lady your quene,' insisting on Arthur's particular bond to the queen
immediately before the contrasting reference to Lancelot. (In this
connection it is relevant to note that Lancelot customarily refers to
Guinevere as 'my lady the quene,' whereas Arthur regularly refers to her
simply as 'my quene'; Lancelot evidently conceives of his relationship to
Guinevere as one of social inferior to superior, contrasting with Arthur's
simple assertion of the bond relationship between husband and wife.)
However, there is subtlety here; it is perhaps not too fanciful to suggest that
the effect of this passage is to cast covert doubt on an overtly expressed
view. The repetition of phrases such as 'peraventure' and 'I dare sey,'
combined with a parallelism of syntax in the sentences within which they
occur, foregrounds doubt about the relationship which, ostensibly, Gawain
is made to favour. The paratactic style, whereby elements are placed side-
by-side, leaves the audience to draw its own conclusions and to make
causal links; Malory gives no overt opinion, thus involving his audience in
the act of moral interpretation. In Field's words, 'Malory . . . has the tact to
remain in the background.'[19]

A further point might be made. As has already been pointed out,
Malory's writing is no 'stencil copy' of his French originals. His choice of
the English prose tradition is an assertion of Englishness which should be
recognized as something positive rather than as an absence of conscious
decision.

[19] Field, *Romance and Chronicle*, p. 116.

III

It has been established in the previous section that Malory's syntax is nearer
to that of the native rather than the French tradition of prose. But closer
study reveals something more about the role of Englishness in the creation
of Malory's prose style. There is good evidence that Malory's taste, in terms
of ethical stance and of stylistic detail, was formed first through the reading
of Middle English verse romances, both alliterative and rhyming,[20] and
powerful echoes of this poetic tradition find their way into his prose. It is
perhaps significant that, in the one section of the cycle where Malory
certainly drew upon native sources, *The Tale of the Noble King Arthur that was
Emperor himself through Dignity of his Hands*, he chose – no doubt to Caxton's
distaste, since he rewrote much of this book – to retain, and even (it seems)
develop, many of the alliterative patterns of the earlier Middle English
verse *Morte Arthure*. Terence McCarthy, moreover, has remarked on the
pervasiveness of alliterative phraseology elsewhere in the cycle:[21] 'most of
Le Morte Darthur reveals a tendency on Malory's part to rely on alliteration,
especially in moments of special tension';[22] and Field has drawn attention
to the use of alliteration at the beginning of *Tristram*.[23] Phrases and clauses
such as 'lay so longe' (15/33; I.11), 'he bete on the basyn with the butte of
his spere' (157/9–10; VI.7), 'the sureté of thys swerde' (520/2; XIII.5), 'brym
as ony boore' (691/36; XX.13) occur throughout the cycle, even if they are
most insistent in the section derived directly from the older alliterative
poem. Here, for instance, is a short passage from part IV of *Tristram*:

> And there by fortune and by grete force that knyght smote downe sir
> Tristramys frome hys horse, and had a grete falle. Than sir Trystramys
> was sore ashamed, and lyghtly he avoyded hys horse and put hys
> shylde afore hys shulder and drew hys swerde, and than sir Trystramys
> requyred that knyght of hys knyghthode to alyghte uppon foote and
> fyght with hym. (295/18–23; IX.10)

The stylistic effect of such alliteration is twofold. On the one hand, it
connects passages of action such as the one quoted above with the older
traditions of alliterative verse, which had always favoured 'set-pieces' to do
with storms at sea or fighting. Chaucer had done something rather similar
in his adoption of the phraseology of the alliterative tradition in *The
Knight's Tale* (especially in the battle-scene at lines A 2604–2619). On the
other hand, it enables the author to make syntagmatic connections between
words, which can sometimes have a thematic significance; thus in this

[20] E. D. Kennedy, 'Malory and his English Sources,' *Aspects of Malory*, pp. 27–55.
[21] T. McCarthy, 'The Sequence of Malory's Tales,' *Aspects of Malory*, pp. 107–124.
[22] McCarthy, 'The Sequence,' p. 110.
[23] Field, *Romance and Chronicle*, chapter IV.

passage the linking of *fortune, force, falle* and *fyght* (as well as *foote*) raises interesting questions about the role of physical combat in Malory's ethical scheme.

McCarthy goes on to argue that

> The cadences of the alliterative rhythm are to a great extent the basis of his prose. Malory writes in short units which, even when the alliteration does not break the surface, it is frequently possible to break down into four beat phrases – like alliterative long lines without the alliteration.[24]

Although it is not necessary to agree entirely with N. F. Blake,[25] who suggests that Malory 'wrote in an alliterative prose,' it is nevertheless plausible to argue that Malory's prose contains echoes of the rhythms of earlier poetry as well as the decoration of older poetic traditions. Something of this can be seen in the following passage, which is here printed as lines of verse:

> 'Alas,' seyde sir Gawayne,
> 'now is my joy gone!'
> And than he felle downe and sowned,
> and longe he lay there
> as he had ben dede.
> And when he arose
> oute of hys swoughe
> he cryed oute sorowfully
> and seyde, 'Alas!'   (686/20–24; XX.10)

Each of the units distinguished in the above passage is roughly comparable with the two-stress half-lines of Old and Middle English alliterative (or, more properly, pure-stress) poetry. It can therefore be argued plausibly that the special ingredient Malory brought to the native prose tradition was to bring the heritage of pure-stress poetry into prose discourse, rather as Ælfric and other late Old English homilists had done five hundred years before.

IV

The reference to Ælfric leads to the next stage in the argument of this essay. Ælfric distinguished between two levels of style, *grande* and *tenue*; and this distinction between a lower and a higher style is one which persists into the later Middle Ages, complicated by certain moral and social associations.[26]

---

[24] McCarthy, 'The Sequence,' p. 112.
[25] N. F. Blake, 'Late Medieval Prose,' in W. F. Bolton, ed., *The Middle Ages*, 2nd ed. (London, 1986), pp. 369–399 (p. 397).
[26] See J. D. Burnley, *A Guide to Chaucer's Language* (Basingstoke, 1983), pp. 199–200.

Malory seems to have been aware of this distinction in speech:

> Wherefore, as me semyth, all jantyllmen that beryth olde armys ought
> of ryght to honoure sir Trystrams for the goodly tearmys that jantylmen
> have and use and shall do unto the Day of Dome, that thereby in a
> maner all men of worshyp may discever a jantylman frome a yoman
> and a yoman frome a vylayne. For he that jantyll is woll drawe hym to
> jantyll tacchis and to folow the noble customys of jantylmen.
> (232/15–20; VIII.3)

The key word here is *tearmys* 'terms,' a technical expression for the gentle
language of moral accomplishment. Malory is aware that there are two
sorts of language, which may be roughly categorized as 'courteous' and
'villainous'; courteous language is – or should be – that of the noble classes
and is characterized by the elevated nature of its subject matter and of the
ethical concerns which inform it, whereas villainous language is base both
in social standing and in moral values. This distinction is well displayed,
for instance, at the beginning of *Sir Gareth*:

> 'The moste noble kynge, kynge Arthure! God you blysse and all your
> fayre felyshyp, and in especiall the felyshyp of the Table Rounde. And
> for this cause I come hydir, to pray you and requyre you to gyff me
> three gyftys. And they shall nat be unresenablé asked but that ye may
> worshypfully graunte hem me, and to you no grete hurte nother losse.
> And the fyrste done and gyffte I woll aske now, and the tothir two
> gyfftes I woll aske this day twelve-monthe, wheresomever ye holde
> your hyghe feste.'
> 'Now aske ye,' seyde kyng Arthure, 'and ye shall have your
> askynge.'
> 'Now sir, this is my petycion at this feste, that ye woll geff me mete
> and drynke suffyciauntly for this twelve-monthe, and at that day I woll
> aske myne other two gyfftys.'
> 'My fayre son,' seyde kyng Arthure, 'aske bettyr, I counseyle the, for
> this is but a symple askyng; for myne herte gyvyth me to the gretly, that
> thou arte com of men of worshyp, and gretly my conceyte fayleth me but
> thou shalt preve a man of ryght grete worshyp.' (177/32–178/6; VII.1)

When Gareth first appears, he requests in knightly fashion a boon, and
Arthur indicates his pleasure at this noble, elevated and ritual request by
using the Middle English second-person pronoun of respect, *ye*. However,
when the comparatively base nature of the boon requested is revealed –
food and drink – Arthur is dismayed, and moves to the pronoun *thou*
which, although it often marks intimacy, is also used to address someone
lower in social position, or, in certain circumstances, to express contempt. It
is not surprising that Kay's opinion of Gareth a few lines later is couched as
follows: 'I undirtake he is a vylayne borne, and never woll make man, for
and he had be com of jantyllmen, he wolde have axed horse and armour,
but as he is, so he askyth' (178/20–22; VII.1).

However, Malory – unlike some of his contemporaries – is not someone who makes a necessary connection between elevated discourse and (to use a contemporary term) 'copiousness' in vocabulary; for Malory, a noble person need not necessarily have an engrossed and florid lexicon. The later Middle Ages saw the appearance in England of two kinds of vernacular text on the verbal arts specifically to do with the inculcation of higher style in language: word lists such as the *Nominale sive Verbale*, and courtesy books such as *The Babees Book* and Caxton's *Book of Curtesye*. But whereas the former are designed to supply the noble (or those aspiring to nobility) with an esoteric, copious and descriptive vocabulary, derived from the prestigious languages Latin and French, the latter are concerned more with linguistic appropriateness – a concern displayed by Chaucer in, for instance, *The Parliament of Fowls*.[27] An author such as Lydgate saw the elevated style as essentially a matter of 'copiousness,' and works such as Lydgate's *A Balade in Commendatioun of Our Lady* show how this was to be achieved:[28] by the use of Latinate aureate diction, which supplied the author with a set of polysyllabic synonyms to give sonority and grandiloquence to his utterance. Malory represents the tradition of the courtesy books; he is in general concerned with the ethical use of language rather than with its potential for engrossment.

Thus we do not find in Malory any real distinction between 'high' (i.e. Latinate) and 'low' (i.e. native) vocabulary comparable to that, for instance, of Lydgate, or of Dunbar in *The Golden Targe* and *The Flyting*. Other than in his use of alliteration, which has already been discussed, Malory's diction is not especially elaborate; the nearest approach he makes to rhetorical effects is in the use of a species of elegant but redundant variation (e.g. the frequent 'ladyes and damesels'), and of stock phrases and proverbs comparable with those which appear in the contemporary Paston letters. Even his more elaborate passages, such as the discussion of virtuous love at the beginning of the 'Knight of the Cart' section in *The Book of Sir Lancelot and Queen Guinevere*, use comparatively simple devices of augmentation:

> For, lyke as trees and erbys burgenyth and florysshyth in May, in lyke wyse every lusty harte that ys ony maner of lover spryngith, burgenyth, buddyth, and florysshyth in lusty dedis. (648/39–41; XVIII.25)

Malory goes on to use several Latinate words, *stabylité, rasure, arace*, but their use seems to be part of the technical language appropriate for the discussion of love; his intention here does not seem to be to heighten his language in the manner of a Lydgate. Rather, he is enacting the sense of spring growth by allowing his use of (especially) verbs to 'burgeon.'

[27] See Burnley, *A Guide*, pp. 179–180.
[28] See J. Norton-Smith, ed., *John Lydgate: Poems* (Oxford, 1966), pp. 192–195.

Malory's lexicon is roughly equally divided between French-derived loanwords and native vocabulary,[29] but there does not seem to be any distinction of register in their use, other than that (as we might expect, given that so many of them are function-words such as 'than,' 'that,' etc.) native words occur more frequently. In passages such as the following, a paratactic grammatical structure is combined with a straightforward, largely monosyllabic vocabulary pared of unnecessary adjectives:

> And so thes four-and-twenty knyghtes sholde dyne with the quene in a prevy place by themselff, and there was made a grete feste of all maner of deyntees. But sir Gawayne had a custom that he used dayly at mete and at supper: that he loved well all maner of fruyte, and in especiall appyls and pearys. And therefore whosomever dyned other fested sir Gawayne wolde comonly purvey for good fruyte for hym. And so ded the quene; for to please sir Gawayne she lette purvey for hym all maner of fruyte. (613/27–34; XVIII.3)

It would be an error to see this avoidance of stylistic variation in register as a lack of technique or sophistication. Critics have found many subtleties to praise in Malory's handling of diction, most notably in his presentation of dialogue. For instance, the way in which speakers violate the principles of efficient communication by refusing to cooperate in conversation can be regarded as a way of demonstrating character, e.g. by answering a question with another question which parallels the vocabulary of the first:

> That aspyed sir Lamerok, that kynge Arthure and his blood was so discomfite. And anone he was redy and axed sir Palomides if he wolde ony more juste. 'Why sholde I nat juste?' seyde sir Palomides.
>   So they hurled togydirs and brake their spearys . . . (405/44–406/4; X.46)[30]

Palomides' rejoinder, an overt refusal to give his potential enemy any information, nevertheless suffices as a response to the challenge covertly made to him; it may be taken as the aggressive response appropriate to a threatened knight. However, it would be anachronistic to see this practice as a way of presenting individuated character in the fashion of a nineteenth-century 'realistic' novelist; Palomides is here behaving as a characteristically heroic knight, demonstrating an appropriate pattern of noble behaviour. The author's purpose is to reveal the moral tensions of a given situation through linguistic usage.

It is not surprising, therefore, that Malory is interested in the functions of conversation beyond the simple communication of overt meaning. For

---

[29] P. J. C. Field, 'The Source of Malory's *Tale of Gareth,' Aspects of Malory*, pp. 57–70 (p. 67).
[30] This example is cited in La Farge, p. 225. For the role of conversational pragmatics in Malory, see also P. Schroeder, 'Hidden depths: dialogue and characterization in Chaucer and Malory,' *PMLA*, 98 (1983), 374–387.

instance, the following dialogue takes place at a moment of crisis for the whole cycle, when slander and strife destroy the amity of the Round Table:

So wyth thes wordis cam in sir Arthur.
'Now, brothir,' seyde sir Gawayne, 'stynte youre stryff.'
'That woll I nat,' seyde sir Aggravayne and sir Mordred.
'Well, woll ye so?' seyde sir Gawayne. 'Than God spede you, for I woll nat here of youre talis, nothir be of youre counceile.'
'No more woll I,' seyde sir Gaherys.
'Nother I,' seyde sir Gareth, 'for I shall never say evyll by that man that made me knyght.'
And therewythall they three departed makynge grete dole.
'Alas!' seyde sir Gawayne and sir Gareth, 'now ys thys realme holy destroyed and myscheved, and the noble felyshyp of the Rounde Table shall be disparbeled.' (674/8–19; XX.1)

The conversation here is marked by brevity and simplicity; the vocabulary, with the exception of exotics such as 'disparbeled,' is for the most part plain. Yet this simplicity does not detract from the power of the passage. In their choric last utterance, Gawain and Gareth speak collectively and performatively, and their lamenting words enact ceremonially the dissolution of the Round Table.

Perhaps the most subtle handling of vocabulary achieved by Malory is in his use of repeated expressions in close proximity to each other. Two passages may be taken to illustrate this practice. The first example is from a dialogue between Arthur, Gawain and Lancelot in the last Tale of the cycle, *The Morte Arthur*. Lancelot is trying to restore his relationship with Arthur and the others of the Round Table who have become his sworn enemies; and one of the means he employs to emphasize his bond of fealty is to repeat constantly the expression *my lorde*. Gawain – who has himself earlier asserted his bond to Arthur by using the triple expression 'my kynge, my lorde and myne uncle' (686/44; XX.10) – is unimpressed, as is indicated by his use of a contemptuous *thou* in response to Lancelot's polite *ye*, and by his own repeated use of the expression *false (recreayed) knyght*; it is moreover noticeable that Lancelot fails to respond directly to Gawain's furious interjections. The failure of conversational interaction between Lancelot and Gawain enacts the ethical breakdown which has befallen the brotherhood of the Round Table.

'. . . And at suche tymes, my lorde Arthur,' seyde sir Launcelot, 'ye loved me and thanked me whan I saved your quene frome the fyre, and than ye promysed me for ever to be my good lorde. And now methynkith ye rewarde me full evyll for my good servyse. And, my lorde, mesemyth I had loste a grete parte of my worshyp in my knyghthod and I had suffird my lady, youre quene, to have ben brente, and insomuche as she shulde have bene brente for my sake; for sytthyn I have done batayles for youre quene in other quarels than in myne

owne quarell, mesemyth now I had more ryght to do batayle for her in
her ryght quarell. And therefore, my good and gracious lorde,' seyde
sir Launcelot, 'take your quene unto youre good grace, for she is both
tru and good.'

  'Fy on the, false recreayed knyght!' seyde sir Gawayn . . .

  '. . . I undirstonde [said sir Láncelot] hit boteneth me nat to seke none
accordemente whyle ye, sir Gawayne, ar so myschevously sett. And if
ye were nat, I wolde nat doute to have the good grace of my lorde
kynge Arthure.'

  'I leve well, false recrayed knyght, for thou haste many
longe dayes overlad me and us all . . .' (688/33–689/28; XX.11)

A second, perhaps more subtle example of such meaningful repetition is
from the beginning of *The Tale of Sir Lancelot du Lake*, where the word *fayre*
is used repeatedly to raise the ethical problem of the difference between
outward appearance and underlying reality. A number of characters use the
word independently, rather like the repeated theme in a passage of music.
Here, for instance, is a conversation between sir Ector de Marys and 'a man
was lyke a foster':

  'Fayre felow,' seyde sir Ector, 'doste thou know this contrey or ony
  adventures that bene here nyghe honde?'

  'Sir,' seyde the foster, 'this contrey know I well. And hereby within
  this myle is a stronge maner and well dyked, and by that maner on the
  lyffte honde there is a fayre fourde for horse to drynke off, and over that
  fourde there growys a fayre tre. And thereon hongyth many fayre
  shyldys that welded somtyme good knyghtes, and at the bole of the tre
  hongys a basyn of couper and latyne. And stryke uppon that basyn with
  the butte of thy spere three tymes, and sone aftir thou shalt hyre new
  tydynges; and ellys haste thou the fayreste grace that ever had knyghte
  this many yeres that passed thorow this foreste.' (150/14–24; VI.2)

Is it perhaps too fanciful to detect a note of annoyance in the foster's repeated
use of *fayre* in picking up Sir Ector's rather patronizing term of address? Or
could it be argued that the foster is deliberately and in 'vilaynous' fashion
goading Sir Ector, by mocking his form of address? Moreover, the foster uses
the term to qualify so many nouns, both abstract and concrete, that we are left
uncertain as to its true denotation. Malory gives us no direct answer to these
questions; we, the audience, have to engage with the situation ourselves, by
analysing the range of possible meanings of the word and coming to our own
decision about its ethical import.[31]

  Such devices of textual cohesion, however they are to be interpreted, lie
at the heart of Malory's artistry. Like all great authors, he has the ability
to recreate everyday vocabulary, to use common words in such a way that

---

[31] A similar example is to do with Malory's use of the word 'swete'; see T. McCarthy,
'Malory's "swete madame",' *Medium Ævum*, 56 (1987), 89–94.

they develop special meanings within the context of his own work. These special meanings cohere to build an ethical lexicon through which his moral concerns and celebration of an imaginary past are covertly furthered – covertly, because Malory seems to have conceived of his function as that of simply the ideological mouthpiece of his intended noble audience. Moreover, in his choice of a native form of expression, Malory was asserting in a deeply conservative fashion the value of these ideological concerns at a time of social ferment, worrying both to himself and to his class.

7

The Malory Life-Records

P. J. C. FIELD

This chapter describes the surviving records of the life of Sir Thomas Malory of Newbold Revel in Warwickshire, who is the most likely author of the *Morte Darthur*. Space, however, prohibits arguing the case for him as against the dozen other Thomas Malorys known from the fifteenth century, and any unknown namesake. The issue has been debated for over a century, and the most important contributions to the debate are listed in the Bibliography at the end of this chapter. My own views are set out in one of the items in the Bibliography, my *Life and Times of Sir Thomas Malory*.

The main part of this chapter is a chronological sequence of the known records of Sir Thomas Malory of Newbold Revel and Elizabeth his wife, with selected records of his parents, his known children and his only known grandchild, the last Malory of Newbold Revel. A summary account of Sir Thomas's life will help to put the records in context.

He was born into a gentry family that had lived for centuries in the English Midlands near the point where Warwickshire, Leicestershire, and Northamptonshire meet. His father, John Malory, was an esquire with land in all three counties, but was primarily a Warwickshire man (Record 1), being twice sheriff, five times M.P. and for many years a justice of the peace for that county. John married Philippa Chetwynd (2), daughter of a family with lands in Warwickshire and Staffordshire, and they had at least three daughters, and one son, Thomas, who was probably born within a year either way of 1416 (4). Almost nothing is known of his upbringing. When his father died in 1433/4 (6–7), he would have been in his mid-teens.

Thomas himself is recorded from 1439 on as a respectable country land-owner with a growing interest in politics (10–14). He dealt in land, witnessed deeds for his neighbours, acted as a parliamentary elector, and by 1441 had become a knight. In late medieval England, taking up knight-hood could be expensive, and doing so may imply political and social ambition. It was perhaps about this time that he married Elizabeth Walsh of Wanlip in Leicestershire, who later in this decade bore him a son Robert, who was to be his heir (24). A discordant note was sounded in 1443: he was charged with wounding and imprisoning Thomas Smith and stealing his goods (17), but the charge apparently fell through. In 1445 he was elected

M.P. for Warwickshire, and in this and the following year served on commissions to assess tax-exemptions in the county (20–2). In 1449, a Thomas Malory was returned as M.P. for the borough of Bedwin in Wiltshire (28). He may have been Sir Thomas of Newbold Revel: Bedwin belonged to a magnate with major interests in Warwickshire, the Duke of Buckingham, who may have wished for another voice in parliament to support the policies he favoured. It was a time of increasing division and unrest in the country, which was eventually to lead to civil war.

It was against that background that the new parliament met in November and December, and dispersed for Christmas on 17 December. Then, with the new decade, Malory's life, for no known reason, underwent a startling change. On 4 January 1450, he and 26 other armed men were said to have laid an ambush for Buckingham in the Abbot of Combe's woods near Newbold Revel (30). This was followed by many other crimes, or at least many well-supported allegations of crimes. Malory seems to have behaved himself while parliament was in session again in London, but it was adjourned to Leicester in April, and the later charges accuse him of committing rape and theft and extortion around Newbold Revel from May to August (32–6).

Despite this, when the next parliament met, in September 1450, a Thomas Malory, who will certainly be the M.P. for Bedwin and may be Sir Thomas of Newbold Revel, was returned to it as M.P. for the borough of Wareham in Dorset (37). It may be no coincidence that Wareham belonged to the Duke of York, who was opposed to Buckingham in the national power struggle: York needed experienced parliamentary help in opposing the government, and Malory needed a protector. Although a warrant was issued during this parliament for his arrest 'for divers felonies' (39), he may have attended until the dissolution in May. A few weeks later, he and various accomplices were alleged to have stolen cattle in Warwickshire (41). Buckingham tried to arrest him, but in the meantime Malory apparently raided Buckingham's hunting lodge, killed his deer, and did an enormous amount of damage (44). He was arrested and imprisoned at Coleshill, but after two days escaped by swimming the moat (45–6). He then reportedly twice raided Combe Abbey with a large band of men, breaking down doors, insulting the monks, and stealing a great deal of money (47–8). He was charged with nearly all these crimes at a court in Nuneaton, over which, despite his own involvement, Buckingham presided (49). By January 1452 Malory was in prison in London (51–2), where he spent most of the next eight years, waiting for a trial that never came.

He was bailed out several times, and on one occasion seems to have joined an old crony on a horse-stealing expedition across East Anglia that ended in Colchester jail (68–70). He escaped from there too, 'using swords, daggers, and *langues-de-boeuf*' (a kind of halberd), but was recaptured and returned to prison in London (72–3). After this date he was shifted frequently from prison to prison, and the penalties put on his jailers for his secure keeping reached a record for medieval England. During Henry VI's insanity, when the Duke of York was Lord Protector, Malory was given a royal pardon (78). This seems to have been the lowest point in his fortunes: the court dismissed his pardon, and he was twice sued for small debts he could not repay (79–80, 84). However, late in 1457, the Earl of Warwick's men bailed him out for two months, and he seems to have been free again briefly in 1459 (86–7, 89). He was moved to a more secure prison when the Yorkists invaded in 1460, but after they had expelled the Lancastrians he was freed and pardoned (92). He was never tried on any of the charges brought against him.

The new decade looked more promising for Malory. He repaid the attentions the Yorkist lords had given him by following them north in 1462 to the siege of the northern castles of Alnwick and Bamburgh, which the Lancastrians had seized (94). The castles were taken, and Malory settled down to a more peaceful life. In 1464 he witnessed a land-settlement for his neighbours, and in 1466 his grandson Nicholas was born (95–6). But by July 1466, King Edward was beginning to be at odds with Warwick's family, formerly his chief supporters, and the Warwickshire knight seems to have changed sides again. In 1468 and again in 1470, he was named in lists of irreconcilable Lancastrians who were excluded from royal pardons for any crimes they might have committed (97–8, 100). Most of those excluded were at liberty; but the *Morte Darthur* shows us that Malory was in prison, completing his work.

Outside prison, the balance of power shifted uncertainly. In October 1470, a sudden invasion brought the Lancastrians back, and among their first acts was freeing those of their party who were in London prisons. Six months later, Sir Thomas Malory of Newbold Revel died and was buried under a marble tombstone in Greyfriars, Newgate, which, despite its proximity to one of the jails in which he had been imprisoned, was the most fashionable church in London (103). On the day of Malory's death, King Edward landed in Yorkshire, and two months later the Yorkists were back in power. When the new administration held the usual enquiry into Malory's estates, the jurors testified that he died owning nothing (105). In a prudent moment, the rash Sir Thomas had made all his lands over, directly or indirectly, to his wife. She was left in possession of them, and he was left to rest in peace until 1547, when Henry VIII had the tombstones in Greyfriars sold for what they would fetch.

Many of the records from which this story is deduced present difficulties of date, attribution, or authenticity. The date of Sir Thomas's death, for instance, was given on his tombstone as 14 March 1471, but the enquiry into his lands after his death (his 'inquisition post mortem') says he died two days earlier, on 12 March. The epitaph is more likely to be right, because the inquisition was formally on behalf of Edward IV, who had landed in England on 14 March after his exile to begin his reconquest. The date in the inquisition may be a device to avert charges that Sir Thomas was in

rebellion against any king who was in England when he died. The same
stratagem was apparently used to protect Richard Boughton of Little
Lawford in Warwickshire and Sir Thomas Gower of Sittenham in Yorkshire,
both of whom were said to have been killed in the Battle of Bosworth in
1485: each man's IPM said he died two days beforehand.[1] Limitations of
space, however, severely restrict explanations of this kind, which must be
pursued in the scholarly writing on Malory's life listed in the Bibliography.

THE DOCUMENTS

Documents are given in order of date. Dates in the form *Jun–Dec 1452* = 'for
the whole of the period from June to December 1452 inclusive'; those in the
form *Jun/Dec 1452* = 'at some time during the period from June to December
1452 inclusive.' Scholarly writings are referred to by short titles; fuller
details will be found in the Bibliography.

1 4 Aug 1406 John Malory 'dominus de fennynewbold' [Fenny Newbold,
    i.e. Newbold Revel, Warwickshire] witnesses a Stretton-under-Fosse
    deed: Warwicks C.R.O. D19/730. This, the first known record of Sir
    Thomas's father, implies John was of age. The silence beforehand and
    numerous records afterwards suggest he had just come of age; if so, he
    was born in 1385. Cf. Field p. 43.

2 1407/1412 A set of heraldic windows is made for the church of Grendon
    in Warwickshire, commemorating Sir Thomas's mother's family, the
    Chetwynds of Grendon and of Ingestre, Staffordshire: see Field pp. 51–2.
    The windows themselves have perished, but a surviving seventeenth-
    century sketch shows they contained the only known image of any
    medieval Malory taken from life, a picture of Sir Thomas's father John
    Malory and his wife Philippa (Chetwynd). That picture is the first
    evidence for John and Philippa's marriage, but it is uninformative about
    individuality, except that it shows John wearing a beard (all the other
    laymen are clean-shaven). Its main interest, however, lies in the fact that it
    and the other pictures are meant not to represent the individuality of their
    subjects but to make a statement about their subjects' place in this world
    and the next.

3 10 Nov 1412 John Malory agrees to arbitration in a dispute with the
    Chetwynd family: *Ancient Deeds* ii 117. The dispute is most likely to have
    been over dividing the estate of his mother-in-law, Aline Lady Chetwynd:
    cf. Field pp. 45, 51.

---

1 Dugdale p. 100, Wedgwood s.v. Gower. (For abbreviations and bibliography in this
   chapter, see below pp. 128–30.)

4 1415/18   Birth of Thomas, only known son of John Malory esquire of Newbold Revel and his wife, Philippa Chetwynd. For the date, see Field pp. 62–4. Thomas must be John's son because he inherited the family estates when John had surviving daughters, and Philippa's son if she and John were married by 10 Nov 1412 (cf. no. 3 supra).

5 19 Jun 1423   John and Philippa Malory of the diocese of Coventry and Lichfield are granted an indult to have Mass said before daybreak: *Calendar of Papal Registers* (1417–31) p. 315.

6 4 Dec 1433   John Mallory of Newbold Revel grants a rent of 12 pence and 3 capons to three local men: P.R.O. WARD/2/1/3/2. Among the witnesses is Eustace Burneby, John's son-in-law. John's seal bears a variant on the Revel arms. This is the last known record of him; his death (by 8 Jun 1434: cf. no. 7) probably left Thomas in his mid-to-late teens.

7 8 Jun 1434   Philippa widow of John Malory is party to a settlement for the marriage of Isobel her daughter and Edward son of Sir Edward Doddingsels of Long Itchington, Warwickshire: *C.C.R.* (1429–35) 314.

8 1436   Philippa widow of John Malory holds land worth £60 a year in Warwickshire: P.R.O. E179/192/59.

9 14 May 1437   Pardon to Philippa, widow and executrix of John Malory of Fenny Newbold: P.R.O. C67/38, m. 1. This is a routine precaution for a prudent executor.

10 23 May 1439   Thomas Malorre esquire witnesses a settlement of property in Warwickshire for Sir Philip Chetwynd: *C.C.R.* (1435–41) 268. There may have been other Thomas Malorys in the Midlands at this time, but a Thomas Malory in a Chetwynd settlement must be Sir Philip's cousin from Newbold Revel, of whom this is the first known record.

11 1 Sep 1440/31 Aug 1441   Robert Vincent of Swinford, Leicestershire, apparently mortgages his lands there to his brother-in-law Thomas Malory of Newbold Revel: Vinaver p. 117 from Burton p. 279, and cf. Nichols iv 361.

12 8 Oct 1441   A Warwickshire vicar grants rights in land in his parish to Sir Thomas Malare and others: P.R.O. E326/10717. The kind of trusteeship involved was part of the staple of social relationships in the fifteenth century. This is the first known record of Sir Thomas as a knight.

13 28 Dec 1441   Return by the Sheriff of Northamptonshire recording the election of M.P.s for that county; Sir Thomas Malery heads the list of 88 electors: P.R.O. C219/15 Part 1. This implies he was a Northamptonshire resident, which suggests he was in possession of the family lands around Winwick in Northamptonshire, but not of their more important estates around Newbold Revel. The most plausible explanation of that is that he had married and that the Winwick lands had been settled on him and his wife, but that his mother still held Newbold Revel. Sir Thomas's only recorded wife, Elizabeth, was a Walsh of Wanlip in Leicestershire; they will have been married by 5 Feb 1448: see Field p. 136 and no. 24 infra.

14 28 Jun 1442　Sir Thomas Malory witnesses a second settlement for Sir Philip Chetwynd and his wife Joan (Burley): Chetwynd Chartulary pp. 316-17.

15 Jul–Aug 1442　Sir Philip Chetwynd is Mayor of Bayonne in south-west France: *Proc. & Ord. P.C.* v 193–4. A junior post with his cousin could have provided Sir Thomas with the knowledge of that area shown towards the end of the *Morte Darthur*.

16 10 Aug 1443　Sir Thomas Mallore witnesses the sale by his distant cousins, the Malorys of Walton-on-the-Wold, Leicestershire, and Tachbrook Mallory, Warwickshire, of the manor of Botley, Warwickshire: S.B.T. DR37/Box 50/2938.

17 10 Oct 1443　Sir Thomas Malory of the parish of Monks Kirby, Warwickshire, and Eustace Burneby of Watford 'in the same county' [*recte* Northamptonshire] are accused of insulting, wounding, imprisoning, and robbing Thomas Smythe at Spratton, Northamptonshire: P.R.O. CP40/731 m. 278 d; 732 m. 414.

18 10 May 1444　Sir Philip Chetwynd dies: Chetwynd Chartulary pp. 261–4, 311–16.

19 31 Jul 1444–31 Jul 1445　Thomas Mallory (no rank) leases the Stretton-under-Fosse tithe corn from and is paid an annuity by Monks Kirby Priory: P.R.O. SC6 1039/18. This will be Sir Thomas of Newbold Revel – it is not unusual for accounts like this to omit a knight's title: Field p. 88n.

20 late Jan 1445–9 Apr 1446　Sir William Mountford and Sir Thomas Malory are M.P.s for Warwickshire. The original returns being lost, their election must be inferred from the next record. Parliament met 25 Feb 1445–9 Apr 1446, with intermissions.

21 3 Jun 1445　Mountford and Malory are appointed to a parliamentary commission for assessing tax-exemptions in Warwickshire: *C.F.R.* (1437–45) 324–30.

22 14 Jul 1446　The commission for tax-exemptions is reorganized; Mountford and Malory are reappointed: *C.F.R.* (1445–52) 31, 36.

23 11 Jun/29 Sep 1446　Sir Thomas Malory is paid an instalment of a 20-mark annuity by the keepers of the lands of Henry Duke of Warwick deceased: P.R.O. E368/220/107–8.

24 7 Nov 1447/5 Nov 1448　Birth of Robert, son of Sir Thomas Malory of Newbold Revel. See no. **105**.

25 9 Oct 1448　Sir Thomas Malory is party to a law-suit with Sir Robert Harcourt and others: P.R.O. KB27/750 m. 48d.

26 1 Sep 1448/31 Aug 1449　Sir Thomas Malory acquires Robert Vincent's lands outright: as no. **11**.

27 9 Oct 1449　Sir Thomas Malory and Sir Robert Harcourt restart their law-suit: P.R.O. KB27/754 m. 61d.

28 14 Oct 1449   Thomas Malory (no rank) is returned as M.P. for Bedwin, Wiltshire: *Return*. Sir Thomas Malory of Newbold Revel's connections with Buckingham, who was lord of Bedwin, and the way in which his movements fit in with the sessions of this parliament suggest he was the man elected; the absence of a rank suggests the contrary: see Field pp. 94–7.

29 6 Nov 1449   Parliament meets; prorogued 17 December.

30 4 Jan 1450   Sir Thomas Malory of Fenny Newbold allegedly tries to murder the Duke of Buckingham in the Abbot's woods at Combe, Warwickshire: see no. **49**. What evidence there is points to Buckingham's having been well-disposed to Malory before this: he had been Sir Philip Chetwynd's patron, it would have been difficult for Malory to be elected M.P. for Warwickshire if he had been hostile, and he may even have helped Malory become M.P. for Bedwin: Field pp. 95–7. The allegation, whether true or false, shows they had (suddenly) become enemies.

31 22 Jan 1450   Parliament meets; it is prorogued on 30 March, and adjourned to Leicester on 29 April.

32 23 May 1450   Sir Thomas Malory allegedly rapes Joan Smith at Coventry: see no. **49**. The charge is not of abduction but of rape in the modern sense: it says *cum ea carnaliter concubit*, 'he carnally lay with her.' It was, however, brought not by Joan under common law, but by her husband under a statute of Richard II intended to make elopement into rape even when the woman consented: see Field p. 106.

33 31 May 1450   Sir Thomas Malory allegedly extorts money by threats from two residents of Monks Kirby: see no. **49**.

34 5/8 Jun 1450   Parliament is dissolved.

35 6 Aug 1450   Sir Thomas Malory allegedly rapes Joan Smith again and steals £40-worth of goods from her husband in Coventry: cf. nos **32** and **49**.

36 31 Aug 1450   Sir Thomas Malory allegedly commits extortion from a third Monks Kirby resident: see no. **49**.

37 2 Nov 1450   Thomas Malery (no rank) is returned as M.P. for Wareham, Dorset: *Return*. Sir Thomas Malory of Newbold Revel's movements suggest he was the man elected; the absence of a rank suggests he was not; he might have owed his election to the Duke of York, who was lord of Wareham: see Field pp. 98–9.

38 6 Nov 1450   Parliament meets, prorogued on 18 December, meets again 20 Jan 1451.

39 15 Mar 1451   A warrant is issued for the arrest of Sir Thomas Malory: P.R.O. KB 29/83 m.3; Baugh p. 7n.

40 29 Mar 1451   Parliament is prorogued, meets again 5 May, and is dissolved 24 May.

41 4 Jun 1451   Sir Thomas Malory of Fenny Newbold allegedly steals 7 cows, 2 calves, 335 sheep, and a cart worth £22 at Cosford, Warwickshire: see no. **49**.

42 13 Jul 1451   A warrant is issued for the arrest of Sir Thomas Malory and John Appleby his servant: *C.P.R.* (1446–52) 476.

43 13/25 Jul 1451   Buckingham takes 60 men from his Warwickshire estates to arrest Sir Thomas Malory: McFarlane pp. 91–2. The size of his retinue suggests he expected Malory to have a good deal of local support.

44 20 Jul 1451   Sir Thomas Malory allegedly steals 6 does and commits £500-worth of wanton damage in the deer park at Caludon, Warwickshire: see no. **49**.

45 25 Jul 1451   Sir Thomas Malory is arrested and imprisoned at Coleshill, Warwickshire, in the house of the sheriff, Sir William Mountford (who had previously been Malory's fellow-M.P.): see no. **49**.

46 27 Jul 1451   Sir Thomas escapes by swimming the moat at night: see no. **49**.

47 28 Jul 1451   Sir Thomas and accomplices allegedly rob Combe Abbey of £46 in money and £40-worth of ornaments: see no. **49**.

48 29 Jul 1451   Sir Thomas and a hundred accomplices allegedly rob Combe of another £40 in money and various valuable objects: see no. **49**.

49 23 Aug 1451   Sir Thomas is charged at Nuneaton with nearly all the preceding crimes: P.R.O. KB9/265/78, m. 3; Hicks pp. 93–7. The principal charge was an attempt to murder Buckingham, who presided over the proceedings, which were held in the area of his greatest power, instead of in the county town, Warwick, as they should have been. It does not follow that the charges were false.

50 5 Oct 1451   Before the case against Sir Thomas can be tried at Warwick, the assize town, it is transferred to the Court of King's Bench at Westminster: P.R.O. KB9/265/78, m. 3.

51 Michaelmas Term 1451   Sir Thomas is charged in the King's Bench with breach of the peace and rape: Baugh pp. 5–6.

52 27 Jan 1452   Sir Thomas is brought from Ludgate Prison to the King's Bench charged with the Nuneaton offences, pleads not guilty, and is returned to Ludgate: P.R.O. KB27/763, m. 23; Hicks p. 97, Baugh p. 29.

53 31 Jan 1452   Sir Thomas is charged in the King's Bench with the damage at Caludon Park; he pleads not guilty: P.R.O. KB27/763, m. 23; Baugh p. 20.

54 9 Feb 1452   Sir Thomas is presented for trial in the King's Bench but no jury appears; the case is deferred until 26 April and he is returned to Ludgate: P.R.O. KB27/763, m. 23; Hicks p. 98.

55 26 Feb 1452   A Leicestershire land deal shows that Sir Thomas Malory was once a feoffee of William Malory of Saddington: Leicestershire C.R.O. DE2242/6/64.

56 26 Apr 1452   Sir Thomas is presented for trial again, no jury appears and the case is deferred (with successive later deferments until May 1454 q.v.); he is sent to the Marshalsea of the King's Bench: P.R.O. KB27/763, m. 23; Hicks p. 98; Baugh p. 9.

57 20 May 1452   Sir Thomas agrees to abide by the arbitration of Thomas Bishop of Ely in all quarrels between himself and John Duke of Norfolk: P.R.O. KB27/764, m. between 52d and 53d.

58 26 May 1452   Sir Thomas borrows £3 from Robert Overton: see 28 June 1456.

59 21 Oct 1452   Sir Thomas is bailed to Sir John Baskerville of Eardisley, William Cecil esquire of London, Thomas Ince esquire of Stanford Rivers, and John Leventhorpe esquire of Southwark, until 3 February 1453, after which the marshal of the Marshalsea of the King's Bench is to keep him safe on penalty of £2000: P.R.O. KB27/766 m. 45d Rex; see Field pp. 108–9. This transaction may be an attempt to bring Malory back into Warwickshire society. If Baskerville represented Buckingham and some of the others represented Norfolk, as seems likely, the noblemen most powerful in Warwickshire presumably wanted Malory to have a chance to compromise in whatever issues were at stake; the huge penalty on the marshal shows someone was determined to keep him locked up if the attempt did not work.

60 25 Oct 1452   Sir Thomas Malory of Newbold Revell enters into a bond for £200 that he, Philip Burgh, and Thomas Barton keep the peace towards William Venour [Keeper of the Fleet Prison] and his household: C.C.R. (1447–54) 396. Malory may have been trying, as was often attempted, to effect a transfer from the King's Bench prison to the more comfortable conditions of the Fleet: Field p. 109.

61 ? Oct/Dec 1452   Sir Thomas and other Warwickshire gentry witness a Monks Kirby Priory grant on '13 October 1453': Lichfield Joint Record Office, MS. B/A/11, fol. 54^{r-v}. On the date, see Field pp. 109–10.

62 ? 21 Jul 1452/22 Mar 1454   Sir Thomas allegedly steals 4 oxen from Katherine Lady Peyto at Sibbertoft, Northamptonshire: P.R.O. C1/15/78. On the date, see Field pp. 91–3, 110–11.

63 2 Feb 1453   The King's Bench orders Sir Thomas's goods to be distrained: Hicks p. 107.

64 26 Mar 1453   The Duke of Buckingham, Sir Edward Grey of Groby, and the Sheriff of Warwickshire and Leicestershire are commissioned to arrest Sir Thomas Malory: C.P.R. (1452–61) p. 61.

65 6 Oct 1453   Malory appears in the King's Bench and is committed to the Marshalsea of the King's Bench again: Baugh p. 9.

66 4 Feb 1454   Malory is again presented for trial and returned to the Marshalsea; the penalty for his escape is reduced to £1000: Baugh p. 9.

67 8 May 1454   Sir Thomas is again presented for trial; no jury appears and

he is bailed until 29 October to Sir Roger Chamberlain of Framlingham, John Leventhorpe esquire of London, Edward Fitzwilliam esquire of Framlingham, Thomas Boughton esquire of Lawford, William Worsop esquire of Framlingham, John Valens esquire of Framlingham, Thomas Ince esquire of Essex, Ralph Worthington gentleman of Framlingham, Edmund Whateley gentleman of London, and John Hathwick gentleman of Harbury: P.R.O. KB27/763, m. 23; KB9/83/25d; Hicks p. 98; Baugh pp. 8–9; Field p. 112. This may represent a more comprehensive attempt to bring Malory back into the fold, with the sureties representing variously Buckingham, Lord Grey of Groby, Norfolk, and Richard Neville, the (relatively new) Earl of Warwick.

68 21 May–2 Jul 1454   John 'Aleyn' or 'Addelsey,' Sir Thomas's servant, allegedly steals horses from Tilty Abbey and elsewhere near Great Easton, Essex: Baugh p. 23. Aleyn is presumably the John Appleby alleged to have been involved in some of Malory's other crimes: cf. no **42**.

69 9–21 Jul 1454   Sir Thomas allegedly feloniously shelters 'Aleyn' at Thaxted and Braintree on 9 and 10 July, and later plans with him an unsuccessful attempt to rob William Grene of Gosfield and others: Baugh p. 24

70 16 Oct 1454   Sir Thomas is arrested and jailed at Colchester: Baugh p. 24.

71 29 Oct 1454   Sir Thomas fails to appear in the King's Bench to answer his bail: Baugh p. 10.

72 30 Oct 1454   Sir Thomas escapes from Colchester gaol, using swords, daggers, and *langues de boeuf*; the King's Bench orders the Keeper of Colchester Gaol to produce him on 18 November: Baugh p. 26.

73 18 Nov 1454   Sir Thomas is duly produced in the King's Bench, and committed to its Marshalsea on penalty of £1000: Baugh pp. 10–13.

74 27 Jan 1455   Sir Thomas is again produced for trial; successive deferments until 8 June (but he actually appeared on 15 June): Baugh p. 9.

75 19 May 1455   Sir Thomas is transferred from the Marshalsea of the King's Bench to the Tower: Baugh p. 13.

76 15 Jun 1455   Sir Thomas appears in the King's Bench, trial is set for 13 October, and he is returned to the Tower under a penalty of £2000: Baugh p. 13.

77 13 Oct 1455   Sir Thomas appears in the King's Bench, no jurors appear, and he is returned to the Tower: Baugh pp. 9, 13.

78 24 Nov 1455   Sir Thomas Malory of Fenny Newbold is granted a pardon: P.R.O. C67/41, m.15.

79 30 Jan 1456   Sir Thomas is produced in the King's Bench by the Lieutenant of the Tower, presents his pardon and offers as sureties Roger Malory gentleman of Ruyton, John Benford gentleman of London, William Cliff gentleman of London, Walter Boys saddler of London, Thomas Pulton tailor of London, and David John tailor of London. His pardon and his obscure sureties are dismissed, and he is committed to the Marshalsea of the King's Bench: Baugh p. 13; Field p. 116.

80 28 Jun 1456   Robert Overton sues Sir Thomas, who is said to be in the Marshalsea of the King's Bench, for 60 shillings lent on 26 May 1452: Baugh p. 26.

81 Jan/Nov 1456   Sir Thomas is transferred 'for more secure custody' from the Marshalsea to Newgate. See Field p. 118, and add that if the location in the previous item is genuine, the transfer presumably took place after 28 June 1456.

82 3 Jul 1456   Sir Thomas borrows money from Thomas Greswold: Baugh p. 28.

83 24 Jan 1457   Sir Thomas is transferred from Newgate to Ludgate Prison on penalty of £1000: KB9/87, m. 17; Hicks p. 100.

84 12 May 1457   Thomas Greswold sues Sir Thomas for his debt, which the latter admits, and is awarded damages: Baugh pp. 28–9.

85 Michaelmas Term 1457   Sir Thomas is transferred from Ludgate Prison to the Marshalsea of the King's Bench: Hicks pp. 100–1; Baugh p. 29.

86 19 Oct 1457   Sir Thomas is released on bail until 28 December to William Neville Lord Fauconberg, William Bridgeham esquire of Bridgeham, Yorkshire, and John Clerkson esquire of Arundel: KB9/87, m. 17; Hicks p. 101. Fauconberg was Warwick's uncle and principal lieutenant.

87 28 Dec 1457   Sir Thomas returns from bail: KB9/87, m. 17; Hicks p. 101.

88 1457/8   Payments involving the Malorys of Newbold Revel in the ministers' accounts for Monks Kirby Priory include one for the obsequies of Thomas Malory junior, presumably Sir Thomas's son: P.R.O. SC6/1107/7.

89 Easter Term 1459   Sir Thomas Malory is said to have been at large in Warwickshire since Easter: the King's Bench orders the Marshal to keep him safe on penalty of £100: KB9/87, m. 17; Hicks p. 101.

90 Hilary Term 1460   Sir Thomas is transferred from the Marshalsea of the King's Bench to Newgate: KB9/87, m. 17; Hicks p. 102.

91 July 1460   A Yorkist invasion from Calais seizes London; Sir Thomas is probably freed: Field pp. 122–3.

92 24 Oct 1462   General pardon for Sir Thomas Malory on Edward IV's first pardon roll: P.R.O. C67/45, m. 14. The pardon entry gives his name and the date; the wording of his copy will be that of the model pardon that begins the roll. The model pardon is dated 9 January 1462: that Malory waited so long after that to take out his own pardon shows he felt secure under the new government.

93 Michaelmas Term 1462   Sir Thomas Malorre, Thomas Walsshe esquire of Oneleppe [= Wanlip, Leicestershire], and Philip Dand settle land in

Winwick on Robert Malorre esquire son of Sir Thomas and Elizabeth wife of Robert: P.R.O. CP40/806 m. 62. Elizabeth was a Pulteney of Misterton, Leicestershire: see Field p. 136. This transaction will be part of the settlement for Robert and Elizabeth's marriage.

94 Oct 1462–Jan 1463   Thomas Malery takes part in Edward IV and the Earl of Warwick's expedition against the castles of Alnwick, Bamburgh, and Dunstanborough: 'Brief Notes' p. 157; Scofield i 263–6.

95 12 Sep 1464   Sir Thomas Malory witnesses the marriage settlement of John, son of William Feilding, and John's wife Helen, daughter and coheir of Thomas Walsh esquire: Nichols iv 368. Sir Thomas was probably Helen's uncle and in some sense her guardian: Field p. 130.

96 2 Aug 1466/26 Jul 1467   Birth of Nicholas, son of Robert Malory, son of Sir Thomas Malory of Newbold Revel and Elizabeth Lady Malory, according to her IPMs. See no. 112.

97 14 Jul 1468   Sir Thomas Malory is among fifteen people excluded by name in the model pardon at the head of the pardon roll for Edward IV's second general pardon: P.R.O. C67/46, m. 39.

98 16 Jul 1468   Pardon to William Paston exemplifying the pardon of 14 July: B.L. Add. Ch. 17248. For examples dated 24 August, 1 November, and 1 December 1468, and 12 February 1469, see Martin p. 166, Nottingham City Corporation Archives C.A. 4173, Hicks p. 71, and P.R.O. Chester 2/141 m. 9.

99 4 Mar 1469/3 Mar 1470   Sir Thomas Malory completes *Le Morte Darthur* in prison: Caxton fol. ee vj^r.

100 22 Feb 1470   Sir Thomas Malory and others are excluded in the model pardon at the head of the pardon roll for Edward IV's third general pardon: P.R.O. C67/47, m. 9.

101 3 Mar 1470   See 4 March 1469 supra.

102 12 Mar 1471   Death of Sir Thomas Malory of Newbold Revel according to his IPM; cf. nos 103 and 105.

103 14 Mar 1471   Death of Sir Thomas Malory of Newbold Revel according to his epitaph: B.L. MS. Cotton Vitellius F.xii, fol. 284^r. The original tombstone was destroyed, but its inscription survives in this early sixteenth-century transcript, which calls him *valens miles* ('a valiant knight') of the parish of Monks Kirby in Warwickshire and says he died on 14 March 1470, which (since the year began on 25 March) is what is now called 1471. Cf. no 102.

104 26 Jun 1471   Writ to Northamptonshire requiring an IPM on Sir Thomas Malory: P.R.O. C140/36/12, *C.F.R.* (1471–85) p. 2.

105 6 Nov 1471   IPM on Sir Thomas Malory, held at Northampton, says he died 12 March 1471 holding no lands in the county, and his heir is Robert his son aged 23+: P.R.O. C140/36/12. The absence of lands will mean

they were held in some form of trust, and the death-date may be a legal fiction (see nos **102–3** above).

106 1469/83 Copying of the only known version of the *Morte Darthur* not deriving from the edition Caxton published in 1485: see no. **99** and Hellinga. This copy, 'the Winchester Manuscript' (it was discovered at Winchester College), is now B.L. Additional MS. 9678; for a photographic facsimile see the Bibliography, s.v. *The Winchester Malory.*

107 1478/79 Elizabeth Lady Malory holds Winwick of Coventry Priory: Hicks p. 56n from 'The First Roll of the Pittancer,' among the Reader MSS in Coventry Free Library. These manuscripts were destroyed by fire in 1940.

108 Michaelmas 1479 Lady Malory pays Coventry Priory 5 marks rent for the manor and vill of Winwick: Birmingham Reference Library MS 168237.

109 30 Sep or 1 Oct 1479 Lady Malory dies, according to her IPMs. See no. **112**.

110 4 Nov 1479 Commission appointed to enquire into the lands of Robert Malory esquire deceased: *C.P.R.* (1476–85) p. 183.

111 7 Nov 1479 Writ of *diem clausit extremum* for Robert Malory to Warwick-shire and Northamptonshire.

112 25 Jul 1480 IPM on Elizabeth widow of Sir Thomas Malory held at Northampton, says she died 1 October 1479 holding for life a messuage and a virgate in Winwick worth £1 annually of the king in chief by knight service, and for life the manor of Winwick worth £10 annually of an unknown lord by an unknown service; her heir is Nicholas son of Robert son of Sir Thomas and herself aged 14+. On 27 July an IPM held at Ryton-upon-Dunsmore in Warwickshire said that she died 30 September 1479 holding the manor of Newbold Fenne alias Newbold Ryvell worth £6.13s.8d of Richard Duke of York and Anne his wife, daughter and heir of John [Mowbray 7th] Duke of Norfolk [d.1476] in right of Anne, a ward of the king, holding the manor in chief by service of one knight's fee; her heir is Nicholas as above, aged 13+. On 27 July an IPM held at Lutterworth in Leicestershire said that she died 30 September 1479 holding the manor of Swynnerford [Swinford] worth £2.13s.4d and a messuage and 2 virgates in Stormefield [modern Starmore] worth £1.6s.8d both of an unknown lord by an unknown service; her heir is Nicholas as above, aged 13+. The three IPMs are P.R.O. C140/75/46; translated Hicks pp. 108–11. They provide the most detailed evidence of Sir Thomas's family lands.

On Nicholas's age, the Warwickshire and Leicestershire inquisitions match a little better than the Northamptonshire one with later proceedings over the Malory lands.

113 7 Jul 1480/3 Mar 1481 Thomas Mansfield clerk, Lady Malory's executor, accuses Robert Forest, a Coventry brewer, in Chancery of obstructive litigation and intimidation intended to avoid paying a debt of £7.19s.0d: P.R.O. C1/60/102.

114 10 Oct 1480   Nicholas Malory's wardship and marriage are granted to Margaret Kelem: *C.P.R.* (1476–85) p. 220.

115 1481   Nicholas Malory's muniments are delivered to William Catesby: P.R.O. E40/14705.

116 31 Jul 1485   Caxton publishes *Le Morte Darthur*: Caxton fol. ee vj^r.

117 6 Feb 1486–Michaelmas Term 1487   Sir Thomas's surviving feoffee recovers possession of his Leicestershire lands: Nichols iv 362.

118 1480/1513   A heraldic window is made for the parlour at Newbold Revel, showing the coats of arms claimed by Sir Thomas's grandson Nicholas. The window is lost, but a seventeenth-century sketch survives: Field pp. 136, 167–9.

119 22 Jan 1513   Nicholas Malory dies: P.R.O. C142/27/115–16, 28/41, and 30/85.

120 1656   Dugdale's Antiquities of Warwickshire p. 56 gives a short life of Sir Thomas Malory of Newbold Revel, from which all modern accounts have been developed. The account is identical in the expanded edition by William Thomas (1730), p. 83; republished in facsimile (Manchester, [c. 1970]). It does not mention the *Morte Darthur*. Dugdale's book also contains pictures of the church windows at Grendon (1730 edn, p. 1105) and of the heraldic window at Newbold Revel (p. 83), on which see nos 2 and 118 respectively.

ABBREVIATIONS

Ancient Deeds	*Calendar of Ancient Deeds*
B.L.	London, British Library Reference Division
Bodl.	Oxford, Bodleian Library
C.C.R.	*Calendar of Close Rolls*
C.P.R.	*Calendar of Patent Rolls*
C.F.R.	*Calendar of Fine Rolls*
C.R.O.	County Record Office
IPM	inquisition post mortem
List of Sheriffs	P.R.O. Lists and Indexes 9
List of Escheators	P.R.O. Lists and Indexes 72
P.R.O.	London, Public Record Office
S.B.T.	Stratford-upon-Avon, Shakespeare Birthplace Trust

SELECT BIBLIOGRAPHY

Printed Records and Calendars

Acts of Chapter of the Collegiate Church of SS. Peter and Wilfrid, Ripon, A.D. 1452–1506. Surtees Society Publications 64 (1875).
'Brief Notes': 'Brief Notes of Occurrences under Henry VI and Edward IV.' In *Three Fifteenth-Century Chronicles*, ed. James Gairdner. Camden Society Publications, 1880.
Caxton, William, ed. Sir Thomas Malory, *Le Morte Darthur*. Westminster 1485.
Chetwynd Chartulary: William Chetwynd. 'The Chetwynd Chartulary,' ed. G. Wrottesley. *William Salt Archaeological Society Publications* 12 (1891), pp. 244–336.
Farnham *Notes*: George Farnham. *Medieval Leicestershire Village Notes*. 6 vols. Leicester 1929–33.
Feet of Fines: Warwickshire Feet of Fines, ed. Ethel Stokes *et al*. Dugdale Society Publications 11, 15, 18 (1932–43).
Gibbons, Alfred. *Early Lincoln Wills*. Lincoln 1888.
Hunt, Philip. *Notes on Medieval Melton Mowbray*. Grantham 1965.
Leeds Archives Department, Vyner Papers.
Ministers' Accounts of the Collegiate Church of St Mary, Warwick, 1432–85, ed. D. Styles. Dugdale Society Publications 26 (1969).
Proc. & Ord. P.C.: *Proceedings and Ordinances of the Privy Council of England* [1386–1461], ed. [N.] H. Nicolas. 7 vols. London 1834–37.
Return: Return of the Name of Every Member of the Lower House of Parliament of England, Scotland, and Ireland [1213–1874]. House of Commons Parliamentary Papers for 1878, vol. LXII. 2 parts plus index. London 1878–89.
Rot. Parl.: *Rotuli Parliamentorum*. 7 vols. London 1832.
Stocks, J. E. *Market Harborough Parish Records*. 2 vols. London 1890–1926.
The Winchester Malory, ed. N. R. Ker. Early English Text Society, ss, vol. 4. London 1976.

Scholarly Debate

Aspects of Malory, ed. Toshiyuki Takamiya and Derek Brewer. Cambridge 1981.
Baugh, A. C. 'Documenting Sir Thomas Malory.' *Speculum* 8 (1933) 3–29.
Burton, William. *The Description of Leicester Shire*. London 1622.
Carpenter, Christine. *Locality and Polity*. Cambridge 1992.
Dugdale, Sir William. *The Antiquities of Warwickshire*. London 1656. 2nd edn, rev. William Thomas, 2 vols. London 1730.
Field, P. J. C. *The Life and Times of Sir Thomas Malory*. Cambridge 1993.
Griffith, Richard R. 'The Authorship Question Reconsidered: A Case for Thomas Malory of Papworth St Agnes, Cambridgeshire.' *Aspects of Malory*, pp. 159–77.
Hellinga, Lotte. 'The Malory Manuscript and Caxton.' *Aspects of Malory*, pp. 127–141.
Hicks, Edward. *Sir Thomas Malory: His Turbulent Career*. Cambridge, Mass., 1928.
McFarlane, K. B. 'The Wars of the Roses.' *Proceedings of the British Academy*, 50 (1964) 87–119.
Martin, A. T. 'The Identity of the Author of the *Morte Darthur*.' *Archaelogia*, 56 (1898) 165–82.
Matthews, William. *The Ill-Framed Knight: A Skeptical Enquiry into the Identity of Sir Thomas Malory*. Berkeley, Calif., 1966.

Nichols, John. *The History and Antiquities of the County of Leicester*. 4 vols. London
    1795–1807.
Roskell, J. R. *The Commons in the Parliament of 1422*. Manchester 1954.
Scofield, Cora L. *The Life and Reign of Edward IV*. 2 vols. London 1923.
VCH(Y)NR: Victoria County History, Yorkshire: North Riding. 3 vols. London 1968.
Vinaver, Eugène. *Malory*. Oxford 1929.
Wedgwood, Josiah, and Anne Holt. *History of Parliament: Biographies of Members of
    the Commons House 1439–1509*. London 1936.

PART II

THE ART OF THE *MORTE DARTHUR*

Beginnings: The Tale of King Arthur *and* King Arthur and the Emperor Lucius

ELIZABETH ARCHIBALD

Medieval writers made little distinction between what we would call history and legend; Arthur appeared in Celtic folktales, in Latin and vernacular chronicles and 'historical' accounts of early English rulers, and also in Latin and vernacular narratives of adventure starring either the king himself or individual knights of his court which are categorized by modern critics as romances.[1] Since Arthur is the king of Britain, his rise and fall, together with his famous knights, are political events as well as private adventures and triumphs and tragedies. Malory's second tale, *King Arthur and the Emperor Lucius,*[2] belongs unequivocally to the public, political realm: it describes the war between Britain and Rome, in which the deeds of individual heroes are motivated by the desire for a British victory (as well as personal glory, of course), and might be considered an epic rather than a romance. But the first tale, *The Tale of King Arthur,* is a mixture of public and private, wars and individual quests, Realpolitik and magic. Arthur is not the focus of each episode, nor is this tale self-contained. It is a tale of beginnings (both of characters and of relationships), and also of endings, actual and foretold: prophecy is often used to foreshadow events to be recounted in later tales.[3]

---

[1] See Antonia Gransden, *Historical Writing in England, II, c. 1307 to the Early Sixteenth Century* (London, 1982); E. K. Chambers, *Arthur of Britain* (London, 1927); J. S. P. Tatlock, *The Legendary History of Britain* (Berkeley, 1950); T. D. Kendrick, *British Antiquity* (London, 1950); *Arthurian Literature in the Middle Ages,* ed. R. S. Loomis (Oxford, 1959). Definitions of romance are notoriously problematic: see for instance J. Finlayson, 'Definitions of Middle English Romance,' *Chaucer Review,* 15 (1980), 44–62, 168–81.

[2] This form of the title of the second tale is commonly used by critics, and is suggested by the colophon at the end of the tale.

[3] On the question of the arrangement of the *Morte Darthur,* and whether or not it was intended to constitute a single text or a series of distinct tales, see D. S. Brewer, '"the hoole book,"' in *Essays on Malory,* ed. J. A. W. Bennett (Oxford, 1963), pp. 41–63; Stephen Knight, *The Structure of Malory's Arthuriad* (Sydney, 1969); Andrea Clough, 'Malory's *Morte Darthur*: The "Hoole Book",' *Medievalia et Humanistica,* n.s. 14 (1986), 139–56; and Carol Meale's chapter in this volume.

I *The Tale of King Arthur*

The beginning of the story as we have it may well seem abrupt.[4] Malory
makes no statement of his intentions or themes or sources; he gives no
historical or pseudo-historical background, of the kind we find in the
opening stanza of *Sir Gawain and the Green Knight,* for instance.

> Hit befel in the dayes of Uther Pendragon, when he was kynge of all
> Englond and so regned, that there was a myghty duke in Cornewaill
> that held warre ageynst hym long tyme, and the duke was called the
> duke of Tyntagil. And so by meanes kynge Uther send for this duk,
> chargyng hym to brynge his wyf with hym, for she was called a fair
> lady and a passynge wyse, and her name was called Igrayne. (3/1–6;
> I.1)

Nothing is said of Arthur here; it is assumed that the references to Uther
and Ygrayne will be enough to make the subject matter clear. There is no
scene-setting: we are not told that Uther is unmarried and has no heir, for
instance. Nor is there any reference to the 'historical' era in which all this is
happening.

Caxton fills in a number of these gaps in the preface to his printed edition
of the *Morte Darthur,* but Malory apparently plunges us *in medias res.* His
style is spare, in every sense. We get no description of any of the three
characters introduced here, except that Ygrayne was beautiful and wise;
and we shall get no descriptions of any other characters, except for odd
details which are relevant at particular points in the plot, such as Gawain's
superhuman strength which waxes and wanes with the sun (96/18–25;
IV.18 – its origin is only explained much later, during the war against
Lancelot [704/8–18; XX.21]). It is, as it were, a world photographed in
black and white rather than colour. But from the very beginning there is a
great deal of dialogue, and it is this which allows for some characterization,
as well as conveying important information to the reader: so in this opening
scene we hear Ygrayne's warning to her husband in direct speech (an
example of her wisdom), rather than being told of it by the narrator. Malory
may be an omniscient narrator, but he seldom favours us with his
knowledge. Much in these tales, and in the work as a whole, remains
mysterious and unexplained: this is sometimes the result of Malory's
conflation and adaptation of his sources, but it is also characteristic of his
narrative style. P. J. C. Field notes that 'Malory's commentary on his
characters rarely goes beyond what could be provided in a few words by
any observer without special insight,' and in relation to explanations he

---

[4] The first folios of the Winchester manuscript of the *Morte Darthur* are missing, so we
have to depend on Caxton for the opening pages (in Vinaver's edition square brackets
mark this section, ending at 13/36).

comments that 'Malory as narrator is always present, but he faces towards the story.'[5]

In the *Tale of King Arthur* there are various layers of plot. The main one is Arthur's rise to greatness: in the course of this tale he establishes his rule, subduing all opposition, and also establishes the Round Table fellowship which is to be the hallmark of his reign. We meet key members of his family, who will recur in many other episodes (and who of course appear in other Arthurian texts): Guinevere, Gawain, Morgan le Fay, Mordred. We are also introduced to a number of themes which are featured frequently in medieval romance: identity and the family, feuds and betrayals, love, magic, chivalry and the pursuit of adventure and 'worship.'

Identity and family are both very important in romance.[6] Arthur is conceived in clandestine circumstances; he is sent away to fosterparents, and does not discover his own identity till he is grown up. He then repeats this pattern by begetting Mordred on his own half-sister, Morgause. Both Arthur and Torre discover their true parentage and are consequently elevated to a much higher station. There are also tragic discoveries about relationships. Arthur learns too late that the Queen of Orkney is his sister, after Mordred has been conceived. Balin learns too late the identity of his beloved brother, when they have wounded each other mortally in battle. Pellinor learns too late that the lady he failed to help was his illegitimate daughter. When Merlin pronounces Pellinor's destiny, to be failed in a desperate situation by his best friend and to be abandoned to die by the man he trusts most, Pellinor hopes for the best (75/ 26–32; III.15): 'God may well fordo desteny.' But prophecies of disaster all come true; they strike gloomy notes among the triumphs and celebrations of the Round Table in the early books.

It is not only the tale of King Arthur, although his role here and in the next tale is larger and more active than anywhere else in the *Morte Darthur* until the tragic civil war recounted in the final tale. Some indication of the range of protagonists is given by the titles generally used for the main episodes in *The Tale of King Arthur*: 'Merlin,' 'Balin or the Knight with the Two Swords,' 'Torre and Pellinor,' 'The War with the Five Kings,' 'Arthur and Accolon,' and 'Gawain, Ywain and Marhalt.'[7] Arthur plays a central

---

[5] *Romance and Chronicle: A Study of Malory's Prose Style* (Bloomington, 1971), pp. 148 and 153.

[6] See for instance the arguments of Northrop Frye in *The Secular Scripture: A Study of the Structure of Romance* (Cambridge, Mass., 1976), esp. chs. 4 and 5.

[7] It should be noted that these titles were assigned by Vinaver, usually on the basis of the linking passages in the text itself, such as 'THUS ENDITH THE TALE OF BALYN AND BALAN . . .' (59.8; II.19). As Larry D. Benson points out, the manuscript offers no authority for Vinaver's last three sections, nor does Caxton divide the text in this way: see *Malory's Morte Darthur* (Cambridge, Mass., 1976), p. 30; Knight, pp. 36ff; and Meale's comments in this volume, p. 14. Nor is Vinaver always consistent: 'Torre and Pellinor' is described in the explicit as 'The Wedding of King Arthur,' and Field uses this rubric in his revised third edition of Vinaver's text.

role in the first, fourth and fifth sections, which deal with the establishment of his rule and subsequent challenges to it; the other three recount the adventures of individual knights of his court, in which he plays very little part.

'Merlin,' the first section, covers the 'facts' of Arthur's early life: his conception (aided by magic), his birth and secret fostering, his startling feat of drawing the sword from the stone, his coronation, and his subsequent struggle against the rebellious northern kings. He begets two illegitimate children, Borre (not mentioned again until the list of Round Table knights in 'The Healing of Sir Urry'), and Mordred, the product of a brief incestuous affair with his unrecognized half-sister, the Queen of Orkney. In subsequent sections Arthur marries Guinevere, and uses her dowry, the Round Table, to found his famous chivalric fellowship. He consolidates his power, defeating five rebel kings and also his own knight Accolon, the lover and agent of Morgan le Fay, Arthur's treacherous half-sister. And when the country is not at war, his knights go out on adventures and quests, the 'matter' of chivalric romance, returning to Camelot to recount their deeds to the king and queen.

But the story of Arthur's rise to power and the beginning of the Round Table adventures is not told in a clear chronological fashion. Throughout the *Tale of King Arthur*, and indeed throughout the whole of the *Morte Darthur*, there is a constant tension between random and often incomprehensible adventures which come the way of knights errant or knights idling at court (such as the arrival at Camelot of the hart, the brachet and the lady at the beginning of 'Torre and Pellinor'), and prophesied events or clearly motivated struggles (Arthur and the rebel kings, Arthur and the Romans). It is often remarked that Malory disliked the French interlace style of romance-writing, in which the plot consists of many narrative threads which are interwoven, so that the adventures of the various characters are constantly interrrupted, and all the sub-plots proceed at a very leisurely pace. Generally he prefers to undo this complex interlace structure in favour of complete, discrete episodes and concise narration of action.[8] The *Tale of King Arthur* is largely derived from a thirteenth-century French prose romance, the *Suite du Merlin* (sometimes referred to as the *Huth Merlin*), composed after the influential Vulgate Cycle; Malory has simplified and abbreviated it considerably.[9] But even so there is still interlace within some of the six sections of the tale, and between them. We are introduced to a number of important characters and themes very

[8] See Benson, *Malory's Morte Darthur*, pp. 39f.; he argues that this is typical of English romance writers generally, and was an increasing trend all over Europe by the fifteenth century.

[9] The *Suite du Merlin* has been edited as *Merlin* by G. Paris and J. Ulrich, 2 vols, SATF (Paris, 1886). On Malory's use of some details from English Arthurian texts in his first tale, see E. D. Kennedy, 'Malory and His English sources,' in *Aspects of Malory*, ed. T. Takamiya and D. S. Brewer (Cambridge, 1981), pp. 27–55.

rapidly, but the introductions and explanations are often not completed in the first instance.

This is particularly apparent in the account of the birth of Mordred and Arthur's attempt to kill him; this ought to be a key episode, one would have thought, since Mordred is fated to be Arthur's nemesis. Yet Malory devotes curiously little space to it, and inserts many other scenes, some only partially developed, between Mordred's conception and Arthur's decision to kill him. After the terse account of Arthur's fatal encounter with his sister, which is described very briefly without any moral commentary (27/35–44; I.19), the king has a disturbing dream of griffins and serpents which ravage his land. He goes out hunting, and encounters the Questing Beast (though it is not named at this point), hotly pursued by a knight who later turns out to be King Pellinor, and who commandeers Arthur's horse. Then Merlin appears to Arthur in several disguises and teases him before becoming serious and revealing the awful sin of Mordred's incestuous conception, which will cost Arthur his life and his kingdom (29/32–6; I.20). In the course of this explanation Merlin also reveals Arthur's parentage, hitherto a mystery, and there is a recognition scene between the king and his mother (30/8–31/6; I.20–21; this episode in other romances might be the first stage of the happy ending). Throughout these scenes there is a great deal of dialogue, and constant change of focus – from Arthur's sin to his reunion with his mother, from his encounter with Pellinor (who will appear again soon as his adversary) to his trying conversations with the disguised Merlin.

This quick-shifting focus is continued in the next episodes. A strange knight wounds the newly knighted Gryfflet. After a brief visit from Roman envoys demanding tribute (a thread casually abandoned here which will be picked up and developed at length in the next tale), Arthur goes to find the knight, and encounters Merlin on his way. During his battle with this unidentified knight the king's sword breaks, and he is only saved from death by the intervention of Merlin, who introduces the two: the stranger is Pellinor. Merlin then takes Arthur to get a new sword, Excalibur, from a lake where it is held up by a mysterious arm (35/2–31; I.25). Merlin explains that it belongs to the Lady of the Lake, who gives it to Arthur together with a magical scabbard. On the way back they pass Pellinor again: Arthur wants to fight him, but Merlin prevents it. These adventures impress the knights at court:

> So they com unto Carlion, whereof hys knyghtes were passynge glad. And whan they herde of hys adventures, they mervayled that he wolde jouparde his person so alone. But all men of worship seyde hit was myrry to be under such a chyfftayne that wolde putte hys person in adventure as other poure knyghtis ded. (36/21–5; I.25)

Once the Roman wars are over, Arthur will seldom 'putte hys person in adventure' like this. Suddenly another challenge arrives, from King Royns of North Wales who wants Arthur's beard to fill the one gap on a cloak made of the beards of defeated kings: Arthur returns a defiant message, but this plot too is summarily abandoned, for the 'Merlin' episode ends with a return to the problem of Mordred (37/10–25; I.27).

In a brief paragraph, Malory describes Arthur's decision to kill all children born around May Day (his unwanted son's birthday, according to Merlin), in the hope of getting rid of his infant nemesis. The babies, including Mordred, are put into a ship which is wrecked; but destiny preserves Mordred, who is found and raised by a good man. The brief description of Arthur's darkest hour, his Herod-like Massacre of the Innocents which earns both him and Merlin the hostility of many lords, is awkwardly sandwiched between Arthur's defiant response to Royns' challenge and Royns' furious reaction, the raising of an army 'as hit reherseth aftir in the BOOKE OF BALYNE LE SAVEAGE that folowith nexte aftir' (37/27–8; not in Caxton). With that the section ends, leaving many loose threads untied; and in fact the next section focuses not on Arthur and his affairs, but on a new character, Balin, though references to Royns continue.

Malory moves at a brisk pace through this complex series of scenes, but he also uses them skilfully to foreshadow actions to come; the narrator himself prophesies through the words and actions of his characters, signalling to the reader some of the persons and adventures to appear later, and so does Merlin. Such comments are fuel for the argument that even at this early stage Malory planned to write about the whole of the Arthurian legend, not just a part of it. So in the first episode Merlin refers to the story of the brothers Balin and Balan, which follows later in this tale (27/1–5; I.18). Arthur's meeting with King Pellinor produces a reference to his successor as pursuer of the Questing Beast, Sir Palomides, who will be a prominent character in *The Tale of Sir Tristram* (28/38–40; I.19), and to Pellinor's two sons Perceval and Lamorak, who will be the best knights in the world apart from one other, not named here but obviously Lancelot (34/36–40; I.24). There are also red herrings which suggest that Malory sometimes changed his plans, such as Merlin's remark that Pellinor will tell Arthur the name of his fatal son begotten in incest (34/40–1), and the narrator's comment that Mordred's rearing and arrival at court will be described later (37/21–2; I.27). Neither of these two episodes is in fact included in the text as we have it today. Perhaps Malory was following a source text without considering the larger implications.[10]

After 'Merlin' there is much less interlace, and the action is simpler to follow, though not every mystery is satisfactorily unravelled. Balin, a poor knight from Northumberland, is able to draw another sword of destiny from a sheath, but the damsel who brought the sword to court demands it

---

[10] For instance the French book which he mentions early on as failing to identify the churchyard where the sword in the stone appeared (7/27–8; I.5).

back, warning him that there will be dire consequences if he keeps it (39/4–40.9; II.2). Jill Mann has underlined the significance of Balin's reply, 'I shall take the aventure . . . that God woll ordayne for me' (40/3–4; II.2):

> It is not a matter of stoic suffering or iron resistance; it is an attempt to stretch the self to embrace the utmost reach of possible events. The knight does not try to close the distance between himself and events by fitting them to himself, mastering them so that they become a mere expression of himself; instead he achieves union with them by matching himself to them, by taking into himself, accepting without understanding, their mysterious inevitability and his enigmatic responsibility for them.[11]

Adventure is the proper activity of knights, but often they have no idea what they are getting themselves into. They must entrust themselves to chance, and sometimes to fate – for though God is frequently invoked in the *Morte Darthur*, and the Arthurian world is a Christian one, much of the story is strongly fatalistic. Malory explores cause and effect, tragic coincidences and painful choices; but some events are predestined and ineluctable, such as Mordred's destruction of Arthur's world (it is striking that Arthur never discusses his sin of incest with a priest, or contemplates atoning for it through penance, a strategy which brings a happy ending, at least in a spiritual sense, in many other medieval incest stories).[12]

Balin's tragic story both begins and ends in this section of *The Tale of King Arthur*, but his actions have long-term consequences, for he maims with a mysterious spear King Pellam, keeper of the Grail Castle (this 'dolorous stroke' is connected to the Waste Land theme so often explored in the Grail legends); the narrator explains that the maimed king will eventually be healed by Galahad in the Grail Quest (53/27–54.13; II.15–16). Balin then unwittingly kills his beloved brother, by whom he himself is killed. Merlin puts Balin's fatal sword into another stone, and foretells that Galahad, Lancelot's son, will be the man to draw it out; Malory adds that this 'ys rehersed in THE BOOKE OF THE SANKGREALL' (58/30–44; not in Caxton; and see 517/12–520/13; XIII.2–5). Thus this mysterious opening adventure which ends so tragically points forward to the Grail Quest, the first phase of the tragic fragmentation of Arthur's fellowship, in which Galahad's perfection highlights the imperfections of other knights (notably his father Lancelot) which lead to civil war and the end of the Arthurian world.

The motif of the drawing of a sword of destiny is used three times in *The*

---

[11] Jill Mann, '"Taking the Adventure": Malory and the *Suite du Merlin*,' in *Aspects of Malory*, ed. Takamiya and Brewer, pp. 71–91 (the quotation is taken from p. 90).

[12] On the relationship between Arthur's incest and other medieval incest stories, see Elizabeth Archibald, 'Arthur and Mordred: Variations on an Incest Theme,' in *Arthurian Literature VIII*, ed. R. Barber (Cambridge, 1989), pp. 1–27; and for a more general survey of medieval incest stories see Archibald, 'Incest in Medieval Literature and Society,' *Forum for Modern Language Studies*, 25 (1989), 1–15.

Tale of King Arthur; and a sword also plays an important part in 'Arthur and Accolon.' Arthur entrusts his magic scabbard to his half-sister Morgan le Fay; she secretly makes a copy, which she returns to the king, and gives the original to her lover Accolon, a knight of the Round Table (this is described in the story of Balin [49/32–38; II.11]). She then engineers a battle between Arthur and Accolon, who fight as champions for two brothers, Outlake and Damas, who are at odds over an inheritance; neither Arthur nor Accolon knows his opponent's identity. Morgan sends copies of Excalibur and the scabbard to Arthur; in the battle he is saved only by the intervention of the Lady of the Lake, who retrieves Excalibur for him (87/6–14; IV.10). Accolon is fatally wounded, but before he dies he tells Arthur about Morgan's enmity: 'for ye shall undirstonde that kynge Arthur ys the man in the worlde that she hatyth moste, because he is moste of worship and of prouesse of ony of hir bloode' (88/9–11; IV.11). Admiration for 'worship and prouesse' is of course the hallmark of Arthurian society. Morgan is shown here as doubly perverse: she despises the values dearest to the Round Table, and she particularly dislikes them in her own brother. Family ties mean nothing to Morgan: after Accolon dies, she shows her treacherous nature again by trying to kill her husband King Uriens; their son Ywain prevents her, calling her a fiend (90/38; IV.13), and she escapes to the land of Gore. Morgan's treachery and malice towards Arthur and his court are well attested in medieval romance: she turns out to be responsible for all Gawain's trials in *Sir Gawain and the Green Knight*, and in the very next section of *The Tale of King Arthur* she is at it again, sending a poisoned cloak to Arthur, who again is saved from disaster by the Lady of the Lake (93/14–94/17; IV.15–16).

The stories of Balin and Accolon foreshadow themes and patterns which will be crucial later in the *Morte Darthur*. Balin's story deals with inexorable destiny and senseless slaughter. His fatal encounter with his beloved brother points forward to Lancelot's unwitting killing of Gareth, Gawain's brother and Lancelot's devoted friend, which triggers the war between Arthur and Lancelot, and thus the end of the Round Table fellowship and the Arthurian world. In 'Arthur and Accolon' too we find brothers quarrelling (Outlake and Damas): it is to resolve their quarrel that Arthur fights Accolon, a knight of his own fellowship, another presage of the collapse of loyalties and the civil war to come at the end of the story. In this episode Arthur is betrayed by a woman he loves and trusts, his own sister: this points forward in two ways. Arthur will be betrayed by Guinevere through her affair with Lancelot, a Round Table knight like Accolon; and he will also be betrayed by Mordred, his own son, whom he has left as regent while fighting Lancelot in France. Earlier in the tale Merlin prophesies several times about the disasters to come. His prophecy of the final battle against Mordred to be fought on Salisbury Plain comes immediately after Arthur has sent the scabbard to Morgan (49/32–42; II.11); and when Arthur proposes to marry Guinevere, Merlin warns him that she and Lancelot will fall in love (59/36–39; III.1 – Merlin also mentions the Grail Quest here).

The description of Arthur's wedding to Guinevere is interrupted after the delivery of the Round Table (a gift to Arthur from her father, and the most important aspect of the marriage in this account) by some chivalric quests featuring Sir Torre (the illegitimate son of King Pellinor), Pellinor himself, and also the newly knighted Sir Gawain, who first enters the story here (61/3ff; III.3ff). Sir Torre's true parentage is revealed when he is brought to court to be knighted by his supposed father, a cowherd, after which he undertakes his first chivalric adventure. It emerges that his mother, a peasant, was raped by Pellinor, but this is no obstacle to Torre's acceptance as a knight: it is emphasized that he is a fine looking young man who does not resemble his foster-family at all and rejects menial labour. In his case, as in Arthur's, the dubious circumstances of his birth are no bar to chivalric success. In the Arthurian world, lineage is all: Merlin comments that Torre 'ought to be a good man for he ys com of good kynrede as ony on lyve, and of kynges blode' (62/9–10; III.3). After the wedding of Arthur and Guinevere, Merlin prophesies 'a straunge and a mervailous adventure' (63/23–4; III.5). Sure enough, into the hall rush a white hart, a black brachet (hunting dog) and thirty couple of hounds: a knight gets up and takes away the brachet, whereupon a lady rides in and complains to Arthur that her dog has been taken, only to be removed herself by another armed knight who suddenly rides into the hall. Gawain is ordered to bring back the white hart, Torre the hound and the first knight, and Pellinor the lady and the other knight. In fact they do not complete these quests, and we never receive any explanation for the mysterious appearance and actions of the animals, the lady or the abductor.

Each of Arthur's knights has disturbing experiences involving women during his quest: Gawain beheads a lady by mistake; Torre finds himself forced by his promise to a lady into killing a knight who has already asked for mercy; and Pellinor refuses to stop and help a lady who, after her death, turns out to have been his illegitimate daughter. In view of these adventures, it is perhaps not surprising that when the three quests are ended and goods and land are distributed to all the knights of the Round Table, they are made to swear an important oath:

> [Arthur] charged them never to do outerage nothir mourthir, and allwayes to fle treson, and to gyff mercy unto hym that askith mercy, uppon payne of forfiture of their worship and lordship of kynge Arthure for evirmore; and allways to do ladyes, damesels and jantilwomen and wydowes socour: strengthe hem in hir ryghtes, and never to enforce them, uppon payne of dethe. Also, that no man take no batayles in a wrongefull quarell for no love ne for no worldis goodis. (75/38–44; III.15)

This passage seems to have been added by Malory to his sources, and to encapsulate his views on proper chivalric behaviour.

Certainly Gawain does not appear in this tale as the flower of chivalry, but as an impetuous and vengeful character, a foreshadowing of his role later in the *Morte Darthur*, and especially at the end in the war against Lancelot. When Pellinor is seated at the Round Table, Gawain, who hates Pellinor for slaying his father, King Lot, tells his brother Gaheris that he will kill him in revenge; the prudent Gaheris advises him to wait (63/2–18; III.4), but later they do kill Pellinor, and later still his son Lamorak, the lover of their mother Morgause. The bonds of the Round Table fellowship are not strong enough to cancel out the epic mentality of feuding and revenge. In the final episode of this tale, 'Gawain, Ywain and Marhalt,' the three knights meet three damsels sitting by a fountain, who explain that 'We be here . . . for this cause: if we may se ony of arraunte knyghtes to teche unto strong aventures' (97/35–6; IV.19). Each knight chooses a damsel, and each rides in a different direction from the nearby crossroads. When Gawain and his damsel set out, they come to a manor and Gawain asks the old knight who lives there 'if he knewe of any aventures,' and is promised 'mervelos aventures' (98/17–19; IV.19). Ominously, when the three knights meet again after the year of adventures, 'the damesell that sir Gawayne had coude sey but lytyll worshyp of hym' (109/12–13; IV.28): this is because of his caddish behaviour in the affair of Pelleas and Ettard, which earns him Pelleas' undying hatred (99/41–104.38; IV.20–23).

The desire to gain 'worship' is a key factor in all these adventures, and one of the principle aims of Arthurian knights. When Arthur establishes his Round Table fellowship, he asks Merlin to find him 'fyfty knyghtes which bene of moste prouesse and worship' (60/28–9; III.2). The opposite of worship is 'disworship,' much to be dreaded. When the lady appeals to Arthur to have her brachet retrieved at the feast after the knighting of Torre and Gawain, Arthur refuses to act, and is glad when she leaves 'for she made such a noyse' (63/40–1; III.5). But Merlin forces him to take the adventure seriously: 'Nay,' seyde Merlion, 'ye may nat leve hit so, thys adventure, so lyghtly, for thes adventures muste be brought to an ende, other ellis hit woll be disworshyp to you and to your feste' (63/42–4). This episode marks the first appearance in the *Morte Darthur* of the tradition well known in other Arthurian romances (notably *Sir Gawain and the Green Knight*), that Arthur would not begin a feast before he had seen some marvel. And at the end of their quests, the three knights involved, Torre, Pellinor and Gawain, each return to Camelot and recount their adventures, another Arthurian tradition repeated throughout the *Morte Darthur*.

Magic and the supernatural are closely associated with the Arthurian legend, and appear in many forms in this tale – good, bad, and baffling. Merlin's magic is necessary for Arthur to be conceived, for the rebel kings to be defeated, for Lot to be killed rather than Arthur, for the explanation of Arthur's dream and Mordred's birth. Yet Merlin is not infallible: although he foresees his own fate ('he scholde be putte into the erthe quyk'), he becomes infatuated with the damsel of the Lake, teaches her all his arts, and is trapped under a stone by her in fulfilment of his own prophecy – the enchanter enchanted (76/5–77.16; IV.1). Nor are enchantresses invulnerable: the second Lady of the Lake rescues Arthur from Accolon and warns him about Morgan's gift of the poisoned mantle, but the first Lady, who gives him Excalibur, is murdered by Balin. In later tales Arthur does not have the benefit of such wise advisers, but has to make his own decisions and interpret events as best he can. Morgan's power seems much more threatening, because it is exercised unpredictably, and often her agency is only revealed at a late stage, as when she transports Arthur, Urien and Accolon on a magic ship and then separates them (82–4; IV.6–8). Since she is hostile to Arthur, her magic always seems negative.

Then there is magic which remains unexplained. The supernatural is chillingly evoked in the story of Balin: he pursues an invisible knight, Garlon, whose interference in Balin's affairs is never explained; when he finally kills Garlon, it leads to the dolorous stroke against King Pellam. Before Balin fights his unrecognized brother to the death 'he herd an horne blowe as it had ben the dethe of a best. 'That blast,' said Balyn, 'is blowen for me, for I am the pryse, and yet am I not dede' (55/44–56.2; II.17). Balin's interpretation is correct, yet we never discover why the fates are pursuing him; it seems particularly baffling that he should be virtuous enough to draw the Lady of the Lake's sword, and then should precipitate one disaster after another.

The invisible knight who plagues Balin and is eventually slain by him is the brother of King Pellam, and it is while the king is pursuing him that Balin finds the spear and strikes the dolorous stroke. Family plays a very large part in Malory's text; the characters are constantly discovering unexpected relationships, or getting involved in quarrels because of offences against the families of others. The Lady of the Lake is motivated by revenge in demanding the head either of Balin or of the damsel who brought the sword won by Balin: 'I take no force though I have both theire hedis: for he slew my brothir, a good kynght and a trew; and that jantillwoman was causer of my fadirs deth' (40/41–4; II.3). Balin responds by cutting off her head, on the grounds that 'my modir was brente thorow hir falsehode and trechory' (41/20–1; II.3). Arthur does not rule this motive inappropriate, but merely says that Balin should not have beheaded the Lady in the king's presence. Merlin then arrives, and contributes further information: the false damsel who brought the sword wants to be revenged through Balin on her own brother, an excellent knight, for killing her lover (42/18–29; II.4–5). When a damsel asks Sir Torre for a gift during his first quest, it turns out to be the head of Sir Abelleus. When Torre urges her to be merciful, she refuses:

'I may nat, for he slew myne owne brothir before myne yghen that was a bettir knyght than he, and he had had grace; and I kneled halfe an owre before hym in the myre for to sauff my brothirs lyff that had done

hym no damage, but fought with hym by adventure of armys, and so
for all that I coude do he strake of hys hede.' (70/19–24; III.11)

Complex family feuds are of course a feature of other kinds of literature,
such as epic. In medieval romances which focus single-mindedly on an
individual quest, family relationships are not usually foregrounded in this
way. But the prose romances with their interlace structure allow for a much
larger cast of characters, who are constantly crossing each other's paths, or
having to deal with the consequences of actions committed by relatives. In
the Arthurian world, these family relationships are further complicated by
the rival loyalties of the Round Table fellowship, itself a sort of extended
family network. In later adventures, especially the Grail Quest, knights
frequently have to choose between the claims of a relation and some other
person in distress (see for instance the episode in which Bors has to decide
whether to rescue his captured brother or a maiden about to be raped
[567/35 ff; XVI.9–11]).

I have said that there are endings in this first tale as well as beginnings,
some of them ominous for the rest of the story. Merlin disappears to his
living death, leaving Arthur without an omniscient adviser. The killing of
Lot in battle gives rise to the feud between the Orkney brothers and King
Pellinor's family. Balin's obstinacy leads to his own death, and his dolorous
stroke leads to the Grail Quest, which radically changes the self-image of
chivalry for the knights involved. Most gloomy of all, Arthur's 'day of
destiny' is already predestined in the first episode, when Merlin explains
the full circumstances and significance of the conception of Mordred. As for
the ending of the tale itself, it points forward, though not apparently to
further tales by Malory: he seems to be encouraging his readers to have a
go at telling more of the story. And there is much more to tell: the explicit
names two major heroes of the Arthurian world who have not yet played a
part in the story (as well as supplying a fascinating detail about the author,
who was also a knight, but 'a knyght presoner'):

> AND THIS BOOKE ENDYTH WHEREAS SIR LAUNCELOT AND SIR
> TRYSTRAMS COM TO COURTE. WHO THAT WOLL MAKE ONY MORE
> LETTE HYM SEKE OTHER BOOKIS OF KYNGE ARTHURE OR OF SIR
> LAUNCELOT OR SIR TRYSTRAMS; FOR THIS WAS DRAWYN BY A
> KNYGHT PRESONER, SIR THOMAS MALLEORRÉ, THAT GOD SENDE HIM
> GOOD RECOVER. AMEN.
>
> (110/9–13; not in Caxton)

Much critical ink has been spilt over the problem of this ending. Did
Malory already intend to write more tales, or was *The Tale of King Arthur*
initially written as an independent work?[13] Lancelot features prominently
in the next tale, and indeed throughout the rest of the *Morte*; and Tristram,

---

[13] See note 3 above.

the equal of the Round Table knights though never actually one of their number, plays an important part in the tale named after him, the fifth in Vinaver's edition. The ending of *The Tale of King Arthur* may reflect some of Malory's uncertainty about the directions his narrative would take.

II *King Arthur and the Emperor Lucius*

The next tale begins with the arrival at court of these two heroes, Lancelot and Tristram.

> Hyt befelle whan kyng Arthur had wedded quene Gwenyvere and fulfylled the Rounde Table, and so aftir his mervelous knyghtls and he had venquyshed the moste party of his enemyes, than sone aftir com sir Launcelot de Lake unto the courte, and sir Trystrams come that tyme also, and than kyng Arthur helde a ryal feeste and Table Rounde. (113/1–5; V.1 – abbreviated)

Malory gives the minimum of information about them: clearly he expects his readers to know who they are and where they came from (there are a number of prophetic references to Lancelot in *The Tale of King Arthur*). This opening could introduce any kind of quest or adventure, and suggests that Lancelot and Tristram may be the protagonists. But in fact *King Arthur and the Emperor Lucius* plunges straight into the Roman war.

Unlike the first tale, which combines history and romance in a series of loosely connected episodes, not all of which feature Arthur very prominently, this second tale is entirely focused and single-minded. It also represents a striking change of source: whereas in the previous tale Malory depended heavily on French sources (and said so frequently), this tale is based almost entirely on the Middle English Alliterative *Morte Arthure*, though Malory does not actually name it.[14] He turns it into prose, but retains much alliteration; in many places his prose can easily be divided into lines of alliterative verse.[15] This alliterative trend is visible from the very beginning. When the envoys from Rome arrive to demand tribute, they address Arthur in alliterative phrases: 'Crownyd kynge, myssedo no messyngers, for we be com at his commaundemente, as servytures sholde'

---

[14] There are editions of the Alliterative *Morte Arthure* by Valerie Krishna (New York, 1976), by Mary Hamel (New York, 1984), and by Larry D. Benson (with the Stanzaic *Morte*) in *King Arthur's Death* (Indianapolis and New York, 1974), 115–238. On Malory's treatment of his sources see Mary E. Dichmann, '"The Tale of King Arthur and the Emperor Lucius": The Rise of Lancelot,' in *Malory's Originality*, ed. R. M. Lumiansky (Baltimore, 1964), pp. 67–90; Benson, *Malory's Morte Darthur*, esp. pp. 39–59; and Kennedy, 'Malory and His English Sources,' esp. pp. 40–2.

[15] Vinaver marks many examples with line breaks in his edition, though there are more, as Terence McCarthy has pointed out: see his 'Malory and the Alliterative Tradition,' in *Studies in Malory*, ed. James W. Spisak (Kalamazoo, 1985), 53–85.

(113/14–15; not in Caxton). The first three alliterative phrases are borrowed from lines 125, 126 and 131 of the comparable speech in the Alliterative *Morte*. Elsewhere Malory borrows complete lines, each with three alliterating words; and sometimes he invents his own alliteration without help from his source. This style did not find favour with all his readers; Caxton reduced the alliteration by heavy editing (in Vinaver's three volume edition, Caxton's text is printed beneath that of the Winchester manuscript for comparison).[16] Alliterative verse requires a broad vocabulary of synonyms for frequently recurring words, many of which were rare in other forms of Middle English; but Malory at least does not seem to have thought that his audience would be put off.

This tale, like all of Malory's work, is characterized by spareness of description. In the Alliterative *Morte*, twenty lines are devoted to Arthur's arming before his battle with the giant of Mont St. Michel (lines 900–19), and thirty to a grotesque description of the giant (lines 1074–1103); Malory devotes two lines to the arming (120/13–14; V.5), and three and a half to the giant (121/32–36; omitted in Caxton). Similarly the coronation in Rome, like the earlier coronation in London, is described in a single brief sentence which merely states the fact (145/14–17; V.12; and 10/29–31; I.7); such an event would have been an elaborate set piece in French romance.

Not only did Malory make the surprising decision to write a prose version of an English alliterative poem, while retaining much of the alliteration, but he also made a radical change to the function of the Roman war in the Arthurian legend.[17] It is a fundamental part of the chronicle tradition as far back as Geoffrey of Monmouth, and almost always comes at the end of Arthur's story (though in Hardyng's chronicle it precedes the Grail Quest). In romance texts it is often replaced, or overshadowed, by the campaign against Lancelot. The Roman war occurs early in Arthur's history in the Vulgate *Estoire de Merlin*. In the *Mort Artu* the Roman expedition is very brief, and interrupts the campaign against Lancelot; the triumph of the emperor's defeat and death is muted by the news of Mordred's treachery, which makes Arthur hurry back to Britain. In the Stanzaic *Morte* the Roman war is omitted entirely. In the chronicle tradition and in the Alliterative *Morte*, the Roman campaign is Arthur's last great adventure, the crowning glory of his reign from one point of view: he challenges and defeats the power of Rome with all its historical and

---

[16] There has been much critical debate about the relationship between the versions of this tale in the Winchester manuscript and Caxton's printed edition, and the authorship of the revisions: see John Withrington, 'Caxton, Malory, and the Roman War in the *Morte Darthur*,' *Studies in Philology* 89 (1992), 350–366.

[17] For further comment see Kennedy, 'Malory and his English Sources'; Felicity Riddy, *Sir Thomas Malory* (Leiden, 1987), pp. 42–3, and her chapter in this volume; also Lesley Johnson, 'King Arthur at the Crossroads to Rome,' in *Noble and Joyous Histories: English Romances, 1375–1650*, ed. Eiléan Ní Cuilleanáin and J. D. Pheifer (Blackrock, Co. Dublin, 1993), pp. 87–111.

symbolic connotations. But it is also a fatal expedition, since Mordred is left as regent in England, and takes the opportunity to steal both the throne and the queen. In Geoffrey, in Wace, in Laȝamon, in the Alliterative *Morte*, Arthur receives the news of Mordred's treachery just before he reaches Rome itself, and hurries home for the final battle, in which he and most of his men perish. The expedition against the Romans can thus be seen, as it is in the Alliterative *Morte*, as a demonstration of excessive pride and lust for conquest, a form of hubris which leads to a terrible fall. Malory, however, makes this a fairly early campaign, and a complete success for Arthur, the culmination of his ascent to power.[18] Like the historical Charlemagne, he is crowned in Rome: 'And at the day assigned, as the romaynes me tellys, he was crowned Emperour by the Poopys hondis, with all the royalté in the worlde to welde for ever' (145/14–17; V.12 – slightly abbreviated). But he takes no further interest in his continental empire, nor is any further reference made to it. He dispenses land to his knights and leaves 'good governaunce' in Rome, and they all return to England, where Guinevere and the other ladies are waiting for them. It is the knights who urge Arthur to go home, for a rather unchivalric reason: 'we woll beseche youre good grace to reles us to sporte us with oure wyffis.' Arthur agrees, with the comment that 'inowghe is as good as a feste, for to attemte God overmuche I holde hit not wysedom' (146/1–5; V.12). This almost seems to be a response to the moralizing emphasis on hubris in the Alliterative *Morte*, where Arthur's lust for conquest is presented as a major factor in his downfall (Mordred is not Arthur's illegitimate son in the alliterative version).

The other significant change in the handling of the Roman war is that Malory pushes Lancelot into the limelight. In Geoffrey and his followers, Lancelot does not appear at all; in the *Mort Artu*, Arthur is besieging Lancelot in France when he is suddenly called away to the Roman war, in which Lancelot takes no part. In the Alliterative *Morte* Lancelot is present, but plays a minor role; he is not identified as Guenevere's lover – in this version of the story Mordred actually marries the queen, as in Geoffrey, and makes her pregnant (lines 3550–2). Mordred is not mentioned at all in Malory's version of the war; Cador of Cornwall and Baudwyn of Britain are left as joint regents. Many feats and speeches from the Alliterative *Morte* are transferred to Lancelot (often from Gawain), to stress the prowess and courage of the newly arrived knight; and Bors, Lancelot's kinsman, is also given a larger part, perhaps to prepare for his starring role in the Grail Quest, and his importance as Lancelot's cousin and confidant in the two final tales.

Malory follows much of the plot of the Alliterative *Morte* very closely. So his Arthur too has a significant adventure on the way to meet the Roman

---

[18] Vinaver has suggested that Arthur's continental campaign in Malory was modelled on that of Henry V: see his introduction to this tale in the three volume edition, pp. 1367–8.

forces, when he seeks out and destroys the giant of Mont St. Michel who has raped and murdered the Duchess of Brittany, wife of Arthur's cousin Howell. In this episode, as in the source (and in versions all the way back to Geoffrey), Arthur has no trouble dispatching the monster, who is referred to in a running joke borrowed from the alliterative text as a saint (e.g. 120/22; omitted in Caxton); but much of the detail in the poem is omitted or reduced (the elaborate description of the monster, Arthur's arming). This victory establishes Arthur's martial credentials yet again; from the beginning of this tale he is constantly referred to as 'the Conqueror,' a title not used by Malory in the other tales, though common in the Alliterative *Morte*.

Gawain, Arthur's nephew, plays a large part in Malory's version, as in the sources. The first encounter with the Romans is triggered when Gawain is offended by the insulting comments of Gaius, the Emperor's cousin, and kills him (124/19–21; V.6); here as elsewhere in Malory, Gawain is presented as impulsive and quick-tempered. Gawain and his party manage to defeat the attacking Romans, and take many prisoners. But whereas in the alliterative text it is Sir Cador who is in charge of escorting the prisoners to Paris, a move which attracts a Roman ambush, in Malory it is Lancelot. When he hears that sixty thousand Romans are waiting to ambush them, he refuses to flee:

> 'Nay, be my fayth,' sayde sir Launcelot, 'to turne is no tyme, for here is all olde knyghtes of grete worshyp that were never shamed. And as for me and my cousyns of my bloode, we ar but late made knyghtes, yet wolde we be loth to lese the worshyp that oure elders have deservyd.' (128/3–6; omitted in Caxton)

Lancelot and Cador dub some knights in order 'worshyp to wynne' (128/17–18); in the Alliterative *Morte* this is done by Cador alone. Needless to say, Lancelot distinguishes himself prodigiously in the battle, astonishing both the Britons and the Romans (129/43–130.4; V.7). Cador reports this to Arthur when they return:

> 'Sir,' seyde sir Cador, 'there was none of us that fayled othir, but of the knyghtehode of sir Launcelot hit were mervayle to telle. And of his bolde cosyns ar proved full noble knyghtes, but of wyse wytte and of grete strengthe of his ayge sir Launcelot hath no felowe.' (130.18–21; V.7 – slightly abbreviated)

When Arthur hears of their feats, he weeps at the risks they took, and argues that in the face of such odds it would have been reasonable to flee, rather than shameful; but Lancelot insists that they would have incurred eternal shame, and Cleges and Bors support him (130/28–35; V.7).

These changes to Malory's source are significant in several ways. First, Lancelot is established here as the best knight (a role attributed to Gawain in texts where Lancelot either does not appear, or does not play any major role). He will remain peerless throughout Malory's tales, except for the *Tale of the Sankgreal* where spiritual values replace earthly chivalry, and Lancelot's illegitimate son Galahad becomes the best knight and achieves the Grail Quest, with Perceval and Lancelot's cousin Bors. Lancelot is humiliated on several occasions during the Grail Quest; yet a hermit tells him that 'of a synner erthely thou hast no pere as in knyghthode nother never shall have' (555/11–12; XV.4), and later he is allowed to perform a miraculous cure on Sir Urry, who has been told that his enchanted wounds can only be healed by the best knight in the world (663-8; XIX.10–12). Second, the importance of acquiring 'worship' and avoiding shame is stressed yet again. This is the motivating force behind all Malorian chivalry; the same ideas are present in the Alliterative *Morte*, but are not expressed by these keywords which resonate throughout Malory's *Morte Darthur*. And thirdly, the frequent reference to Lancelot's cousins is important. He is not part of Arthur's family, but has his own loyal clan. At the end of the *Morte Darthur*, when conflicting loyalties and tragic accidents create divisions between Lancelot and Arthur and Gawain, Lancelot's clan will stand by him, fighting for him against the king both in England and in their native France; this destroys the Round Table fellowship for ever.

In the next encounter with the Romans, all Arthur's men distinguish themselves, and so does the king himself, who kills the Emperor: 'For evir kynge Arthur rode in the thyckeste of the pres and raumped downe lyke a lyon many senators noble' (134/27–8; V.8). After routing the Roman army, he and his men work their way through Flanders, Lorraine, and Germany on their way to Italy. Gawain returns to centre stage when he fights and captures a brave and noble Saracen, Priamus, who is later converted and made a knight of the Round Table; this battle occurs in the source, but not Priamus' baptism and acceptance as a Round Table knight, an addition typical of Malory's interest in chivalry and fellowship.

Next the victorious forces enter Italy; they capture Milan and cities in Tuscany. Here Malory tones down the ferocity of these events in the Alliterative *Morte*, where Arthur's actions are described as cruel and destructive, creating great bitterness among the people (lines 3150–63). Senators and cardinals come from Rome to beg for peace and make arrangements for his coronation. At this point in the alliterative *Morte* Arthur has a very important dream about the wheel of Fortune, which he recounts to his men when he wakes up (lines 3230ff). He sees six kings who have fallen off the wheel, and two who are clinging to it. Arthur dreams that Fortune, a beautiful woman, lifts him up onto a throne for a little while, but then spins the wheel so that he falls off. His philosopher explains the dream (lines 3394ff): the eight men are the classical, biblical and medieval heroes known as the Worthies (traditionally Arthur was the ninth); the king's fall from the wheel is a prophecy of disaster to come, the result of Arthur's violence and destruction and 'surquidrie' (pride). The philosopher urges Arthur to repent – but the very next morning a messenger arrives with news of Mordred's treacherous actions, and the king and his army leave at once for Britain. Malory omits this dream, of course, since in his account the Roman war does not lead straight into the final struggle against Mordred;[19] instead it is the climax of Arthur's early reign, the final trophy which marks him as the greatest king in the world – he has done nothing of which he should repent. The tale is nearly at an end: he is crowned without any mishap, and distributes land to his heroic knights (including Sir Priamus), and they all return to England.

The English sometimes used the legend of Arthur's Roman expedition as supporting evidence in political claims. In the later Middle Ages historians were worried by it, since they could find no records of it in continental chronicles.[20] As historiography developed, the veracity of the Arthurian legend was challenged, and by the mid-sixteenth century there were many who argued that it had no basis in historical fact. But for Malory, the Roman campaign was crucial in establishing the reputation of Arthur and his knights throughout Christendom. This is the last time that we see them acting (and fighting) together, until the disastrous civil war which destroys the Round Table fellowship and the Arthurian world. In the two tales that follow, *The Tale of Sir Lancelot* and *The Tale of Sir Gareth*, individual knights are singled out as protagonists; then in *The Book of Sir Tristram* the adventures of various knights errant are interlaced, as they are in *The Tale of the Sankgreal* too. These tales could not possibly be described as 'epic' or 'history'; wars are replaced by tournaments, and the focus is on individual adventure and reputation, not national struggles. The first two tales establish Arthur as a mighty warrior and the respected leader of the best knights in the world. In *The Tale of King Arthur* King Pellinor overhears a northern spy giving his impressions of Arthur's court: 'there have I bene and aspied the courte of kynge Arthure, and there ys such a felyship that they may never be brokyn, and well-nyghe all the world holdith with Arthure, for there ys the floure of chevalry' (74/15–18; III.14). This verdict is repeated at the beginning of the next tale by the Roman envoys when they return to their imperial master:

> 'And of all the soveraynes that we sawe ever he is the royallyst kynge that lyvyth on erthe, for we sawe on Newerys day at his Rounde Table nine kyngis, and the fayryst felyship of knyghtes ar with hym that durys on lyve, and thereto of wysedome and of fayre speche and all royalté and richesse they fayle of none.' (116/28–32; V.2)

---

[19] A very brief version of this dream, without any interpretive commentary, is used instead in Malory's last tale, on the night before the final battle with Mordred (711/19–29; XXI.3); it also occurs in this position in the Stanzaic *Morte*, and two nights before the same battle in the *Mort Artu*.

[20] For full discussion of the changing status of the Arthurian legend from the Middle Ages to the Renaissance, see Kendrick, *British Antiquity*.

In the first two tales Malory shows us the establishment of Arthur as king of Britain, his defeat of all his political enemies (Lot and his allies, Morgan and Accolon, and the Romans), his marriage and the establishment of the Round Table, and the chivalric débuts of Gawain and Lancelot. The presence of so many great knights at court gives ample opportunity for many variations on chivalric themes. The stage is now set for adventures and marvels, and they are found in abundance in the tales that follow.

9

The Tale of Sir Gareth *and the* Tale of Sir Lancelot

I

Near the end of the *Morte Darthur*, under royal edict of banishment, Lancelot prepares to leave King Arthur's court 'for ever' (697/41; XX.17). Having unwittingly killed Gareth and Gaheris in the melée of battle, he faces their brother Gawain's wrath. In answer to Gawain's accusations that he has killed his brothers 'traytourly and piteously,' Lancelot avers his abiding love for the dead Gareth:

> 'And wete you well, sir Gawayne, as for Gareth, I loved no kynnesman
> I had more than I loved hym, and ever whyle I lyve . . . I woll bewayle
> sir Gareth hys dethe, nat all only for the grete feare I have of you, but
> for many causys whych causyth me to be sorowfull. One is that I made
> hym knyght; another ys, I wote well he loved me aboven all othir
> knyghtes; and the third ys, he was passyng noble and trew, curteyse
> and jantill and well condicionde . . . And as Jesu be my helpe, and be
> my knyghthode, I slewe never sir Gareth nother hys brother be my
> wyllynge, but alas that ever they were unarmed that unhappy day!'
> (695/42–696/11; XX.16)

This attestation of love, admiration, and grief, not in Malory's known sources and very likely invented by him, punctuates one of the most moving moments in the whole of the *Morte Darthur*. At the same time, it powerfully refocuses our experience of two much earlier tales in the *Morte Darthur* – the paired tales of Sir Lancelot and Sir Gareth, which are the third and fourth 'works' in Eugène Vinaver's edition.

Almost fifty years ago, Vinaver argued that Malory had designed his several 'tales' in the *Morte Darthur* not as 'a single work, but as a series of eight separate romances.'[1] Vinaver did not deny that the eight tales he had identified contribute in some way to the 'hoole book.' But he did insist that Caxton, not Malory, had been responsible for presenting the *Morte* as a

---

[1] *The Works of Sir Thomas Malory*, ed. E. Vinaver, 3 vols (Oxford, 1947), I, xxxv; the statement is in the 3rd edition, rev. P. J. C. Field (Oxford, 1990), I, xxxix.

single work 'subordinate to an imaginary principle of all embracing dramatic "unity"' (xli). His strongest pieces of evidence for Malory's 'cutting the threads' in his source 'tapestry,' were not only the explicits of the Winchester manuscript but also the relatively independent *Tale of Sir Lancelot* and *Tale of Sir Gareth*.

The continuing debate over the question of unity in the *Morte* cannot be definitively resolved since the text offers no unequivocal statement on the subject of authorial 'intention.' Yet the companion tales devoted to Sir Lancelot and Sir Gareth provide intriguing evidence as to how individual tales in the *Morte* contribute, *by means of their compositional separateness*, to the whole book's tragic effect. In this chapter, I want to consider anew the form and content of *Gareth* and *Lancelot* as they further the stylistic and moral commitments of the text as a whole. In its general contours, my approach is not a new one. But I believe the question of the 'separateness' of these two tales in relation to the *Morte* as a whole has not yet been satisfactorily addressed as it bears on two crucial issues: (1) the specific *generic* affiliations of each of the two tales; and (2) the impact of the two tales, as Malory configured them, on the *Morte Darthur*'s distinctive tragic effect.

More than many other parts of Malory's 'book,' the tales of Sir Lancelot and Sir Gareth have the appearance of being self-contained units. Each fiction details the adventures of a single great knight who bears a special relationship not of filial but of chivalric love to the other. And both of them are organized rather on the pattern of the twelfth-century French verse *roman d'aventure* than on the interlaced, historical model of the thirteenth-century prose Vulgate Cycle – two points to which I shall return. In addition both tales celebrate moments of stability and glory in the history of King Arthur's Round Table. The best knights, bent on proving themselves and thereby winning worship, are free to do so 'in all turnementes, justys, and dedys of armys' (149/6–7; VI.1). Though the opening phrase of the *Tale of Lancelot* marks the political history of Arthur's realm, the *Tale* itself turns not on historical matters but on Lancelot's character within the context of a series of marvelous adventures. *The Tale of Sir Gareth* begins in a spirit of celebration, when the Round Table is 'moste plenoure' (177/1;VII.1), and the temporal order is measured not by the course of political events but by the cycle of the liturgical feasts – Pentecost, the Assumption of the Virgin Mary, Michaelmas. Within this ritual framework, the episodes are highly patterned, characterized by repetitions that support the self-contained, 'completed' impression of the tale as a whole.

At the same time, however, for us as readers, the intersection of the tales of Lancelot and Gareth with the *Morte*'s ending is essential to the whole book's tragic impact. When, in the passage quoted at the beginning of this chapter, Gareth is killed and Lancelot accused, the text invites us to recall the unswerving virtue of, as well as the love between, the two great knights. We are made to see: (1) that the moral worth of Lancelot and

Gareth, including their love for each other, transcends historical circumstance and even death; and (2) that the tragedy of the whole book lies in the inability of even the best knights to stay the dark forces of jealousy, lust, gossip, anger, enchantment, treachery, ignorance, misunderstanding, misrecognition, raw ambition, and sheer mischance in the circumstantial world they inhabit. As Lancelot poignantly comments just before he leaves Arthur's court for the last time: 'Howbehit I wote well that in me was nat all the stabilité of thys realme, but in that I myght I ded my dever' (699/7–9; XX.18).

Lancelot's summary of his career crystallizes the tragedy of the Arthurian world as Malory represents it: even in the best of societies, destructive, often malevolent forces will eventually destabilize the power of individual goodness. In Malory's argument, Lancelot's banishment does not signal a change in his character, or, as the Vulgate Cycle would have it, a punishment for the sin of adultery. Instead, it participates in the asymmetry between good and evil in the world. Even before the *Tale of Lancelot*, which fully demonstrates its hero's supremacy among Arthur's knights, Malory has already granted Lancelot privileged status as *primus inter pares*. Whenever, in the early pages of the *Morte*, he is mentioned, he is the 'trewest' lover (45/15; II.8), the 'beste knyght' (58/25; II.19) and 'moste man of worship of the worlde' (76/38–9; IV.1). The tale devoted to him, then, brings into full focus the nature of his 'noblesse,' 'jantylnesse,' and 'curtesy,' showing as it does his extraordinary courage in helping both men and women in need. In a parallel way, Sir Gareth, who is the subject of the *Morte*'s fourth tale, enters the narrative as a young would-be knight already in command of his own greatness and needing only a public arena in which to prove himself. His narrative, which unfolds as a romance of a particular kind, gives him the opportunity to prove his nobility both of body and of heart. And he, like Lancelot, remains unerringly noble until he is cut down by chance, killed accidentally by Lancelot, the man he most loves in the world.

No tales in the *Morte Darthur* show more clearly than those of Lancelot and Gareth Malory's moral essentialism in conceiving and drawing his hero-knights. Like the Anglo-Saxon hero, Beowulf, but unlike, for example, the Lancelot of the French Vulgate Cycle, Malory's ideal knights have a specific, unalterable moral valence from the beginning to the end of the *Morte*. Both the third and the fourth tale dramatize their respective hero's inborn honour and prowess. The French knight and the British knight, bound together as master to protégé, manifest their physical as well as their moral strength in a series of unexpected, often bizarre adventures. And, by this means, they both win worship. In this regard, the two tales mirror each other much as two paintings in a diptych might, each one reflecting on and intensifying the content and form of the other, and together exemplifying Malory's best hopes for chivalry.

Malory's essentialism, moreover, enables the unfolding of a kind of

tragedy that has little to do with either Aristotelian or Christian notions of
the heroic or the tragic. In saying this, I do not mean to suggest that Malory
consciously set about replacing established literary models of heroism or
tragedy with something new. He was not himself an academic man of
letters but, as he characterizes himself, a prisoner-knight. His distinctive
tragic vision in the *Morte* seems to stem from personal experience and
from a clearcut system of moral values, as these inform and are informed
by his reading of Arthurian romance. The tragedy Malory unfolds in the
Morte does not show us great characters undone by their own flaws (the
Aristotelian paradigm). Nor does it offer us Christian heroes who succumb
to sin (the Christian paradigm). Instead, the best knights in the world fall to
forces largely beyond their control, leaving behind them only the memory
of their greatness and the painful, irreversible fact of their loss to the
Arthurian kingdom. What the tales of Lancelot and Gareth show us is the
heroic generosity, strength, and courage of their protagonists in contexts
relatively free of familial and political constraints. Configured as virtually
independent *romans d'aventure*, they celebrate their heroes' innate,
unchangeable nobility of heart. Over the course of the whole *Morte Darthur*,
however, as Malory pursues the historical trajectory of the French Vulgate
Cycle, even the best knights become increasingly entangled in the rancour
and pettiness of the king's court and family. Though this entanglement
never undoes their virtue, it does finally destroy them.

II

To discover how Malory shaped the tales devoted to Sir Gareth and Sir
Lancelot, and to what end, we must first ask what his likely sources were
and how he seems to have adapted them for his own purposes. These
questions are easier to answer for the *Tale of Sir Lancelot* than for the *Tale of
Sir Gareth*. Yet the answers for the latter tale bear heavily on the way we
respond in relation to the former. For this reason, I want to begin with the
fourth rather than the third tale. By opening up the vexed problem of the
'lost source' for the *Gareth*, we shall be better equipped to ask how and why
Malory reworked his known sources in shaping his *Lancelot*.

No single source has yet been found for the *Tale of Sir Gareth*, and this has
led more than one scholar to suggest that Malory invented the story himself.
R. H. Wilson and P. J. C. Field, on the other hand, have argued that internal
evidence in the *Tale* points to a source now lost, which Malory adapted for
his own purposes.[2] Whatever the case – and clearly this is a question
inviting further study – the *Tale* as we have it intertwines two distinct

---

[2] See R. H. Wilson, 'The "Fair Unknown" in Malory,' *PMLA*, 58 (1943), 1–21; P. J. C. Field,
    'The Source of Malory's *Tale of Gareth*,' in *Aspects of Malory*, ed. T. Takamiya and D. S.
    Brewer (Cambridge, 1981), pp. 59–70.

storylines. The first of these, as Field has ably shown, involves a traditional folktale motif in which a younger brother competes with an older brother in a contest to demonstrate his prowess, and we shall examine that pattern later on. Before doing so, however, I want to consider the dominant second story, that of the *bel inconnu* or 'Fair Unknown' – which seems to have entered the orbit of French Arthurian romance as early as the twelfth century.[3] To the 'Fair Unknown' tradition, Malory's tale owes two of its key elements: (1) the hero who refuses to reveal his name or parentage and wins his chivalric fame incognito; and (2) the positive treatment of erotic love as magical, transformative, and unending.

The motif of the young hero hiding his identity is, in an important sense, the hallmark of the 'Fair Unknown' group of romances. The pattern is as follows: a strong and handsome young man, the *bel inconnu*, appears suddenly at court, usually on a major religious feast, and asks King Arthur for a gift or gifts. Yet in spite of his request for favours, he will tell nothing of his biographical identity when the king asks who he is. As a result, he is given a nickname under which he earns his fame.[4] In several versions too the hero earns his worship partly by enduring mockery, whether for a short or long time, from a damsel who regards him as too young or too lowborn to perform great deeds.

Malory's *Tale of Sir Gareth* recapitulates this storyline in a way that links it to all extant versions of the *bel inconnu* story, including 'La Cote Male Tayle' embedded in the *Morte's Book of Sir Tristram*. In *Gareth*, on the *Tale's* first feast of Pentecost, King Arthur awaits a 'grete mervayle' so that he and his court can begin eating. Suddenly a very tall young man enters the hall, leaning on the shoulders of two other men, as if he could not support himself. Then, straightening up easily, he addresses the king, asking him for three gifts. On this Whitsunday, however, he requests only one gift – food and drink for the next year. In a move fundamental to the 'Fair Unknown' romances, the king, recognizing that the youth must come from 'men of worshyp,' asks 'what is thy name . . .?' By thus demanding to know Gareth's

---

3   Usually included in the list of romances belonging to the 'Fair Unknown' group on the basis of common themes, narrative patterns, and characters are the following: the twelfth-century verse fragment called by Gaston Paris *'Le vallet a la cote mal taillie,'* Renaut de Beaujeu's early thirteenth-century verse *Le Bel Inconnu*, Wirnt von Gravenberg's German *Wigalois* (1204–10), the Middle English verse *Libeaus Desconus* (c.1350), the Italian *Cantari di Carduino* (c.1375), and the story of *La Cote Mal Taile* told in the French prose *Tristan* and translated by Malory as part of his long *Tale of Sir Tristram*. Other romances sometimes linked to the group are the Welsh *Peredur*, Chrétien de Troyes' *Perceval*, and Chaucer's *Wife of Bath's Tale*.

4   Differences of detail separate one romance from another in the group. For example, in some versions, the young man knows his lineage and refuses to divulge it, while in others, he genuinely does not know who his parents are. And in some versions, the 'Fair Unknown' seeks to be knighted, while in others he has already been knighted when he arrives at Arthur's court. For a detailed comparison of differences and similarities in the various versions, see R. H. Wilson, 'The "Fair Unknown".'

identity, Arthur raises a question that will resonate in several ways both within the *Tale of Sir Gareth* and over the course of the *Morte Darthur* as a whole.

Within the *Tale* as romance, in a fairytale mood, Gareth's masking of his
identity sets in motion his manipulation of Arthur's court as well as his
own royal family. From the start, Gareth knows who he is and it is he who
largely controls the play between his biological and his knightly identity.
He withholds his name and lineage in order to 'prove' to his public,
without depending on family connections, that he is a worthy knight. By
remaining incognito, Gareth opens the way for the scorn of Sir Kay, who
relegates him to the kitchen and nicknames him Beaumains. His refusal, a
year later, to reveal his identity renders him vulnerable to mockery by the
damsel, Lynet, whose adventure Gareth takes despite her protestations.
With an astonishing self-confidence, he insists on pursuing the quest, even
though Lynet persistently denigrates his manifest victories. The entire tale,
then, turns on the interplay between Beaumains' many demonstrations of
his prowess and the largely comedic difficulties surrounding his refusal to
say who he is. This refusal introduces a delightful dramatic irony for the
audience. It also issues in several 'romantic' recognition scenes: one by one,
Gareth's ladylove, his brother, his uncle, his mother, and his opponents in
battle discover the unexpected but seemly congruence of great knightly
virtue with high birth.

Besides giving the tale an aura of comedy and romance, Gareth's hiding
of his identity until he has proved himself serves some of the *Morte
Darthur*'s deepest interests. Perhaps most importantly, his insistence on
remaining incognito supports the author's essentialist conception of
knighthood, to which I have already alluded. One or two moments in the
Tale suggest that its immediate source may have been a *bildungsroman* in
which a young hero *learns* to be a great knight.[5] Yet Malory offers no overt
hint of biographical development or growth for his hero. Instead, his *Tale*
shows that Gareth's greatness is innate. From the start, he is physically and
morally strong *and* he belongs to a noble family. For Malory, there is a
necessary link between aristocratic lineage and knightly achievement. Yet,
while great knights will come of high birth, not all men of high birth are
great knights. As Gareth hides his family identity, he deliberately separates
himself from his family, and particularly from his brother, Gawain. In one
encounter after another, without reference to his lineage, he earns his place
among the best knights in the world. When, at last, his ladylove, his
opponents, and his family learn that he is the son of King Lot and Queen

---

[5] For example, when Gareth takes on the Red Knight of the Red Lands, the narrative
suggests that the young knight, responding to the Red Knight's wiliness, learns to be
prudent: 'And the Rede Knyghte was a wyly knyght in fyghtyng, and that taught
Bewmaynes to be wyse . . .' (198/40–1; VII:17). For an interesting account of a latent
psychological pattern of development in the *Tale*, however, see Derek Brewer, 'The Story
of Gareth,' in *Symbolic Stories* (Cambridge, 1980), pp. 100–111.

Morgause of Orkney, they are filled with joy. And this joy marks the *heightening* of Gareth's honour. The worship he has earned both enhances and is enhanced by his parentage.

A second element linking the *Tale of Sir Gareth* to the *bel inconnu* tradition is Malory's (and possibly his source's) treatment of women and sexual love. To a large extent, the love interest in the *Tale*, and the women who catalyze it, determine its fairytale-like tonality. In the 'Fair Unknown' romances, love centers on what Jean Frappier has called 'l'amour arthurien.'[6] This is a concept, Celtic at base, which Frappier has distinguished as a generic feature of a number of early French Arthurian fictions. The underlying Celtic mythos, borrowed and rationalized by several twelfth-century northern French poets, involves a *fée-amante* or fairy lover who draws to her and inspires a chosen mortal. Endowed with magical powers, the lady orchestrates a series of adventures or tests designed to catalyze the transformation of the knight's moral life. Erotic desire and fulfilment, moreover, participate centrally in this transformation, and indeed the perfection of the hero's destiny *requires* that he love. Falling totally and irrevocably in love, he takes his *fée-amante* as bride or mate and lives happily ever after.[7]

In the romances it shapes, including the *Tale of Gareth*, the concept of 'l'amour arthurien' licenses writers to celebrate sexual love as spontaneous, delightful, ennobling, and lasting for women and men alike. In *Gareth*, a powerful woman both arouses and shares her lover's erotic desire, and it is chiefly to the love she inspires that the *Tale* owes its idealizing, poetic quality. Certainly, the *Morte Darthur* as a whole is thoroughly patriarchal, masculine, and epic in its structure, and *Gareth* fully participates in these interests. Its affective core is, as we shall see later on, the relationship between Gareth and Lancelot. Yet the *Tale*'s poetic delight springs from its celebration of heterosexual love. In addition, the treatment of women and sexuality in *Gareth* (and presumably its source) seems to have given Malory a model more compelling than the negative model of seductive women and sinful love proposed by the Vulgate Cycle's *Lancelot*. Not only does he 'translate' this model into his *Tale of Gareth*; as I shall argue later on, he may also have borrowed its aura as he set about delineating Lancelot's love for Guinevere in the preceding *Tale of Lancelot*.

In the *Tale of Sir Gareth*, the erotic love-interest centers on the exquisitely beautiful dame Lyonesse, who is besieged and held captive by the Red Knight of the Red Lands. Her need initiates Gareth's important first quest as a knight, and her beauty wins his undying love. To be sure, Lyonesse

---

[6] 'Le Concept de l'amour dans les romans arthuriens,' in *Amour Courtois et Table Ronde* (Geneva, 1973), pp. 43–56

[7] Such is the concept of love that animates romances as different from each other as Chrétien de Troyes' *Yvain*, Marie de France's *Lanval*, Béroul's *Tristan*, Renaut de Beaujeu's early thirteenth-century verse *Le Bel Inconnu*, and, *mutatis mutandis*, Malory's *Tale of Sir Gareth*.

does not appear in person until nearly the midpoint of the narrative (Chapter 16 of Caxton's 36 chapters). But it is her plight, first presented to King Arthur's court by her sister Lynet, that sets in motion both Gareth's knighting and his taking of her 'adventure.'[8]

Gareth's unswerving desire to pursue the quest Lynet has outlined, in spite of her mockery, appears at first to be no more than youthful fervor driving him to begin his knightly life. Underlying this appearance of accidental circumstance, however, we can discern vestiges of the Celtic mythos. As the tale unfolds, Gareth's determination seems more and more to participate in a magical destiny, offered by Lyonesse and recognized, however imperfectly at first, by her knight.[9] This same sense of destiny hovers over Gareth's first glimpse of Lyonesse as he prepares to take on the Red Knight of the Red Lands in her defence. In one of those economical, sharply focused conversations characteristic of Malory's own style, Lynet unites Gareth's 'trial' with his initiation into love:

> 'Sir . . . loke ye be glad and lyght, for yondir is your dedly enemy, and at yondir wyndow is my lady, my sistir dame Lyones.'
> 'Where?' seyde Bewmaynes.
> 'Yondir,' seyde the damesell, and poynted with her fyngir.
> 'That is trouth,' seyde Bewmaynes, 'she besemyth afarre the fayryst lady that ever I lokyd uppon, and truly,' he seyde, 'I aske no better quarell than now for to do batayle, for truly she shall be my lady and for hir woll I fyght.' (197/19–27;VII.16)

The lady first seen from a distance resembles the perpetually inaccessible *domna* of the troubadours. Yet all of Lyonesse's subsequent behavior aligns her much more closely with the *fée-amante* associated with *l'amour arthurien*.

One important sign of this connection occurs after Gareth's victory over the Red Knight of the Red Lands. Even though he has completed his assigned adventure, Lyonesse refuses to grant her champion her love. From a window on high, she issues her orders to Gareth:

> 'Go thy way . . . for as yet thou shalt nat have holy my love unto the tyme that thou be called one of the numbir of the worthy knightes. And

---

[8]   Gareth's quest begins at King Arthur's court on Pentecost, when Lyonesse's sister Lynet arrives and asks the king for one of his knights to take on her sister's adventure. Arthur refuses to ask one of his knights to help her, because Lynet will not reveal her sister's name. But then Gareth demands the two gifts Arthur had promised him on the previous Pentecost. As one gift he asks that he be given the adventure Lynet has proposed, and, as the other, that he be knighted by Sir Lancelot. Arthur grants both requests, and Gareth rides out after Lynet, despite her strong protestations that he is a mere 'kychyn page' (301).

[9]   To be sure, Lyonesse seems not to know who Gareth is, and she expends considerable effort to learn his identity from his dwarf. But this narrative withholding of the young knight's identity probably belongs to a later development of the originally Celtic love story in which the motif of the 'Fair Unknown' has been added to the motif of the fairy lady's love-trial.

therefore go and laboure in worshyp this twelve-monthe, and than ye shall hyre newe tydyngis.' (201/18–21; VII.19)

Lyonesse's command clearly belongs to the 'love-trial' typical of the Celtic story-type, and one would expect the tale's next segment to detail Gareth's exploits for the following year. In fact, dame Lyonesse, and possibly Malory's source, set aside the promised storyline.[10] Lyonesse's command turns out to be a ruse designed to send Gareth away until she has learned more about his identity. Yet, in spite of truncating the year-long test, the *Tale* deprives its *fée-amante* neither of her power over her chosen lover nor of her erotic desire.

Once she has found out what his 'ryght name' is and 'of what kynrede he is commyn' (202/15–16; VII.19), and accepted these as appropriate to her own stature, Lyonesse is prepared to give him her heart (and herself). But first she insists on playing an identity game of her own. Up to this point in the story, Gareth has seen Lyonesse only from a distance. When he next meets her in her brother Gringamour's castle hall, it is she who chooses to stage herself, as Gareth has been doing elsewhere in the *Tale*. Self-consciously 'arayde lyke a prynces,' she refuses to reveal her identity. In choosing to play with Gareth in this way, Lyonesse does not reject the received feminine stereotype in the courtship game, focused as it is on the woman as beautiful object. Yet she does claim subjective control over it. Because she does not introduce herself, Gareth does not recognize her. But her beauty inspires in him the same burning love he had felt on first seeing her from afar. So much is he captivated that he wishes 'the lady of this Castell Perelus were so fayre as she is' (204/20–1; VII.21). The elegant joke, in which we as readers fully participate, is that the two ladies are, in fact, one.[11] No matter what the lady's guise, so the implied argument goes, the *fée-amante* will be able to exert the same power over her chosen mate. Concomitantly, Gareth as lover will, because of his magical destiny (and, in Malory's argument, his innate goodness), remain ever faithful to his fairy lady.

The sequence that follows this game gives us one of the rare celebrations of erotic passion in Malory's *Morte*. The very next moment of the *Tale* involves us in the delicate and amusing consequences of the 'hoote love' Gareth and Lyonesse feel equally for each other. Both lovers yearn to go to bed together even before their marriage. Yet, because they are 'yonge bothe and tendir of ayge,' they do not know how to conceal their plan. Lynet, who

---

[10] This uncompleted trial year may suggest that Malory was, in fact, working from a direct source and that he chose to eschew narrative consistency because he was more concerned with his hero's chivalric identity than with the love-trial *per se*.

[11] Oddly, there is a potential for mistaken identity and betrayal in this play, even though it is almost immediately passed over. Gareth gives his heart to the 'second' lady before he knows that she is identical with the first.

seems to be the only one in the situation concerned about the dangers to female honour of premarital sex, is 'a lytyll dysplesed,' thinking her sister 'a lyttyl overhasty' (205/27–28; VII.22). What Lynet does here, in effect, is to identify and seek to protect for her sister the only route to honour available to women in the Middle Ages.[12] And she succeeds in her effort, though not without magic, and not without comedy.

On the appointed night, when Lyonesse has just managed to slip into Gareth's bed and the two have begun to kiss, Lynet arranges for an armed knight to interrupt them. Despite not being armed himself, Gareth reaches for his sword, attacks the knight, and cuts off his head. As is nearly always the case in the *Tale of Sir Gareth*, potential tragedies of a kind that involve revenge and death in other parts of the *Morte* are here averted by magic. Lynet enters the scene, takes a special ointment, reattaches the knight's head to his body with it, and puts the healed knight in her chamber. Malory is generally concerned with 'breffing' his tales, including this one. Yet he plays this comedic scene once again. On a second attempted night of love, Gareth's slaying of a second visitor knight is still more gruesome than the first, and Lynet's healing of him all the more wondrous. In the second case, Gareth not only cuts off the knight's head; he also cuts it into 'gobbettis' and throws them out the window into the castle moat. This time, Lynet's healing involves retrieving the 'hondred pecis' of head, reamalgamating them with her ointment, *and* rejoining them to the knight's body. We might assume that, in doubling the bedroom/healing scene, Malory was passively following his source. Yet it is tempting to suppose that he did not 'bref' the tale at this point – or even that he invented the second scene – because he himself found that the magic enhanced his hero's charm for his readers and also confirmed his election as a great lover-knight.

Lynet's healing skills are of a piece with Lyonesse's own forms of magic. Not only has she drawn her chosen love and future husband to herself by some mysterious force aligned with a secret destiny; she also possesses a magical ring, which has several powers. The *Tale* brings the ring into play for the great tournament, designed by Gareth and called by Lyonnesse, ostensibly to select her husband. This ring, which becomes the comedic fulcrum for the tournament, allows its wearers to change colours and saves them from losing blood. By giving the ring to Sir Gareth, Lyonesse ensures that he will take the prize in the tournament and win her hand. Like Iseult's magical potion in the Tristan romances, the ring seems to be a vestige of the original Celtic mythos, signalling the otherworldly power the *fée-amante* uses to win or protect her chosen lover. In the case of the *Tale of Sir Gareth*, however, this function has been suppressed in favor of the *Tale's* dominant interest. The magic grants Gareth one more means of delaying

---

[12] On women and honor in the Middle Ages, see Julian Pitt-Rivers, 'Honour and Social Status,' in J. G. Peristiany, *Honour and Shame: The Values of Mediterranean Society* (Chicago, 1966), pp. 19–77.

the revelation of his biographical identity in favor of exhibiting his chivalric prowess. During the day of the tournament, Gareth remains as he has always been: courageous, strong, and victorious in fighting. Only his armour changes from green to blue to white to red to black so 'that there myght neyther kynge nother knyght have no redy cognysshauns of hym' (215/34–35; VII.29).

In the event, in Malory's argument, Gareth succeeds in overcoming the Red Knight of the Red Lands and liberating Lyonesse *both* because he is a great knight *and* because he loves his lady. Malory's essentialist conception of his hero works against his permitting his hero an actual transformation of the kind that belongs to the Celtic love-mythos. Instead, the *Tale* shows us how *fine amor* as 'pure love' simply draws out and enhances the great knight's 'Jantylnesse' as a quality already inherent in his character. In fact, neither the ring nor the tournament is essential to the unfolding of the plot. Long before she calls the tournament, Lyonesse has already chosen Gareth as her mate and declared that she will have no one else. And Gareth has already proved himself one of the greatest knights of the world. Yet Malory devotes five chapters (by Caxton's count) to Gareth's triumphant proof of his knightly prowess. The quintessentially ceremonial joust owes its character entirely to Gareth and Lyonesse's playfulness as, together, they manipulate Arthur's court for their own delight. The tournament does not make possible but simply confirms the young knight's right to his chosen lady. In addition, it sets the tone for the triple marriage that concludes the *Tale*.

As I have been suggesting, neither the love interest nor the elements of magic in the *Tale of Sir Gareth* alter the character the *Tale*'s hero possesses from the beginning. Yet the atmosphere they encourage defines the dominant mood of the romance, setting it somewhat apart from the political concerns of the *Morte Darthur* as a whole. The positive treatment of erotic love, moreover, grants sexual fulfilment a legitimate place in the life of the great knight. Gareth's love life plays no part in the *Morte*'s subsequent narrative. In fact, neither Lynet nor Lyonnesse ever reappears after the fourth tale. Yet the erotic spirit celebrated in the *Tale of Gareth* indirectly ennobles Lancelot's parallel love for Guinevere. Faced with the Vulgate Cycle's condemnation of Lancelot and Guinevere for adultery, Malory cannot entirely exonerate the illicit lovers. As we shall see when we turn to the *Tale of Lancelot*, however, he does everything in his power to align their love with 'l'amour arthurien' informing his *Tale of Gareth* and to separate it from the heavy-handed moralizing of the thirteenth-century prose *Lancelot*.

Up to this point I have focused on the themes and motifs of the *bel inconnu* tradition as these enter into Malory's *Tale of Sir Gareth*. Now I want to consider another story-type embedded in *Gareth* – the folkloric motif of the younger brother who competes with his older brother. More than a century ago, H. O. Sommer suggested that *Gareth* must have originated as a folk-tale, which either Malory or a predecessor had then adapted to the

Arthurian cycle. P. J. C. Field has recently refined Sommer's hint, arguing that, from a structural point of view, Malory's tale conforms to a specific folktale pattern.[13] In this story type, a younger brother sets out to demonstrate that he can compete with an already well-known older brother. Undertaking a series of adventures, he concludes the 'proof' of his prowess by fighting with his older brother in an evenly matched battle. The outcome involves recognition that the younger brother is worthy of his older brother's praise and can be judged his equal. Field also argues that Malory's immediate source would 'almost certainly [have been] about Gawain and Gareth' ('Source,' p. 61). Pervasive signs in *Gareth* support the younger brother theory and, in particular, Field's hypothesis concerning the likely identity of the two brothers, if indeed Malory was working from a single source. Gawain, as the eldest of the Orkney brothers, plays a prominent role in Malory's tale. He is the first to see Gareth when he arrives at King Arthur's court, though he fails to recognize his youngest brother (as he does for most of the tale). Gawain is also the first to express anger at Kay's insulting treatment of the youth, offering him food and drink beyond what Kay gives him in the kitchen. Moreover, in the course of the tale, Gareth engages twice in battle with Gawain. The second of these two encounters perfectly exemplifies the folktale pattern and also completes it. Standing alone, Gareth sees an armed knight riding towards him on horseback. He mounts his horse and the two run together 'as thundir' (221/36; VII.34). Gawain wounds Gareth, and both of them then dismount, engaging in a two-hour sword battle on foot. At last Lynet comes upon the scene and reveals the identity of both knights: 'Sir Gawayne!' she cries out, 'leve thy fyghtynge with thy brothir, sir Gareth!' (221/42; VII.34).

The recognition scene that follows upon Lynet's announcement is a touching one. Gawain throws away his shield and sword, runs to Sir Gareth, takes him in his arms, kneels down, and asks his mercy. Gareth answers his brother's gestures of love by kneeling down himself and likewise begging mercy. Both rise up, then, embracing each other and weeping. Gawain's words of admiration, addressed to his younger brother, bring the folktale pattern to its appropriate conclusion:

> 'Alas! my fayre brother . . . I ought of ryght to worshyp you, and ye were nat my brother, for ye have worshipte kynge Arthure and all his courte, for ye have sente mo worshypfull knyghtes this twelve-monthe than fyve the beste of the Rounde Table hath done excepte sir Launcelot.' (222/12–16; VII.34)

Once Gawain has given his brother 'worship' – a worship earned not by right of birth but by prowess – the scene is set for his wider recognition. King Arthur, having been told the news of the combat by Lynet, arrives

---

[13] 'The Source of Malory's *Tale of Gareth*.' See note 2 above.

with his entourage at the 'lytyll hyllys syde' where the two brothers are sitting. He too is overjoyed and weeps at finding Gareth. His tears, like Gawain's, signal love and admiration. Then Gareth's mother, Morgawse, enters the scene and swoons. This touching concord in Arthur's family, focused as it is on the youth who has amply earned the title *Sir* Gareth, adds to the celebratory tone of the tale as a whole. In the *Tale's* concluding sequence, the two plots – the younger brother story and the 'Fair Unknown' romance – come together more or less neatly. And the disguise motif, functioning in both plots to heighten the dramatic irony, also intensifies the spirit of joy in the recognition scenes.

If Malory's *Tale of Sir Gareth* involved simply combining elements of the *bel inconnu* story-type with the younger brother folktale pattern, we would have an idealizing *roman d'aventure* on the pattern of Chrétien de Troyes' romances or Marie de France's lais. And, if Malory had a source, this may possibly have been more or less its character. But the tale as Malory presents it deviates from both traditional patterns in significant ways. First of all, Gareth's refusal – as a 'Fair Unknown' hero – to reveal his name opens the way for small and large misunderstandings within his own family. Secondly, in Malory's version of the younger-brother folktale motif, Gareth competes with two elder 'brothers' rather than one: Gawain, who is his blood-brother, and Lancelot, who is his chosen mentor. These deviations, which are closely related to each other, make *Gareth* less 'pure' in its character as a *roman d'aventure*. At the same time, they deepen the tale by connecting it to the historical trajectory of the *Morte Darthur* as a family tragedy.

At least two scenes of familial tension cast their shadow over the otherwise joyful tale, both of them directly related to Gareth's hiding of his identity. The first such episode occurs when Gareth's mother comes to King Arthur's court some time after her youngest son has embarked on his quest for worship. Her other three sons, Gawain, Agravain, and Gaheris all greet and embrace her, and she then asks about Gareth. Morgause, who has apparently received news of her son's service as a kitchen boy in Arthur's household, chastises the king for slighting his nephew. In a sentence that will reverberate painfully much later on within the context of the *Morte's* closing movement, Gawain declares: 'A, dere modir, I knew hym nat' (209/35; VII.25). The family discomfort in this scene is considerable, but it ends, as do many others like it in the *Morte Darthur*, without resolution. Arthur simply commands Morgause: 'Sister . . . lat this langage now be stylle' (210/31; VII.25).

A second brief episode likewise records familial distress over misrecognition, but this time at a deeper level. At the end of the great tournament orchestrated by Gareth and called at Lyonesse's request, Gareth enters the lists no longer wearing the magical ring that has hidden his identity up to this point in the jousting. For the first time in the tale he is publicly recognized and named by the heralds: 'This is sir Gareth, kynge

Lottys son of Orkeney!' Immediately following the heralds' announcement, Gareth, surprisingly, smites down Sir Sagramour and *'his brother* sir Gawayne' (218/6–7; VII.30). To this act of violence, Gawayne responds, 'A, brother . . . I wente ye wolde haue smyttyn me so' (218/8–9; VII.30). When Gareth hears this, he struggles to leave the mêlée of the joust and flees. Gawain then pursues him into the forest, but in vain.

This scene is fraught with mystery as to Gareth's motivation in striking his brother. Did Gareth recognize Gawain or did he not? Why, when his brother speaks to him, does he leave without a word? Malory provides no narrative commentary to ease our readerly discomfort over the family tension. Gareth's attack on Gawain may well have been accidental: he may simply not have recognized his brother because of his armour. Gawain's response to the blow, however, abruptly interrupts Gareth's manipulative game, commenting on his violation (whether unintentional or not) of family loyalty. Gareth is apparently so upset by what his brother has said that he pushes his way through the crowd and flees into the woods.

To add to the confusion surrounding this scene, the text poses a slight but significant editorial problem. What does Gawain, in Malory's account, actually say to Gareth? The Winchester Manuscript, which Vinaver follows in his edition, has Gawain say, 'I wente ye wolde have smyttyn me.' Caxton's edition, on the other hand, reads: 'A, brother . . . I went ye wolde not haue stryken me.' Vinaver, noting that 'either reading is possible,' prefers the Winchester text. But Caxton's reading seems to me much more likely to reflect the original text, calling attention as it does to Gawain's sense of Gareth's sacred responsibility not to harm a member of his own family.

If we assume that Caxton's is the better reading, however, there remains the further problem of Gareth's silence and flight in response to Gawain's direct address. A writer more self-consciously literary than Malory might well have had Gareth echo Gawain's earlier plea to his mother in an extenuating defense like, 'A, dere brother, I knewe thee nat!' Such closure would have produced a neatly symmetrical (and easily analyzed) rhetorical pattern. Yet the very *absence* of closure allows the episode to participate in a more ominous and more lifelike moral pattern of unresolved tensions in the extended royal family. And it is this underlying dissonance – often involving significant silences – that will eventually precipitate the fall of the Round Table.

If Gareth's discomfiting skirmish with Gawain casts a shadow over the fairytale quality of the *bel inconnu* romance, it also participates in Malory's disruption of the younger brother folktale. In what may be his most systematic addition, if he was in fact working from a source, Malory involves Lancelot *as well as* Gawain in the proving of Gareth. And he does so, I think, to show that Lancelot is more worthy to be Gareth's 'brother' than Gawain is. As Field has noted, Malory's insertion of Lancelot makes his *Gareth* 'less authentic than some of its cognates.'[14] But the very disturbance of the traditional pattern may provide us with information about Malory's deepest commitments.[15] As Lancelot competes with Gawain for Gareth's admiration at every turn, Malory tests his young hero against *two* 'brothers' rather than one. By this means, the English author can set two kinds of brotherhood – chivalric and biological – in competition with each other.

The *Tale* first compares Gawain and Lancelot soon after Beaumains arrives at court, when both knights protest Kay's mockery of him. As the text puts it, perhaps following its source: 'Thereat was sir Gawayne wroth.' Then, in what looks like Malory's deliberate doubling, the narrator adds: 'And in especiall sir Lancelot bade sir Kay leve his mockyng.' In the same episode, the text grants Lancelot the power of greater personal presence than Gawain by giving him direct speech: 'for I dare ley my hede,' he says, 'he shall preve a man of grete worshyp' (178/28; VII.2). Even more tellingly, when both Lancelot and Gawain privately offer Beaumains meat and drink, the narrator adds a comparative evaluation of his own:

> But as towchyng sir Gawayne, he had reson to proffer hym lodgyng, mete, and drynke for that proffer com of his bloode, for he was nere kyn to hym than he wyste of; but that sir Launcelot ded was of his grete jantylnesse and curtesy. (179/3–6; VII.2)

Over the course of the *Tale*, the narrator's preference for Lancelot over Gawain coincides again and again with Gareth's, and always on the basis of nobility of heart.

Even in its smallest details the text seems to emphasize Gareth's privileging of the French knight over his own family, as if there were a spiritual gravity drawing him to Lancelot and away from the Orkneys. As Gareth is about to leave the court, for example, syntactic as well as narrative force links Arthur and Gawain together as those who are to be left behind, and sets Lancelot apart as the one whom Gareth asks to follow him: 'And ryght so he . . . toke his leve *of* kyng Arthure and sir Gawayne and *of* sir Launcelot, *and prayde hym to hyghe aftyr hym*' (180/25–7; VII.3; emphasis added). Malory is not a consciously 'literary' stylist in the academic rhetorical tradition, and it is risky to credit him with a meticulous or self-conscious use of syntax. Yet in cases such as this one, the almost palpable moral weighting of his characters seems to have compelled his highly nuanced management of language. The double use of the preposition 'of,' slight though it is as a signal of meaning, manages to separate the family

---

[14] 'Source,' 61.

[15] P. J. C. Field attributes this 'disturbance' of the younger brother story to Malory's general tendency in the *Morte* to make 'more of Lancelot's friendship with Gareth' than his sources, and to make 'Gawain's part smaller and less creditable and Lancelot's bigger and more creditable' ('Source,' 61).

group, Arthur and Gawain, from the chivalric group, Lancelot and Gareth.[16]

In what appears to be a systematic doubling at the more obvious level of the folktale plot, Malory gives Lancelot, like Gawain, two chances to do battle with Gareth. In the first encounter, near the beginning of the tale, just after Gareth has left Arthur's court, he takes Lancelot on and does so well in the fight that his opponent is afraid of losing. The French knight stops the battle and compliments Gareth on his prowess. Gareth then asks to be knighted, at which point Lancelot requires that he reveal his identity. This episode of the two 'brothers' battling each other should, in the folkloric pattern, take place near the *end* of the story, as Gareth's comparable fight with Gawain properly does. Yet Malory locates his young hero's contest with Lancelot at the start of his adventure and ties it to Lancelot's knighting of him. If, as seems likely, Malory has invented Lancelot's 'brotherly' role in the *Tale of Sir Gareth*, he has done so to dramatize his belief that the best knights will recognize each others' greatness instinctively and will naturally gravitate towards each other.

Lancelot's second chance to do battle with Gareth occurs during the same great tournament for Lyonesse's hand in which Gareth, perhaps accidentally, strikes Gawain down. In this case, Malory himself may have added the scene we are about to consider in order to further his distinction between Lancelot and Gawain as 'brothers' competing for Gareth. In an encounter that contrasts sharply with Gareth's subsequent attack on Gawain, the *Tale* records a delicate mutual recognition between Lancelot and Gareth, *in spite of* Gareth's disguises. Observing the prowess of the 'knyght with the many coloures,' King Arthur asks Lancelot to take him on in battle. But Lancelot refuses, and for noble reasons. The unknown knight is doing so well that Lancelot does not want to keep him from deserved 'worship'; moreover, he guesses that this may be the best beloved of Lyonesse and decides that the young lover should have the honour for the day. For his part, Sir Gareth, recognizing Lancelot (as in the same tournament he seems not to recognize Gawain), refuses to strike at him: 'No stroke wolde he smyte sir Lancelot.' From this behavior, Lancelot concludes: 'That aspyed sir Launcelot and demed hit sholde be the good knyght sir Gareth' (216/35–6; VII.29). What Malory here dramatizes is a magnetic love between two great knights, drawn to mutual recognition, in spite of armour, in spite of disguises, because of their noble actions. At this moment, the *bel inconnu* love/disguise romance and the younger brother folktale achieve a perfect equilibrium. Gareth as lover-knight reveres and is revered by his chosen chivalric 'brother' even as, in his magical disguise, he successfully competes for his lady love.

---

[16] One hesitates to analyze Malory's prose in microscopic detail in the way one might study the prose style of, say, Flaubert or Henry James. Yet in cases where the author's deepest concerns are at issue, such analysis seem to me both appropriate and rewarding.

Yet, in spite of such moments as this, Malory's poetic *roman d'aventure* never quite manages to erase the family tensions that pull the fairytale down to earth and bind it to historical continuation. Near the end of *Gareth* the narrative records the young hero's definitive rejection of his eldest blood-brother because Gawain is *'evir* vengeable' and given to murder. As the text puts it:

> For *evir aftir* sir Gareth had aspyed sir Gawaynes conducions, he wythdrewe hymself fro his brother sir Gawaynes felyship, for he was *evir* vengeable, and where he hated he wold be avenged with murther: and that hated sir Gareth. (224/20–23; VII.34; emphasis added)

This indirect discourse, almost certainly Malory's invention, is of a piece with the other hints of family tension in the *Tale of Sir Gareth* to which I have already called attention.

By no coincidence, it follows immediately upon another likely Malorian comment:

> For there was no knyght that sir Gareth loved so well as he dud sir Launcelot; and *ever* for the most party he wolde *ever* be in sir Lancelottis company. (224/16–19; VII.34; emphasis added)

The unalterable civilization of the heart binding Gareth to Lancelot – here condensed in a single sentence – is, for Malory, the *raison d'être* for his romance of Gareth. But the text's concomitant assertion that Gareth *'evir* after' avoided his blood-brother undercuts the dominant spirit of romance in the *Tale*, pointing darkly towards the last movement of the *Morte Darthur*. In the end, it will be Gawain's vengeance that forces Lancelot's wrongful banishment after he has mistakenly killed his beloved Gareth. From this teleological perspective Gareth's romance can be remembered only as a passing moment of innocence, chivalric goodness, and glory.

III

We may never know for certain whether Malory invented the *Tale of Sir Gareth* or reshaped an existing narrative to suit his agenda. But we do know, for the most part, which materials he had ready to hand in making his *Tale of Lancelot*. His principal sources were two long French prose romances – the Vulgate Cycle *Lancelot* and the noncyclic *Perlesvaus*.[17] What Malory does in transforming the French texts involves much more than giving, as Eugène Vinaver once argued, a 'moderately continous account of Lancelot's

---

[17] On the sources for the *Tale of Sir Lancelot*, see R. H. Wilson, 'Notes on Malory's Sources,' *Modern Language Notes*, 66 (1951), 22–66; and 'Malory and the Perlesvaus,' *Modern Philology*, 30 (1932), 13–22.

adventures' or 'telling a good story.'[18] In form a more or less self-contained *roman d'aventure* along the lines of the *Tale of Sir Gareth*, the *Tale of Sir Lancelot* gives us Malory's single most concentrated tribute to his hero as the best 'of ony synfull man of the worlde' (520/32–33; XIII.5). It also provides óne of the clearest examples in the *Morte Darthur* of the English author's art in fashioning his eulogy to Arthurian knighthood. By the way he selects and configures the *Tale*'s episodes, he encapsulates in narrative the qualities of heart and the conduct he regards as *essential* to the best knight in the world. His conception of Lancelot, like his view of Gareth, is simple and whole from the outset. It is not the hero who develops and changes in the various adventures Malory chooses to concatenate, but his public's (and the *Tale*'s readers') understanding of what his greatness involves.[19]

The Vulgate *Lancelot*, unlike Malory's English sources, would have offered him a clear directive for celebrating Lancelot as the hero not only of a tale devoted to him but also of the *Morte* as a whole. Most manuscripts of the prose *Lancelot* begin with a rubric explaining what the reader (usually of a large, expensive folio volume) can expect to find:

> *Cest le liure de messire Lancelot du lac* ou que sont contenuz *tous les faiz et les chevaleries de luy* et de lavenement du saint graal & la queste de celuy faite et acheuee par le bon chevalier Galaad Parceval le galois et Boor en la quelle furent les bons chevaliers Lancelot Tristan & Palamides. (Bibliothèque Nationale MS fr. lll, 15th c., fol. 1; emphasis added)

> (This is the book of my lord Lancelot du Lac in which all his deeds and chivalric conduct are contained and the coming of the Holy Grail and his quest (which was) made and achieved by the good knights, Galahad, Perceval the Welshman, and Bors, on which (quest) were the good knights, Lancelot, Tristan, and Palomides.)

In fact, the French *Lancelot* includes not only its hero's 'faiz & chevaleries' but also an elaborate biography: the story of his childhood and youth in a politically unsettled milieu; his indoctrination into chivalry; his entry into King Arthur's court; his passion for Guinevere; the quest of the Grail; sometimes the death of King Arthur.[20] Yet it may well have been the initial

---

[18] *Works*, 3rd ed. (1990), pp. 1408 and 1412.

[19] As Derek Brewer has put it, 'the series of adventures all illuminate the image of Lancelot' ('Malory's "Proving" of Sir Lancelot,' *The Changing Face of Arthurian Romance*, ed. Alison Adams, *et al.* [Cambridge, 1986], p. 128). See also R. H. Wilson, who, on the basis of his source studies, concluded that Malory 'had a mental picture of his character as a whole' early on in his translating project and that he 'deliberately altered the narrative he was translating' in order to further this picture (*Characterization in Malory: A Comparison with his Sources* [Chicago, 1934], p. 49.

[20] The colophon in this manuscript includes under the title 'le liure de messire launcelot' not only all that one finds in the *incipit* but also 'la mort du roy artus en la quelle queste furent plus autres chevaliers. Cest assavoir launcelot du lac tristan et palamides compaignons de la table ronde' (fol. 299^v).

rubric that encouraged Malory, already committed to Lancelot as the 'moste man of worship of the wórlde' (76/38–39; IV.1), to search his French source exclusively for the moral inscape of his hero's 'faiz' and 'chevaleries.'

As if to provide an introduction improving upon the rubricated summary that typically begins the French book, Malory offers his readers two related frames through which to approach his *Tale*. The *explicit* for the preceding tale of Arthur and Lucius reads: 'And here folowyth afftir many noble talys of sir Launcelot de Lake' (146).[21] More importantly, the *Tale* itself begins with a paragraph telescoping Lancelot's lifelong achievement in terms specifically of his 'dedys of armys' and his 'chevalry':

> Sone aftir that kynge Arthure was com from Rome into Ingelonde, than all the knyghtys of the Rounde Table resorted unto the kynge and made many joustys and turnementes. And som there were that were but knyghtes encresed in armys and worshyp that passed all other of her felowys in prouesse and *noble dedys*, and that was well proved on many.
>
> But in especiall hit was prevyd on sir Launcelot de Lake, for in all turnementes, justys, and *dedys of armys*, both for lyff and deth, he passed all other knyghtes, and at no tyme was he ovircom but yf hit were by treson other inchauntement. So this sir Launcelot encresed so mervaylously in worship and honoure; therefore he is the fyrst knyght that the Freynsh booke makyth mencion of aftir kynge Arthure com from Rome. Wherefore quene Gwenyvere had hym in grete favoure aboven all other knyghtis, and so he loved the quene agayne above all other ladyes dayes of his lyff, and for hir he dud many *dedys of armys* and saved her frome the fyre thorow his *noble chevalry*. (149/1–15; VI. 1; emphasis added)

This is a passage as powerful in its economy as any in the *Morte Darthur*. Giving a specific gravity to each word and each proper name as he seeks to capture the essence of his hero's career, Malory invites us to value *all* of Lancelot's 'dedys of armys' and 'noble chevalry,' including his saving of Guinevere, as both indivisible and 'marvelous.'[22] Malory's opening summary, it seems to me, holds within it most, if not all, of the principles governing the *Tale*'s construction. I shall therefore return to it often in what follows, using it as a basis for analyzing several aspects of his 'romance' of Lancelot. Malory's method of searching the Vulgate *Lancelot* and the *Perlesvaus* for materials is, as Larry D. Benson has observed, somewhat forced and mechanical.[23] Yet the very rigor with which he limits his

---

[21] Moving from the plural to the singular, the third tale concludes: 'Explicit a Noble Tale of Sir Launcelot du lake' (Vinaver, p. 173).

[22] The words 'mervalous' and 'mervalously,' connected in the Vulgate Cycle with the divine, are, in Malory, transferred to individual knights, and pre-eminently to Lancelot.

[23] *Malory's Morte Darthur* (Cambridge, Mass., 1976), p. 91.

subject bespeaks the clear, totalizing vision he had of his ideal knight.[24]

At the start of this chapter I suggested that the tales devoted to Lancelot and Gareth follow more the pattern of the twelfth-century French *roman d'aventure* than the biographical model of the Vulgate Cycle. Now I want to take this argument a step further. There is, I think, some reason to suppose that Malory was using either his *Tale of Sir Gareth* or its immediate source as a partial model for framing the *Tale of Sir Lancelot*. Several elements in his presentation of Lancelot, including the configuration of the *Tale*'s first paragraph, seem to align his hero with the 'Fair Unknown' tradition. Whether or not this is the case, Lancelot, as Malory presents him in the *Tale*, achieves an almost mythic splendor. Like Gareth, he stands as an icon of knightly 'bestness,' more or less isolated from the political entanglements governing the *Morte* as a whole.

The opening presentation of Lancelot offers us an event not unlike the moment in Arthur's hall at Pentecost when Gareth, as the 'Fair Unknown,' suddenly arrives and stands up straight before his chosen audience. Lancelot is, of course, not technically a 'Fair Unknown.'[25] He has been mentioned at several points earlier in the *Morte*, and his first appearance at Arthur's court has been noted.[26] Yet before this point in the narrative, he has been mainly part of a large canvas, a background figure in the political history of King Arthur. When Malory introduces him to us at the start of his *Tale*, we know almost nothing of his biographical past, nor do we know how he has learned to be a great knight. Now, suddenly, he emerges, luminous, flawless, complete, as if from the recesses of a half-darkened stage. He simply *is* foremost in 'dedys of armys' 'thorow his noble chevalry.'

Within the *Tale*'s drama, moreover, the motif of deliberately hidden identity, used by Gareth and other 'Fair Unknown' heroes, plays a significant role. Altering his French source at two different points, Malory twice has Lancelot *choose* to disguise himself before performing deeds of arms. In the first instance, in the midst of the *Tale*'s initial long sequence, Lancelot agrees to fight on behalf of King Bagdemagus in a tournament against the king of North Wales. In the French Lancelot, it is King

---

[24] Derek Brewer has called useful attention to the traditional or 'archaic' quality of this sort of 'timeless' characterization. Though my emphasis differs from Brewer's, his reading of the *Tale*, and of Lancelot within it, complements my own. See 'Malory's "Proving" of Sir Lancelot,' pp. 123–136.

[25] Interestingly enough, near the beginning of the 'Fair Unknown' story of the Cote Mal Tayle in Malory's *Tale of Sir Tristan*, Lancelot is loosely linked to the type of the *bel inconnu*. In a passage Malory has translated from the French prose *Tristan*, Mordred rebukes the damsel who mocks La Cote, saying of Lancelot: 'For in lyke wyse syr Launcelot du Lake, whan he was fyrste made knyght, he was oftyn put to the worse on horsebacke, but ever uppon foote he recoverde his renowne and slew and defowled many knyghtes of the Rounde Table' (287/14–17; IX. 4).

[26] The summary description of Lancelot's arrival at Arthur's court, which begins the second tale (Vinaver 111/3–5), does not appear in Caxton. There are, however, various prophetic references to him in the preceding parts of the *Morte*.

Bagdemagus who causes the hero and his horse to be furnished with
'couvertures blanches' (white armature) and it is he who orders a white
shield for him.[27] By contrast, in Malory, Lancelot himself commands
Bagdemagus to provide the white armour and unmarked white shield,
specifically as a disguise:

> 'But, sir, ye shall sende unto me three knyghtes of youres suche as ye
> truste, and loke that the three knyghtes have all whyght sheldis and no
> picture on their shyldis, and ye shall sende me another of the same
> sewte; and we four wyll oute of a lytyll wood in myddys of bothe
> partyes com, and we shall falle on the frunte of oure enemys and greve
> hem that we may. And thus shall I not be knowyn what maner a knyght
> I am.' (155/8–14; VI.6)

Here Lancelot shares Gareth's sense of drama, disguising himself so that a
great chivalric performance will precede the triumphant revelation of his
biographical identity.

In a second episode, imported by Malory from another part of the French
source into his *Tale's* opening sequence, Lancelot saves Kay from three
knights who have attacked him. The two Arthurian knights then retire to
sleep in the same room, after which Lancelot, awakening before Kay, leaves
to seek further adventures. In the Vulgate account, the hero mistakenly
dons Kay's armour rather than his own.[28] Malory's text, by contrast,
implies that Lancelot deliberately takes Kay's armour: 'And sir Launcelot
toke sir Kayes armoure and his shylde and armed hym' (164/1–2; VI.11). In
this case, it is not Lancelot but Kay who explains the advantage to be gained
by what appears to be a playful switching of armour:

> 'Now, be my fayth, I know welle that he woll greve som of the courte
> of kyng Arthure, for on hym knyghtes woll be bolde and deme that hit
> is I, and that woll begyle them.' (164/6–9; VI.11)

In the event, the disguise has just the effect Kay predicts. Lancelot
encounters two different sets of knights, the second of which includes
Ywain, Sagramour, the hero's own foster brother Ector, and King Arthur's
nephew Gawain.

As we would expect, both groups mistake Lancelot for Kay to their
regret. Defeating the knights in the first group, but refusing to reveal
his identity, Lancelot commands that they yield themselves to 'dame
Gwenyvere' as prisoners, telling her that Sir Kay has sent them. The second
encounter is more complicated than the first because the knights involved
include both Lancelot's and King Arthur's family circle. In the Vulgate
account, the fight is given a tragic coloring as Lancelot, failing to recognize
his opponents, seriously wounds them. When at last he learns their identity,

---

[27] Micha, IV, 191.
[28] Micha, V, xcix, 18, pp. 285–86.

he rides away filled with sorrow.[29] And indeed the French Vulgate Lancelot's pain in learning what he has done bears a striking resemblance to Gareth's comparable sorrow in Malory's *Gareth*, after he has struck two of the same knights, Gawain and Sagramour. But when the English author reconfigures the Vulgate scene for his *Lancelot*, there is no such tragic foreshadowing of the misrecognitions that will mark the concluding tragedy of the *Morte*. Lancelot retains *his* disguise, but he explictly knows the identity of at least one of his opponents, Sir Sagramour. And the episode ends not with sadness but with a recognition scene not unlike similar moments in the *Tale of Sir Gareth*. The four knights celebrate the victor as 'a man of grete myght' and Gawain declares: 'I dare ley my hede hit is sir Launcelot: I know hym well by his rydyng' (166/24–25; VI.13).

I do not here have space to explore fully the motif of hidden identity in the *Tale of Sir Lancelot* as it contributes to the triumphant unveiling of the hero's character. Suffice it to say that this motif is a key feature of Malory's romance. In almost every encounter, questions about Lancelot's identity preface or follow the demonstration of redoubtable prowess just as they do in the *Tale of Sir Gareth*. As in *Gareth* too, the motif of hidden and revealed identity heightens the wonder of the observing public and, concomitantly, the lustre of the worship won.

A second principle governing Malory's choice of episodes in the *Tale of Lancelot* and articulated at the end of the *Tale*'s opening summary has to do with Lancelot's love for Guinevere:

> [Because of his great deeds of arms] quene Gwenyvere had hym in grete favoure aboven all other knyghtis, and so he loved the quene agayne above all other ladyes dayes of his lyff, and for hir he dud many dedys of armys and saved her frome the fyre thorow his noble chevalry. (149/12–15; VI.1)

This reference at the end of the *Lancelot*'s introduction to a much later event in the *Morte Darthur* supports Derek Brewer's contention that Malory's storytelling is archaic or traditional. Here, as at many points, the text requires us to 'hold the whole story of Launcelot and Gwenyvere, if only cloudily, simultaneously in mind.'[30] At the same time, the passage also gives what may seem disproportionate attention to the relationship between Lancelot and his queen, and in terms that run directly counter to the French Vulgate Cycle.

As Malory unfolds the nature of Lancelot's 'chivalric' love in the *Tale* (and in the *Morte* as a whole), he substantially revises the French text's account and, concomitantly, its attitude towards women generally. Making the relationship between the queen and her knight neither lustful nor sinful

---

[29] Micha, V, xcix, 27–28, pp. 292–93.
[30] 'Malory's "Proving"' p. 125.

as it is in the French *Lancelot*, Malory characterizes Lancelot's devotion to Guinevere, and hers to him, as singular and unswerving. Augmenting his principal source with several discourses on their love, the English author seems eager to conform their relationship, as far as possible, to the positive concept of *'amour arthurien'* that governs the *Tale of Sir Gareth*. At the same time, perhaps because of the strongly negative character given to the love affair in the Vulgate version, Malory chooses not to dramatize the relationship in Lancelot's tale, permitting only talk about it. Nor does he allow it a sexual component of the kind that delights us in *Gareth*.

Three passages original with Malory in the *Tale of Sir Lancelot* provide important evidence of his effort to ennoble the love relationship between his hero and the queen. The first of these occurs early in the *Tale*, after Lancelot has been captured by four sorceress-queens, including Morgan le Fay, all of whom wish to take him as 'peramour.' While the episode is drawn from the French *Lancelot*, Malory makes several alterations, including Lancelot's response to the queens. In the French version, he simply refuses them, thinking to himself in private that he could never choose one of the 'vielles' (old women) over the queen who is 'fontainne de biauté.'[31] By contrast, Malory has Lancelot publicly celebrate Guinevere's fidelity to King Arthur: 'And as for my lady, dame Gwenyvere, were I at my lyberté as I was, I wolde prove hit on youres that she is the treweste lady unto hir lorde lyvynge' (152/18–20; VI.3).

Not long after this, the Lancelot–Guinevere relationship again surfaces, this time in a conversation between Lancelot and a damsel whom he is serving. The point of the conversation – original with Malory – is specifically Lancelot's courtesy to women in relation to rumours of his affair with Guinevere. The damsel first praises Lancelot in terms that surely echo Malory's idealized conception of him: 'for the curteyst knyght thou arte, and mekyste unto all ladyes and jantylwomen that now lyvyth' (160/35–6; VI.10). She then observes, however, that he is wifeless and that there is gossip as to why this is so: 'hit is noysed that ye love quene Gwenyvere, and that she hath ordeyned by enchauntemente that ye shall never love none other but hir' (160/40–2; VI.10). In response, Lancelot notes the impossibility of stopping rumours, rejects marriage as unsuitable to adventuring knights, and condemns adultery, lechery and love 'peramours' (161/1–11; VI.10). No hint in this passage suggests that Lancelot is dissembling. And indeed all of his conduct in his *Tale* confirms the truth of his assertions.

In a third episode later on in the *Tale*, drawn not from the Vulgate *Lancelot* but the thirteenth-century prose *Perlesvaus*, Guinevere's name is once again invoked. In a macabre scene set in the 'Chapell Perelus' Lancelot takes a sword from the side of the dead Sir Gilbert the Bastard. Just beyond the

---

[31] Micha, IV, lxxviii, 8, p. 178.

chapel yard, a damsel stops him and demands the sword on pain of death. Lancelot, with his customary fearlessness, declares 'I leve hit not . . . for no thretyng' (168/18; VI.15). And, in a response original with Malory, the damsel responds, 'and thou dyddyste leve that swerde quene Gwenyvere sholde thou never se' (168/19–20; VI.15). Asking for a kiss, she is once again rebuffed by Lancelot, at which she tells him that, had he kissed her, he would have died. She then confirms what we already know: 'there may no woman have thy love but quene Gwenyver' (168/31–32; VI.15). Neither of these references to Guinevere appears in the source scene, where the damsel simply avers her own desire for Lancelot. Yet it is worth noting that the treatment of Lancelot's love for Guinevere in the *Perlesvaus* corresponds strikingly to Malory's. In the French text, for example, even after Guinevere's death, Lancelot refuses the love of the 'plus bele damoisele' of a kingdom, explaining his reasons in terms of a perpetual devotion that closely parallels the feelings Malory grants him in the *Morte Darthur*:

> vostre amor aim je mout, e vostre bienvoilance; mais vos ne les autres damoiseles ne devriez jamais avoir fiance en moi, se je metoie si tost en noncaloir l'amor a qui mis cuers estoit obeïsanz, por la valor e por la cortoisie qui herbegie estoit en soi.[32]

> (I greatly like your love and your well-wishing; but neither you nor other damsels should ever have faith in me if I so quickly set aside as nothing the love to whom my heart was obedient on account of the worth and the courtesy lodged in her.)

Despite his known borrowings from it, we cannot be sure just how well Malory knew the whole of the *Perlesvaus* any more than we can know for sure whether or not he had a source for his *Tale of Sir Gareth*. Yet it is not unlikely that at least one and possibly both narratives encouraged him in his own wish to make Lancelot's love for Guinevere a noble rather than an ignoble part of his chivalric character.

To extend his image of Lancelot as a devoted, 'jantyl,' and 'curteys' lover, Malory chooses to include in his *Tale of Sir Lancelot* several episodes demonstrating his hero's solicitude towards women in distress. In these instances (which by no accident foreshadow his rescue of Guinevere from the fire), the text portrays Lancelot specifically as a 'saviour.' In each case, by his prowess and his courtesy, he liberates 'ladies, damsels, and gentlewomen' from oppression of various kinds. The first such episode of this kind occurs just after the *Tale*'s long opening sequence in which Lancelot defeats the cruel Sir Tarquin, thereby freeing many Arthurian knights from prison. The damsel who has led Lancelot to Tarquin's castle now asks for his help against 'a knyght that dystressis all ladyes and jantylwomen, and at the

---

[32] *Perlesvaus*, ed. W. A. Nitze and T. A. Jenkins, 2 vols (Chicago, 1932–7), lines 7535–7538, pp. 315–16.

leste he robbyth them other lyeth by hem' (160/7–9; VI.10). In a striking addition to his source, Malory has Lancelot express outrage at so flagrant a violation against knighthood: 'What? . . . is he a theff and a knyght? And a ravyssher of women? He doth shame unto the Order of Knyghthode, and contrary unto his oth' (160/10–12; VI.10). After Lancelot cleaves his head and neck 'unto the throte,' Malory has the damsel articulate what must have been his own rationale for including and shaping the scene: 'lyke as Terquyn wacched to dystresse good knyghtes, so dud this knyght attende to destroy and dystresse ladyes, damesels and jantyllwomen' (160/29–31; VI.10). What Malory here offers is a morally pointed summary of the episodes he has recorded up to this point in the *Tale*. He intended, the commentary implies, to show his hero devoted equally to saving both men and women.

In a second episode immediately following this one, Lancelot delivers 'three score of ladyes and damesels' from imprisonment and forced labour as silk workers. Since the French *Lancelot* has the hero free both men and women, it seems clear that Malory altered his source specifically for the sake of showing Lancelot's salvation of women.

One further episode showing Lancelot's solicitude for ladies in distress I want to reserve for later discussion. In it, we shall see, Lancelot tries to save a wife oppressed by her husband, but, because of a trick, he fails and the husband manages to cut off the lady's head.

The women whom Lancelot saves both in the *Tale of Sir Lancelot* and in the course of the whole book are generally represented as vulnerable and needy. As such, they fall well within the patriarchal value system of the *Morte Darthur* as a whole. Yet paradoxically, in Malory's account, they also play a major role in generating adventures for the hero, inspiring great deeds, and allowing him to manifest his kindness as well as his strength. Malorian epic heroes, including Lancelot and Gareth, need women as fully as they do men. Above all, Lancelot needs Guinevere, as Gareth needs Lyonesse, in order to practise 'jantylnesse' and draw out fearlessness. In the *Tale of Sir Lancelot*, love catalyzes chivalric greatness in a way that it also does in the *Tale of Sir Gareth* and the *Perlesvaus*, but explicitly does not in Malory's principal French source, the Vulgate *Lancelot*.

In his *Tale*, Malory goes to some trouble to balance Lancelot's kindness to 'jantylwomen' with parallel acts that involve his saving of knights in distress. The *Tale's* first long sequence, condensed from the Agravain section of the Vulgate version, centers on the hero's battle with the cruel Sir Tarquin, who holds a number of King Arthur's knights prisoner. By means of might, Lancelot defeats and kills Tarquin, thereby freeing his friends. Yet, instead of taking the credit directly, he characteristically disappears, leaving Gaheris to release his fellows from the dungeon and thereby eliciting praise in his absence. Within this same sequence, Lancelot also manages to assist King Bagdemagus in the tournament discussed above and, in a comic scene of misidentification, to staunch the wounds of

Sir Belleus (Malory's name for him), whom he has hurt in a sword fight. In this latter case, Malory alters his French source in order to stress Lancelot's saving mercy and his healing power. In the Vulgate episode, Lancelot kills the knight who has attacked him in the dark. Malory's hero, by contrast, both allows the knight to live and stops his bleeding. As is his wont, Malory has the vanquished knight celebrate his conqueror's prowess and gentility:

> '. . . this knyght is a good man and a knyght of aventures . . . And whan that I yelded me unto hym he laffte me goodly, and hath staunched my bloode' (154/4–7; VI.5).

Perhaps the most impressive healing episode is one Malory apparently imported into the Vulgate narrative from the *Perlesvaus*. The English author may well have been drawn to it, in part at least, because it allowed him to show Lancelot as saviour in a particularly touching way. Melyot, who has killed Sir Gilbert, has also been wounded himself. A sorceress has told Melyot's sister that her brother will not be healed unless his wounds are touched with a sword and the bloody cloth in which Sir Gilbert's corpse is wrapped. As Melyot's friend, Lancelot takes upon himself the healing mission, confronting horrific spectacles in the Chapel Perelous in order to secure the requisite sword and cloth. The healing scene involves a sort of miracle:

> Than sir Launcelot lepe unto hym and towched his woundys with sir Gylbardys swerde, and than he wyped his woundys with a parte of the bloody cloth that sir Gylbarde was wrapped in; and anone an holer man in his lyff was he never. (169/6–9; VI.15)

Malory's economy of style intensifies the pathos of the moment even as it dramatizes Lancelot's participation in a miraculous act of healing. It is an act, moreover, which anticipates the magnificent 'Healing of Sir Urry' much later on in the *Morte*.

'. . . At no tyme was he ovircom but yf hit were by treson other inchauntement' (149/8–9; VI.1). Thus, by means of a subordinate clause in the opening paragraph of the *Tale of Sir Lancelot*, Malory introduces a dark note in the otherwise triumphant portrait of his *Tale*'s hero. I want to look now at the workings of treason and enchantment in several episodes of the *Lancelot* as they lead the hero to actual- or near-failures. As with the *Tale of Sir Gareth*, so with *Lancelot*, the ideality of the romance world is systematically countered by a sinister underside. We have already seen how in *Gareth* this darker aspect is tied to the young hero's family, and particularly his eldest brother, Gawain. In *Lancelot*, the evil resides in those who enchant or betray. They are perennially, inexplicably possessed by evil and, at the same time, they either hate or lust for Lancelot. Like Gareth, Lancelot is not undone by the negative forces in his *Tale*. He manages more often than not to escape his predators by wit or daring or the help of others. But not always.

In Malory's implied argument, treachery and enchantment activate the courage of the best knights, but, unlike ordinary threats from attacking knights, they can also undermine their honor. The reason for this, the text suggests, is that those who practice enchantment and treason operate according to systems of value outside the honor code authorized for epic heroes in the *Morte*. It is their manifest 'otherness' in terms of their behaviour that defines them as ontologically evil.[33] In Malory's vision, their presence as 'evil' because 'other' – beyond rational control – absolutely compromises the hero's sense of triumph. It also points, however, indirectly, to the particular character of the *Morte*'s concluding tragedy.

Those who, in the *Tale*, enchant or try to enchant Lancelot include the four sorceress-queens who capture him, and the damsel at the Chapel Perilous, who wants him dead and embalmed so that she can enjoy his body. All five of these ladies use their skill in sorcery, each one hoping to gain Lancelot as paramour. And all of them fail, though not without causing the hero distress. Malory seems to have included both of the sorceress-episodes at least in large part to raise the question of his hero's honour as it relates to his love for Guinevere. In each case, the enchantresses give Lancelot the chance to assert his single-hearted devotion to his queen.

If feminine magic threatens Lancelot, his honor can also be undermined by petty tricksters. Like the enchantresses, the tricksters have no intention of acting honorably. In one episode involving this kind of treachery, a certain Sir Phelot has his wife trick Lancelot into taking off his armour to rescue her falcon.[34] While he is thus unprotected, Phelot rides out, sword in hand, planning to kill him. The episode provides Lancelot (and Malory) the opportunity to condemn as shameful deliberately unequal combat: 'That were shame unto the . . . thou an armed knyght to sle a nakyd man by treson' (170/7–8; VI.16). By extraordinary ingenuity, the details of which I omit for want of space, Lancelot manages not only to save his own life but also to cut off Phelot's head. Defending what he has done to Phelot's wife, he enunciates the chivalric principle permitting his action: 'with falshede ye wolde have had me slayne with treson' (170/28–29; VI.16). As is very often the case with Malory's prose, each word weighs in the denunciation.

---

[33] On this subject, see Fredric Jameson: 'Evil . . . continues to characterize whatever is radically different from us, whatever by virtue of precisely that difference seems to constitute a real and urgent threat to my own existence' (*Political Unconscious: Narrative as a Socially Symbolic Act* [Ithaca, 1981], p. 115). I owe this point as it relates to Morgan le Fay to Geraldine Heng, 'The Feminine Subtext in Malory,' in Keith Busby and Erik Kooper, eds, *Courtly Literature. Culture and Context* (Amsterdam, 1990), p. 293. The 'traitors' Lancelot encounters in his *Tale* and elsewhere participate, like Morgan, in this moral and ontological 'otherness' which perennially threatens Arthurian knighthood. In characters like Gawain, who 'evir' follow their passions rather than the nobler rules of Arthurian chivalry, Malory represents a potentially lethal combination of 'sameness' and 'otherness.' Gawain is more dangerous than either enchantresses or tricksters because he operates *within* the system and yet catalyzes its destruction.

[34] This is an episode that may well be original with Malory; see Wilson, 'Notes,' p. 23.

Moreover, it is just such 'falshede' and 'treson,' with all the pettiness and passion generating them, that will triumph in the concluding sections of the *Morte Darthur*. Sadly, they will coincide with and reinforce the deeper treason of certain of Arthur's knights, who, driven by passion or ambition, will undermine Lancelot from within the system.

On a second occasion along similar lines, a trickster-knight actually succeeds in dishonoring Lancelot by lying to him.[35] In an episode Lancelot himself regards as one of the darkest in the *Tale*, he seeks to help a lady pursued by an armed knight. With righteous indignation, he challenges the knight in noble terms: 'Knyght, fye for shame, why wolte thou sle this lady? Shame unto the and all knyghtes!' (170/43–44; VI.17). The knight defends himself, claiming that his lady has been unfaithful to him. But she protests her innocence and begs Lancelot, 'the worshypfullest knyght of the worlde,' to protect her. Lancelot agrees, and to ensure her safety, he places himself between the two antagonists. But the knight plays a trick. Warning Lancelot (falsely) to look behind him at men-at-arms riding after him, he pulls his horse next to the lady's and cuts off her head. Lancelot's response is astonishingly economical in the precision of its accusation: 'Traytoure, thou haste shamed me for evir!' (171/23–24; VI.17). He then pulls out his sword to slay the knight (whom Malory names Pedevere). Yet, as frequently happens in the *Tale*, Lancelot relents in response to his victim's plea for mercy. As penance, he requires Pedevere to bear the head and body of his lady to Queen Guinevere, and he agrees to do so. The sequence ends with the lady's burial at Rome under the Pope's direction. In this case, Lancelot's mercy to the knight-murderer allows him to repent and reform. In the end, he not only comes dutifully to Arthur's court but also turns to a holy life as a hermit. Yet a woman under Lancelot's protection has died in spite of his efforts. The dishonour he suffers because of Pedevere's unfair play, the text suggests, will permanently mar his reputation as a knight.

IV

As I have been arguing through the course of this chapter, the hero's triumph in both the *Tale of Sir Lancelot* and the *Tale of Sir Gareth* is in part a triumph of generic traditions Malory had discovered in his French sources. Configuring the two tales as Arthurian *romans d'aventure* incorporating the mythos of the *bel inconnu*, Malory provides space for heroic virtue to shine, largely unencumbered by the weight of political and family history. Like the *Tale of Sir Gareth*, the *Tale of Sir Lancelot* concludes in triumph. Coming home two days before Pentecost, still wearing the disguise – armour he had taken

---

[35] R. H. Wilson argued that this episode, usually considered 'of doubtful origin,' is, in fact, based on materials Malory could have found in some manuscripts of the Vulgate Lancelot ('The Prose Lancelot,' pp. 1–13).

from Kay, Malory's hero engenders a joyful recognition scene of the kind that also concludes *Gareth*. Public recognition at King Arthur's court by all those whom Lancelot has defeated, helped, and healed enables the narrative to confirm very simply the worship he has won: 'And so at that tyme sir Launcelot had the grettyste name of ony knyght of the worlde, and moste he was honoured of hyghe and lowe' (173/7–8; VI.18).

By the last movement of the *Morte Darthur*, however, the circumstances of history have overwhelmed the idealism of romance. And the chivalric love binding Lancelot to Gareth bows to death and destruction. In conclusion, let me recall the passage I quoted at the start of this chapter. Lancelot's pain-filled 'Alas' uttered in the wake of his accidental slaying of Gareth records the personal cost of the political upheaval tearing the Arthurian kingdom apart. And it weighs the more heavily because we recall the two tales Malory had devoted much earlier in the *Morte* to the beauty of Lancelot's and Gareth's essential, unalterable nobility of spirit.

10

The Book of Sir Tristram de Lyones

HELEN COOPER

The Book of Sir Tristram de Lyones supplies the middle third of Malory's great work. In the Winchester manuscript, it occupies almost 200 of the 480 surviving folios. It falls to the *Tristram* to display Arthurian chivalry at its height, and it is accordingly by far the most substantial single section of the *Morte*. The layout of the manuscript lends its structure an ease of flow that Caxton's firm chapter divisions and Vinaver's even firmer section arrangement disguise; the three different structural schemes, together with a summary of the contents of the *Book*, are given in an appendix at the end of this chapter.

The story of Tristan as it is best known now could not have made such a substantial contribution in terms of either length or significance. In its twelfth- and thirteenth-century metrical forms, in Anglo-Norman, French and German, it was essentially a story of private love, with little or no Arthurian reference and no apparent scope for displaying the broad patternings of chivalrous action that Malory required. The shift took place in the thirteenth-century French prose version of the *Tristan*, a work so successful that it superseded the original, simpler version for the later Middle Ages. A number of the eighty-odd surviving manuscripts were copied as luxury items in the fifteenth century, and the audience for the work was widened still further through its printing in 1489, just four years after Caxton printed the *Morte* itself. Translations or adaptations appeared in a number of European languages, including several versions in Italian, and it was a major influence on many of the major Spanish and Italian romantic epics of the Renaissance.[1] In Englishing the prose *Tristan*, Malory was bringing insular vernacular literature up to date with the fashions of the continent.

Malory's respect for his source also shows in his treatment of it: although his version is, on Vinaver's estimate, only about a sixth the length of his

[1] Boiardo's *Orlando inamorato*, Ariosto's *Orlando furioso* and Tasso's *Rinaldo* all show clear influence from the prose *Tristan*; so do the Spanish *Amadis de Gaule* and, in a rather different spirit, Cervantes' *Don Quixote*. Spenser also introduces the young Tristram into the *Faerie Queene* (VI.ii).

original, he does not subject it to such drastic processes of excision and rearrangement as he practises elsewhere. Precise source study is none the less unusually difficult for the *Tristram*, because none of the numerous extant French manuscripts represents the particular form of the work known to Malory:[2] his exemplar seems to have had close affinities successively with a number of different surviving manuscripts,[3] and one cannot be certain that any of the extant copies contain the French in just the form that he encountered it. There are none the less a number of changes of emphasis or phrasing that are consistent across the whole of the *Book* but that appear in none of the known French manuscripts, and in these instances it seems safe to speak of Malory's own invention. He greatly reduces the overt sexual element of the prose *Tristan*, for instance, as he also does in his account of Lancelot and Guinevere; it is the intensity and faithfulness of their love, not the tabloid detail of what happened when, that matters. Such changes add up to a significant reinterpretation of the whole work.

The prose *Tristan* provided Malory with what he needed to give the sense of the long continuance of Arthur's reign between the turmoils of its founding and its collapse and downfall. The *Tristram*'s spacious exposition of chivalric action, knightliness and love is essentially celebratory, but it also turns ominous. The key word of the whole *Book* is 'fellowship,'[4] with its sense of knightliness as companionship; but such an ideal also means that the worst treachery may come from within. The incorporation into the fellowship of the Round Table of Tristram, the greatest knight of the world outside Arthur's circle and barely second even to Lancelot, represents the high point of Arthurian chivalry; but it is also the structural watershed of the whole work. Only shortly after this, there occurs the first event in its

---

[2] The difficulty is compounded by the fact that there is still no full critical edition of the prose *Tristan*. The facsimile *Tristan: 1489*, with introduction by C. E. Pickford (London, 1978), is closely cognate to Malory's exemplar for the first part of the *Book*: see Vinaver's and Field's notes, *Works*, p. 1469. An edition of *Le Roman de Tristan en prose* has been under way for some years, the first part edited by R. L. Curtis (Munich, 1963; Leiden, 1976; both reprinted with the third volume, Arthurian Studies 12–14, Cambridge, 1985), later parts by Philippe Ménard and others (Textes Littéraires Français, Geneva, 1987–), but these are not based on manuscripts close to Malory. The essential studies of the French text are by Eilert Löseth, *Le Roman en prose de Tristan*, Bibliothèque de l'Ecole des hautes Etudes 82 (Paris, 189–91), which includes a detailed summary (with variants) of all the complexities of the story; and Emmanuèle Baumgartner, *Le 'Tristan en prose': Essai d'interprétation d'un roman médiéval* (Geneva, 1975), which refines some of Löseth's conclusions about the text as well as constituting a valuable critical study.

[3] See Baumgartner, pp. 85–6 on the affiliation of the manuscripts closest to Malory (Paris, Bibliothèque Nationale fonds fr. 103, 334 and 99; London, British Library Add. MS 5474).

[4] See Elizabeth Archibald, 'Malory's Ideal of Fellowship,' *Review of English Studies*, n.s. 43 (1992), 311–28; and Dhira B. Mahoney, 'Malory's "Tale of Sir Tristram": Source and Setting Reconsidered,' *Medievalia et Humanistica*, n.s. 9 (1979), 175–98, esp. 181. This is one of the most sympathetic studies of Malory's *Tristram*; another is the chapter in Larry D. Benson's Malory's *Morte Darthur* (Cambridge, Mass., 1976), pp. 109–34.

destruction, when Gawain and three of his brothers, Agravain, Gaheris and Mordred, murder the 'good knyght' Sir Lamorak in pursuit of a blood-feud over the death of their father, King Lot; the preceding action in the vendetta, Gaheris' murder of their mother Morgause, Lamorak's mistress, is still more gruesome, though it is accorded less symbolic weight (420/5–18, 427/22–5; X.54, 58; 377/41–378/6; X.24). In the French Vulgate Cycle, it was the quest for the Holy Grail that led to the downfall of the Round Table by showing up the inadequacies of earthly chivalry by contrast with the demands of the divine; Malory, who treats the Grail rather as a celebration of what it is possible for Arthurian knighthood at its highest to achieve, locates the cracks that lead to the break-up of Arthur's fellowship within his great exposition of chivalry in the *Tristram*. In the murder of Lamorak, the worse side of human nature – jealousy, false sense of honour, hatred – wins out decisively over the knightly qualities of recognizing and loving the good; the claims and interests of the kin-group are put above those of loyalty to Arthur and the whole fellowship of the Round Table; and the specific divisions in the fellowship that cause its final downfall – the jealousies of Mordred and Agravain, Gawain's pursuit of a family feud regardless of the cost to Arthur – are most clearly foreshadowed.

The architectonics of the *Tristram* are shaped by these events, and by the final assembly at court which brings together Tristram with his newly reconciled rival Palomides, Lancelot on his recovery from madness, and Lancelot's son Galahad; but these episodes take up little narrative space. Instead, Malory follows the adventures of a large cast of characters, either interlaced or as autonomous narrative blocks within the larger structure of the *Book*, in a way that shows as much concern with definitions of chivalry and models of chivalric behaviour as with event for its own sake. Such an interest was a marked feature of the thirteenth-century development of Arthurian romance; both the prose *Tristan* and the *Lancelot* offered the reader a kind of *education sentimentale*. Malory shifts the emphasis of his own version, however, to stress models of male companionship rather than heterosexual love. His knights ride alone only briefly, between longer periods of keeping company with each other. The 'good knyghtis' seek each other, support each other, praise each other and 'infelyship' with each other, with all the extra dynamism lent by the conversion of the noun to an active verb. The transgressions of this code of companionship, which increase in frequency and violence as the book progresses, therefore become all the more disturbing. Such an effect directly contradicts reader expectations of archetypal Arthurian romance – expectations fulfilled generously by much of the *Tristram* with its narrative imagery of perilous forests and chance encounters. Gratification of this kind may account for the great popularity of the prose *Tristan*; but if Malory offers the reader such satisfaction at the start of the *Book*, he goes on to disrupt it by the substitution of images of dangerous hatred and deliberate injury.

In narrative form, the *Tristram* is a world to itself. For the first time in the

Morte Darthur, the point of view is initially from outside the magic circle of the Round Table, in a way that enhances its desirability. Both the epic action of the establishment of Arthur's kingdom and its downfall, and the tight focus of the early tales of knights errant, would be inappropriate here. Battles are replaced by tournaments, which are poised between being courtly entertainments that attract knights from miles around, sporting events in which league tables of chivalric prowess are drawn and redrawn, and, increasingly as the *Book* progresses, opportunities for the working out of life-or-death rivalries. Formal quests are scarce, their completion even scarcer; Palomides' intermittent pursuit of the Questing Beast, its achievement infinitely deferred, is typical. Tristram, the great huntsman, frequently goes hunting but never catches anything; on several occasions, he is away on the hunt when he is most needed for chivalric action at home.[5] The knights errant who meet each other in the undefined landscape of the dangerous forest and even more dangerous harbourage seldom have any obvious reason for being there, and the adventures that they find along the way often appear less sought after than run into. The downplaying of significant narrative event is reflected in the deferral of climax that results from the frequent diversion of one line of adventurous pursuit by a different one.[6] 'Now leve we . . . and turne we' is a much-repeated formula of transition between different knights, as one path of narrative is abandoned in favour of another in a curiously self-referential mapping of narrative structure onto topography and teleology.

Within this pattern of interlace and broken threads, three inset and more or less self-contained stories stand out like individual letters from a carpet page of the Book of Kells. The first of these is the story of La Cote Male Tayle (*cote mal taillé*, 'ill-fitting coat,' the insulting epithet given him by Kay); this is an account of the proving of a young and untried knight very like that of Gareth. The second is the story of Alisaunder the Orphan, the outline of which provides a close parallel to the enclosing story of Tristram even though Tristram himself does not appear in it. Alisaunder, like Tristram, is a nephew of King Mark, and incurs his uncle's implacable enmity – in Alisaunder's case, because Mark has murdered his father out of jealousy and wants to get rid of the child as well. Alisaunder's mission to avenge his father, a mission parallel to that of La Cote Male Tayle, is never fulfilled; at the very end of his tale, indeed, we are informed briefly that Mark kills him, just as he will eventually kill Tristram, though revenge for both deaths is predicted in the action of Alisaunder's son Bellynger. The third story again offers parallels with Tristram's experiences though its

---

[5] See also Corinne J. Saunders, 'Malory's *Book of Huntynge*: the *Tristram* Section of the *Morte Darthur*,' *Medium Ævum* 62 (1993), 271–85.

[6] See Jill Mann, *The Narrative of Distance, The Distance of Narrative in Malory's Morte Darthur*, William Matthews Lectures (London, Birkbeck College, 1991), pp. 2–8, 23–6, 29–30, on the nature of the*Tristram* narrative.

overt narrative links are rather with the story that follows, the Grail quest, to which it functions in effect as a prologue: this is the account of Lancelot's enchantment-induced affair with Elaine that results in the birth of Galahad.

Galahad's arrival at court, the event that both ends the *Tristram* and begins the *Grail*, is firmly locked into the time scheme of the final books. Most of the events of the *Book of Sir Tristram*, by contrast, can seem rather free-floating within the larger story of Arthur, or even within the time-scheme of the *Tristram* itself. Malory does, however, go to some pains to integrate references to the story of Tristram into the earlier books of the *Morte*, indicating how its events run concurrently with the history of the Round Table,[7] to an extent that suggests that he did indeed think of the *Morte* as a single history and not a series of independent romances.[8] The adventures of Marhalt at the end of *The Tale of King Arthur* conclude with the note that Tristram would kill him 'many dayes aftir' (109/40; IV.28). Tristram takes part in the tournament at the Castle Perilous at the end of the *Tale of Sir Gareth*, before he is installed as a Knight of the Round Table (212/43–213/2; VII.26), and his warm relationship with Gareth in the *Tristram* is rooted in his earlier recognition that Gareth will 'preve a full noble knyght' (217/16–17; VII.29). After the deaths of Launceor and Columbe in the story of Balin, Merlin adds to the inscription on their tomb the prophecy that Tristram and Lancelot will fight there, and the prophecy is recalled at the time of the combat (45/11–18; II.8; 350/7–10; X.5). Their arrival at court together is mentioned after the first round of Arthur's battles against his enemies, including King Claudas, and before the war with Lucius (113/1–5 [excised from Caxton, V.1]); and it is apparently at the same juncture that Elaine comes to the court (485/20–7; XI.6, 7), in the episode that results in Lancelot's madness.[9] Malory accounts for Tristram's absence from the war with Lucius by the fact that he had just left the court with Mark (118/3–5; V.3 (though Caxton's text is confused here)]; 375; X.22). The two major narrative strands of the later part of the *Book* – Lancelot's recovery from madness, and Palomides' final reconciliation with Tristram and his christening – come together as all three come to court for the feast of Pentecost, the same feast at which the young Galahad arrives to start the

---

[7] A number of romance writers, Malory included, saw the intervals of peace in Arthur's pseudo-historical career as the times when the adventures of the knights could be slotted into the time scheme of the chronicles: see Ad Putter, 'Finding Time for Romance: Mediaeval Arthurian Literary History,' *Medium Ævum* 63 (1994), 1–16.

[8] Malory is particularly generous in supplying cross-references to the *Tristram*: see Murray J. Evans, 'Ordinatio and narrative links: the impact of Malory's tales as a "hoole book",' in *Studies in Malory*, ed. James W. Spisak (Kalamazoo, 1985), pp. 29–52.

[9] This chronological ordering is not fully consistent, however, over the *Morte* at large or within the *Tristram* itself, where time can shrink or expand by as much as a generation according to the requirements of the story. As so often, Malory is more concerned with thematic consistency than with precise historical or novelistic verisimilitude: that there should be temporal cross-references matters more than the plausibility of their detail.

adventures of the Grail quest. By the time of the 'Great Tournament' at Westminster (647/1–2; XVIII.23), Tristram is dead.

Malory makes 'no rehersall of the thirde booke' of Tristram (511/4; XII.14), not necessarily because he did not have a copy, but because much of its material duplicates the story of the Grail quest as found in the Vulgate Cycle, and it is that version that he uses next. But Tristram's removal from the narrative does not mean that he is lost from memory: his name continues to echo through the later stages of the work, where it serves as a reminder of the increasing damage done to the fellowship that he so ardently admired. An account of his death is first given in the course of the episode where the company of the Round Table is seen together for the last time, in the middle of the great roll-call of knights who attempt to heal Sir Urry in the *Book of Sir Lancelot and Queen Guinevere*. The whole passage amounts to a reprise of many of the adventures of the knights of the Round Table, but this central part of the roll-call evokes, not the prowess of those present, but the sense of loss for those who were once of the fellowship and who have been killed by treachery:

> Than cam in . . . sir Bellyngere le Bewse that was son to the good knyght sir Alysaundir le Orphelyn that was slayne by the treson of kynge Marke.
>
> Also that traytoure kynge slew the noble knyght sir Trystram as he sate harpynge afore hys lady, La Beall Isode, with a trenchaunte glayve, for whos dethe was the moste waylynge of ony knyght that ever was in kynge Arthurs dayes, for there was never none so bewayled as was sir Trystram and sir Lamerok, for they were with treson slayne; sir Trystram by kynge Marke, and sir Lamorake by sir Gawayne and hys brethirn.
>
> And thys sir Bellynger revenged the deth of hys fadir, sir Alysaundir, and sir Trystram, for he slewe kynge Marke. And La Beall Isode dyed sownyng uppon the crosse[10] of sir Trystram, whereof was grete pite. And all that were with kynge Marke whych were of assente of the dethe of sir Trystram were slayne, as sir Andred and many othir.
>
> Than cam sir Hebes, sir Morganoure, sir Sentrayle, sir Suppynabiles, sir Belyaunce le Orgulus that the good knyght sir Lamorak wan in playne batayle . . . (666/23–40; XIX.11)

Tristram is remembered after his death as being of Lancelot's party, and so his name can be used to enforce the division of the fellowship: in Gawain's feud against Lancelot over the deaths of Gareth and Gaheris, many knights side with Lancelot 'for sir Lamorakes sake and for sir Trystrames sake' (679/36; XX.5). The end of the *Book of Sir Tristram* itself may be a moment of supreme fellowship and harmony, but the stories of Lamorak and Tristram belong with the larger tragic movement of the history of Arthur.

---

[10] The account given in the French would lead one to expect 'cors' (body) rather than 'crosse,' as Tristan suffocates her with his dying embrace.

The sense of fellowship in the *Tristram* is conveyed partly by the sheer number of significant characters, many of whom serve as the focus of narrative interest at some point in the *Book*. The cast is led by Tristram and Lancelot, each of whom is associated with two women, the two Isoldes with Tristram, Guinevere and Elaine with Lancelot. Also important are Lamorak, Palomides and Dinadan, whose major contributions to the whole history of Arthur are, like Tristram's own, largely contained within the *Tristram*; Gareth, Gawain's 'good' brother; and two who appear in the inset tales devoted to them, La Cote Male Tayle and Alisaunder the Orphan. The vast supporting cast includes various kin groups, notably Gawain and his other brothers Agravain, Gaheris and Mordred, and the kin of Lancelot (Ector, Bors, Blamour and Bleoberis), with bit parts for the brothers of Lamorak and Palomides.[11] There is also a series of villains, notably King Mark and Sir Breunis Sans Pité – to whom, as the book progresses, should be added Gawain and his three brothers. Importantly, evil is represented not by anything alien, like the Giant of St Michael's Mount, but by men who belong outwardly to the same social grouping as the heroes.

Tristram himself is largely defined in terms of his relationships with these other knights and of their evaluations of him. Only at the start of the *Book* is he seen acting as an individual, though his actions there establish him as one of the supreme exponents of Malory's great virtue of knightliness. His first notable action is to forgive his stepmother for her attempted murder of him, and to persuade his father to do likewise. The episode sets a model for the rest of the book, of reconciliation as one of the highest of knightly actions, though it is a model that on later occasions Tristram himself has more difficulty in living up to. His stepmother, one could say (neither Malory nor Tristram indulges in psychological speculation), poses no threat to his sense of himself; but with potential rivals in chivalry and love such as Lamorak and Palomides, final harmony is harder to achieve,[12] though all the more striking when it does come. Tristram's credentials in terms of physical prowess are established by his first combat, with Sir Marhalt; by contrast, his characterization as a lover is long delayed. At first Isolde herself is more in love with him than he with her: as Malory puts it in a passage unparalleled in his source, 'The joy that La Beale Isode made of sir Trystrames ther myght no tunge telle, for of all men erthely she loved hym moste' (257/16–18; VIII.23). Yet it is after this that Tristram finds himself

---

[11] On the importance of kinship and the genealogies of the various families, see Ruth Morse, 'Sterile Queens and Questing Orphans,' *Quondam et Futurus*, 2 (1992), 41–53.

[12] Tristram and Palomides' love–hate relationship resulting from their competition as lovers of Isolde is part of the fabric of the whole book, though they are distinguished by Tristram's comparatively greater readiness to show fellowship towards Palomides. Tristram's attitude to Lamorak is more variable, but perhaps because of narrative discontinuities rather than because Malory is making a thematic point (276; VIII.38; 295–6; IX.11).

in sexual rivalry with Mark, the Cornish knight Segwarides and Bleoberis over Segwarides' wife, Isolde apparently forgotten. Only after drinking the love-potion on the ship that is bringing Isolde to marry Mark does Tristram fully reciprocate her love, 'the whyche love never departed dayes of their lyff' (258/15; VIII/24); and even that does not prevent his marriage to Isolde le Blaunche Maynes, Isolde of the White Hands, when he had 'allmoste forsakyn' his own love, a phrase that seems to be Malory's addition (273/16; VIII.36), though the belated memory of Queen Isolde does prevent his consummating the marriage.

Love is surprisingly downplayed in the *Book of Sir Tristram*, in contrast with its supreme importance in the early metrical versions of the story. It can be acute to the point of death: Faramon's daughter dies for love of Tristram and Keyhydyns for love of Isolde, but both deaths occur as asides in the narrative and Malory does not spend either time or sentiment on them (234/17–18; VIII.5; 302/38–40, 474/24; IX.16, X.86).[13] Far greater expression of love comes from the unrequited Palomides than from Tristram; and the most poignant and circumstantial scene of falling in love occurs not in the main narrative but in one of the inset tales, when Alis and Alisaunder see each other:

> And than he put of his helme, and whan she sawe his vysage she seyde,
> 'A, swete Fadir Jesu! The I muste love, and never othir.'
> 'Than shewe me youre vysage,' seyde he.
> And anone she unwympeled her, and whan he sawe her he seyde,
> 'A, Lorde Jesu! Here have I founde my love and my lady! And therefore, fayre lady, I promyse you to be youre knyght, and none other that beryth the lyff.' (397/2–9; X.38–9)

The love of Tristram and Isolde is largely treated as a given of the story, or expressed in action rather than speech: in Tristram's madness when he believes Isolde to be unfaithful, or her attempted suicide when she thinks she has lost him. It is Palomides, not Tristram, who takes 'suche a rejoysynge' at the sight of her watching the tournament at Lonezep

> that he smote downe, what wyth his speare and wyth hys swerde, all that ever he mette, for thorow the syght of her he was so enamered in her love that he semed at that tyme that and bothe sir Trystram and sir Launcelot had bene bothe ayenste hym they sholde have wonne no worshyp of hym. (448/12–16; X.70)

---

[13] The reference in Vinaver's numbering by Caxton's chapter division is IX.17, as he subdivides Cowen's chapter IX.13; Vinaver's numbering from chapter 14 to the end of Book IX is therefore one chapter ahead of the Penguin edition. The confusion arises over a disparity between Caxton's chapter rubrics and his numbering of chapters in the text. All references here follow the numbering of the chapter divisions in Cowen's edition of Caxton.

Here as elsewhere in the *Morte*, however, love comes below chivalric prowess in Malory's scale of values. Isolde's role gets a fair proportion of its significance from the fact that she is, not Tristram's lover, but allied to the 'felyship' round him when they are in England together; and her relationship with Brangwain shows a female version of the same comradeship and concern (in striking contrast to the French versions, where she tries to kill her). Malory gives almost as much narrative emphasis to dismissals of love as to assertions of its power or value: Segwarides comments on his wife's unfaithfulness that he 'woll never hate a noble knyght for a lyght lady' (275/11; VIII.38); and after Dinas's paramour has eloped with another knight and taken two of his hunting-dogs with her, 'sir Dynas cam home and myste hys paramoure and hys brachettes, than was he the more wrother for hys bracchettis, more than for hys lady' (337/24–6; IX.39). Intense love carries with it more sense of tragedy than of fulfilment: most of the lovers of the story – Tristram and Isolde, Lancelot and Guinevere, Lamorak and Morgause – are heading for disaster, and they are backed by a cast of unrequited lovers for whom love is equated with suffering: Palomides, Faramon's daughter, Keyhydyns, the Sir Matto whose only function in the story is to have run mad for love (306/34–7; IX.18). Elaine does, in a way, get her man – Lancelot – but he makes it very clear that she can never have his heart. Dinadan is not going against the tenor of the narrative when he prays God to defend him from love, 'for the joy of love is to shorte, and the sorow thereof and what cometh thereof is duras [=hardship] over longe' (424/11–13; X.56).

Palomides plays the most extensive part after Tristram himself across the whole of the *Book*. He is defined by three roles: as the follower of the Questing Beast; as a pagan who is Christian in heart but who has sworn to fight seven battles before he is christened; and as the hopeless lover of Isolde, forever torn between jealousy of Tristram and admiration of his supreme knightliness. He is second to Tristram in prowess as well as love, from the moment early in the *Book* when Tristram, thinly disguised as 'Tramtrist,' defeats him at the jousts in Ireland out of 'grete envy' of his love for Isolde (239/9; VIII.9), to the concluding combat when Tristram strikes his sword out of his hand. Palomides can overcome Tristram only by unfair means, such as striking him before he is ready (318/25–8; IX.27). The combats between them, even in the ceremonial context of tournaments, can be of extraordinary violence: at the tournament at the Castle of Maidens, Palomides first attempts to ride down Tristram after he has been unhorsed, and then Tristram, rehorsed, 'gate hym by the nek with hys bothe hondis, and pulled hym clene oute of hys sadle, and so he bare hym afore hym the lengthe of ten spearys, and than he lete hym falle at hys adventure' (326/24–7; IX.32). But their relationship is much more complex and interesting than this. Palomides may from time to time declare Tristram to be his mortal enemy, but he is equally ready to acknowledge Tristram's pre-eminence.[14] The ambivalence is acknowledged to Tristram by Palomides himself: 'I wote nat what eylyth me, for mesemyth that ye ar a good knyght; and that ony other knyght that namyth hymselff a good knyght sholde hate you, me sore mervaylyth' (426/29–32; X.57). He is never so happy, or so successful, as when he is in Tristram's company (467/35–6; X.82), and he takes it for granted that Tristram will avenge him if he is killed (435/2–3; X.62). Yet he tries to injure Tristram by treachery at the tournament at Lonezep, and suffers grievously for it: he spends the night weeping, so that when Tristram, Gareth and Dinadan come to wake him in the morning,

> they founde hym faste aslepe, for he had all nyght wacched. And it was sene uppon his chekes that he had wepte full sore.
> 'Say ye nothynge,' seyde sir Trystram, 'for I am sure he hath takyn angir and sorow for the rebuke that I gaff hym, and La Beall Isode.' (462/17–21; X.78)

He has indeed 'takyn sorow': he leaves their company, and laments bitterly that 'I ded nat knyghtly, and therefore I have loste the love of her and of sir Trystram for ever' (467/31–2; X.82). Even this is not final, however. In the closing section of the *Book*, he fights against Tristram the seventh combat that will fulfil his oath and is reconciled with him, Tristram standing as his godfather at his christening. They ride on to Camelot for the feast at which Lancelot returns to the court after his madness and Galahad takes his place in the Siege Perilous: the moment at which not only the various knights and the various threads of narrative of the *Tristram* come together in a climactic display of Christian fellowship, but after which the society of the Round Table is 'departed and dysceyvirde' (510/42; XII.14) as spiritual knighthood pulls away from its earthly forms.

Palomides tries to cheer himself up at one point by assuring Dinadan – and himself – that Tristram is a 'hardyer knyght' than Lancelot (366/28; X.16); but Malory promptly negates the statement by having Dinadan, Tristram's most loyal but also clear-eyed supporter, elicit the information that Palomides and Lancelot had scarcely encountered each other. To everyone else, Lancelot and Tristram are comparable, and Malory never ceases to compare them or to have his other characters speak of them in the same breath. They are first equated early in the book, by a damsel who believes that only Lancelot could have done the deeds of arms that Tristram, as Tramtrist, achieved at the tournament in Ireland; he replies that he

> 'was never of suche proues. But in God is all: He may make me as good a knyght as that good knyght sir Launcelot is' (241/24–6; VIII.10).

The rest of the *Book* chronicles that comparison, both in others' evaluation

---

[14] See e.g. 372/20; X.20; 465/9–11; X.80; 325/5–14; LX.31; 363/32–4; X.14; 465/26–8; X.80.

of the two and in the interweaving of their adventures. Tristram promises early on that 'as sone as I may I woll se sir Launcelot and infelyshyp me with hym, for of all the knyghtes in the worlde I moste desyre his felyshyp' (262/9–11; VIII.27). They have several near-encounters, sometimes anonymously, in which their admiration for each other is increased; but although they are seeking each other – in effect, questing for each other – their meeting is deferred until they encounter by the great stone, the 'perowne,' beside Camelot, by chance in narrative terms (Tristram believes Lancelot to be Palomides) although it has been prophesied by Merlin (45/11–18; II.8). There they fight for four hours before they exchange names, 'and aythir kyste other an hondred tymes' (351/10; X.5). It is in Lancelot's company that Tristram arrives at Arthur's court and is installed as a knight of the Round Table, in the central thematic and narrative climax of the *Book*.

The equivalence of the two knights is mirrored in the parallelism of their stories. This is scarcely surprising when the early form of the romance of Lancelot was partly modelled on that of Tristan, and later the prose *Tristan* was in turn modelled on the prose *Lancelot*; but Malory stresses the similarities further. Each of them loves the queen who is the wife of his overlord; Isolde speaks of the four of them as being the only lovers in the land (267/21–4; VIII.31). Both run mad in the forest, Tristram when he believes Isolde to be in love with Keyhydyns, Lancelot when Guinevere dismisses him for his unfaithfulness with Elaine; both continue to demonstrate their physical prowess even in their madness; and they are finally recognized as they sleep in a garden, Tristram by Isolde, Lancelot by Elaine. It may have been a concern to emphasize these parallels that led Malory to alter the discovery of Tristram in line with the Lancelot episode, and indeed to bring the whole story of Lancelot and Elaine within the larger structure of the *Book of Sir Tristram* rather than attaching it to the Grail. Smaller episodes also mirror each other. In the inset story of Alisaunder, he is kin to Tristram, his beloved Alis is kin to Lancelot. On a number of occasions they take on adventures intended for the other: Tristram fights the thirty knights that Morgan has set to lie in wait for Lancelot (311–12; IX.22); he acts to defend Lancelot's honour from the slur that Gawain is the better knight (422; X.55); and Lancelot rescues Palomides from death even as Tristram is riding 'a grete pace' to do the same (471/25; X.85). Tristram's relationship with Lancelot's kin itself follows the curve of the story from fellowship towards destruction: first, 'for that jantyll batayle' in which Tristram refuses to kill Blamor 'all the bloode of sir Launcelott loved sir Trystrames for ever' (257/10–11; VIII.23), but later 'sir Launcelottis bretherne and his kynnysmen wolde have slayne sir Trystram bycause of his fame' (476/43–4; X.88).

Lancelot provides the highest model by which any knight can be evaluated, and that Tristram is effectively his peer marks him out as extraordinary in Malory's hierarchy of knightliness. In decisive contrast,

Tristram's closest companion in the later parts of the *Book* is an apparently inadequate sidekick, the delightful 'good knyght' Dinadan. He is determined to steer well clear of love (and succeeds), and almost equally determined to steer well clear of violence (at which he fails miserably). He has the potential for becoming a kind of Sancho Panza; he has indeed often been read as someone who undermines the high chivalric ideology of the Arthurian world, who provides a critique from within it or below it just as the spiritual demands of the Grail quest will show its inadequacies from the divine perspective. Yet this is not how Malory presents him:[15] the numerous authorial comments on the quality of his knighthood are all of them positive, as if to counter any suspicions that his refusal to throw himself in the way of danger might cause. He knows very well that he does not have extraordinary strength and is therefore likely to get hurt, so his courage represents an impressive overcoming of fear, not the casual self-confidence of the physically supreme. He has to be bullied into some of his greatest exploits, such as supporting Tristram against Morgan's thirty knights; but when there is no one to provide the bullying, he will accept superior odds unhesitatingly. He first enters the narrative to request a joust with Tristram in which he knows he will be defeated; when the formidable Palomides is seeking the wounded Tristram to destroy him, Dinadan is prepared to take him on, to 'do to hym what I may, and yf I be slayne ye may pray for my soule' (327/24–5; IX.33); and he would rather tackle Lancelot himself (the equivalent of throwing yourself in front of a Sherman tank) than allow the wearied Tristram to be shamed (458/4–26; X.76). His love for and service of Tristram is his primary motivation: exceptionally in the work, he belongs to no kin group, and although he is a Knight of the Round Table (423/44; X.56) he is never seen acting as part of Arthur's affinity, the immediate support group around the king. His independence in choosing whom he serves reinforces the sense of moral probity that Malory has him carry.

Dinadan is the only one of Malory's male characters who consistently understands how to relate to people other than by combat or kinship; he operates by intelligence and sympathy rather than brute force. He is also given a degree of inner life – of motivation and of unspoken thoughts – unusual in the *Morte*. He knows when not to speak, as in the restraint of his answer to Tristram over Palomides' prowess at the tournament at Lonezep:

> 'Sir, hit is his day,' seyde sir Dynadan, and he wolde sey no more unto sir Trystram, but to hymself he seyde thus: 'And sir Trystram knew for whos love he doth all this dedys of armys, sone he wolde abate his corrage.' (448/28–31; X.70)

---

[15] Vinaver is among the most ardent advocates of Dinadan's role as constituting an attack on chivalry: see his notes in the 3rd edition of the *Works*, pp. 1474–5, 1487–8, 1491–2, 1511–3. Baumgartner rejects such a reading of him even in the French prose *Tristan*, believing that he functions rather to distinguish true knight-errantry from false (*Le Tristan en prose*, pp. 183–7).

Yet he will incur Tristram's anger himself so as to needle him into fighting, for the greater good of his reputation (450/36–451/9; X.71–2). He alone can persuade the angry Lancelot to confide in him out of 'grete truste' (381/44; X.27); and their intimacy shows itself more light-heartedly in that he is quite prepared to address Lancelot with the insulting 'thou' and to call him an 'olde shrew' (407/22; X.47). Lancelot, whom Malory elsewhere always takes seriously, responds with his one practical joke of the whole work, when he disguises himself as a damsel in order to get close enough to the wary Dinadan to unhorse him (410; X.49).

Dinadan's most significant function, however, is to serve as a touchstone of good knightliness for Malory's other characters. His down-to-earth streetwiseness is offset by an unerring and emphatically expressed sense of right and wrong. His own qualities are recognized both by narrative and spoken comment. Malory notes in his own voice that he is 'a good knyght on horsebacke' (357/26; X.10), and 'the meryste knyght amonge felyship that was that tyme lyvynge' (407/10–11; X.47). Tristram, who 'in aspeciall loved sir Dynadan passyngly well' just as Dinadan loves Tristram, speaks of him as 'a noble knyght of his hondis'; and the court 'was glad of sir Dynadans commynge home, for he was jantyll, wyse and a good knyght' (373/1–3; X.20, 423/19; X.56). 'All good knyghtis lovyth his felyship' in a way that gives him a special place in the book's great study of knightly comradeship (423/20; X.56). There are however exceptions to this warmth of response. Dinadan himself

> had suche a custom that he loved all good knyghtes that were valyaunte, [but] he hated all tho that were destroyers of good knyghtes. And there was none that hated sir Dynadan but tho that ever were called murtherers. (379/29–32; X.25)

Those who are most called murderers by Malory are Gawain and his brothers, the killers of Lamorak, whom Dinadan greatly loves; and he himself suffers the same fate, at the hands of Agravain and Mordred, whom he saved from Breunis Sans Pité:

> And aftir, in the queste of the Sankgreal, cowardly and felonsly they slew sir Dynadan, whyche was a grete dammage, for he was a grete bourder and a passynge good knyght. (379/42–4; X.25).[16]

Dinadan is the first to point out the dangers of Agravain and Mordred's hatred of Lancelot (428/20–4; X.58), which is later to cause the destruction of Arthur and the Round Table; but the proleptic murder of Dinadan –

---

[16] A single French manuscript adds more detail of the events leading up to Dinadan's death. In despair after the murder of Tristan, he attempts to wreak vengeance on Mark but fails. After being mortally wounded by Agravain and Mordred, he dies in Lancelot's arms, and is buried beside Palomides (Bibliothèque Nationale ms fonds fr. 24400; summarized in Baumgartner, *Le Tristan en prose*, pp. 257–9).

reported even before their killing of Lamorak – is, apart from Merlin's early prophecies, the first premonition of the collapse of the chivalric order.

The gulf between good knights and others – characterized most often as murderers, traitors, cowards, or false or shameful knights – is exemplified throughout the *Book*. Gawain and his brothers start on a par with Arthur's other knights, but as the work progresses Gareth is increasingly marked out as different. He emphatically dissociates himself from the actions of his brothers, and his moral distance from them is recognized by his fellows: in Dinadan's words: 'Sir Gawayne and his bretherne, excepte you, sir Gareth, hatyth all good knyghtes of the Rounde Table' (428/18–20; X.58). The other villains of the *Book* – Mark, his nephew Andret, and the thug errant Sir Breunis Sans Pité – are treated as villainous from their earliest appearances. Mark may come to Arthur's court, but he can never be assimilated into its fellowship; Breunis is always an outsider, encountered only in fleeting moments in the forest, where his unknightliness is matched only by his skill in speedy escapes. Mark's readiness to say fair words while planning evil deeds is especially condemned, and gets an appropriate come-uppance in the insulting lay that Dinadan composes and has sung at the Cornish court. Where the good knights promote fellowship through love for each other, the villains are marked by destructive hatred, unable either to love the good or to put any social or political bonds above their own jealousy.[17] Nor is good knightliness necessarily the norm: jealousy of Lancelot's prowess makes him widely 'behated' even though his magnanimity should make him loved by all good knights. The female equivalent of the false knights in the *Tristram* is Morgan, an exemplar of treason in her desire to destroy Lancelot and Arthur, and an 'enemy to all trew lovers' (270/33; VIII.34) both in her attempts to reveal Lancelot's love for Guinevere through the magic horn and emblematic shield and in her lust for Lancelot and Alisaunder – a lust that serves to define true love by contrast just as murder is contrasted with true knightly prowess.

Much of the *Tristram* is a book of concealed identities and mistaken purposes. Tristram fights Lancelot in the belief that he is Palomides;

---

[17] There is one very curious episode in the *Tristram* in which an anonymous 'stronge knyght,' later identified as Lancelot, pursues a career of destructive carnage in the forest similar to that of Sir Breunis (347–8; X.3). The reason for it seems to lie in Malory's fondness for explanation and identification: in the French, the knight is never identified. Malory's naming of him seems to be designed to explain his strength in combat; the whole episode is profoundly atypical of Lancelot's actions and knightly *credo* everywhere else. Unlike the murder of Lamorak it has no reverberations elsewhere in the work, and such insulation from the rest of the narrative prevents it from functioning as another example of villainy located this time within the model of all chivalry, Lancelot himself. It does, however, furnish ammunition for critics who wish to see the whole *Tristram* as an indictment of the shallowness of chivalric values: see e.g. Maureen Fries, 'Indiscreet objects of desire: Malory's "Tristram" and the necessity of deceit,' in *Studies in Malory*, ed. Spisak, pp. 87–108. For a contrary (though still unresolved) reading, see Jill Mann, *The Narrative of Distance*, p. 25.

Morgan's magic horn ends up in the wrong court; Breunis Sans Pité is never recognized until it is too late; Lancelot makes love to the wrong woman, twice. With so many of the knights concealing their names from each other for so much of the time, the suggestion of unexpressed meaning that Malory's style can convey in the closing books here tends to be transferred to the surface of the narrative: there is more going on than meets the eye of the beholding knight, but the reader is likely to be in the secret. This might seem to imply dramatic irony, but such effects are only brief and highly localized. The result is rather an avoidance of irony, a stylistic clarity that says just what it means and no more – or, very often, rather less. Malory's mastery of the laconic style is strikingly demonstrated in the *Tristram*:

> And so this damysell cam by sir Palomydes, and he and she had language togyder whych pleased neythir of them. (330/6–7; IX.35)

> And then he raced of his helme and smote of his hede. Than they wente to souper. (401/4–5; X.41; cf. 402/41–3; X.43]

The book is especially rich in concise antitheses with a proverbial resonance to them:

> Thoughe there were fayre speche, love was there none. (246/28; VIII.14)

> He that hath a prevy hurte is loth to have a shame outewarde. (246/32–3; VIII.14)

> 'Thoughe a marys sonne hath fayled me now, yette a quenys sonne shal nat fayle the!' (269/38–9; VIII.33)

> Many spekyth behynde a man more than he woll seye to his face. (279/10–11; VIII.40)

> [Tristram] seyde but lytyll, but he thought the more. (299/38; IX.14)

> Harde hit ys to take oute off the fleysshe that ys bredde in the bone. (337/16–17; IX.38)

> Manhode is nat worthe but yf hit be medled with wysdome. (428/33–4; X.59)

Many of these are without parallel in the French, as are the similes Malory adds for his knights, as they charge like thunder (249/32, 298/11; VIII.17, IX.13) or clash like wild boars (298/14, 503/20; IX.13, XII.7) – phrases where the formulaic quality emphasizes the closeness of each encounter to a single model of chivalric combat. Elsewhere he adds authenticating detail, such as that Tristram and Segwarides' wife 'soupede lyghtly' before going to bed, and are found by her husband 'by candyll-lyght' (245/24, 33; VIII.14); or the notorious twenty thousand pounds that the search for the mad Lancelot costs Guinevere (505/19; XII.9).

Such stylistic features reflect a broader realism in the *Tristram*, a realism that co-exists with the fantastic encounters of unnamed knights errant in forest glades. Malory moves into the present tense of his own world for his praise of Tristram as the founder of the art of hunting, or for his lament on the evils of sickness for a prisoner (232/10–20; VIII.3; 333/11–18; IX.36). He writes the detailed accounts of tournaments for a culture where such events were of immediate importance.[18] The values celebrated in the Arthurian world had become the institutionalized chivalric fantasies of the later Middle Ages; but in so far as the *Morte Darthur* is a book about the state of England, the *Tristram* offers one of the closest analogies to the troubled fifteenth century. The supernatural is limited to a handful of episodes (only the love-potion and Morgan's horn outside the story of Lancelot and Elaine); the motivating force of the many actions instead becomes a web of shifting allegiances, inspired most often at the start of the *Book* by motives of political loyalty or personal admiration, but giving way increasingly to hatred and envy – words that begin to take over dominance from 'fellowship.' The *Tristram* sets up a pattern of affinities, sometimes feudal (headed by Arthur or Mark), but often family-based, around Lancelot, the sons of Lot (including Gawain) or of Pellinor (including Lamorak). All these groups can be at odds with each other, or within themselves. Arthur himself is incapable of controlling the feud between the families of Lot and Pellinor, even though all the protagonists belong to his own affinity, and Gawain's behaviour as an over-mighty baron in the *Tristram* costs the king support in the final feud with Mordred. At this earlier point in the work the political issues do not affect the crown itself; but the Wars of the Roses were fuelled by just such local faction-fighting and private vendettas as the *Tristram* shows getting increasingly out of hand. The models of good and bad knighthood offered by the book were not the escapism of an age of declining chivalry, but an implied appeal to those who wielded political and military power at any social level to use it for good. Malory's recalling of the deaths of Tristram and Lamorak in the last books of the *Morte* is not just an expression of nostalgia, but a recognition of the complexities of the political turmoil in which he and his readers had played a part.

APPENDIX. THE STRUCTURE OF THE *TRISTRAM*

The length of the *Book of Sir Tristram* makes subdivision essential. Caxton breaks it into four books and 201 chapters, including a mammoth 88-chapter tenth book; Vinaver offers instead a fifteen-part division intended to fit the outlines of the individual stories more closely. In the notes to his three-volume edition, he states that Malory 'indicated here and there the

---

[18] See Benson, *Malory's Morte Darthur*, pp. 137–45, 167–85.

main divisions of the narrative, and by following the *explicits* and *incipits* in the Winchester MS it is possible to split the whole work into a number of well-defined sections' (III.1444). One cannot be certain that the manuscript divisions are in fact authorial, though they are certainly more so than Caxton's arrangement; but Vinaver's implication that the divisions of his own edition follow those of the manuscript is to an extent misleading. The *Tristram* section of the manuscript is divided up by 38 large capitals, often accompanied by transition formulas and occasionally also by blank lines. Caxton always supplies chapter divisions at these points, but only half of Vinaver's section divisions coincide with the divisions indicated by such initials in the manuscript (his sections II, VI, IX, X, XI, XII and XIII do not), and on several occasions he does not even give a paragraph break at these points (at the end of Winchester's 1, 2 and 10). Elsewhere he tidies up or redivides the transition formulas, and capitalizes them too.

The table below outlines the structure of the *Book of Sir Tristram* as the Winchester manuscript presents it, with two emendations. One capital, corresponding to the start of Caxton's X.35, seems to be a scribal error resulting from the confusion of Anglides' spoken 'Now –' with the opening of the standard transition formula, and is omitted. I have on the other hand included a division at one point (22, the middle of Caxton's X.40) where there is a major transition formula of the kind usually signalled by a capital but where none is on this occasion provided. I have retained one capital that does not mark a significant narrative division, at the end of Winchester's section 14 (Caxton's IX.43), where the curious mid-episode colophon presumably marked a volume division in Malory's French source (or its own exemplar). I have grouped together (as 12 [+ 1], 22 [+ 5]) capitals that mark off the separate days of play at the tournaments at the Castle of Maidens and Surluse; the capital that introduces the second day of the tournament at Lonezep, however, also marks the shift from Palomides' companionship with Tristram to his hostility, so I have treated it as a full structural division.

This pattern of capitalization results in 31 sections as given below. My numbering of the Winchester sections is on the left, headed 'MS'; the Caxton numbering as given by Cowen is in the next column, with an asterisk to show where Vinaver's text adds one to the chapter numbers (see note 13); the corresponding text of Vinaver's edition is given in the third column, and a plot summary on the right.

MS	Caxton	Vinaver	Summary
1	VIII.1–6	I Isolde the fair 229/1–236/mid-3	Tristram's birth and upbringing; preparations for the fight with Marhalt
2	VIII.7–28	I contd. 226/3–263/mid-5	Tristram's combat and sojourn in Ireland; rivalry over Segwarides' wife; arrival in Cornwall with Isolde

MS	Caxton	Vinaver	Summary
3	VIII.29–35	I contd. 263/5–272/34	Isolde's marriage to Mark and abduction by Palomides; Lamorak and Morgan's horn; Tristram taken with Isolde
4	VIII.36–7	I concluded: II Lamorak de Galys 272/35–274/38	Tristram's marriage to Isolde le Blaunche Maynes and its report at court; Lamorak's shipwreck in Nabon's country
5	VIII.38–41	II concluded III incipit 274/39–282/4	Tristram in Nabon's country; reconciliation with Lamorak
6	IX.1–4	III La Cote Male Tayle 282/5–287/21	La Cote Male Tayle's initial adventures
7	IX.5–9	III concluded 287/22–294/14	La Cote Male Tayle joined by Lancelot; concluding adventures
8	IX.10–*13	IV Tristram's Madness 294/16–299/16	Miscellaneous incidents concerning Tristram, Lamorak and Palomides
9	IX.*14–*21	IV contd 299/17–310/34	Tristram's madness, recovery and exile from Cornwall
10	IX.*22–*24	IV contd 310/35–315/mid-26	Tristram's defeat of 30 knights; warned against Morgan by Gawain
11	IX.*25–*28	IV concluded 315/26–320/32	Preparations for the tournament at the Castle of Maidens
12 [+1]	IX.*29–*35	V Castle of Maidens 320/36–331/31	Two days of tournament
13	IX.*36–*39	V concluded VI Round Table 331/32–339/12	Imprisonment of Tristram, Palomides and Dinadan by Darras; Mark's jealousy; their release
14	IX.*40–*43	VI contd 339/13–343/26	Tristram and Morgan
15	X.1–6	VI concluded 343/27–352/43	The combat of Tristram and Lancelot; Tristram joins the Round Table
16	X.7–10	VII King Mark 353/2–358/10	Mark comes to England
17	X.11–15	VII contd 358/11–364/35	Mark's arrival at Arthur's court
18	X.16–27	VII contd 364/36–382/12	Adventures of Lamorak and Palomides; Gaheris' murder of Morgause; Mark's letter to Arthur and Dinadan's revenge
19	X.28–3	VII concluded 382/13–388/16	Tristram in Cornwall; Dinadan's lay sung to Mark
20	X.32–5	VIII Alexander the Orphan 388/18–392/26	Birth and knighting of Alisaunder

MS	Caxton	Vinaver	Summary
21	X.36–mid-40	VIII concluded 392/27–398/42	Alisaunder's adventures, love and death
[22] [+5]	X.mid-40–49	IX Tournament at Surluse 399/2–411/2	Announcement of tournament and the various days' jousting
23	X.50	IX explicit X Joyous Gard 411/3–412/36	Tristram imprisoned by Mark
24	X.51	X contd 412/37–415/9	Tristram released
25	X.52–4	X contd. 415/10–420/22	Tristram and Isolde to England; news of Lamorak's death
26	X.55–73	X concluded XI Red City XII Tournament at Lonezep 420/23–453/33	Adventures of Tristram, Dinadan, Palomides and Gareth, including Palomides' exploits at the Red City, and the first day's jousting at Lonezep
27	X.74–88	XII contd XIII Sir Palomides 453/34–477/14	Palomides' hostility to Tristram; they agree to fight
28	XI.1–14	XIV Launcelot and Elaine 477/16–495/27	Lancelot's affair with Elaine, to the healing of Percival and Ector by the Grail
29	XII.1–8	XIV contd 495/28–504/18	Lancelot's madness, recovery, and discovery by Percival and Ector
30	XII.9–10	XIV concluded 504/19–506/11	Lancelot returns to court
31	XII.11–14	XIV explicit XV Conclusion 506/12–511/10	Palomides' combat with Tristram and christening; Galahad to court

11

Malory and the Grail Legend

JILL MANN

The Grail first enters literature in the *Conte del Graal* of Chrétien de Troyes.[1] The title of this romance, which is given to it by Chrétien himself (line 66), seems to invest the Grail with a central importance. But when it makes its first appearance in the narrative, it is simply one of a number of striking features in the courtly procession which passes before the astonished Perceval as he sits at dinner talking to his host, the maimed Fisher King (lines 3190–253). First comes a boy holding a white lance, its point constantly dripping blood which falls on the boy's hand. Then there follow two other boys, holding candlesticks of gold, inlaid with black enamel-work. Behind them comes a girl, holding between her hands 'un graal,' made of gold and set with precious stones, which emits a light so brilliant that it eclipses the twenty candles in the two candlesticks. Then comes another girl, carrying a silver carving-dish. One after another all these figures pass before Perceval and disappear into another room. With each course of dinner, the grail (and by implication the rest of the procession) passes by again.

To a modern reader, the most disconcerting feature of this narrative sequence is probably the use of the indefinite article: '*a* grail,' not '*the* Grail.' Not, that is, a unique object, designated by a proper name which labels it while leaving it uncategorized, enigmatic in nature. Instead, it is one of a class, even if it is a particularly splendid example of its kind. The definite article used in the title of the romance turns out not to indicate the grail's uniqueness, but simply to refer to the particular grail which figures in this story. 'Graal' is a rather uncommon word in Old French, but it is attested, with the meaning 'bowl' or 'dish'.[2] Helinand of Froidmont, a Cistercian monk writing in the late twelfth century, in the course of discussing the Grail legend defines a grail (Latin *gradalis, gradale*) as 'a wide and slightly hollow dish,' on which luxurious foods are served up to

[1] *Le Roman de Perceval ou le conte du Graal*, ed. Keith Busby (Tübingen, 1993). Subsequent references to the line-numbers of this edition are given in the text.
[2] Tobler-Lommatzsch, *Altfranzösisches Wörterbuch*, s.v. gräal.

the wealthy.[3] Chrétien's Grail is thus not the chalice or goblet familiar from Pre-Raphaelite painting or Wagnerian opera; nor is there anything intrinsically 'holy' about it. It is not carried by a priest or an acolyte, as would be proper for an object of a liturgical or religious nature, but by a girl. And however wonderful is the light that emanates from it, it is not as evidently puzzling as the bleeding lance which precedes it, and which seems to call even more urgently for some kind of explanation.

What gives the Grail its importance in Chrétien's romance is not its status as a sacral object, nor a previous history in Celtic myth or Christian legend, but Perceval's failure to ask about it. With the best of motives, he restrains his curiosity in obedience to the instructions of Gornemant, the 'preudome sage' who had earlier impressed on him that he must not speak too much (lines 3244–7; cf. lines 1648–56). Next day, he awakes to find the castle deserted, and on riding away he meets a girl lamenting over the headless body of a knight, who questions him closely on the previous night's events. When he reveals that he had put no question to his host about the procession that had passed before him, she denounces him as 'Perceval the wretch'; had he done so, she tells him, the Maimed King would at once have been cured. What is more, she continues, further ills will befall him and others as a result. And she blames his failure on his sin in leaving home and abandoning his mother, who has since died of grief (lines 3545–611). This denunciation is later repeated and extended by the Loathly Damsel who accuses Perceval in front of Arthur's court (lines 4610–83). The enigma of the Grail is thus a matter of narrative function, rather than of the properties of an object: the enigma lies in the contrast between the unambiguous boldness with which Perceval's guilt is asserted, and the difficulty of defining this guilt in terms of normal moral criteria. The most obvious reason for this difficulty is that the sequence of cause and effect which binds sin to disastrous consequence is obscure. Abandoning his mother may in itself be reprehensible, but it is difficult to see how this could have become the *cause* of his failure to ask the question; nor is it possible

---

[3]   *Chronicon, Patrologia Latina*, 213, col. 815: 'Gradalis autem sive gradale Gallice dicitur scutella lata, et aliquantulum profunda; in qua pretiosae dapes cum suo jure divitibus solent apponi gradatim, unus morsellus post alium in diversis ordinibus; et dicitur vulgari nomine graalz, quia grata et acceptabilis est in ea comedenti; tum propter contentum, id est ordinem multiplicem pretiosarum dapum.' ('"Gradalis" or "gradale" is in French the name of a wide and slightly hollowed dish, in which rich foods and their sauce are customarily carried to the wealthy in stages, one delicacy after another in different courses, and it is called "grail" in the common tongue because it is pleasing ("grata") and welcome to the one who eats from it, and also on account of its content, that is, the varied succession of rich foods.') One may suspect that Helinand's explanation of why a grail is so called is largely derived from a combination of close reading of Chrétien's *Perceval* and the employment of etymological ingenuity; but it is noteworthy that he does not take the word to be a proper name, even though the rest of his account shows that he is familiar with the legend that identifies the grail in the Perceval story with the vessel used to collect Christ's blood.

to understand how asking the question might have brought about the Maimed King's cure. In the second place, it seems unfair that Perceval should incur such blame when his fault is the result of trying his hardest to practise the rules of conduct which he has been taught.

The enigma of Perceval's guilt is never resolved. But a clue to understanding its significance within the narrative is supplied by Chrétien's own comment on Perceval's resolute silence: 'I fear he may suffer for it, because I have heard it said that one can as easily be too silent on occasion as speak too much' (lines 3248–51). The question that Perceval is reproached for having failed to put is not 'what is the grail?,' but 'who is served from the grail?' (lines 3244–5, 4660–1, 6379–80). This question is answered directly and without ceremony at a later point in the romance (lines 6417–31), when a hermit tells Perceval that the grail carries a single consecrated wafer which for twelve years has been the sole sustenance of the Fisher King's father (who, like the hermit himself, is revealed to be Perceval's own uncle). It is thus not the answer to the question, but the *timing* of the question, that is the heart of the mystery. That is, the mystery which Perceval fails to penetrate is the mystery of courtly tact – the knowledge of when to speak and when to be silent. This is a knowledge which resides, not in rules that can be taught and learned, but in the instinctive responses of the courtly heart. The art of speaking and of being silent is one of the rituals and practices of court life which the Grail procession invests with mystique and wonder, a wonder heightened by the fact that Perceval has been brought up as a rustic in the woods, far away from civilized life. If the bleeding lance is a 'marvel' (line 3202), so too is the lavish array of exotic fruits, wines and spices served at dessert: 'the young man marvelled greatly at all this, since he was unschooled in it' (line 3334–5). Courtly life becomes the object of awe and admiration as it is presented through the eyes of the untutored youth.

The consecrated wafer is the only feature in Chrétien's narrative which connects the Grail with religious ritual. Whether he intended to develop this aspect of the Grail must remain uncertain, since he left the *Conte del Graal* unfinished. But the various poets who wrote continuations of his romance seized on this detail and linked it with the enigmatic bleeding lance, in such a way as to create a religious pseudo-history for both objects.[4] The Grail, now first called 'the holy grail' (p. 112), is said to be the vessel in which the blood flowing from the crucified Christ was collected (p. 160); the lance is identified as that with which Longinus pierced Christ's side (pp. 131–2). But at the same time the décor of the Grail procession remains courtly rather than religious: the Grail, and sometimes the lance too, is still carried by a girl (pp. 112, 180, 191), and it still forms part of the ritual of a

---

[4] *The Continuations of the Old French Perceval of Chrétien de Troyes*, ed. William Roach *et al.*, 5 vols in 6 (Philadelphia, 1949–83). The *Continuations* are also accessible in a translation-cum-summary appended to the translation of Chrétien's *Perceval* by Nigel Bryant (Cambridge, 1982). References in the text will be to the page-numbers of this translation.

courtly dinner, on one occasion serving up seven courses of food while magically circulating among the diners of its own accord (p. 130). Meanwhile, the image of the bleeding lance, the agent of wounding which is itself wounded, is doubled in the appearance of a broken sword, which lies on the breast of a dead man whose bier is carried in the procession (p. 112). Gawain twice tries to mend this broken sword and fails (pp. 113, 131); Perceval tries and succeeds (p. 192).

The *Continuations* of the *Conte del Graal* thus adumbrate a religious history of the Grail, but fail to co-ordinate the bric-à-brac of proliferating imagery into a meaningful whole. It was Robert de Boron's *Estoire du Graal* which first shaped these scattered elements into a coherent narrative, by identifying the Grail as the vessel used by Christ and his disciples at the Last Supper, later passing into the hands of Joseph of Arimathea, who collected in it the blood from Christ's body as he prepared it for burial.[5] The *Estoire* then goes on to relate how the Grail then became an object of veneration, the centre of a cult maintained by Joseph's descendants. It is this conception of the nature of the Grail and its history which reappears in the French prose *Queste del Saint Graal*, the immediate source of Malory's *Tale of the Sankgreal*.[6] Towards the end of this narrative, Galahad, Perceval and Bors, along with nine other knights from other countries, see the Grail in the castle of Corbenic; it is again accompanied by the bleeding lance, which is now set upright in it. The Grail is then used as a Eucharistic vessel in the ceremony of the Mass; the celebrant (identified as Joseph, the son of Joseph of Arimathea) places in it a wafer, which is miraculously transformed into the figure of a child, and then becomes bread again. Joseph then vanishes, and out of the Grail comes a man who has (in Malory's words) 'all the sygnes of the Passion of Jesu Cryste bledynge all opynly' (603/26–7; XVII. 20), who administers the Host to the knights. Finally, he identifies the Grail as 'the holy dysshe wherein I ete the lambe on Estir day' (603/39–40; XVII. 20) – that is, the vessel used in the Last Supper, when Christ identified the bread and wine he gave to his disciples as his own body and blood (Matt. 26: 26–8; Mark 14: 22–4; Luke 22: 19–20). It is this occasion which is both commemorated and recreated in the Mass, when the consecration of bread and wine by the priest transforms them into the body and blood of Christ.

In both the French *Queste* and Malory, the Grail is thus a Eucharistic vessel.[7] The mystery that surrounds it is a religious mystery: it renders visible the transformation of bread and wine into body and blood, a trans-

---

[5] Robert de Boron, *Le Roman de l'Estoire dou Graal*, ed. William A. Nitze, (Paris, 1971).

[6] *La Queste del Saint Graal*, ed. A. Pauphilet (Paris, 1978); translated as *The Quest of the Holy Grail* by P. M. Matarasso (Harmondsworth, 1969).

[7] W. E. M. C. Hamilton, 'L'interprétation mystique de La Queste del Saint Graal,' *Neophilologus*, 27 (1942), 94–110; Jean Frappier, 'Le Graal et la chevalerie,' *Romania*, 75 (1954), 165–210, (p. 166).

formation which is normally accessible to Christians only on the plane of belief. But why, one might ask, should such a penetration of the mystery of the Eucharist be the goal and climax of knightly endeavour? The conventional answer to this question is that the author of the French *Queste* was offering a challenge and a corrective to the secular ethos of chivalry which was celebrated in the verse and prose romances of his time. The knights in the *Queste* are frequently lectured by hermits on the distinction between the 'earthly chivalry' ('chevalerie terriane') in which they have been engaged hitherto, and the 'heavenly chivalry' ('chevalerie celestiel') which is demanded in the quest of the Grail. Critics of Malory have likewise seen his *Sankgreal* as the point at which the worldly values of the Round Table are judged by religious standards and found wanting; Lancelot's adultery is there revealed as the flaw which robs him of his pre-eminence, and which will lead eventually to the collapse of the whole Arthurian world in the *Morte*.[8]

Such interpretations of both the *Queste* and Malory are in the main following the lead of Albert Pauphilet, who in a widely influential book argued that the French *Queste* is deeply permeated by Cistercian spirituality; for him, it represents a monastic attempt to appropriate the idiom of chivalric romance for religious ends.[9] The parallels with Cistercian writings and practice which Pauphilet claims are, however, weak and unconvincing, and there are other serious objections to this view of the *Queste*, the most powerful of which is that the early Cistercians, as Jean Frappier has observed, did not write romances;[10] the austerity of their order, which led even to the banishment of all church ornament, would hardly have tolerated engagement in so frivolous a pastime as the

---

[8] See, for example, Charles Moorman's analysis of the relation between Malory's *Sankgreal* and the French *Queste* in *Malory's Originality*, ed. R. M. Lumiansky (Baltimore, 1964), pp. 184–204.

[9] *Etudes sur la Queste del Saint Graal* (Paris, 1921; repr. 1980), pp. 53–84.

[10] 'Le Graal et la chevalerie,' p. 195; Frappier says of the author of the *Queste* 'il ne saurait être question de voir en lui un moine de Cîteaux, ne fût-ce que pour cette raison péremptoire que les Cisterciens n'écrivaient pas des romans.' This argument is reinforced and extended by Pauline Matarasso, *The Redemption of Chivalry: A Study of the Queste del Saint Graal* (Geneva, 1979), pp. 225–8, but she still clings to a belief in the 'Cistercian bias' (p. 224) of the *Queste*, although the examples she cites are no more convincing than Pauphilet's (pp. 218–24); she tentatively concludes that the *Queste* may have been written by 'a Cistercian seconded from his abbey to some lay or ecclesiastical dignitary' (p. 241).
    On the exclusion of profane literature (including classical Latin poetry) from Cistercian libraries, see further Anne Bondelle, 'Trésor des moines. Les Chartreux, les Cisterciens et leurs livres,' in *histoire des bibliothèques françaises: Les bibliothèques médiévales du VIᵉ siècle à 1530*, ed. André Vernet (Paris, 1988), pp. 64–81; Birger Munk Olsen, 'The Cistercians and Classical Culture,' *Cahiers de l'institut du moyen-âge grec et latin*, 47 (1984), 64–102; Christopher R. Cheney, 'Les bibliothèques cisterciennes en Angleterre au XIIᵉ siècle,' *Mélanges Saint Bernard: XXIVᵉ Congrès de l'Association Bourguignonne des Sociétés Savantes, Dijon 1953* (Dijon, n.d.), pp. 375–82.

composition of vernacular fiction, even for religious ends. It is significant that Helinand of Froidmont mentions the Grail legend only to dismiss it as not worth wasting time on.[11] Emmanuèle Baumgartner has also stressed that the *Queste* was manifestly conceived and written in close relation to the prose *Lancelot*;[12] the first appearances of the Grail occur in the latter half of that work, as a kind of prelude to the *Queste*.[13] In only four of the forty-three manuscripts of the *Queste* does the work appear alone; usually it is either part of the whole Vulgate Cycle, or preceded by the end of the *Lancelot* or followed by the *Mort Artu*.[14] That is, the *Queste* is not conceived as a religious alternative to the secular prose romances, but as forming a continuum with them. Forty years ago, Jean Frappier presented a powerful case for reversing Pauphilet's view of the relation between chivalry and religion: that is, instead of representing an attempt to appropriate chivalry for religious ends, the Grail romances use religion as a means of exalting the dignity of the knightly class.[15] They create a 'messianic chivalry, pre-destined, worthy of approaching, almost without intermediaries, the mysteries of the faith and of achieving knowledge of the divine'(p. 170). The *Queste* in particular propagates, in Emmanuèle Baumgartner's words, 'a class gospel' ('un évangile de classe,' p. 146).

Against the background of this view of the Grail romances, it is worth re-posing the question: why should the mystery of the Eucharist be the goal and climax of knightly endeavour? The answer, I suggest, lies in the central elements of this religious mystery, the body and blood which are the con-centrated symbols of Christ's redemptive suffering. For body and blood are also the central elements of the knightly experience: it is through hazarding his body in combat and shedding blood – both his own and his opponent's – that the knight realizes his worth and that of his fellows. Just as Christ's bodily suffering was, miraculously and mysteriously, the means through which redemption was accomplished on the spiritual plane, so the knight's bodily exploits are the vehicle through which his spiritual worth is realized. And blood is almost the only important bodily element in these exploits: the descriptions of knightly combat make no mention of muscles, nerves, sinews, sweat, pus, for example. The knightly body is represented in quasi-stylized form as a vessel containing blood, and in this it resembles the Grail itself.[16]

---

[11] Helinand complains that he cannot find a Latin version of the Grail legend, nor is it easy to find a complete version of the story in French. He prefers therefore to translate 'more probable and useful' things ('verisimiliora et utiliora') into Latin (*Patrologia Latina*, 213, col. 815).

[12] *L'Arbre et le pain: essai sur La Queste del Saint Graal* (Paris, 1981), pp. 12, 21.

[13] *Lancelot*, ed. A. Micha, 9 vols (Paris, 1978–83), II, 376–7; IV, 205–6, 270–1; V, 255–6, 267–71; VI, 204–5.

[14] Baumgartner, *L'arbre et le pain*, pp. 11–12.

[15] See n. 7. Further references are given in the text.

[16] Charlotte C. Morse draws attention to the vessel-motif that links the Grail with the human body in *The Pattern of Judgment in the Queste and Cleanness* (Columbia, 1978); see esp. p. 16.

What the knight sees in the Grail vision is thus the apotheosis of his own existence.

The adventures of the Grail Quest thus follow, in intensified form, the pattern of the knightly adventure in general, which I have outlined on other occasions: they enact an elaborate interplay of distance and closeness, fragmentation and integration, separation and union.[17] Distanced from his world by his inability to understand the mysterious laws that govern it and produce its often bizarre events, the knight attempts to engage with it on the plane of physical action, using his body as the medium through which his destiny will be revealed. Coming together with his fellow-knights, in extreme and violent form, in single combat, he ruptures the bodily integrity of his opponent and loses his own; but this rupture on the bodily plane often, paradoxically, leads to fellowship and union between the two combatants. The pursuit of an adventure is an attempt to close the gap between himself and the enigmatic challenges posed by the outside world, but it severs the knight from the fellows he leaves behind at court. At the close of the adventure, the movement is reversed and he is reintegrated into that fellowship.[18]

These patterns are repeated throughout the Arthurian narrative, but the Grail Quest sacralizes them by re-enacting them in a religious form. The French *Queste* is a symbolic narrative composed of a whole repertoire of images of wounding and healing, separation and union – images which reach a climactic expression in the final visions of the Grail, as we shall see. Malory's *Sankgreal* reproduces this symbolic narrative, but makes its patterns even clearer, not only by significant change at certain moments, but also by drastically reducing the religious interpretations of the narrative which in the *Queste* are regularly delivered by hermits and other religious. These religious commentaries not only blur the narrative line, but also tend to reduce its symbols to a set of cryptograms, whose imagistic power is discarded as they are decoded into moral instruction. In minimizing the role of these religious expositions, Malory makes the world of the *Sankgreal* consistent with that of the rest of his work: a world of pervasive enigma, in which explanation or understanding comes, if at all, fitfully and too late to have any bearing on action – a world in which the knight must engage in adventure without any clear notion of the consequences or character of his

---

[17] Jill Mann, '"Taking the Adventure": Malory and the *Suite du Merlin*,' in *Aspects of Malory*, ed. Toshiyuki Takamiya and Derek Brewer (Cambridge, 1981), pp. 71–91, 196–207; 'Malory: Knightly Combat in *Le Morte D'Arthur*,' *The New Pelican Guide to English Literature*, ed. Boris Ford, vol. 1, Part One: *Medieval Literature: Chaucer and the Alliterative Tradition* (Harmondsworth, 1982), pp. 331–9; *The Narrative of Distance, The Distance of Narrative in Malory's Morte Darthur*, The William Matthews Lectures 1991 (London, 1991).

[18] The deeper resonances of the word 'felyship' in Malory, as compared with the *Queste*'s 'compaignie,' are explored by Elizabeth Archibald, 'Malory's Ideal of Fellowship,' *Review of English Studies*, n.s. 43 (1992), 311–28.

involvement. And here as elsewhere, adventure is heuristic: it reveals a knight's pre-existing worth rather than offering an opportunity to acquire it. Galahad's superiority is not a result of his trying harder, or of his resisting temptations more successfully; on the contrary, it is manifested in the fact that he is simply not tempted, as Perceval and Bors are.[19] His pre-eminence consists in his wholeness, which is his from the beginning, and which the events of the narrative are designed to express.

The symbolic patterns I have attempted to describe are immediately visible in the opening sequence of the *Tale of the Sankgreal*. The fellowship of the Round Table, assembled for the feast of Pentecost, is made complete by the arrival of Galahad, who occupies the one empty seat, the Siege Perilous. His arrival is heralded by the miraculous appearance of gold letters on each seat bearing the name of the knight to whom it belongs; the Siege Perilous bears an inscription declaring that it will be 'fulfylled' on this very day (516/33–44; XIII. 2). The letters on the Siege Perilous are then covered with a silk cloth, which is removed on Galahad's arrival, revealing that the original inscription has been replaced by Galahad's name (518/41–4; XIII. 4). The removal of the cloth represents the unveiling of a destiny, a moment of fulfilment, both for Galahad and the Round Table, which is imaged in the removal of this symbolic barrier. This moment of fulfilment is celebrated in the joust which is requested by King Arthur, so that he may see the Round Table 'holé togydirs.'

> 'Now,' seyde the kynge, 'I am sure at this quest of the Sankegreall shall all ye of the Rownde Table departe, and nevyr shall I se you agayne holé togydirs, therefore ones shall I se you togydir in the medow, all holé togydirs! Therefore I woll se you all holé togydir in the medow of Camelot, to juste and to turney, that aftir youre dethe men may speke of hit that such good knyghtes were here, such a day, holé togydirs.' (520/39–44; XIII. 6)

The fourfold repetition of 'holé togydir(s)' is Malory's own intensification of the single word 'ensemble' in the *Queste* (p. 13). But the sense of unity and completeness here is strengthened by the very thing that also undermines it – namely, Arthur's melancholy reference to the imminent departure of his knights on the quest of the Grail, and his conviction that they will never again be re-assembled as a whole. The appearance of the Grail at the evening supper consecrates the completion of the Round Table, the eradication of its one remaining gap, but it also initiates the quest which will scatter the fellowship, and sever some of its members from it for ever. And it introduces another barrier to be eradicated, a distance to be closed, in the form of the white samite covering that hides the Grail from view. Gawain is moved to initiate the quest because 'we myght nat se the Holy

---

[19] Cf. Matarasso, *The Redemption of Chivalry*, p. 85 n. 96.

Grayle: hit was so preciously coverde' (522/11–12; XIII. 7). He proposes to pursue the Grail, not in order to take possession of it, but in order to see it 'more opynly than hit hath bene shewed here' (522/16–17; XIII. 7). The motive for the quest is the same impulse towards closeness that characterizes knightly engagement in adventure elsewhere. But this impulse towards closeness – again, as elsewhere – opens up a gap in another direction: Gawain's vow to undertake the quest provokes Arthur's bitter lament over 'the departicion of thys felyship' (522/30; XIII. 7); 'For whan they departe frome hense I am sure they all shall never mete more togydir in thys worlde, for they shall dye many in the queste'(522/26–8; XIII. 7). The dual meaning of 'departe' in Middle English – 'to leave' and 'to separate' (*MED* 1a, 2a) – makes every departure in Malory's narrative a poignant image of severance, the loss of a fellowship temporarily achieved. But the departure on the Grail Quest is a 'departicion'of a more final kind, precisely because it is a quest for a wholeness which is only to be realized elsewhere.

The veiling of the Grail is mirrored in the veiling of Galahad's identity. The *Sankgreal* opens with Lancelot being summoned away from the court to bestow the order of knighthood on the young Galahad, whom he does not know to be his son. When Galahad arrives at court, the revelation of his identity is adumbrated in the scene at the jousting where Guinevere asks him to remove his helmet, and surmises from his facial resemblance to Lancelot that they are father and son (521/19–23; XIII. 7). But the final recognition of their relationship is deferred until later; until it takes place, there is another barrier towards whose removal the narrative aspires, another kind of wholeness which the quest can achieve.

The processes by which Galahad acquires his sword and his shield offer yet more images of wholeness and the loss of wholeness. The sword arrives at court before Galahad does: set in a stone which floats, miraculously, in the river, it bears an inscription proclaiming that it can be drawn out only by the knight for whom it is destined, who will be 'the beste knyght of the worlde' (517/25; XIII. 2). Declining to make the attempt, Sir Lancelot further reveals that 'who that assayth to take hit and faylith of that swerde, he shall resséyve a wounde by that swerde that he shall nat be longe hole afftir' (517/31–3; XIII. 2). This prediction is proved true on Gawain, who attempts to withdraw the sword, and is later severely wounded by Galahad with it (578/3–18; XVII. 1). Galahad, in contrast, withdraws the sword without difficulty and without suffering harm; his bodily invulnerability, that is, functions as the outward testimony of an inner perfection. Galahad then explains that the sword is the one with which Balin le Sauvage killed his brother Balan, 'thorow a dolerous stroke that Balyn gaff unto kynge Pelles, the whych ys nat yett hole, nor naught shall be tyll that I hele hym' (520/11–13; XIII. 5). This explanation, which is Malory's own addition, makes the coming of Galahad into the completion of a history; the wound opened up by Balin is to be healed by Galahad. Himself the embodiment of a perfect wholeness, he is also the one who makes whole, and who brings the unfinished narrative to fulfilment.

The shield that Galahad later acquires likewise functions as a testimony to his wholeness. It too is destined for 'the worthyest knyght of the worlde' (525/18–19; XIII. 9), and is hedged about with a warning that 'no man may bere hit aboute his necke but he be myscheved other dede within three dayes, other maymed for ever' (525/4–6; XIII. 9). And again this prediction is fulfilled on another knight – in this case, King Bagdemagus, who takes the shield and is immediately wounded, near fatally, by a knight in white armour (525/26–33; XIII. 9). The white knight then bids Bagdemagus' squire carry the shield to Galahad, who takes possession of it without further ado (525/38–526/18. XIII. 10). His pre-eminence is demonstrated in his ability to remain invulnerable while bearing the shield, but this invulnerability is not a consequence of his superior strength or skill in combat; it is simply intrinsic to his being.

The events that follow also function as demonstrations of this quasi-magical wholeness. Bagdemagus's squire Melyas is knighted by Galahad, and asks if he may accompany him 'tyll that som adventure departe us' (529/2–16; XIII. 12). The severance of their temporary fellowship duly takes place a week later, when they come to a cross which (symbolically) 'departed two wayes' (529/22; XIII. 12), bearing a warning of the perils threatening the knight who takes either of them. Against Galahad's advice, Melyas insists on taking the left-hand path, the more arduous of the two. It leads him to a meadow in which stands a table set with food, and a chair with a golden crown on it. Melyas takes away the crown, and is then challenged by another knight who deals him an apparently fatal wound. Galahad arrives on the scene and engages with Melyas's assailant and a second knight, both of whom he overcomes. He then takes Melyas to an abbey so that he may be confessed; Melyas receives the Eucharist, and the tip of his opponent's spear is pulled from his body. He swoons, but does not die, and the monk who is tending to him declares that he can heal him within seven weeks (529–31; XIII. 13).

The events in this short narrative sequence are shaped by a symbolic logic which works to contrast Melyas's vulnerability with Galahad's wholeness. The symbolic character of the narrative is made clear when a monk explains that Melyas's wound is due to his failure to make confession before being knighted (531/14–17; XIII. 14). The left-hand path which he took signifies 'the way of synnars and of myssebelevers' (531/20; XIII. 14); the pride that led him to separate from Galahad, and the covetousness that led him to take the crown, are signified in the two knights against whom Galahad fought (531/26–32. XIII. 14). The relation between narrative event and interpretation here, as elsewhere in the *Sankgreal*, is of a rather unusual kind. On the one hand, the interpretation is not far-reaching enough to convert the narrative into a full-blown allegory, such as Deguileville's *Pilgrimage of the Life of Man*: the two knights *signify* the two deadly sins which affect Melyas, but that is not to say that they *are* those sins. Yet at the same time the interpretation resists assimilation into a fully mimetic mode – that is, a mode in which ethical significance is intrinsic to the actions portrayed rather than symbolically expressed by them. Melyas's failure to be confessed may be deplorable, but it is not easy to see why it should be a cause of his being physically wounded. And if the left-hand path is in some literal sense 'the way of synnars and of myssebelevers,' why does Galahad urge Melyas to let him take it? Melyas does not become a sinner and a misbeliever by virtue of choosing a path that is intrinsically wicked; rather, this path becomes the way of sinners and misbelievers because the sinful Melyas chooses it. Again, if Melyas's covetousness in taking the crown is reprehensible, why does Galahad attack the knight who reproves Melyas for this action and tries to stop him? This narrative sequence is thus not designed to present a series of ethical choices which function as examples for everyday life; rather, like the final vision of the Grail, it manifests a spiritual reality on a physical plane, even though the relation between the spiritual and the physical remains inaccessible. So the lack of confession and the sin of pride manifest themselves in a physical separation from Galahad ('pryde ys hede of every synne: that caused thys knyght to departe frome sir Galahad' [531/26–7; XIII. 14]) and a physical wound; confession, conversely, 'makes whole' the spiritual wound and so initiates the process of physical healing.

The processes by which Galahad acquires first his sword and then his shield thus invest the knight's equipment with a special mystique. His arms are not merely the tools of his trade, but sacral objects which mark out his special destiny. The crown which Melyas takes seems, like the sword in the stone, to offer itself to all comers, but when he carries it off he finds that, like the sword, it chooses its owner, rather than the reverse. A king does not become king by seizing a crown; rather, the crown marks him out as the one who already is king. So it is with the knight: Galahad's arms are the symbols of a destinal election. This destinal role is reinforced by the account of the shield's history which the white knight gives Galahad: it goes back to the days of Joseph of Arimathaea, and was made for King Evelake to do battle against the Saracens. At the outset of the battle, it is covered with a cloth, which is removed at the most critical moment to reveal the figure of a crucified man. This image of suffering wins the battle, and also heals a man whose hand has been severed (526–7; XIII. 10). Later, when Joseph of Arimathea is dying, he makes a cross on the shield with his own blood, and declares that no one will be able to own it with impunity but Galahad, the good knight, 'laste of my lynage' (527/36–9; XIII. 11). Again we have the unveiling of a destiny – a destiny expressed in an image of bodily suffering that conquers and heals. And this bodily suffering is elided with the knight's hazarding of himself in combat. Religious history thus finds its culmination in the knight; chivalry can trace its history back to the foot of the Cross.[20]

[20] Baumgartner, *L'Arbre et le pain*, p. 38.

The dual role of blood, as symbol of both wounding and healing, is evident not only in the story of the shield but also elsewhere in the *Sankgreal*. The bleeding spear which accompanies the Grail, and which enigmatically unites the active and passive versions of wounding into a single image, is at the centre of this symbolic role. It is with the blood that drips from this spear that Galahad anoints the Maimed King and makes him 'an hole man' (604/19; XVII. 21), after he and his companions have seen the man bearing the signs of Christ's Passion 'bledynge all opynly' emerge from the Grail (603/27; XVII. 20). Bors's vision of the bird which dies giving blood for the life of its young is another image of the dual role of blood (564/34–40; XVI. 6); so is the death of Perceval's sister, who consents to give a basinful of blood to heal a leper lady (591–2; XVII. 11). The simultaneity of wholeness and severance, bound together like substance and shadow, is expressed in the vocabulary Malory uses here: 'Than asked she her Saveoure, and as sone as she had reseyved Hym the soule *departed* frome the body. So the same day was the lady *heled* whan she was anoynted with hir bloode' (592/28–30; XVII. 11; my italics).

Blood also creates a wholeness of another kind, as we are reminded when Galahad and Perceval find the tombs of the sixty maidens who have likewise died as a result of giving blood for the leper lady: the tombs bear their names 'and of what bloode they were com off. And all were of kyngys bloode . . .' (593/24–5; XVII. 12). Lineage and kin, the links created by blood, take on a special importance in the *Sankgreal*, working in both a horizontal and a vertical direction: blood-relationship intensifies fellowship into a mystical bond; blood-lineage is the carrier of destiny. Galahad is, as we have seen, the last of Joseph of Arimathaea's line; he is also the last knight of Solomon's kindred, as Perceval's sister reveals in her explanation of the three spindles on the ship (584/31–2, 586/12; XVII. 5, 7). The knightly stress on lineage unites with biblical genealogy to give a religious sanction to chivalry.[21] The quest for the Grail reveals kin relationships: Perceval finds an aunt and a sister, Lancelot a son.

Like blood, the body is an image of wholeness, expressed in the form of virginity. Galahad's perfection is manifested above all in the fact that he is 'a clene virgyne above all knyghtes' (600/22; XVII. 18), and it is the magical power of his virginity that works to heal King Mordrains and restore his youth (600/15–26; cf. 584/32; XVII. 18; XVII. 5). Similarly, the blood that Perceval's sister is required to give must come from 'a maydyn, and a clene virgyne in wylle and in worke, and a kynges doughter' if it is to heal the leper lady (591/32–3; XVII. 11). It is because the intact, inviolate, virgin body is an image of spiritual wholeness that sexual temptations loom so large in the adventures of the Grail knights. Perceval is tempted by a lady who turns out to be a fiend in disguise; she plies him with food and drink, and then offers him her love. Perceval is ready to succumb, but he is saved by 'adventure and grace'.

> And than sir Percivale layde him downe by her naked. And by adventure and grace he saw hys swerde ly on the erthe naked, where in the pomell was a rede crosse and the sygne of the crucifixe therin, and bethought hym on hys knyghthode and hys promyse made unto the good man tofornehande, and than he made a sygne of the crosse in his forehed. And therewith the pavylon turned up-so-downe and than hit changed unto a smooke and a blak clowde. (550/11–17; XIV. 9)

It is significant that Perceval is not saved by a moral struggle culminating in a deliberate choice, but rather by a semi-instinctive physical reaction prompted by chance – by adventure. The linking of 'grace'with 'adventure' fixes its meaning as 'good fortune' (*MED* 3c) rather than 'God's grace' (*MED* 1a); it is chance rather than God's will that is the operative force. Here, no less than in knightly combat, adventure works to reveal destiny. The symbolic nature of this scene is brilliantly conjured up by Malory's use of the word 'naked,' the adjective applied to both Perceval and his sword. The word 'naked' makes the sword the image of the knight himself, again making his weapons the symbolic expression of his destined role. The 'naked' sword is both vulnerable and dangerous – unprotected by its sheath, but at the same time ready to strike, to inflict a wound. So Perceval's naked body bespeaks vulnerability, the precarious fragility of his virginity, and yet it also bespeaks his openness to the power of 'adventure' and 'grace.' It is his nakedness before the workings of chance that releases the power that saves him. Coming to his senses, Perceval punishes his unruly flesh by wounding himself in the thigh, so that 'the blode sterte aboute hym' (550/29–30; XIV. 10). The physical wound paradoxically heals his spiritual wound, the acknowledgement of guilt re-creates wholeness on the spiritual plane.

Bors too is tempted by the offer of love from a lady who threatens to commit suicide, along with twelve of her gentlewomen, if he rejects her (571/6–24; XVI. 12). The pressure is increased by the additional threat that rejection will also entail the death of his cousin Lancelot (570/3–5; XVI. 11). Bors's response is to reflect 'that levir he had they all had loste their soules than he hys soule' (571/20–1; XVI. 12). The strange element of detachment in this reflection is also present in his assessment of the dilemma with which he is confronted – significantly, 'at the departynge of . . . two wayes' (567/35–6; XVI. 9) – when he sees his brother Lionel, bound and bleeding, being led away on a horse by two knights on one hand, and on the other, a maiden about to be raped by a knight. Agonized, Bors decides to rescue the maiden, but he represents her plight not in terms of the physical or emotional trauma of rape, but in terms of the loss of virginity, whose very vulnerability gives it a quasi-magical status: 'if I helpe nat the mayde she ys shamed, and shall lose her virginité which she shall never gete agayne'

(568/16–18; XVI. 10). The claims of virginity here over-ride the claims of blood; bodily wholeness entails separation, albeit accompanied by great emotional distress, from the bonds created by fellowship and kinship. The separateness which is the condition of this bodily wholeness is imaged both in Bors's prefatory dream of the two lily flowers which are 'departed' by a good man (566/17–18; XVI. 8), symbolizing the maiden and the would-be rapist (572/41–573/1; XVI. 13), and in the issue of the final combat between the indignant Lionel and the reluctant Bors, when they are dramatically separated by a fiery cloud from heaven, and a voice commands Bors 'go hens and beare felyship no lenger with thy brothir' (576/31; XVI. 17). He is told to make his way to the sea, and join Perceval; the fellowship of the Grail, founded on bodily integrity, supersedes natural blood-ties.

The narrative imagery of wholeness and separation is woven into complicated and paradoxical patterns, as this sequence of adventures shows. Wholeness never brings unalloyed fulfilment; it always entails a corresponding separation, the rupture of another kind of unity, which imbues it with a sense of nostalgia or yearning. Malory inherits much of this complex narrative imagery from the *Queste*, although, as we have seen, he is also capable of extending and refining it. But his most imaginative development of the Grail narrative is in his conception of the role of Lancelot and his relation to Galahad. It is here that the *Sankgreal* achieves an emotional power which goes far beyond anything in the French source.

If Galahad embodies inner wholeness, Lancelot embodies an inner fragmentation. As Galahad's wholeness is expressed in his virginity, Lancelot's fragmentation resides in his relationship with Guinevere. The split at the centre of Lancelot's being can be seen in the comments made to Gawain by the hermit Nacien.

> '. . . as synfull as ever sir Launcelot hath byn, sith that he wente into the queste of the Sankgreal he slew never man nother nought shall, tylle that he com to Camelot agayne; for he hath takyn upon hym to forsake synne. And ne were that he ys nat stable, but by hys thoughte he ys lyckly to turne agayne, he sholde be nexte to encheve hit sauff sir Galahad, hys sonne; but God knowith hys thought and hys unstablenesse. And yett shall he dye ryght an holy man, and no doute he hath no felow of none erthly synfull man lyvyng.' (563/16–24; XVI. 5)

These words have no parallel in the French *Queste*, and they have often been attributed to Malory's partisan attachment to Lancelot, and consequent reluctance to admit that in the Grail Quest his hero becomes a failure. The function of Nacien's speech is not to salvage Lancelot's reputation, but to show Lancelot as riven by a fundamental contradiction. The impression that Nacien's words give is not of qualification, of demotion to second-best, but of paradox; what is taken away with one hand is immediately restored with the other, in a way that makes it impossible to arrive at a single unified view. The two occasions when Lancelot himself is lectured by a hermit show the same disorienting oscillation between praise and blame, producing the same sense of contradiction and paradox as fundamental to his being (538/30–42, 555/10–13; XIII. 19, XV. 4).

Lancelot's inner fragmentation expresses itself in the events of the Grail Quest in terms of distance. Early in the quest, he has a vision of the Grail which appears before a sick knight and heals him; but throughout this vision he is 'half wakyng and half slepynge' (536/39; XIII. 18) and so is distanced from the wholeness it represents. Even in his final, most satisfying vision of the Grail, he has to watch from the chamber door, and when he tries to enter, invisible hands carry him outside and leave him in a trance before the door (597/6–13; XVII. 15). His distanced relation with his son Galahad is another sign of the lack of integration in his being. The distance is strikingly evident in the manner of Galahad's begetting: Lancelot is led by enchantment to believe that he is lying with Guinevere, when in fact it is Elaine to whom he is making love. Yet it is this action, which is at the furthest point of remove from his true self, that paradoxically produces the unflawed wholeness embodied in Galahad. Just as wholeness is never achieved without an accompanying severance, so fragmentation can miraculously issue in wholeness. Without Lancelot's adultery, Galahad's purity would not come into being.

If the Grail Quest lays bare the fragmented nature of Lancelot's being, it also allows him to achieve his own kind of wholeness. The first means to this end is confession: Lancelot cannot repair the fracture in his selfhood, but in openly acknowledging its existence, he eradicates the split between his outer reputation – his 'worship,' in Malory's words – and his inner being. The second way in which he achieves wholeness is in the mutual acknowledgement of his relationship with Galahad, which, significantly, is the prelude to his final vision of the Grail. As Baumgartner has aptly observed with reference to the Grail narrative as a whole,[22] the quest for the Grail frequently turns into a quest for Galahad, who thus becomes a displaced figure of the Grail itself. So Lancelot's meeting with Galahad is a moving celebration of wholeness, symbolized in the mysterious ties of blood. Malory gives this scene an especial emotional power by altering the narrative of the *Queste* in one significant detail: in the *Queste*, Lancelot is alone on the ship which bears the dead body of Perceval's sister, and one night hears the arrival of a stranger knight who then identifies himself as Galahad. In Malory, Lancelot goes ashore, 'for he was somwhat wery of the shippe' (594/20–1; XVII. 13); he then hears a knight going past him into the ship, whom he follows and accosts. Simple as this change of detail is, it nevertheless has a profound impact on the emotional charge of the ensuing recognition. For it introduces a distance, small but potentially decisive, between Lancelot and the recognition of his son. Removing Lancelot from

---

[22] *L'Arbre et le pain*, p. 56.

the direct trajectory of Galahad's path creates the momentary possibility that the meeting may not be realized, that father and son will pass each other by, without ever acknowledging their relationship. The poignancy created by this sense of potential severance fills the recognition, when it is after all achieved, with a surge of emotional relief.

> And than he lystened and herde an hors com and one rydyng uppon hym, and whan he cam nyghe hym semed a knyght, and so he late hym passe and wente thereas the ship was. And there he alyght and toke the sadyll and the brydill, and put the horse frome hym, and so wente into the shyppe.
> And than sir Lancelot dressed hym unto the shippe and seyde, 'Sir, ye be wellcom!'
> And he answerd, and salewed hym agayne and seyde,
> 'Sir, what ys youre name? For much my herte gevith unto you.'
> 'Truly,' seyde he, 'my name ys sir Launcelot du Lake.'
> 'Sir,' seyde he, 'than be ye wellcom! For ye were the begynner of me in this worlde.'
> 'A, sir, ar ye sir Galahad?'
> 'Ye, forsothe.'
> And so he kneled downe and askyd hym hys blyssynge. And aftir that toke of his helme and kyssed hym, and there was grete joy betwyxte them, for no tunge can telle what joy was betwyxte them. And there every of them tolde othir the aventures that had befalle them syth that they departed frome the courte. (594/21–39; XVII. 13)

The separate paths that their adventures have followed are united in their re-telling and their convergence on this moment of union. Yet even here, distance is maintained in the formal mode of address – 'sir Lancelot,' 'sir Galahad' – which reinforces the awareness of the preciousness and rarity of union.

The final reunion of Lancelot and Galahad is followed by their final separation: after they have spent half a year in adventures together, a knight armed in white bids Galahad leave the ship, and a heavenly voice tells them that they will not meet again before the Day of Judgement. Lancelot's response counterpoints the continuing bonds of blood with the finality of separation:

> 'Now, my sonne, sir Galahad, sith we shall departe and nother of us se other more, I pray to that Hyghe Fadir, conserve me and you bothe.'
> (595/29–30; XVII. 14)

The 'departure' between father and son hangs over Lancelot's following vision of the Grail like a shadow, making the end of Lancelot's quest both severance and fulfilment.

The same is true of the original ending which Malory invents for the *Sankgreal* as a whole. After relating the death of Galahad, then of Perceval, the French *Queste* finally tells how Bors returned to King Arthur's court and related the adventures of the Grail, which were written down and kept in the library at Salisbury. Malory follows his source up to this point, but whereas the *Queste* ends with a reference to its own genesis in the fictive records at Salisbury, Malory introduces a completely original exchange between Bors and Lancelot. It is an exchange which emphasizes the permanent severance of Galahad and Perceval from the Round Table fellowship, sundered from it by death in a distant city, on the other side of the sea. But it is an exchange which also emphasizes wholeness, in the reassembling of the 'hole courte' of Arthur at the conclusion of the Quest, in its reminiscence of the time that Lancelot and Galahad spent together, in its reminder of the ties of blood that link Galahad, Lancelot and Bors, and in Lancelot's final moving affirmation that he and Bors will never again 'depart in sundir' so long as they live.

> And anone sir Bors seyde to sir Launcelot,
>   'Sir Galahad, youre owne sonne, salewed you by me, and aftir you my lorde kynge Arthure and all the hole courte, and so ded sir Percivale. For I buryed them both myne owne hondis in the cité of Sarras. Also, sir Launcelot, sir Galahad prayde you to remembir of thys unsyker worlde, as ye behyght hym whan ye were togydirs more than halffe a yere.'
>   'Thys ys trew,' seyde sir Launcelot, 'now I truste to God hys prayer shall avayle me.'
>   Than sir Launcelot toke sir Bors in hys armys and seyde,
>   'Cousyn, ye ar ryght wellcom to me! For all that ever I may do for you and for yours, ye shall fynde my poure body redy atte all tymes whyle the spyryte is in hit, and that I promyse you feythfully, and never to fayle. And wete ye well, gentyl cousyn sir Bors, ye and I shall never departe in sundir whylis oure lyvys may laste.'
>   'Sir,' seyde he, 'as ye woll, so woll I.' (607/39–608/9; XVII. 23)

Perfect wholeness, as represented by the full vision of the Grail granted to Galahad and his companions, is achieved only briefly, but fragmentary images of that wholeness are woven into the texture of knightly experience, sudden flowerings of fulfilment which bring renewed longing in their train.

The last two books of Malory's work trace the slow disintegration of the Round Table fellowship and the final loss of the wholeness which it had embodied. Yet just before he begins the final book, Malory introduces a powerful image of wholeness in 'The Healing of Sir Urry,' an episode which has no counterpart in the French source. It is an episode which, as Mark Lambert has noted, constitutes a kind of narrative pun on the word 'hole':[23] the wounded knight Sir Urry seeks to be made whole by 'the beste knyght of the worlde' (663/34; XIX.10), the whole court attempts to heal him. The

---

[23] *Malory: Style and Vision in Le Morte Darthur* (New Haven, 1975), p. 63.

long roll-call of names emphasizes the wholeness of the Round Table
fellowship, assembled one last time before the imminent end. Only
Lancelot is absent, but he arrives just as all the other knights have tried and
failed. Persuaded by Arthur to try in his turn, not out of presumption, but
'for to beare us felyshyp, insomuche as ye be a felow of the Rounde Table'
(668/5–6; XIX.12), Lancelot prays to God to preserve his 'symple worship
and honesté' (668/23–4; XIX. 12), searches Sir Urry's wounds, and heals
him. Lancelot's 'worship' is proved on the body of Sir Urry, as the
perfection of Galahad and Perceval is proved in acts of bodily healing. The
healing of Sir Urry is a kind of secular counterpart to the final visions of the
Grail in the *Sankgreal*, the first of which leads to the healing of the Maimed
King, and the second of which leads to Galahad's absorption into the
'feliship' of heaven (604, 606/22, 39; XVII. 20–22). But here too wholeness is
counterpointed by separation, in the diverging responses to the healing of
Sir Urry.

> Than kynge Arthur and all the kynges and knyghtes kneled downe and
> gave thankynges and lovynge unto God and unto Hys Blyssed Modir.
> And ever sir Launcelot wepte, as he had bene a chylde that had bene
> beatyn! (668/33–6; XIX. 12)

The court rejoices; Lancelot weeps. This divergence at the very heart of the
climactic moment of healing and fellowship expresses with delicate
poignancy the precariousness and the preciousness of wholeness.

Malory, like the author of the *Queste*, sees the Grail narrative as the
apotheosis of chivalric experience. But what for the French author is a story
of chivalric success acquires in Malory a note of nostalgia and longing. In
the French *Queste*, Galahad's role is to 'put an end to' the adventures of
Logres, as if they were an unpleasant interruption to normal life. In Malory,
the ending of adventures brings sadness as well as a sense of fulfilment.
The dominant mood of his work – particularly towards its end – is elegiac.
If he celebrates the Arthurian world, he celebrates it as something lost for
ever, severed from the present by death and time. But the elegiac mood
goes deeper still: it mediates a view of life as a constantly frustrated search
for wholeness which is no sooner found than lost again. The *Sankgreal*
situates the full realization of wholeness beyond earthly experience; its
necessary condition is the severance from the world effected by death. So
the 'death and departynge' of King Arthur and his knights makes possible
the completion of the 'hoole book' that relates their adventures; earthly
wholeness is realized only on the plane of narrative.

12

The Ending of the Morte Darthur

C. DAVID BENSON

Nothing so becomes the *Morte Darthur* as its ending. The fall of the Round
Table is the climax of the Arthurian story and shows Malory at the height of
his powers. He consistently reshapes the traditional story to dramatize his
central themes (honour, fellowship, love) and to make us share the emotions
of his principal characters. Their tragedy is of such nostalgic nobility that the
reader does not experience fear and pity so much as longing and comfort.
The end of the *Morte Darthur* celebrates the greatness of the Arthurian world
on the eve of its ruin. As the magnificent fellowship turns violently upon itself,
death and destruction also produce repentance, forgiveness, and salvation.

The final sections of the Winchester Manuscript, which Vinaver calls *The
Book of Sir Launcelot and Queen Guinevere* and *The Most Piteous Tale of the
Morte Arthur Saunz Guerdon* (XVIII–XXI in Caxton), are often read in isola-
tion from the rest of the work and have been edited separately. The power
of the last act of the Arthurian drama used to be attributed to a lost French
original, but Malory is now justly given credit for the skill with which he
rearranges, cuts, and adds to his two principal sources, the French prose *La
Mort Le Roi Artu* (hereafter *Mort Artu*) and the English Stanzaic *Le Morte
Arthur* (hereafter Stanzaic *Morte*).[1] The result is a narrative that is at once
more emotional and more symbolic.

Modern readers are often surprised and delighted by the extent to which
they are able to identify with Malory's human creations, as though they
were characters in a novel or movie. Most medieval writers maintain a
certain critical distance from even their most sympathetic figures. Whatever
the narrator and the reader may feel, we are asked to judge the moral
conduct of Francesca or Brunetto Latini in the *Inferno*, just as Chaucer
demands with Criseyde or the *Pearl*-poet with Gawain. Perhaps because he
lacked formal literary training, Malory's response to his characters is more
direct and emotional. Never much of a systematic thinker, he repeatedly
appeals to our hearts rather than to our heads.

---

[1] For the use of these sources, see R. H. Wilson, 'Malory, The Stanzaic *Morte Arthur*, and
the *Mort Artu*,' *Modern Philology*, 37 (1939), 125–38; and E. Talbot Donaldson, 'Malory
and the Stanzaic *Le Morte Arthur*,' *Studies in Philology*, 47 (1950), 460–72.

The human sympathy that so distinguishes the *Morte Darthur* is balanced by its symbolic episodes. These symbols may suggest the Bible, as does the serpent whose bite initiates the final battle, or the Bible and classical literature, as does the apple of discord that first threatens Queen Guinevere with shameful death, or archetypal myth, as does the killing of Arthur by his own son. These moments are rarely original with Malory. His skill is in recognizing their potential when they appear in his sources (especially the Stanzaic *Morte*) and then making them more prominent and powerful, as he does by having the scavengers despoil their victims after the last battle under moonlight (714/22–7; XXI.4).

The final sections of the *Morte Darthur* form a discrete unit that brings the story of the Round Table to a close, and the thematic and narrative relationship between these last sections are increasingly recognized by scholars. Yet for all their interconnections, the two parts differ in structure. Whereas the final part is a continuous narrative of the fall itself, the penultimate one is composed of five separate narratives whose various events and settings prepare us for that fall. The penultimate part sums up the achievements and limitations of the Arthurian world in anticipation of its destruction.

I

The opening narrative of the penultimate section, 'The Poisoned Apple,' shows Malory's deftness in rearranging a relatively minor episode in his sources. Nothing much happens here except the accidental death of a minor knight, but the mood, characters, and issues that characterize the ending as a whole dominate Malory's retelling. We are immediately made aware that these are indeed the final days of the Round Table: the Grail Quest, the last great communal adventure, is over, and it is only 'the remenaunte' (611/6; XVIII.1) that reassembles at court. That remnant is still glorious, however, and Malory reintroduces those who will play leading roles in the final act: Arthur and Guinevere welcome back Lancelot and Bors (Lancelot is not present in the *Mort Artu* and no such reunion occurs in the Stanzaic *Morte*), and then Gawain is named in connection with Agravain, who will precipitate the final division. The resumption of the love between Lancelot and Guinevere, which determines so many subsequent events, is also soon mentioned: 'and so they loved togydirs more hotter than they dud toforehonde, and had many such prevy draughtis togydir that many in the courte spake of hit' (611/16–7; XVIII.1).

Lancelot and Guinevere are Malory's two greatest characters and their brief scene together at the beginning of this section suggests something of their complexity. On the Quest, Lancelot for once did not surpass all other knights because he was more devoted to Guinevere than to God (611/12–5; XVIII.1). He now tries to balance these two loves. While resuming the affair, he also performs good works for other women 'for the plesure of oure

Lorde Jesu Cryst' (611/23; XVIII.1) and avoids the queen's company for fear of 'sclawndir and noyse' (611/25; XVIII.1). But Guinevere will accept no half measures. She accuses him of not loving her and banishes him from the court, which he accepts with his usual stoicism. At the end of the scene, Lancelot defines himself precisely when he says that on the Quest he saw 'as much as ever saw ony synfull man lyvynge' (611/35–6; XVIII.1). He is the best knight of this world, not the next.

In contrast to the courteous, modest Lancelot, Guinevere is all temperament, quick to take offence (612/19–21; XVIII.2). Her unjust dismissal of her lover, as Bors notes, is characteristic of her fickleness: 'for many tymys or this she hath bene wroth with you, and aftir that she was the first that repented hit' (612/42–4; XVIII.2). In the next episode, the queen reaches new extremes of unreasonableness, as she repeatedly wishes for Lancelot's death because of his supposed unfaithfulness with the Fair Maid of Astolat, only to declare at the end that he might have saved the Maid's life if he had been nicer to her! This Guinevere may seem like an anti-feminist stereotype, but Donaldson rightly notes 'a force and dignity' in her that is not in Malory's two sources and that will enable her to respond to the coming tragedy.[2]

The dinner that Guinevere holds for Arthur's knights in the 'Poisoned Apple' episode emphasizes the fellowship of the Round Table. This is not only the primary institution of the Arthurian world but a central concept in Malory's book, as Elizabeth Archibald has recently reminded us.[3] But even as the fellowship is celebrated, we are shown its limitations. Being human, it is subject to discord. The agent is a poisoned apple, offered not by a goddess or by Satan but by a knight who desires revenge for the death of a kinsman. His sneak attack is a debased example of the chivalric honour at the heart of the Arthurian world, and its intended victim, Gawain, will seal the destruction of the fellowship with a similar act of revenge. More discord follows when Guinevere is wrongly held responsible and threatened with burning at the stake.

In fact, nothing bad happens to the central characters. A certain Patryse eats the poisoned apple instead of Gawain, and Guinevere is rescued by Lancelot after which the true villain is unmasked. 'The Poisoned Apple' ends with 'grete joy' and 'many merthys' (620/40–1; XVIII.7), and thus asserts the glory of the Arthurian world just before its fall. The very last words of the tale 'all was forgyffyn' (621/23; XVIII.8), look to the deeper repentance and mutual forgiveness that the major characters finally achieve.

Despite this relatively happy resolution, the forces that will cause the fall of the Round Table are clearly foreshadowed. Despite the queen's

---

[2] Donaldson, p. 462.
[3] 'Malory's Ideal of Fellowship,' *Review of English Studies*, n.s. 43 (1992), 311–28.

exonerated, the knights' deep distrust of her will later return when more justified charges are brought against her. Even more unsettling is the implication of Lancelot's final speech in the 'Poisoned Apple.' In response to Arthur's gratitude, Lancelot expresses his obligation to both king and queen: 'My lorde . . . wytte you well y ought of ryght ever to be in youre quarell and in my ladyes the quenys quarell to do batayle, for ye ar the man that gaff me the hygh Order of Knyghthode, and that day my lady, youre quene, ded me worshyp' (620/21–4; XVIII.7). What Lancelot seems unable to imagine is a quarrel in which king and queen would be on opposite sides, thus producing those conflicts of loyalties that many have seen as the central theme of the ending. Such a conflict will soon appear as a result of the last word in the quotation: 'worshyp.' Worship, or honour as we would say, is noble but not necessarily moral, as Lancelot reveals when he tells Arthur that he had promised the queen 'ever to be her knyght in ryght othir in wronge' (620/29–30; XVIII.7).

The second narrative in this part, 'The Fair Maid of Astolat,' continues the foreshadowing of the destruction of the Arthurian fellowship. For example, Gareth's heroic deeds earn him comparison to and praise from Lancelot (637–8; XVIII.18), but it will be Lancelot's accidental killing of Gareth that causes Gawain's implacable enmity in the final part.[4] Lancelot's apparently whimsical decision to fight in a tournament 'ayenste the kynge and ayenst all hys felyship' (622/22–3; XVIII.9) is a preview of more serious divisions. In fact, Lancelot never again fights on Arthur's side. The internecine warfare of the final battles is also anticipated by the terrible wounds that a disguised Lancelot accidently receives from his closest ally Bors. Lancelot quotes a proverb, 'there ys harde batayle thereas kynne and frendys doth batayle ayther ayenst other' (634/32–3; XVIII.16), whose full horror will only be apparent when the closest of friends and kin no longer battle each other in disguise but with the full knowledge of who it is they are attacking.

If tournaments suggest a potential for destruction, that other central activity of the Arthurian world, romantic love, is presented as fatal. The love that Elaine, the Fair Maid of Astolat, feels for Lancelot is immediate and total. She is as sweet and devoted as Guinevere is moody and fickle, resorting to none of the tricks or deceptions of her English or French models.[5] Yet for all its sincerity, the Fair Maid's passion is worldly and sensual, as her offer to be Lancelot's wife or paramour reveals. On the point of death from unrequited love, she is told by her confessor to leave such secular thoughts, but she defends her feeling, asking 'Am I nat an erthely

---

[4] Lancelot is apparently not personally responsible for the death of Gareth in the Stanzaic *Morte*, 1959–65.

[5] Felicity Riddy, 'Structure and Meaning in Malory's "The Fair Maid of Astolat,"' *Forum for Modern Language Studies*, 12 (1976), 361–2, notes the innocence of the world of Astolat in contrast to Arthur's court.

woman?' She goes on to assert that her love does no offence to God, 'for He fourmed me thereto, and all maner of good love comyth of God.' Her only offence, she says, is loving 'oute of mesure,' which she cannot control, having 'no myght to withstonde the fervent love, wherfore I have my deth!' (639/31–640/2; XVIII.19). The priest offers no reply.

Any moral theologian could find the holes in Elaine's argument, but her assertion that loyal romantic love is not repugnant to God is echoed throughout the end of the *Morte Darthur*. Human passion is always potentially tragic because it is necessarily contingent, unlike the unchanging love of God, but it is not easily controlled. Bors wishes that Lancelot would reciprocate Elaine's passion (635/9–13. XVIII.16), thus satisfying both her and orthodox morality, but he recognizes that he cannot. Human love has its own laws. As Lancelot tells Guinevere when she criticizes him for not being nice enough to Elaine, 'I love nat to be constrayned to love, for love muste only aryse of the harte selff, and nat by none constraynte' (641/36–8; XVIII.20).

The next two narratives, 'The Great Tournament' and 'The Knight of the Cart' (the first apparently original with Malory and the second displaced from its usual place in the Arthurian sequence and radically reshaped), tell us more about two of the most important themes of the ending: honour and the relationship of Guinevere and Lancelot. 'The Great Tournament,' a different tournament from that in the 'Fair Maid,' has moments that approach slapstick (such as the accidental wounding in the buttocks of Lancelot by a huntress), but its predominant tone is chivalric and elegiac. On the eve of the breakup of the Round Table we are given a roll call of its noble knights (644–5; XVIII.23), a list that also includes Agravain and Mordred. Lancelot once again fights against the king and his party, and Gareth joins him against his kinsmen, making even more excruciating his later accidental killing by Lancelot during the rescue of the queen. Questioned by Arthur, Gareth defends his choice to fight with Lancelot here on the grounds of honour. ' 'My lorde,' seyde sir Garethe, 'he [Lancelot] made me knyght, and whan I saw hym so hard bestad, methought hit was my worshyp to helpe hym' ' (648/16–7; XVIII.24).

The great importance of honour in the *Morte Darthur* was first argued by D. S. Brewer, who showed that it is 'the strongest single motivating force in the society which Malory creates.'[6] Gareth demonstrates that it can transcend family and nationality (Lancelot is French), but despite its high idealism, honour must not be confused with Christian or even secular morality: it is often opposed to truth and even to life itself. Honour is about responsibility and reputation rather than virtue. The honourable man must assert the good name of those for whom he is responsible, even (perhaps especially) if he knows that they do not deserve it. To do the honourable

---

6 *The Morte Darthur. Parts Seven and Eight*, ed. D. S. Brewer (London, 1968), p. 25.

thing may well be self-destructive, as in many Roman or Victorian English historical anecdotes. Arthur warmly applauds Gareth's behavior: 'ye say well, and worshypfully have ye done, and to youreselff grete worshyp' (648/21–22; XVIII.24), but soon a similar concern with 'worshyp' will cause Gareth's murder and destroy Arthur's court. Brewer notes the tragic paradox of the ending in which the same honour 'which has created the good society brings about its collapse.'[7]

'The Knight of the Cart' is a version of Chrétien de Troyes's great poem of courtly love, *Le Chevalier de la Charrete*, which Malory knew from the prose *Lancelot*. Malory moves the story to a much later point in the Arthurian saga and uses it both to explore the love of Guinevere and Lancelot and to replay the themes of 'The Poisoned Apple' in a darker mode. While out maying with unarmed men and women, Guinevere is captured by the love-sick Meleagant, who holds her prisoner in his castle until Lancelot learns of the abduction and sets out to rescue her. 'The Knight of the Cart' inhabits a more realistic landscape than the romance fantasy of previous versions. There is no sword bridge, Meleagant's kingdom does not suggest the otherworld (it is only seven miles from Westminster), and Lancelot's ride in the cart does not demonstrate that he will endure any shame for Guinevere – it is merely an efficient way to reach the queen.

'The Knight of the Cart' makes explicit the physicality of Lancelot and Guinevere's passion. This may seem hardly necessary, but in fact the only time during the last two parts of the *Morte Darthur* when we see the lovers actually making love is when Lancelot breaks into the queen's chamber: 'So, to passe uppon thys tale, sir Launcelot wente to bedde with the quene and toke no force of hys hurte honde, but toke hys plesaunce and hys lykynge untyll hit was the dawnyng of the day; for wyte you well he slept nat, but wacched' (657/33–6; XIX.6). As the quotation indicates, Lancelot has hurt his hands while breaking the window bars to get to the queen, and the blood he leaves in her bed is discovered by Meleagant who accuses her of adultery. The charge is as serious as in the 'Poisoned Apple' and more accurate. Lancelot can defend the queen on a technicality because Meleagant charges her with adultery with the knights of her chamber; if Meleagant had noticed the glove that Lavayne makes to hide Lancelot's wound (657/40–1; XIX.6), a detail original in Malory, he might have guessed the whole truth. Even more ominous is the implication that the cowardly Meleagant's love for Guinevere is a version of Lancelot's own illicit devotion, just as Meleagant's abduction is a preview of Lancelot's taking the queen away from the court when she is finally put to the stake.

The relationship of Lancelot and Guinevere is one of Malory's primary interests during the final episodes. It is the subject of an early scene in the

[7] Brewer, p. 30.

penultimate part, as we have seen, and the last section of the final part. Near the center of these two parts, 'The Knight of the Cart' is prefaced with a discussion of romantic love by the narrator. As in the speech by the Fair Maid of Astolat, such love is presented as not necessarily hostile to God: 'But firste reserve the honoure to God, and secundely thy quarell muste com of thy lady. And such love I calle vertuouse love' (649/19–21; XVIII.25). Malory complains about the lack of stability in modern love ('sone hote sone colde'), whereas in Arthur's days, couples could love together for seven years 'and no lycoures lustis was betwyxte them, and than was love trouthe and faythefulnes' (649/22–9; XVIII.25). Lest we think that Malory is praising only physical restraint, he concludes by asserting that Guinevere 'was a trew lover, and therefor she had a good ende' (649/34–5).

The meaning and coherence of this praise of love in general and the relationship between Lancelot and Guinevere in particular have been the subject of much critical debate. To give just one example, is 'vertuouse love' that which is practised by a 'trew lover'? Roger Sherman Loomis, in a critical move that would solve many other literary cruxes, suggested that the author might have been drunk when he wrote it.[8] Because he is not a trained rhetorician, Malory tends to become obscure, not to say confused, during non-narrative passages like these, but Mark Lambert is surely right that the important thing is not the consistency of the argument but its earnest tone.[9] Larry Benson has noted the 'passion and lyricism' of this passage, as with the similar speech of the Maid of Astolat, and argues that Lancelot's love of Guinevere is presented as 'a positive virtue,'[10] though, in fact, it is only the queen's true love and virtuous end that are explicitly praised.

The two great passions of medieval literature – the love of God and erotic love – are both present in the *Morte Darthur* but neither engages the author's deepest response. Malory keeps the outer forms of both without their inner energy. Perhaps the most remarkable aspect of Malory's 'Knight of the Cart,' especially if we have Chrétien's poem in mind, is the moderation of Lancelot's desire. The 'obsessive love for Arthur's Queen' mentioned by Brewer is simply not evident, for, as Felicity Riddy notes, 'Malory sees Lancelot as a warrior, rather than as a lover.'[11] Chrétien's Lancelot is totally obsessed with the queen, even with cuttings from her hair, but Malory tells us little about the erotic, except for a few general

---

[8] *The Development of Arthurian Romance* (New York, 1964), p. 175.
[9] *Malory: Style and Vision in Le Morte Darthur* (New Haven, 1975), p. 146, n. 28. For two recent examples of interpretations of this passage, which perhaps try too hard to find consistency in Malory's thought, see Beverly Kennedy, 'Malory's Lancelot: "Trewest Lover, of a Synful Man,"' *Viator*, 12 (1981), 409–56; Peter Waldron, '"Vertuouse Love" and Adulterous Lovers: Coming to Terms with Malory,' *Sir Thomas Malory: Views and Reviews*, ed. D. Thomas Hanks, Jr. (New York, 1992), pp. 54–62.
[10] Larry D. Benson, *Malory's Morte Darthur* (Cambridge, Mass., 1976), p. 231.
[11] Brewer, p. 10; Riddy, p. 365.

phrases about the heat of the couple's love at the beginning of the 'Poisoned Apple' and the brief scene of the knight and queen in bed, which I discussed above. Lambert has shrewdly observed that the passion of Lancelot for Guinevere is not made real to us, and that the knight we see 'is long-suffering rather than lustful.'[12]

Malory's Lancelot is not particularly interested in sex. When he refuses Elaine of Ascolot in the *Mort Artu*, the French Lancelot gallantly declares that he would certainly consider himself fortunate to receive her love if his heart were free, but that instead he has left it in the best of places – i.e. with Guinevere (pp. 41–2). In the same situation, Malory's Lancelot presents himself as uninterested rather than otherwise engaged. To the Maid's offer of marriage, he responds, 'I caste me never to be wedded man' (638/20; XVIII.19), and to her request that he be her paramour, his shocked reply is that it would be an evil reward for her father and brother's goodness toward him (638/22–3; XVIII.19). Significantly, he says nothing about either the Maid's appeal to him or his heart being otherwise engaged.

Human love is highly valued by Malory, but not erotic passion. The only character who deeply feels such desire, the Fair Maid of Astolat, is presented sympathetically, but she dies early and unrequited. The extreme sexual jealousy that Guinevere feels toward the Maid in Malory's sources, a jealousy fed by Gawain's report that Lancelot had granted her his love, is much reduced in the English work, just as it does not reproduce Arthur's strong jealousy from the *Mort Artu*. Malory is more interested in friends and comrades than in sexual relationships. In contrast to the Maid of Astolat's difficulties with Lancelot, her brother easily forms a strong chivalric relationship with him. In the final part of his book, Malory even casts doubt on whether or not Lancelot and Guinevere were in bed together when surprised by Agravain and Mordred (his two sources are explicit that they were). As we shall see, the couple are described more like knightly comrades than courtly lovers. Lancelot's love for Guinevere is a given and serves to define him as secular and sinful rather than as the Grail knight he might have become, but that love in the *Morte Darthur* is only superficially sexual.

The Book of Lancelot and Guinevere concludes with another tale apparently original with Malory, 'The Healing of Sir Urry,' which, on the eve of the fall, celebrates the achievements of Arthur's court and of its greatest knight. Sir Urry arrives in Arthur's court with terrible wounds that sorcery has made unhealable except by the best knight in the world. The attempt to cure him occasions a list of knights and adventures that is a final reprise of the glories of the Round Table. After all others have tried and failed, Lancelot makes a dramatic entrance, though he is modesty itself and afraid of presumption. He acts only on Arthur's command and after praying to the Trinity: 'Thou

[12] Lambert, pp. 200, 205.

masyste yeff me power to hele thys syke knyght by the grete vertu and grace of The, but, Good Lorde, never of myselff' (668/24–26; XIX.12). When Urry is cured, Lancelot weeps like a beaten child.

The healing of Urry does seem to suggest some kind of divine approval for Lancelot despite his adultery, as Larry Benson argues, but much about this scene remains mysterious, such as the reason for his tears.[13] And we ought to recognize the limits of Lancelot's apotheosis. Reaffirmed as the greatest of Arthur's knights, his achievement remains of this world. He neither reaches nor attempts any spiritual union with God, and his miracle is purely physical – he cures wounds, not souls. The salvation he offers is bodily. He is a chivalric hero rather than a religious saint or courtly lover.

II

In contrast to the many different stories of the penultimate part, the final part of the *Morte Darthur* is a continuous narrative of the fall of the Round Table. If all human institutions must disappear, few do so with as much heroism, nobility, love, and emotion as Arthur's court. The flower imagery in Malory's opening May description suggests the coming ruin. The season is usually one in which the heart of every man and woman 'rejoysyth' because of 'somer commynge with his freyshe floures,' but in this May begins 'a grete angur and unhappe' that only ends with the destruction of the 'floure of chyvalry' (673/1–8; XX.1). The beautiful but transitory Arthurian garden is inhabited by serpents, two 'unhappy knyghtis whych were named sir Aggravayne and sir Mordred,' whose 'prevy hate' toward Guinevere and Lancelot drives them to expose the affair (673/9–13; XX.1).

Such hate is balanced by the way that the fellowship of the Round Table is able to transcend the simple bonds of kinship. Although Gawain is Agravain's brother, he will have nothing to do with his schemes. Recalling Lancelot's many services to the court, including the rescue of the two plotters themselves, Gawain declares, 'I woll never be ayenste sir Launcelot for one dayes dede, that was whan he rescowed me frome kynge Carados of the Dolerous Towre and slew hym and saved my lyff' (673/40–674/2; XX.1). Already we find a sharper irony than in the previous section of the work. The Dolorous Tower, renamed Joyous Garde by Lancelot, is precisely where Gawain will shortly first attack his old friend.

The same scene introduces what becomes an excruciating motif throughout the last part: heroes helpless to avert the disasters they so clearly foresee. As Gawain takes leave of his evil brother, he fully understands what will happen: 'Alas! . . . now ys thys realme holy destroyed and

---

[13] Larry Benson says that Lancelot's healing, which occurs 'after reestablishing his faithful love of Guinevere,' is 'a sign of divine approval. It is surely a sign that Malory did not make a simple equation between the sin of lust and the fall of the Round Table' (p. 228).

myscheved, and the noble felyshyp of the Rounde Table shall be disparbeled' (674/17–19; XX.1). In contrast to Malory's earlier stories, disasters
no longer come unexpectedly or because of disguise; now they are as clear
as they are unavoidable. A few lines later, Bors advises Lancelot not to visit
the queen from a similarly accurate presentiment of danger (675/25–30;
XX.2). But Lancelot does go to the queen's room, and the affair is made
public.

Malory makes clear that Arthur has no interest in such exposure, though
he is forced to sanction Agravain's plot when publicly requested. In
contrast to the jealous obsessive in the French *Mort Artu*, Malory's king
'had a demyng' of the love affair, but he would hear nothing of it 'for sir
Launcelot had done so much for hym and for the quene so many tymes that
wyte you well the kynge loved hym passyngly well' (674/38–41; XX.1).
Later Arthur declares, 'much more I am soryar for my good knyghtes losse
than for the losse of my fayre quene; for quenys I myght have inow, but
such a felyship of good knyghtes shall never be togydirs in no company'
(685/29–32; XX.9). It is not just that Arthur chooses the role of king over
that of husband, but, even more important, that he chooses the love
between comrades over the erotic passion so often celebrated in Arthurian
romance.

A similar choice is made by Lancelot and Guinevere when they are
trapped in the queen's chamber by Agravain, Mordred, and twelve armed
knights. In their dignity, bravery, and concern for each other, the couple,
like Arthur, express chivalric rather than sexual love.[14] In an original
speech as he awaits what he expects will be his certain death, Malory's
Lancelot speaks not about his passion but about his service to one whom he
addresses as 'Moste nobelest Crysten quene' and to whom he promises
protection by his relatives (676/33ff; XX.3). The queen, her extreme fickleness transmuted into extreme courage, insists that if Lancelot is slain, she
will 'take my dethe as mekely as ever ded marter take hys dethe for Jesu
Crystes sake' (677/1–3; XX.3). The religious language associated with
Guinevere is not satirical or hypocritical, but stresses the heroic public role
that she henceforth plays with honour and bravery.

In the fight against Agravain and his allies, Lancelot is more reasonable,
trickier, and deadlier than he is in Malory's sources. He offers to answer
their charge of treason the next day, but when this is refused, he lures one
knight into the queen's chamber to get his armour. In contrast to the one
or two casualties in the sources, Malory's Lancelot kills all except,
unfortunately, Mordred. His victory against such odds is a measure of his
greatness, but the carnage makes reconciliation impossible. The court is
split between Arthur and Lancelot, and the knights begin to choose sides.

---

[14] Lambert, p. 203, compares this part of the *Morte* to the Old English heroic poem, *The
Battle of Maldon*.

Many different causes have been identified as the reason for the fall of the Round Table in the *Morte Darthur*, from divine punishment of sin to a series of unfortunate accidents. Individual characters have also been blamed, and all the major figures can be held responsible to some degree: Lancelot and Guinevere for their affair, Agravain for making it a public scandal, Arthur for sending his queen to the stake, and Gawain for his relentless desire for revenge against Lancelot. The most satisfactory explanation for the fall, however, is the honour or, to use Malory's word, 'worship' that Brewer identified as fundamental to Arthurian society.[15]

Each of the major characters strives to make his actions during the ending follow the dictates of worshipful honour. Even the wretched Agravain and Mordred claim that their hostility to Lancelot is motivated by the shame (the opposite of honour) that his affair does to their king and uncle: 'hit ys shamefully suffird of us all that we shulde suffir so noble a kynge as kynge Arthur ys to be shamed' (673/19–20; XX.1). It is not outside enemies or the villainy and vice of the Round Table that cause its fall, but one of its central values. The Arthurian ideal of fellowship is destroyed by the Arthurian ideal of honour. The *Morte Darthur* is so moving because it is a tragedy of virtue.

The three main heroes of the ending – Arthur, Lancelot, and Gawain – have no choice in what they do if they would remain honourable. Once Agravain and his knights have been killed and the affair between Lancelot and Guinevere exposed, Arthur's public honour demands that he punish his queen whatever his private feelings: '"And now hit ys fallen so," seyde the kynge, "that I may nat with my worshyp but my quene muste suffir dethe," and was sore amoved' (682/9–11; XX.7). Gawain urges the king not to condemn Guinevere so hastily because she may have asked Lancelot to her room 'for goodnes and for none evyll' (682/31–32; XX.7). But Arthur cannot accept that appearances may be deceiving because honour is all about appearance. Goodness and inner motivation have nothing to do with it.

If honour compels Arthur to send Guinevere to the stake, it just as surely forces Lancelot to rescue her. He has no choice. As Bors (a Grail knight!) makes clear, this is not a question of Lancelot's guilt or innocence or even of his love for the queen. Because Lancelot is responsible for the queen's predicament, he would be publicly shamed if he did not act:

> 'And also I woll counceyle you, my lorde, that my lady quene Gwenyver, and she be in ony distres, insomuch as she ys in payne for youre sake, that ye knyghtly rescow her; for and ye ded ony other wyse all the worlde wolde speke you shame to the worldis ende. Insomuch

---

[15] See notes 6 and 7 above. Building on Brewer's analysis, Lambert argues, 'It is Malory himself, not just his characters, for whom honor and shame are more real than innocence and guilt. *Le Morte Darthur* is *of* rather than *about* a shame ethos' (p. 179).

as ye were takyn with her, whether ye ded ryght othir wronge, hit ys now youre parte to holde wyth the quene, that she be nat slayne and put to a myschevous deth. For and she so dye, the shame shall be evermore youres.' (680/16–24; XX.6)

This is as clear a definition of honour (its basis in responsibility, its focus on public reputation, and its indifference to right and wrong) as one can find in the *Morte Darthur*.

Gawain's vengeance against Lancelot, though often condemned by modern commentators as wicked and obsessive, is equally demanded by honour.[16] After the rescue of Guinevere, but before Gawain learns that his brothers Gareth and Gaheris have been slain 'unarmed and unwares' (684/26; XX.8), Malory adds a remarkable speech in which Gawain recognizes that Lancelot had no choice but to act as he did if he would preserve his honour: 'and to say the trouth he were nat of worshyp but if he had rescowed the quene, insomuch as she shulde have be brente for his sake' (686/1–3; XX.9). Gawain continues that he himself and any other knight would have done likewise: 'he hath done but knyghtly, and as I wolde have done myselff and I had stonde in lyke case' (686/3–5; XX.9). After he learns that Lancelot has killed his brothers, Gawain faints and then vows to Arthur 'be my knyghthode, that frome thys day forewarde I shall never fayle sir Launcelot untyll that one of us have slayne that othir' (687/1–3; XX.10). Gawain's response is neither inconsistent nor atavistic. Recognizing Lancelot's opposition to Arthur as knightly, he must now oppose Lancelot to retain his own honour. Previously he refused to avenge the killing of his brother Agravain and two of his own sons because they had acted against his explicit advice, but the innocence of Gareth and Gaheris requires a response. Motive is again irrelevant (Arthur correctly reports that Lancelot did not recognize the two). His relatives were wrongly killed and there is only one honourable course of action. It is in pursuit of the knightly worship he praises in Lancelot that Gawain becomes the other's mortal enemy.

Many critics argue that somehow these conflicts could have been avoided and a more moderate course of action found, but that is not possible. If any of the three heroes were to shirk the demands of honour, he would lose his reputation, his name, and thus his very being. The unbearable tragedy is that each sees the ruin that will result from his necessary action. Although Lancelot's actual killing of Gareth is unwitting, he understands that in rescuing the queen 'peradventure I shall there destroy som of my beste fryndis' (681/4–5; XX.6). Arthur also knows the

---

[16] For example, Brewer refers to Gawain as a 'half-villain' (p. 11), Lambert notes his 'relentless pursuit of revenge' (p. 217), and Benson calls him 'clearly the least virtuous' of the four major characters (p. 241). For a detailed analysis of Gawain's actions as dictated by honour, see my 'Gawain's Defence of Lancelot in Malory's "Death of Arthur,"' *Modern Language Review*, 78 (1983), 267–72.

terrible result of what he must do. Even as he insists that worship demands that Guinevere be put to the stake, he accepts that this will destroy what is closest to his heart: 'for now I am sure the noble felyshyp of the Rounde Table ys broken for ever' (682/7–8; XX.7). In similar fashion, Gawain is forced to break the deep loyalty he had shared with Lancelot, his only peer at the Round Table, knowing, as we have seen, that it must end in the death of one of them (687/1–3; XX.10).

To consider the fall of the Round Table as a series of unhappy accidents that might well have been avoided, as Larry Benson and, to a lesser extent, Mark Lambert argue, is to diminish Malory's tragic vision.[17] He may be a sentimentalist, but, for all his novelistic tendencies, he is a man of the Middle Ages who knows that no one lives happily ever after. The Arthurian court is a human institution and like all things of this world must come to an end: much more fitting that it be brought down by its champions than by its villains, by its virtues than by its vices.

As the Round Table destroys itself in pursuit of its ideals, the ideals themselves necessarily suffer. Fellowship is the first to go. If each side gathers to it 'all that we love and that lovyth us,' as Bors puts it (679/8; XX.5), that must mean that former friends and comrades are now enemies. One of the great achievements of the Arthurian fellowship had been its transcendence of family and nationality, but now such divisions reassert themselves. Gawain seeks revenge for his family, and Lancelot is forced to return to France. The greatest blow to the fellowship is the accidental death of Gareth, who attended the attempted burning of Guinevere unarmed and under protest only because he had been ordered to by his king (and kinsman) Arthur. His deepest affection, as we have seen, is not for his family, but for Lancelot, on whose side he fights in the Great Tournament and to whom he is often compared. That Gareth of all people is killed by Lancelot, however unwittingly, signals the end of the Round Table.[18]

Even honour is put under stress as the heroes seek to follow its dictates. Arthur's worship may demand that he respond to the public revelation of his queen's adultery, but how honourable can it be to put a woman (and one's wife) to the stake? Lancelot notes that the king and Gawain get no honour in attacking him: 'here wynne ye no worshyp, but magré and dishonoure' (687/44; XX.11). Arthur indeed has little heart for the pursuit of his best knight whatever its justification: 'Alas, alas, that ever yet thys warre began!' (691/30; XX.13). Although Gawain's opposition to Lancelot begins as honourable revenge, he becomes increasingly nihilistic and seems

---

[17] See Larry Benson, pp. 239–40: 'But one cannot escape the feeling that save for a series of unhappy accidents the catastrophe might have been avoided' (p. 240). Although Lambert sees a 'tragic multicentricity' (p. 168), he also points to Malory's emphasis on 'luck, fate, fortune, chance, rather than moral responsibility' (p. 162) and claims that even after Gawain's death, 'a happy "Lancelot and Guinevere" ending is still possible' (p. 170).

[18] Lambert, p. 211.

less interested in victory than in self-destruction. Wounded by Lancelot, he challenges him again as soon as he is physically able; struck down once more, he lies on the ground explicitly begging to be killed: 'Traytoure knyght, wyte thou well I am nat yet slayne. Therefore com thou nere me and performe thys batayle to the utteraunce!' (706/39–40; XX.22). Not that Lancelot himself wins much glory in the conflict. He is both reluctant and murderous. He refuses to fight his former companions until their taunts of cowardice become too much for him bear, and then his blows cause Gawain's death.

Amid such sordid events, the nobility of the Arthurian world is redefined. Honour is transformed into a deeper sense of responsibility. As they face death, Malory's principal characters take responsibility for their actions, repent their sins, and forgive their enemies. Sexual desire is left firmly behind, but what replaces it is only superficially Christian. The love the Arthurian heroes finally affirm is neither divine nor erotic, neither *caritas* nor *amor*, but a deep and fully human bond of affection, an earthly *amicitia* of comrades. As their careers and the Round Table come to an end, a new, purified fellowship is born.

A knight is expected to do what honour demands, even if this results in the destruction of those comrades and institutions that he most loves, but in the face of death, the self-assertion of honour gives way to something deeper and more generous. Only then can the 'longing for wholeness' that Jill Mann sees as the root of Malory's poignancy be satisfied: 'the obliteration of fissures, gaps, fragmentation, both within the self, and between the self and the outside world.'[19] It is appropriate that Gawain, whose relentless pursuit of 'worship' is the most extreme, should be the first to show how honour can be transformed. When he recognizes that his wounds are mortal, Gawain tells his affectionate uncle Arthur, who calls him 'the man in the worlde that I loved moste' (709/24–5; XXI.2), that the war and his death are entirely the result of his own faults: 'And all I may wyte myne owne hastynes and my wylfulnesse, for thorow my wylfulness I was causer of myne owne dethe' (709/30–3; XXI.2).[20] Like Cresseid at the end of Henryson's *Testament of Cresseid*, Gawain will blame no one but himself: 'thorow me and my pryde ye have all thys shame and disease' (709/35–6; XXI.2). Gawain's analysis is obviously incomplete, for others are guilty as well, but his willingness to take full responsibility is an advance beyond honour. Honour demands that someone must be attacked to protect or avenge another, whereas Gawain takes all on himself. It is an appropriate return for Arthur's love and allows Gawain to request that

---

[19] *The Narrative of Distance, The Distance of Narrative in Malory's Morte Darthur*, The William Matthews Lectures 1991 (London, 1991), p. 2

[20] Gawain utters no death speech in the Stanzaic *Morte*, which Malory generally follows in this last section; Gawain's speech in the French *Mort Artu* does blame himself but less explicitly (pp. 220–1).

Lancelot come quickly to rescue the king, invoking 'all the love that ever was betwyxte us' (710/18; XXI.2).

As with Gawain's confession of the sin of pride, the last pages of Malory's work have many moments that could be interpreted as strongly Christian. Arthur has an apocalyptic vision of himself in rich clothes suddenly cast from a wheel into 'an hydeous depe blak watir, and therin was all maner of serpentis and wormes and wylde bestis fowle and orryble' (711/23–5; XXI.3). The clear reference here is to the Wheel of Fortune and the punishment of worldly pomp. Arthur then receives another vision directly from God (712/6; XXI.3) that warns him not to fight Mordred the next day; but battle is inadvertently begun when a knight is stung by an adder, suggesting the serpent in the Garden of Eden.

Yet for all their Christian coloring, these references are also strongly mythic and refer to this world rather than the next. Perhaps the most terrible symbolic moment is the mutual slaying of Mordred and Arthur – the horror of which is increased by Malory's original description of how the dying, skewered son pulls himself up the shaft of his father's spear in order to strike the mortal blow against his father (714/8–9; XXI.4). This Oedipal struggle, which Mann calls a 'grotesque parody' of knightly adventure,'[21] mocks the family, chivalric, and personal love at the center of the *Morte Darthur*. The Arthurian world has become a surrealistic nightmare. The king asks 'where ar all my noble knyghtes becom' (713/23–4; XXI.4), but all that can be seen on the battlefield are helpless victims pillaged in the moonlight (714/23–7; XXI.4). Lucan and Bedevere are the only knights that remain with Arthur, but soon Lucan dies more horribly than in Malory's sources – 'he lay fomyng at the mowth and parte of his guttes lay at hys fyete' – (714/41–2; XXI.5); and Bedevere twice tries to keep Excalibur for himself rather than throwing it back into the lake as he promised the failing Arthur.

The orthodox medieval answer to such blows of Fortune and earthly ruin is to turn to the divine. This happens in the *Morte Darthur*, but only super-ficially. Arthur sees the dead Gawain with all the ladies for whom he fought, but though we are told that the vision is sanctioned by God, we learn nothing of Gawain's ultimate fate (711/34–712/12; XXI.3). Arthur himself is carried away by ladies in a mysterious barge either to be buried (716/33ff; XXI.6) or to be taken 'by the wyll of oure Lorde Jesu into another place' (717/29–30; XXI.7) in readiness for his fabled reappearance. Malory constantly uses the language of Christianity and describes his heroes going to heaven, but he has no real interest in the metaphysical. His focus remains on this world and his religion is sentimental.

Malory's sentimental Christianity is seen most clearly in the concluding episode of the book. Despite its title, the *Morte Darthur* does not end with

[21] Mann, p. 33.

the death of Arthur, but with the deaths of his queen and greatest knight. Before their deaths, Lancelot and Guinevere take up religious careers, but they do not reject the Round Table and all its works so much as affirm its deepest values. The last act is initiated by Guinevere. Once she learns that Arthur is dead, she goes with five of her ladies to become a nun. As always, the queen's actions are extreme, but now anything but wilful and selfish. She exchanges the hauteur of a courtly lady for the devotion of a religious: 'but ever she lyved in fastynge, prayers, and almes-dedis, that all maner of people mervayled how vertuously she was chaunged' (718/2–3; XXI.7). But how much has really changed beside her clothing?

When Lancelot returns to England and Guinevere sets eyes on him, 'she sowned thryse' (720/6–7; XXI.9), which suggests the persistence of affection. The speech to her ladies in his presence is revealing. Although she says she hopes to see the face of God after her death and to sit on his right hand, her emphasis is on secular affairs: 'Thorow thys same man and me hath all thys warre be wrought, and the deth of the moste nobelest knyghtes of the worlde; for thorow oure love that we have loved togydir ys my moste noble lorde slayne' (720/15–7; XXI.9). Like Gawain, Guinevere takes the responsibility for the fall of the Round Table upon herself. This is moral but not necessarily Christian, because she does not reject the Arthurian world for something higher so much as insist on its matchless nobility. She describes her adulterous love not as a sin against God but as the cause of the deaths of 'the moste nobelest knyghtes of the worlde' and 'my most noble lorde.' It is her earthly not heavenly lord whom she has injured.

Guinevere concludes by urging Lancelot to return to his realm 'and there take ye a wyff, and lyff with hir wyth joy and blys' (720/30–1; XXI.9). This farewell is reminiscent of the scene at the beginning of the last Book when the lovers were trapped by Agravain and his men and Lancelot told Guinevere that if he were to die she could go to live on his lands. As she had refused to separate her fate from his then, he now refuses to separate his from hers: 'I shall never be so false unto you' (720/36–7; XXI; 9). He will once again follow her, this time into religion, so that even in separation they remain a couple: 'But the selff desteny that ye have takyn you to, I woll take me to, for the pleasure of Jesu, and ever for you I caste me specially to pray' (720/37–9; XXI.9). Jesus is mentioned, but he seems decidedly secondary. The language is religious, but the motive is Lancelot's devotion to the queen ('sythen ye have taken you to perfeccion, I must nedys take me to perfection, of ryght' [721/5–6; XXI.9]). He confirms this by insisting that he would have taken her back to his own realm if she had been willing and by asking for a final kiss.

Guinevere refuses because she knows that things can never go back to the way they were. The kissing has to stop, but their love is not superseded by divine love, though it is transformed. The erotic aspect of their relationship, which Malory never makes prominent, has now completely fallen away. What remains between them is something like chivalric love, the human love of comrades that distinguished the Round Table and that the couple have practised since Agravain's attack.[22] If such knightly love can transcend the claims of kin and nationality, it can also transcend gender. In their separate monasteries, Guinevere and Lancelot are closer than ever.

Just as the queen has her ladies with her, Bors and seven other knights join Lancelot. The result is not a true spiritual community so much as a recreation of the Arthurian fellowship despite their different activities. Lancelot gives up being a knight to become a priest. He prays and fasts rather than fights, and the knights' horses (the very symbol of their vocation) are allowed to go 'where they wolde' (722/16–7; XXI.10).[23]

Nevertheless, the values of the Round Table remain in these religious settings, as we see at the deaths of Guinevere and Lancelot, which Malory greatly develops from his sources. After the queen's death, Lancelot is given a vision that charges him to go and bury her in remission of his sins, but the mission he performs is deeply sentimental: to 'burye hir by her husbond, the noble kyng Arthur' (722/25–6; XXI.10). Just as death transforms the demands of honour, so also it allows king and queen a physical closeness they seem not to have achieved in life.

Lancelot is the last to repent and take responsibility for the Arthurian tragedy. When upbraided for swooning at Guinevere's grave, he says it comes from sorrow rather than any pleasure in sin. He then blames his own faults for what has happened, as did Gawain and Guinevere before him: 'by my defaute and myn orgule and my pryde . . . they were bothe layed ful lowe' (723/27–8; XXI.11). Yet Lancelot's mind is not on God but on the physical bodies of Arthur and Guinevere:

> 'For whan I remembre of hir beaulté and of hir noblesse, that was bothe wyth hyr kyng and wyth hyr, so whan I sawe his corps and hir corps so lye togyders, truly myn herte wold not serve to susteyne my careful body.' (725/23–6; XXI.11)

Lancelot dies with all the marks of sanctity. He predicts the hour of his death, and the Bishop has a vision of him guided by flights of angels to his heavenly rest (724/25–8; XXI.12). But once again Malory's heaven is asserted rather than realized. Gawain, Guinevere, and Lancelot take moral responsibility for their lives as they die, but rather than looking forward to the New Jerusalem, they look back at the glories that were in Camelot.

---

[22] Lambert argues that for Malory there is 'one typical relationship,' one love that ties together all the loyalties in the last tale: these loyalties are all 'variations on the pattern of chivalric loyalty and service' (p. 212).

[23] Larry Benson notes that Malory adds a final passage, found in no other French or English version, that explains that after Lancelot's death the knights who were with him leave the monastery and carry on the life of chivalry as crusaders (pp. 246–7).

The last words on Lancelot are spoken by his brother Ector, not by the Bishop, in praise of Lancelot as a knight, not a saint.

> 'A, Launcelot!' he sayd, 'thou were hede of al Crysten knyghtes! And now I dare say,' sayd syr Ector, 'thou sir Launcelot, there thou lyest, that thou were never matched of erthely knyghtes hande. And thou were the curtest knyght that ever bare shelde! And thou were the truest frende to thy lovar that ever bestrade hors, and thou were trewest lover, of a synful man, that ever loved woman, and thou were the kyndest man that ever strake wyth swerde. And thou were the godelyest persone that ever cam emonge prees of knyghtes, and thou were the mekest man and the jentyllest that ever ete in halle emonge ladyes, and thou were the sternest knyght to thy mortal foo that ever put spere in the reeste.' (725/16–26; XXI.13)

Formally, Lancelot is a 'Crysten' knight, but the noun is clearly more important that the adjective. It is 'earthely knyghtes' who cannot match him. He is praised as the truest lover 'that ever loved woman,' with the significant qualifier, 'of a synful man.' Lancelot is seen as an earthly knight by Ector (and Malory) even after he has been taken away by angels. Along with Gawain and Guinevere, Lancelot is granted heaven at the end of the *Morte Darthur*, but the real immortality for all three comes from their acts in this world, which are never more heroic, loving, and generous than as they leave that world.

PART III

POSTERITY

13

The Reception of Malory's Morte Darthur

A. S. G. EDWARDS

The enduring appeal of the *Morte Darthur* draws on nostalgia for a world that never existed, one in which King Arthur is not dead but alive in his relevance to situations and contexts beyond the imaginings of Thomas Malory. The history of the reception of Malory's work demonstrates this creative vitality over time and medium, finding expression in verse and prose, in painting, architecture and film and extending as far afield as Japan. The sketch of the history of this reception that follows is inevitably highly selective. But it may give some sense of the range and continuity of the appeal of Malory's work.[1]

One obvious but important and revealing aspect of that appeal is the printing history of the work itself. The *Morte Darthur* was one of the very few of the works first printed by Caxton (in 1485) that retained its hold on the reading public in the following centuries. It was reprinted five times after its first publication. Such reprintings testify in various ways to an unusually sustained audience for Malory. There were various factors in such interest. De Worde's 1498 reprint, for example, provides the first illustrations for the *Morte*, a series of twenty woodcuts which he had had executed specifically for his edition. This was the first major work of secular

---

[1] It should be stressed that the reception of Malory's work is part of a much larger and much more complex preoccupation with Arthurian legend in its literary, historical and visual aspects. In what follows I have attempted to discriminate Malory's own contributions to the influence of Arthurian legend from this larger preoccupation. For more general accounts of the influence of Arthurian legend see Howard Maynadier, *The Arthur of the English Poets* (Boston, 1907) and, most valuably, James Douglas Merriman, *The Flower of Kings: A Study of the Arthurian Legend in England between 1485 and 1835* (Lawrence, Kansas, 1973) and Beverley Taylor and Elisabeth Brewer, *The Return of Arthur: British and American Arthurian Literature since 1800* (Cambridge, 1983). I am particularly indebted to these last two works. On Malory's specific influence useful information can be found in Page West Life, *Sir Thomas Malory and the Morte Darthur: A Survey of Scholarship and Annotated Bibliography* (Charlottesville, 1980) and Marilyn Parins, ed., *Malory: The Critical Heritage* (London, 1988); this last is primarily concerned with nineteenth- and twentieth-century scholarly responses to Malory. For discussion of the influence of Malory on art see the excellent book by Muriel Whitaker, *The Legends of King Arthur in Art* (Cambridge, 1990).

literature that de Worde published for which he chose to include a major series of woodcuts.[2] It was an innovation that later editions were to follow. De Worde's own 1529 reprint reuses most of his earlier cuts and adds a few more. Some of these are carried over in their turn to William Copland's 1559 edition, with some replacements. And a very few reappear in Thomas East's edition of 1582, the last illustrated edition, which seems to have recut a number of the earlier pictures to a smaller size and employed some from other sources.[3]

The gradually widening intervals between editions do suggest a slackening of interest in the work over time. The final early printed edition, by William Stansby in 1634, suggests important reasons why this should be so. The Preface announces that

> in many places this Volume is corrected (not in language but in phrase), for here and there, King Arthur or some of his knights were declared in their communications to sweare prophane, and vse superstitious speeches, all (or the most part) of which is either amended or quite left out, by the paines and industry of the Compositor and Corrector at the Presse; so that as it is now it may passe for almost a famous piece of Antiquity revived from the gulph of oblivion, and renued for the pleasure and profit of present and future times.

These asseverations indicate the growing distance between Malory's original audience and the one envisioned for Stansby's edition. Such an audience interestingly was now conceived primarily as 'gentylwomen,' rather than the 'gentylmen' who formed Caxton's prime audience. And Malory is now 'a famous piece of Antiquity' to be restored ('revived') in a form consistent with contemporary taste. It is hard, however, not to suspect some disingenuousness in the announcements of the Preface. For, in spite of its claims to the contrary, Stansby's edition remained unrevised and unexpurgated.[4]

Whatever Stansby's audience of 'gentlewomen' thought of his reprinting, it was the last for over a hundred and fifty years. The next editions do not appear until 1816 and 1817 and they signal the beginnings of modern literary study of the *Morte Darthur*.[5] The late nineteenth and early twentieth centuries saw a renewal of the tradition of regular reprintings, before the discovery of the Winchester manuscript in 1934. It was during this same period that Malory's work was firmly annexed as a text for the scholarly

[2] For discussion and description of these woodcuts see Edward Hodnett, *English Woodcuts 1480–1535* (Oxford, 1973), pp. 14, 309–313.
[3] For a general survey of illustrations in the early editions of Malory see Muriel Whitaker, *The Legend of King Arthur in Art*, pp. 165–72.
[4] For an excellent discussion of Stansby's edition see Tsuyoshi Mukai, 'Stansby's 1634 Edition of Malory's *Morte*,' *Poetica*, 36 (1992), 38–54, to which I am indebted.
[5] For discussion of these see Barry Gaines 'The Editions of Malory in the Early Nineteenth Century,' *Papers of the Bibliographical Society of America*, 68 (1974), 1–17.

community, in the editions of Sommer (1889–91) and Vinaver (1929), and the latter's subsequent edition (first published in 1947), based on the rediscovery of the Winchester manuscript in 1934. While most study of Malory since then has been appropriately based on this manuscript, it is necessary to emphasize the fact that all responses to the *Morte* down to the twentieth century have been based on versions of Caxton's text and that it has its own important culturally inscribed position in the history of the work's reception.

This outline of the bibliographical history of the *Morte Darthur* suggests one dimension of the history of the work's reception, the external record, as it were, revealed in the various editions of the work and their adaptation to meet the demands of new markets. For it is clear that Caxton's edition and its early reprints by de Worde were widely read. Paradoxically, the chief evidence of this is negative: very few copies survive of Caxton's 1485 edition and de Worde's of 1498 and 1529, and those that do are usually imperfect. For such a large work the virtual disappearance of editions is striking. It suggests the degree to which Malory's work, like other early editions of romances, was literally read to destruction.[6] The relative rarity of copies of these earliest editions may go some way to explaining why the earliest recorded evidence of reader response to Malory comes in a manuscript. This manuscript was copied in the second half of the sixteenth century by one John Grinken.[7] It is a compilation of the principal deeds of King Arthur and his knights as they appear in Malory. It seems to be the work of an early Arthurian enthusiast, one concerned to try to reconcile different accounts of the legend.

Otherwise no evidence survives of how contemporary readers responded to the work. The chief indications of response must be found therefore in the evidence of its literary assimilation, the ways in which it which it was referred to, employed and appropriated by writers from the later sixteenth century to the present. Among the most remarkable of these is one that is possibly the earliest. It is preserved in Robert Laneham's account of the entertainment for Queen Elizabeth at Kenilworth Castle for twelve days in July 1575.[8] The entire entertainment was clearly structured around Arthurian legend; but at one point it reveals a specifically Malorian influence. Laneham reports the appearance of a 'sqier minstrel' who 'after a little warbling on hiz harp for a prelude, came foorth with a sollem

---

[6] There is a tantalizing reference in a late fifteenth-century book-list, now bound in British Library MS Royal 15 D. ii, fol. 211, to 'a boke cald mort Artho' which may refer to an early printed edition; see G. F. Warner and J. P. Gilson, *Catalogue of Western Manuscripts in the Old Royal and King's Collections*, 4 vols. (London, 1921), II, 171.

[7] It was sold at Christies (London) 29 November 1978, lot 27 and is now in private hands. It has not been possible to examine this at first hand, but I am most grateful to the owner for kindly answering my questions about it.

[8] *Captain Cox, his Ballads and Books; or Robert Laneham's Letter*, ed. F. J. Furnivall (London, 1890).

song, warraunted for story oout of King Arthurz acts, the first book and 26. chapter, whearof I gate a copy,' which he then prints.[9] It is clear that the ballad derived from one of de Worde's editions of Malory; the minstrel's knowledge of his work also extended considerably beyond the chapter he specifies.[10] A ballad based on a quite recent printed work suggests a degree of oral transmission that reveals the extent of the assimilation of the *Morte* into forms of popular culture. Nor is this the only indication of the swift absorption of Malory's work into oral tradition. It seems to have provided a source for a ballad on King Arthur's death in the seventeenth-century Percy Folio manuscript,[11] and there are other indications of a knowledge of Malory among the ballads in this manuscript.[12]

But interest in Malory was not restricted to popular tradition in the sixteenth and early seventeenth centuries. It seems likely that Philip Sidney knew the work and was to some degree influenced by it in his *Arcadia*.[13] And it is clear that Spenser had read it. *A View of the Present State of Ireland* (1633) mentions Sir Lancelot, who 'wore the sleve of the fayre mayd of Asterothe in a Tvrney, wheareat Quene *Guenover* was muche displeased,' a clear allusion to the episode in The Book of Sir Launcelot and Queen Guinevere (621–42, especially 623–32; XVIII. 8–20).[14] The influence of the *Morte Darthur* on the *Faerie Queene* has often been asserted since Thomas Warton first made the claim in the eighteenth century (see further below). The likelihood of the influence of the earlier great chivalric literary work on the later is very probable, even if the full extent of it is not easy to assess.[15]

Shakespeare's knowledge of the *Morte* is demonstrated in a single aside. It occurs in *2 Henry IV* (1597–8), in Shallow's comment: 'I was then Sir Dagonet in Arthur's Show,' (III. ii. 272), a clear allusion to The Book of Sir Tristram de Lyones (360–62; X.11–12) that may reflect a larger acquaintance with the *Morte Darthur*, evident (it has been argued) elsewhere in *Henry IV*

[9] *Captain Cox*, pp. 41–2

[10] For discussion of this ballad see William Matthews, 'Alliterative Song of an Elizabethan Minstrel,' *Research Studies*, 32 (1964), 135–46.

[11] British Library Add. MS 27879; see Robert H. Wilson, 'Malory and the Ballad "King Arthur's Death,"' *Medievalia & Humanistica*, n.s. 6 (1975), 139–49.

[12] David Fowler points out that the ballad *Clerk Edwards* contains details 'reminiscent of an episode in Malory's *Sir Gareth of Orkney*'; see *A Manual of the Writings in Middle English*, VI, general ed. Albert E. Hartung (New Haven, Conn., 1980), 1799.

[13] See Marcus S. Goldman, *Sir Philip Sidney and the Arcadia*, Illinois Studies in Language and Literature, vol. XVII ([Urbana], 1934), pp. 186–210. While a number of the parallels adduced there lack specific force, their cumulative weight makes the influence of Malory quite probable.

[14] *Spenser's Prose Works*, ed. R. Gottfried (Baltimore, 1949), p. 111/1914–5.

[15] See Mark Lambert, 'Malory,' in *The Spenser Encyclopedia*, ed. A. C. Hamilton (Toronto, 1990), pp. 450–1 for a succinct and authoritative assessment of influence. For an earlier, more sceptical view see Merritt Y. Hughes, 'The Arthurs of the *Faerie Queene*,' *Etudes Anglaises*, 6 (1953), 193–213.

and *Henry V*.[16] The very casualness of the allusion seems to suggest a familiarity on the part of both author and audience with Malory's work.

Such familiarity can also be demonstrated among Shakespeare's contemporaries. Robert Chester's (1566?–1640?) *Love's Martyr* (first published in 1601) was reprinted in 1611 under the title, the *Annals of Great Britaine* with Shakespeare's *Phoenix and the Turtle* and other works. One of these is the '*Birth, Life* and Death of honourable Arthur *King of Brittaine*,' comprising a prose Preface ('To the courteous Reader') followed by a verse history of Arthur largely in six-line stanzas.[17] Both the Preface and the opening sections of the work draw heavily and often verbatim from Malory's work.[18]

Such variegated evidence of the imaginative impact of Malory's work is given some piquancy in view of the evident distaste for the *Morte Darthur* in other cultivated circles. The earliest critical response to it is Roger Ascham's who attacked the *Morte* in a famous passage in *The Scholemaster* (1570):

> In our forfathers tyme . . . fewe bookes were read in our tong, sauyng certaine books of Chevalrie . . . as one for example, *Morte Darthur*: the whole pleasure of which booke standeth in two speciall poyntes, in open mans slaughter, and bold bawdrye: In which booke those be counted the noblest Knightes, that do kill most men without quarell, and commit fowlest aduoulteries by subtlest shiftes: as Sir *Launcelote*, with the wife of King *Arthure* his master: Syr *Tristram* with the wife of King *Marke* his uncle: Syr *Lamerocke* with the wife of King *Lote*, that was his owne aunte. This is good stuffe, for wise men to laughe at, or honest men to take pleasure at. Yet I know, when Gods Bible was banished the Court, and *Morte Arthure* received into the Princes chamber. What toyes the dayly readyng of such a booke, may worke in the will of a yong ientleman, or a yong mayde . . .[19]

The sensational matter Stansby alludes to in his 1634 edition may be a reference to the hardening distaste for romance as a literary form that that had begun with Tudor humanists and which received its fullest expression in Ascham's criticisms.[20] 'Open mans slaughter and bold bawdrye' were not swiftly suppressed as reading matter by this stern intellectual

---

[16] For a detailed examination of this allusion and Shakespeare's possible wider use of Malory see Mary Lascelles, 'Sir Dagonet in Arthur's Show,' *Notions & Facts* (Oxford, 1972), pp. 81–90.

[17] I use the edition of A. B. Grosart (London, 1878), pp. 34–77.

[18] For details see Charlotte d'Evelyn, 'Sources of the Arthur Story in Chester,' *Journal of English and Germanic Philology*, 14 (1915), 75–88 (76–78); Irma Reed White, 'Loves Martyr,' *Times Literary Supplement*, 21 July, 1932, 532.

[19] Ascham, *English Works*, ed. W. A. Wright (Cambridge, 1904), pp. 230–1.

[20] For discussion of the context of the humanist attack see Robert P. Adams, ' "Bold Bawdry and Open Manslaughter": The English New Humanist Attack on Medieval Romance,' *Huntington Library Quarterly*, 23 (1959–60), 33–48.

disapproval. (There were to be two further reprintings of the *Morte* after Ascham published his animadversions on romance.) But growing historical distance and newer literary forms gradually combined to dimish the appeal of Malory's work.

The few seventeenth-century responses largely reflect Ascham's disapproval. The great antiquary William Camden refers to the *Morte Darthur* in his *Remaines of a Greater Work, Concerning Britaine . . .* (1605) citing 'king Arthurs historie' (pp. 61, 71). But otherwise there is only glancing interest of any serious kind in Malory. Although Milton once contemplated the composition of an Arthurian epic, his awareness of the most famous vernacular model is only demonstrated by the use of a detail from in his description of Sin in Book 2 of *Paradise Lost*.[21] This period also provided the most curious evidence of a growing antipathy to the *Morte*. Samuel Butler in *Hudibras* draws on the woodcut frontispiece to Stansby's edition to mock chivalric assumptions, by suggesting that the Round Table was actually Arthur's shirt under which he carried supplies to feed his questing knights:

> . . . For Arthur wore in Hall
> Round-Table like a Farthingal,
> On which, with shirt pull'd out behind,
> And eke before, his good Knights din'd.
> Though 'twas no Table, some suppose,
> But a huge pair of round Trunk-hose;
> In which he carry'd as much meat
> As he and all his Knights could eat,
> When laying by their swords and truncheons,
> They took their Breakfasts or their Nuncheons.[22]

Equally grotesque is the response to Malory revealed in *Chaucer's Ghoast . . . with the History of Prince Corniger*, which was published in 1672. The latter part of this collection, *Prince Corniger*, is a Restoration parody of the *Morte* drawn both in plot and verbal borrowing from an early edition of Malory. The author evidently knew the *Morte* well, but Malory's name is nowhere mentioned. The title *Chaucer's Ghoast* clearly indicates that his name was felt to be a better draw for marketing purposes. The whole curious undertaking suggests the decline in Malory's literary fortunes at this period. But it is the only form of his text to be printed between 1634 and 1816.[23]

It is not until the mid-eighteenth century that we find any more sympathetic engagement with Malory. It has been claimed with justice that

---

[21] See Lynette R. Muir, 'A Detail in Milton's Description of Sin,' *Notes & Queries*, n.s. 3 (1956), 100–1.

[22] Quoted in David Carlson, 'Arthur's Round Table in Hudibras,' *Journal of the Warburg and Courtauld Institutes*, 49 (1986), 261–4.

[23] For a full account of this work – which resists summary – see Paul Hartle, 'Malory "Redivivus"; A Restoration "Morte Darthur,"' *Modern Language Review*, 83 (1988), 10–15, to which I am greatly indebted.

'it is in Warton's *Observations on the Faerie Queene* that Malory makes his entrance into literary criticism.'[24] This work is still remarkable as a first attempt at an historical survey of Middle English literature, a sketch for the later, even more learned and wide-ranging *History of English Poetry*. Warton singles out 'this fabulous history' as 'one romance which Spenser seems more particularly to have made use of' (I, 19).[25] Malory appears in 'SECT. II. *Of Spenser's Imitations from old Romances*' (I, 17–65). He is identified as the source for many of Spenser's Arthurian names and for parts of the *Tale of Sir Tristram* (I, 19–22). His account of the Questing Beast is the inspiration for Spenser's Blatant Beast (I, 22–4) as is the 'superstitious tradition' of the Holy Grail (I, 34–5). He also glosses occasional obscure passages in Spenser by reference to the *Morte Darthur* (I, 32–4). He intersperses these claims of influence with a number of references to the early reputation of Malory's work (I, 27–32, 35–6, 41–2).[26] Warton's study marks the beginnings of scholarly interest in Malory. But it was to be some time before the range of his learning found any responses.

The first reprintings of Malory since Stansby's 1634 edition took place in the early nineteenth century, in 1816 and 1817. The chief stimulus to these reprintings was the interest of Sir Walter Scott and Robert Southey. And the association of Malory's work with such notable men of letters reminds us of the recurrent power of the *Morte Darthur* to provide imaginative stimulus to creative as well as scholarly minds. Scott had read Malory for illustrative passages in his 'Notes to Canto First' of *Marmion* (1808). Here he quotes extensively from a passage of the Grail episode to gloss his occasional Arthurian allusions. He recommends Malory to the 'general reader' who will get 'an excellent idea of what romances of chivalry were. It has also the merit of being written in pure old English; and many of the wild adventures which it contains, are told with a simplicity bordering on the sublime.'[27]

Marmion was the most substantial fruit of Scott's study of Malory.[28] He had contemplated an edition of the *Morte*, but abandoned it in view of Robert Southey's projected one, which did not appear until 1817.[29] Southey himself was among the admirers of Malory who traced his influence back to their childhood: 'it has been my delight since I was a schoolboy.'[30] And

---

[24] David Nichol Smith, 'Warton's History of English Poetry,' *Proceedings of the British Academy*, 15 (1929), p. 76.

[25] I quote from the second edition (1762).

[26] There are occasional references to Malory later in this work; for example I, 213, II, 147, 172.

[27] *Marmion: A Tale of Flodden Field* (Edinburgh, 1808), I, iii–iv; see also *The Letters of Sir Walter Scott*, ed. Herbert Grierson *et al.* (London, 1937), XII, 296–7.

[28] Although a number of other tenuous parallels are adduced by Jerome J. Mitchell, *Scott, Chaucer and Medieval Romance: A Study in Sir Walter Scott's Indebtedness to the Literature of the Middle Ages* (Lexington, Ky., 1987).

[29] For discussion of this episode see the excellent article by Barry Gaines, 'The Editions of Malory in the Early Nineteenth Century' (n. 5 above).

[30] Quoted in Gaines, 3.

his edition was the form in which the *Morte* was most influentially transmitted to, among others, Burne-Jones, William Morris, Dante Gabriel Rossetti and Swinburne.[31]

Oddly enough it does not seem to have been through Southey's edition that his fellow Romantic poets read Malory. Both Keats and Wordsworth owned copies of a slightly earlier, two-volume 1816 edition.[32] The consequences of Wordsworth's study of this edition were not altogether happy. His 'The Egyptian Maid,' composed in 1828, is one of the less fortune results of his interest in medieval literature. Merlin out of 'envious spleen' (25) destroys a ship carrying 'a meek and guileless Maiden' (66), 'a Damsel peerless' (79), to Arthur's court. Nina, the Lady of the Lake, recovers her corpse and commands Merlin to carry it to Arthur's court, where each of the knights tries to restore her to life. Sir Galahad succeeds and the poem ends with a celebration of the pair's marriage.[33] In a slightly defensive headnote Wordsworth states: 'For the names and persons in the following poem see the "History of the renowned Prince Arthur and his Knights of the Round Table;" for the rest the Author is answerable' (p. 232). Wordsworth's indebtedness to Malory may actually go a little further in this poem: the manner of the restoration of the Egyptian maid to life seems to combine elements from two episodes near the end of the *Morte*, the 'Fair Maid of Astolat' and the 'Healing of Sir Urry.' But while Malory provided the impetus to the poem's composition, he did not provide much inspiration. It is a pedestrian piece of work.

It is in fact with the lesser figures of the early nineteenth century that Malory seems to have made the deepest impression. Kenelm Digby's *The Broad Stone of Honour, or Rules for the Gentlemen of England* (1822) quotes Malory at a number of points in a work that has been best described as 'an extraordinary fusion of Scottian medievalism, romantic Catholicism, English and German Gothicism and enthusiasm for chivalric romances and Wordsworthian nature.'[34] Reginald Heber's *Morte d'Arthur* was apparently begun between 1810 and 1812, before the publication of the first nineteenth-century editions of Malory. It continued to preoccupy him intermittently throughout his life, but remained unfinished and unpublished at his death. It is noteworthy as the first post-medieval English attempt at an Arthuriad.[35] Such eccentric and aborted undertakings remain the fullest testimony to Romantic interest in Malory.

It is only in the latter part of the nineteenth and the twentieth centuries that we see the most distinctive sustained creative and critical engagement

---

[31] See further, Gaines, 16–17.

[32] Gaines, 13.

[33] References to the poem are to *The Poetical Works of William Wordsworth*, ed. E. de Selincourt and Helen Darbishire (Oxford, 1946), III, 232–243.

[34] Merriman, *The Flower of Kings*, p. 124.

[35] For description and analysis of this work see Merriman, *The Flower of Kings*, pp. 168–72.

with the *Morte Darthur*. Tennyson provides the first major point of reference. Like a number of others who have left significant evidence of their indebtedness to the work, he first encountered Malory as a child, and the *Morte* remained a fundamental influence from such early works as his own *Morte d'Arthur* (1842), a poem which was later incorporated into the *Idylls of the King* (published between 1859 and 1885). Such influence is so wide-ranging and so pervasive as to preclude any adequate summary treatment, and it has received extensive treatment from modern scholarship.[36] It is clear that Tennyson's indebtedness to Malory was highly complex, deep but not in any sense slavish, a profound inspiration as well as a source. The publication of the *Idylls*, Tennyson's lifelong poetic project, constitutes the greatest acknowledgement of the power of Malory to prompt the poetic imagination.

Such power is confirmed, albeit in very different ways, by Swinburne's *The Tale of Balen*, first published in 1896. Swinburne draws on a single episode in Malory, the narrative of that most accident-prone of knights, Sir Balin, near the end of the *Tale of King Arthur* (37–59; II, chs. 1–19). Balin moves from misfortune to misfortune, often as a consequence of his rash temper, before finally perishing in an act of reciprocal fratricide. The narrative remains quite close to Malory, although its transformation into verse achieves rather jangling effects.[37]

Although Malory was an important influence on William Morris, his treatments of Malorian materials rarely reflect that influence in a very direct way. *The Defence of Guenevere and other Poems* (1858). The title poem and 'King Arthur's Tomb' are re-workings of episodes from concluding sections of the *Morte*: 'The Vengeance of Gawain,' and 'The Dolorous Death . . . of Sir Launcelot and Queen Guinever.' In the first the emphasis falls on the figure of Guinevere as she reflects upon and justifies her love for Lancelot just before she is to be condemned. 'King Arthur's Tomb' takes up the story of their love after Arthur's death. Guinevere has retreated to a nunnery at Glastonbury (not Amesbury as in Malory) where Lancelot visits her. At the heart of the poem (161–392) is Guinevere's penitent recapitulation of their love and its tragic consequences.[38]

American interest in Malory seems to have begun at around this time, possibly prompted by the imaginative renewal of Arthurian writing taking

---

[36] The fullest account of Tennyson's debt to Malory is David Staines, *Tennyson's Camelot: The Idylls of the King and Its Medieval Sources* (Waterloo, Ont., 1982).

[37] For a very sound discussion of Swinburne's treatment see Taylor and Brewer, *The Return of Arthur*, pp. 159–61; they note that 'jogging four-stressed lines in nine-line stanzas, very insistently rhymed, create a trivialising, almost parodic effect' (p. 161).

[38] These poems have been well edited by Margaret A. Lourie, *William Morris, The Defense of Guenevere and Other Poems*, Garland English Texts, no. 2 (New York, 1981), whose notes discuss Morris's specific debts to Malory; see also David Staines, 'Morris' Treatment of his Medieval Sources in *The Defence of Guenevere and Other Poems*,' *Studies in Philology*, 70 (1973), 439–64.

place in Britain. The poet Sidney Lanier produced the first American edition of Malory in 1880, *The Boy's King Arthur. Being Sir Thomas Malory's History of King Arthur and his Knights of the Round Table*, edited, the sub-title redundantly insists, 'for Boys.' The edition proved a popular one, and may well have been the form in which T. S. Eliot read Malory. He lists among the desiderata for Malory studies '. . . a children's edition. Such an edition was in my hand when I was a child of eleven or twelve. It was then, and perhaps has always been, my favourite book.'[39] Both Lanier and Eliot give a curiously American emphasis to a rather tangential earlier nineteenth-century view of Malory. Robert Southey in his 1817 edition also saw it as a precursor of the boy's adventure story:

> . . . were it again modernized [as in the seventeenth century] . . . and published as a book for boys, it could hardly fail of regaining its popularity. When I was a schoolboy I possessed a wretchedly imperfect copy, and there was no book, except the Faery Queen, which I perused so often, or with such deep contentment. (xxviii)

Something of the same view can be found in Charlotte Yonge's *The Heir of Redclyffe* (1888):

> 'What! Don't you know the Morte d'Arthur? I thought everyone did! Don't you, Philip!'
> 'I once looked into it. It is very curious, in classical English; but it is a book no one could read through.'
> 'Oh!' cried Guy, indignantly; then, 'but you only looked into it. If you had lived with its two fat volumes you could not help delighting in it. It was my boating-book for at least three summers.'
> 'That accounts for it,' said Philip; 'a book so studied in boyhood acquires a charm apart from its actual merits.'
> 'But it has actual merits. The depth, the mystery, the allegory – the beautiful characters of some of the knights.'
> 'You look through the medium of your imagination,' said Philip; 'but you must pardon others for seeing a great sameness of character and adventure, and for disapproving of the strange mixture of religion and romance.'
> 'You've never read it,' said Guy, striving to speak patiently. (Ch. X)

There are other children's versions of Malory as well as other even less prob-able adaptations, including such equally gender-specific, if rather different responses as Anne D. Alexander, *Women of the Morte Darthur: 12 of the most romantic of the world's love stories . . . from Malory's Morte Darthur* (1927).[40]

---

[39] 'Le Morte Darthur,' *Spectator*, 23 February, 1934, p. 278. For the possible influence of Malory on *The Waste Land* see Barbara Everett, *Times Literary Supplement*, 3 March, 1972, 249.

[40] There is even detective fiction drawing on the *Morte*; see Phyllis Ann Karr, *The Idylls of the Queen* (London, 1982).

But Malory clearly struck a deeper chord in the American literary imagination. He achieves his most explicit effect in the nineteenth century on Mark Twain's *A Connecticut Yankee in King Arthur's Court* (1889). The novel starts with a reading of 'old Sir Thomas Malory's enchanting book' and the debt to this source is reflected in the interpolation in the narrative of a number of lengthy extracts from the *Morte*, as well as other allusions.[41] Malory clearly provided an important stimulus to Twain's work.

In the early twentieth century, this American interest continued to produce some extensive responses. The poet E. Arlington Robinson composed several long Arthurian poems: *Merlin* (1917), *Lancelot* (1920) and *Tristram* (1927).[42] *Merlin* is set at the moment before the final destruction of the Round Table. At this moment Merlin returns to Camelot from a voluntary exile with his love Vivian. The personal relationship between them stands in contrast to the larger political and historical realities Merlin cannot change. At the end, he departs powerless, with Arthur's fool Dagonet. The mood of pensive reflection Robinson creates here is representative of his approach to Malory. Emphasis is shifted from action to emotion, and narrative invention (as in the Merlin/Vivian story) is combined with a sensitive fidelity to the underlying tone of elegiac powerlessness of the later stages of the *Morte*. The same note is struck in *Lancelot* where he omits all the significant action to create a pensive, emotional Lancelot. In his final major Arthurian poem *Tristram* he moves further from the *Morte* to locate the fate of the two lovers, Tristram and Isolde in a more complex representation of suffering and understanding that treats all the main characters more sensitively than in Malory. Robinson's three poems have been termed, with some justice, 'the most distinguished Arthurian works produced in America.'[43] Malory is clearly an underlying inspiration, but Robinson's treatments take relatively little directly from this source.

In the same period came John Erskine's Arthurian novel, *Galahad* (1926).[44] The novel is subtitled 'Enough of his Life to Explain his Reputation' but is perhaps more concerned with Lancelot's relationship with Guinevere than with Galahad himself. It reshapes parts of Malory's narrative to present an unsentimental, often rather tart picture of the lovers.

John Steinbeck's extended interest in Malory achieved its most explicit expression in his modernization of the first and third sections in the

---

[41] The passages are (according to the Globe edition of Malory (1868) which Twain used): VI. xi (Introduction), I. xxiii (Ch. III), VII. xxviii (Ch. IX) , IV, xvi–xix, xxiv–xv (Ch. XV), IV xxiv–xxv (Ch. XIX), XX.viii (Ch. XLII), XXI. iv (Ch. XLII). There are other allusions to the *Morte* in, for example Ch. XVI (IX.xiii) and Ch. XX (X. xlviii). For discussion of Twain's treatment of Malory see Lesley C. Kordecki. 'Twain's Critique of Malory's Romance,' *Nineteenth Century Fiction*, 41(1986), 329–48.

[42] All are reprinted in Robinson's *Collected Poems* (New York, 1929).

[43] Taylor and Brewer, *The Return of Arthur*, p. 179.

[44] Erskine wrote other Arthurian novels including *Tristan and Isolde* (1932), but they draw less directly on Malory.

Winchester manuscript.[45] But Malory's influence has been discerned in a number of his works, notably *Tortilla Flat*.[46] And Thomas Berger's *Arthur Rex: A Legendary Novel* (1978) employs Malory as part of an ambitious synthesis of various Arthurian materials, including, as well as Malory, new versions of *Sir Gawain and the Green Knight* and *The Wedding of Sir Gawain and Dame Ragnell*. Berger presents a vision of an Arthurian world inexorably doomed by Arthur's incestuous encounter with his half-sister Margawse, an encounter which produced Mordred. He stresses the steady moral and/or physical decay of the main characters all of whom, except for Guinevere, die in the final battle. Berger's reshaping of Malory is strongly determinist, and his characterizations both more sardonic and more psychologically compassionate than those of the *Morte*. It is among the freshest and most knowledgeable re-creations of Malory's work.

The twentieth-century reception of Malory in England has produced little as imaginatively distinctive. Perhaps his most explicit and sustained influence is to be found in the various novels of T. H. White. *The Once and Future King* (1958) completes and assembles in one volume several earlier narratives beginning with *The Sword in the Stone* (1938), narratives which are often quite explicit attempts to offer new versions of Malory's world. (The final narrative is entrusted to Tom Malory, Arthur's page.) Other gifted writers and poets among them C. S. Lewis,[47] Charles Williams,[48] Robert Graves,[49] Herbert Read[50] and T. S. Eliot[51] have offered perceptive insights into Malory in their critical writings, but the evidence of creative engagement seems generally more diffused in modern English writing.

Yet it is clear that Malory's work continues to evoke a range of creative responses, forms of imitation or renewal, among contemporary writers. That King Arthur is not dead, is indeed clearly vitally alive, seems to an important degree due to the lasting imaginative stimulus of the *Morte Darthur*.

---

[45] *The Acts of King Arthur and his Noble Knights* (London, 1976).

[46] See, for example, the various essays in Tetsumaro Hayashi, ed., *Steinbeck and the Arthurian Theme* (Muncie, Ind., 1975).

[47] Most extensively in 'The English Prose *Morte*,' *Essays on Malory*, ed. J. A. W. Bennett (Oxford, 1963), pp. 7–28.

[48] 'Malory and the Grail Legend,' *Dublin Review*, 214 (1944) 144–153.

[49] See, for example, his article 'Kynge Arthur is Nat Dede,' *New Statesman*, 4 December 1954, 745–6, and his Introduction to Keith Baines' modernization of Malory, *Le Morte D'Arthur* (New York, 1962).

[50] 'Sir Thomas Malory and the Sentiment of Glory,' *The Sense of Glory* (Cambridge, 1929), pp. 33–56.

[51] Eliot characterized Malory as 'a kind of crude northern Homer,' *Spectator*, 23 (February 1934), p. 278.

14

A Selective Bibliography of Malory Studies

ELIZABETH ARCHIBALD
A. S. G. EDWARDS

This bibliography is highly selective: it aims to direct the reader to the more significant studies rather than provide a full bibliography. For additional references see the individual chapters of this book and the essays in the Collections of Essays cited below (which have not been separately listed).

EDITIONS

(i) Facsimiles

Sir Thomas Malory: Le Morte Darthur. Printed by William Caxton, 1485. Introduction by Paul Needham. London, 1976. A facsimile of the only complete copy of Caxton's edition.

The Winchester Malory. A Facsimile. Introduction by N. R. Ker. Early English Text Society, supplementary series, no. 4. London, 1976. A full facsimile of the Winchester manuscript.

(ii) Collected editions

The Works of Thomas Malory, ed. Eugène Vinaver, rev. P. J. C. Field. 3rd ed. 3 vols. Oxford, 1990. A complete text, based on the Winchester manuscript.

Malory: Works, ed. Eugène Vinaver. London, 1971. A one-volume complete text, based on the Winchester manuscript.

Sir Thomas Malory: Le Morte D'Arthur. Introduction by John Lawlor, ed. Janet Cowen. 2 vols. Harmondsworth, 1969. A complete text, based on Caxton's 1485 edition.

(iii) Selected editions

The Morte Darthur. Parts Seven and Eight, ed. D. S. Brewer. London, 1968.

The Morte Darthur. The Seventh and Eighth Tales, ed. P. J. C. Field. London, 1978.

King Arthur and his Knights: Selected Tales by Sir Thomas Malory, ed. Eugène Vinaver. London, 1978.

BIBLIOGRAPHY AND REFERENCE WORKS

Dillon, Bert. *A Malory Handbook.* London, 1978.
Kato, Tomomi, ed. *A Concordance to the Works of Sir Thomas Malory.* Tokyo, 1974.
Life, Page West. *Sir Thomas Malory and the Morte Darthur: A Survey of Scholarship and Annotated Bibliography.* Charlottesville, Va., 1980.

BIOGRAPHY

Field, P. J. C. *The Life and Times of Sir Thomas Malory.* Cambridge, 1993. The standard biographical account, including full discussion of earlier ones.

COLLECTIONS OF ESSAYS

Bennett, J. A. W., ed. *Essays on Malory.* Oxford, 1963.
Lumiansky, R. M., ed. *Malory's Originality: A Critical Study of Le Morte Darthur.* Baltimore, 1964.
Spisak, James W., ed. *Studies in Malory.* Kalamazoo, 1985.
Takamiya, T. and D. S. Brewer, ed. *Aspects of Malory.* Cambridge, 1981.

SOURCE STUDIES

Much material is assembled in Benson (see below), in the Collections of Essays noted above and in Vinaver's introduction to each Tale in his three-volume edition. See also:

Donaldson, E. T. 'Malory and the Stanzaic Le Morte Arthur.' *Studies in Philology,* 47 (1950), 460–72.
Mahoney, Dhira B. 'Malory's "Tale of Sir Tristram": Source and Setting Reconsidered.' *Medievalia et Humanistica,* n.s. 9 (1979), 175–98.
Wilson, R. H. 'Malory, the Stanzaic "Morte Arthur" and the "Mort Artu."' *Modern Philology,* 37 (1939–40), 125–38.
Withrington, John. 'Caxton, Malory, and the Roman War in the *Morte Darthur.*' *Studies in Philology,* 89 (1992), 350–66.

STRUCTURE AND UNITY

Brewer, D. S. '"The hoole book."' Bennett, pp. 41–63.
Clough, Andrea, 'Malory's *Morte Darthur*: The "Hoole Book,"' *Medievalia et Humanistica,* n.s. 14 (1986), 139–56.
Evans, Murray J. 'The Explicits and Narrative Division in the Winchester MS.: A Critique of Vinaver's Malory.' *Philological Quarterly,* 58 (1979), 263–81.
———. 'Ordinatio and Narrative Links: The Impact of Malory's Tales as a "hoole book".' Spisak, pp. 29–52.
Knight, Stephen. *The Structure of Sir Thomas Malory's Arthuriad.* Sydney, 1969.
Moorman, Charles. *The Book of Kyng Arthur: The Unity of Malory's 'Morte Arthur.'* Lexington, Ky., 1965.

Olefsky, Ellyn. 'Chronology, Factual Consistency, and the Problem of Unity in Malory.' *Journal of English & Germanic Philology*, 68 (1969), 57–73.

GENERAL CRITICAL STUDIES

Archibald, Elizabeth. 'Malory's Ideal of Fellowship.' *Review of English Studies*, n.s. 43 (1992), 311–28.

Benson, Larry D. *Malory's 'Morte Arthur.'* Cambridge, Mass., 1976.

Brewer, D. S. 'Malory: The Traditional Writer and the Archaic Mind.' *Arthurian Literature*, I, ed. R. Barber (Cambridge, 1981), 94–120.

Davies, R. T. 'The Worshipful Way in Malory.' *Patterns of Love and Courtesy: Essays in Memory of C. S. Lewis*. London, 1966. Pp. 157–77.

Field, P. J. C. *Romance and Chronicle: A Study of Malory's Prose Style*. London, 1971.

Heng, Geraldine. 'Enchanted Ground: The Feminine Subtext in Malory.' *Courtly Literature: Culture and Context*. Keith Busby and Erik Kooper, ed. Amsterdam, 1988. Pp. 148–75.

Lambert, Mark. *Malory: Style and Vision in Le Morte Darthur*. Yale Studies in English, 186. New Haven, Conn., 1975.

Mann, Jill. *The Narrative of Distance The Distance of Narrative in Malory's Morte Darthur*. The William Matthews Lectures 1991. London, 1991.

———. 'Malory: Knightly Combat in Le Morte D'Arthur.' *Medieval Literature: Chaucer and the Alliterative Tradition*. Boris Ford, ed. The New Pelican Guide to English Literature, vol. I, part 1. Harmondsworth, 1982. Pp. 331–9.

McCarthy, Terence. 'Malory and the Alliterative Tradition.' Spisak, 53–86.

———. *Reading the Morte Darthur*. Cambridge, 1988; reprinted as *An Introduction to Malory*. Cambridge, 1991.

———. 'Le Morte Darthur and Romance.' *Studies in Medieval English Romance*. D. S. Brewer, ed. Cambridge, 1988. Pp. 148–75.

Reiss, E. *Sir Thomas Malory*. New York, 1966.

Riddy, Felicity. *Sir Thomas Malory*. Leiden, 1987.

Wilson, R. H. 'Malory's Early Knowledge of Arthurian Romance.' *Texas Studies in English*, 29 (1950), 33–50.

Index

We have not noted titles for Arthurian characters ('King,' 'Queen,' 'Sir'), or included Arthurian place names. Arthurian proper names have been normalized to single, standard forms. Since Arthur is mentioned so frequently we have not attempted to include all references to his name.

Abelleus 143
Accolon 40, 136, 140, 143, 151
adultery 16, 43–50, 51, 65, 82, 93, 155, 163, 175, 207, 217, 226, 229, 233, 236
Ælfric 99, 107
Agincourt 66
Agravain 49, 185, 189, 195, 222, 225, 228, 229–32, 236, 237
Alexander the Great 26
Alexander, Anne D. 250
Alfred, King 97
Alis 41, 190, 193
Alisaunder the Orphan 40, 41, 186, 189, 190, 193, 196, 200
alliteration 83–4, 106–7, 109, 145–6
Alliterative Morte Arthur *see Morte Arthure* (Alliterative)
Allmand, Christopher 67 n. 31
Alvaro de Luna 29
Amadis de Gaule 183 n. 1
Andret 196
Andrew, S. O. 104
Anglides 199
Anglo Saxon Chronicle 22, 97, 98, 101, 102–3
Annales Cambriae 59
Antoine the Bastard of Burgundy 31
Archibald, Elizabeth 44 n. 10, 139 n. 12, 184 n. 4, 209 n. 18, 223
Ariosto 183 n. 1
Armes Prydein 59
Arthur birth 14, 60, 62, 136, 141, 142; death 59, 61, 62–3, 64–5, 170, 235–6, 237, 244; and Guinevere 14, 37, 44, 45, 59, 91–3, 136, 140–41, 147, 151, 230–31, 232–3, 237; historicity of xiv, 11–12, 55–66, 150; and Roman war 60, 62, 64–5, 68–9, 75–6, 83–4, 133, 136, 137, 145–51 passim; legend of return 63, 235; for his relationships with individual characters see under their names (e.g. Lancelot, Gawain etc.)

Ascham, Roger, *The Scholemaster* 245, 246
Auerbach, Erich 39

Babees Book 109
Bagdemagus 172–3, 177, 212
Balan 72, 138, 211
Baldwin of Brittany 73
Balin 50, 72, 83, 135, 138–40, 142, 143, 187, 211
Barbarossa, Frederick 20
Barber, Richard 19 n. 1, 31 n. 18
Barkefolde, John 67
Basin, Thomas, *History of Charles VII* 68, 69–70
Battle of Maldon 94, 230 n. 14
Baudwyn 147
Baumgartner, Emmanuèle 184 nn. 2–3, 194 n. 15, 195 n. 16, 208, 213 n. 20, 217
Bede, *Historia ecclesiastica* 57–8
Bedevere 235
Bedford, John, Duke of 68
bel inconnu see 'Fair Unknown'
Le Bel Inconnu 157 n. 3, 159 n. 7
Bellay, Joachim du 80 n. 15
Belleus 178
Bellynger 186
Benjamin, Walter 55, 61
Bennett, J. A. W. 94
Benson, Larry D. 31 n. 19, 135 n. 7, 136 n. 8, 145 n. 14, 171, 184 n. 4, 198 n. 18, 227, 229, 233, 237 n. 23
Beowulf 20, 94, 95, 155
Berger, Thomas 252
Bernheimer, R. 41
Béroul *see Tristan*
Black Prince 29
Blake, N. F. 4 n. 4, 7 n. 14, 11 n. 25, 107
Blamour 189, 193
Bleoberis 189, 190
Boiardo 183 n. 1
Bondelle, Anne 207 n. 10
Bornstein, Diane 12 n. 32

Borre 13
Bors 82, 144, 147, 148, 189, 206, 210, 214,
    215–16, 219, 222, 223, 224, 225, 230, 231,
    237
Bosworth Field xiv
Boughton, Richard 118
Boulton, D'A. J. D. 23 n. 7
Brangwain 191
Breunis Sans Pitê 32, 189, 195, 196
Brewer, Derek 4 n. 4, 5, 52, 78 n. 11,
    133 n. 3, 158 n. 5, 170 n. 19, 172 n. 24,
    174, 225–6, 227, 231, 232 n. 16
Brewnor 46
Brittany, Duchess of 148
Brooks, Peter 61–2
Bruges 12
Brunetto Latini 221
Brunor 38
Brut 99
Buckingham, Duke of 116
Burgundy 12, 30
Burne-Jones, Edward 248
Burnley, J. D. 107 n. 26, 109 n. 27
Butler, Samuel 246

Cador 64, 147, 148
Camden, William 246
Cantari di Carduino 157 n. 3
Caxton, William, edition of Le Morte
    Darthur xiii–xv, 3–17 passim, 70–71,
    79, 93, 94, 100, 134, 146, 153, 163, 166,
    183, 188–9, 190 n. 13, 199–201, 241–3;
    Book of Curtesye 109
Celtic myth 39, 43, 159, 160, 161, 163, 204
Cely Letters 101
Cervantes 183 n. 1
Chambers, E. K. 133 n. 1
chanson de geste   20, 26
Charlemagne 20, 147
Charles VI 67, 68
Charles-Edwards, Thomas 59 n. 14
Chaucer, Geoffrey xiii, xiv, 78, 97, 100;
    Canterbury Tales 24, Knight's Tale 106,
    Wife of Bath's Tale 157 n. 3; Parliament
    of Fowls 109; Troilus & Criseyde 221
Chaucer's Ghoast 246
Cheney, C. R. 207 n. 10
Chester, Robert, Love's Martyr 245
Chetwynd, Philippa 115
chivalry, Arthurian 16, 34, 93, 179 n. 33,
    183, 184, 194, 198, 223, 238; and
    Christian history 24–5, 28–9, 32, 213;
    earthly/celestial 34, 82, 149, 192, 207–8,
    238; historical xv, 19–32 passim, 198;
    and love 21–2, 26–8, 29, 32–3, 41, 48, 51,
    159–63, 177, 189, 191, 230; Malory's
    view of xv, 24, 31–5, 41–2, 51, 82, 94–5,

141, 149, 155, 158, 171, 183, 184, 185,
    191, 194, 196 n. 17, 198, 220, 238; see also
    knighthood
Chrétien de Troyes 26, 81, 165; Chevalier
    de la Charrete (Lancelot) 226, 227; Conte
    del Graal (Perceval) 157 n. 3, 203–6; Erec
    et Enide 21, 22; Yvain 41, 159 n. 7; see also
    Continuations
Cistercians 207
Claudas 187
Cleges 148
Clough, Andrea 5, 133 n. 3
Columbe 40, 187
companionship, comradeship 184–5,
    194–5, 228, 234, 237; see also fellowship
Continuations of the Old French Perceval
    205
Constantine 64, 66
Copland, William 242
Cornwall, J. C. K. 73 n. 47
La Cote Mal Taile 157 n. 3
La Cote Male Tayle 186, 189, 200
Cowen, Janet 190 n. 13, 199
Crécy 29
Criseyde 221
crusades 24–5

Dagonet 51, 244
Damas 140
Dante, Inferno 221
Darras 200
Dean, Christopher 79 n. 14
Degrevaunt 81
Deguileville, Guillaume de, Pilgrimage of
    the Life of Man 212
Dichmann, Mary E. 145 n. 14
Digby, Kenelm 248
Dinadan 189, 191, 192, 193-6, 200
Dinas 191
disguise 30, 137, 157–8, 165, 168, 172–4,
    180, 195, 224, 230; see also identity
Don Quixote 183 n. 1
Donaldson, E. T. 221 n. 1, 223
Dover 11
dreams and visions 42, 88–9, 137, 142,
    149–50, 217, 235, 237
Duby, George 56 n. 4
Dumville, David 57 n. 7, 58 n. 12
Dunbar, William 97; The Golden Targe
    109; The Flyting of Dunbar and Kennedy
    109
Dyer, Christopher 71 n. 45

East, Thomas 242
Ector (de Marys) 88, 101, 112, 173, 189,
    201, 238
Edward III 29

Edward IV   66 n.30, 117
Edwards, A. S. G.   12 n. 29, 13 nn. 34–5
Elaine (mother of Galahad)   40, 52–3, 187, 189, 191, 193, 198, 201, 217
Elaine (the Fair Maid of Astolat)   15–16, 43, 46, 53, 83, 87, 223, 224–5, 227, 228
Eliot, T. S.   250, 252
Elizabeth, Queen   243
enchanter/enchantress   see magic
Erskine, John   251
Estoire del Saint Graal   63, 75, 206
Estoire de Merlin   146
Ettard   142
Evans, Murray J.   13 n. 36, 187 n. 8
Evelake   213
Excalibur   137, 140, 143, 235

Faerie Queene   183 n. 1, 244, 247
Fair Maid of Astolat   see Elaine
'Fair Unknown,' theme of   76, 157, 159, 165, 166, 168, 180
family   86, 135, 140, 143–4, 149, 156, 158, 165–9, 173, 185, 198, 214, 225, 233
Faramon's daughter   190, 191
fée-amante   159, 160, 161
fellowship   31, 34, 44, 48, 49, 52, 140, 142, 149, 184–5, 188, 189, 193, 196, 209, 210–11, 214, 216, 219, 220, 221, 223, 229, 230, 231, 233, 234, 237
Field, P. J. C.   10, 11 n. 26, 76 nn. 4–5, 77, 80, 85 n. 21, 89 nn. 29–31, 101 nn. 4–7, 101, 104, 105, 106, 110 n. 29, 134–5, 156–7, 164, 166, 167 n. 15, 184 n. 2
Finlayson, John   133 n. 1
Fisher King   203, 205
Flori, Jean   22 n. 5, 23 n. 8
Fortescue, John, The Governance of England   99
Fortune   149, 235
Francesca (da Rimini)   221
Frappier, Jean   159, 206 n. 7, 207–8
Freud, Sigmund   61
Fries, Maureen   196 n. 17
Froissart, Jean   26
Frye, Northrop   135 n. 6

Gaheris   142, 153, 165–6, 177, 185, 188, 189, 200, 232
Gaius   148
Galahad   19, 35, 82, 83, 139, 149, 185, 187, 192, 201, 206, 210–14, 216–19, 220, 248, 251
Galehot   44
Gareth   83, 111, 140, 153–74 passim, 177, 181, 186, 187, 188, 189, 192, 201, 224–6, 232, 233
Garlon   143

Gawain   34, 48, 50, 64, 66, 91, 94, 104–5, 111, 134, 135, 141–2, 147, 148, 149, 151, 153, 164–9, 173–4, 178, 179 n. 33, 185, 188, 193, 195, 196, 198, 200, 206, 210–11, 216, 221, 222, 223, 229–30, 231, 232–5, 236, 238
Geoffrey of Monmouth, History of the Kings of Britain (Historia Regum Britanniae)   21, 60–61, 62, 63, 64, 65, 66, 72 n. 46, 146, 147
Gilbert   175, 178
Girard, René   45
Glastonbury   63
Gordon, Ian A.   98 n. 1
Gornemant   204
Gottfried von Strassburg   27
Gower, John   97
Gower, Thomas   118
Grail Quest   28, 34, 76, 79, 83, 87, 88, 139, 141, 144, 146, 147, 149, 170, 185, 188, 203–20 passim, 222
Gransden, Antonia   133 n. 1
Graves, Robert   252
Gringamour   161
Grinken, John   243
Gromoresom Erioure   81
Gryfflet   137
Guenée, Bernard   70 n. 41
Guesclin, Bertrand du   26
Guillaume d'Orange   20
Guinevere   15–16, 19, 28, 32, 34, 37, 38, 44, 45, 46, 49, 50, 51, 53, 54, 65, 66, 77, 79, 82, 83, 86, 87, 91, 92, 105, 135, 136, 140, 141, 147, 163, 170, 171, 173–7, 179, 180, 184, 189, 191, 193, 196, 197, 216–17, 221, 222–38 passim, 251, 252

Hallewes   39
Hamilton, W. E. M. C.   206 n. 7
Hanning, Robert W.   60 n. 18
Hardyng, John   64 n. 28, 76, 80, 146
Heber, Reginald   248
Hector   see Ector
Helinand of Froidmont   203, 208
Hellinga, Lotte   7, 10, 11 n. 25, 12 n. 32
Heng, Geraldine   179 n. 33
Henry V   66–7, 69–70
Henry VI   66, 68, 117
Henry VII   xiv
Henryson, Robert, Testament of Cressid   234
Higham, N. J.   58 n. 11
Holbein, Hans, the Younger   73
honour   49, 162, 179, 185, 221, 225–6, 231–4, 237; see also worship
'hoole booke'   see Malory, Morte Darthur, unity of

Tennyson, Alfred Lord   249
Torre   141–2, 143
tournaments   25–6, 29–32, 33, 150, 162–3,
    165–6, 168, 190, 191, 198, 199–201, 224
treachery, treason   20, 27, 178–80, 184,
    188, 196, 230
Tristan (in Continental versions)   27, 28,
    34, 35, 162, 170, 183, 193
Tristan (Béroul)   159 n. 7
Tristan (French Prose)   63, 76, 86, 92, 157
    n. 3, 183, 185, 193, 194 n. 15
Tristram (in Malory)   38, 40, 41, 42, 43, 46,
    47, 63, 83, 144–5, 183–201, 251
Troy   12
Tucker, P. E.   51, 52
Twain, Mark   251

Ullman, Walter   69 n. 39
Urban II, Pope   24
Uriens   140
Urry   17, 149, 188, 219–20, 228–9
Uther   44, 63, 134

Vale, Juliet   29 n. 15
Valentine, Lucia   8 n. 17
Vayssière, A.   30 n. 17
Vinaver, Eugène   3–17 passim, 34, 37,
    68–9, 75, 85, 87–8, 89, 101 n. 8, 103,
    135 n. 7, 145, 153, 166, 169, 183,
    194 n. 15, 198–201, 221, 243
Vulgate Cycle   63, 76, 95, 136, 154, 155,
    156, 159, 163, 171–5, 185, 188, 208; *see
    also Estoire del Saint Graal*; *Estoire de
    Merlin*; (*Le Livre de*) *Lancelot* (*du Lac*);
    La Mort le Roi Artu

Wace   147
Waldron, Peter   227 n. 9
Wars of the Roses   xiv, 55, 72, 198
Warton, Thomas   244; *Observations on the
    Faerie Queene* 247
Warwick, Duke of   117
White, T. H.   252
Wigalois   157 n. 3
William I   22
Williams, Charles   252
Wilson, R. H.   77 n. 9, 93 n. 32, 156,
    157 n. 4, 170 n. 16, 179 n. 33, 221 n. 1
Winchester Manuscript (British Library
    MS Additional 59678)   3–17 passim,
    134 n. 4, 154, 166, 199–201, 242
Withrington, John   11 n. 27, 146 n. 16
Wolfram von Eschenbach, *Parzival*   25,
    28–9
Woodville, Anthony, Lord Scales   31
Worcestre, William   71 n. 43
Worde, Wynkyn de   241, 242, 243
Wordsworth, William   248
'worship'   135, 140, 142, 148–9, 154,
    155, 157, 159, 164, 171, 174, 181, 217,
    220, 224, 226, 231–3, 234; *see also*
    honour
Wulfstan   99

Ygrayne   63, 134
Yonge, Charlotte   250
York, Duke of   116, 117
Ywain   140, 173

Zarnecki, George   42 n. 9

Howell, of Britanny   148
Humphrey, Duke of Gloucester   68
Huth Merlin   see Suite du Merlin

identity (motif of hidden identity) 135,
    157– 8, 161, 164, 165, 168, 172, 173, 174,
    196–7, 211; *see also* disguise, recognition
    scenes
incest   136, 137, 139, 252
interlace   93, 136–8, 144, 150, 154, 185, 186
Ironside   81
Iseult (in Continental versions)   27, 28, 34,
    35, 162
Isolde (La Belle Isolde, wife of Mark, in
    Malory)   38, 40, 41, 43, 46, 47, 189–91,
    193, 199–201, 251
Isolde (le Blaunche Maynes, wife of
    Tristram, in Malory)   40, 43, 189, 190,
    200

Jacques de Lalaing   26
Jameson, Fredric   179 n. 33
Jeste of Sir Gawayne, The   81
John of Salisbury   55, 56 n. 3
Johnson, Lesley   65 n. 29, 146 n. 17
Jones, Gwyn   95 n. 36
Joseph of Arimathea   206, 213, 214
Juan II, of Castile   29

Kato, Tomomi   4 n. 3
Kay   158, 164, 167, 173, 181
Keats, John   248
Keegan, John   67
Keen, Maurice   19 n. 1, 25 n. 10, 56 n. 4
Keiser, George   13 n. 34
Kells, Book of   186
Kendrick, T. D.   133 n. 1, 150 n. 20
Kennedy, Beverly   227 n. 9
Kennedy, E. D.   91–2, 93, 106 n. 20,
    136 n. 9, 145 n. 14, 146 n. 17
Ker, Neil   8, 9
Keyhydyns   41, 46, 190, 191, 193
kin-groups, kinship   48, 54, 185, 189, 193,
    194, 214, 216, 229; *see also* family
Knight, Stephen   133 n. 3, 135 n. 7
knighthood   19–35 passim, 55–6, 93;
    Malory's view of   158, 170, 185, 189, 193,
    194, 195, 196; and church 23–5; *see also*
    chivalry

Lady of the Lake   50, 137, 140, 142
La Farge, Catherine   38, 48, 51, 52,
    104 n. 18
Lambert, Mark   52, 102, 219, 227, 228,
    230 n. 14, 231 n. 15, 232 n. 16, 233,
    237 n. 22
Lambeth Homilies   99

Lamorak   46, 138, 142, 185, 188, 189, 191,
    195, 196 n. 17, 198, 200–201
Lancaster, Henry, Duke of, *The Book of
    Holy Remedies*   28
Lancelot   15–16, 19, 28, 32, 34, 40, 41, 42,
    45, 48, 49, 51, 52, 53, 54, 63, 64, 65, 73,
    75, 77, 79, 83, 86, 87, 88, 93, 94, 95, 101,
    105, 111, 138, 139, 144–5, 146, 147–9,
    151, 153–6, 163, 166–9, 169–81 passim,
    184, 185, 187, 188, 189–98 passim, 200,
    207, 211, 215, 216–17, 220, 222–38
    passim, 251
Lancelot en prose (in the Vulgate Cycle)
    23, 51, 63, 76, 77, 83, 86, 87, 88, 92, 159,
    169, 170, 171, 172–3, 174, 175, 177, 185,
    193, 208, 226
Laneham, Robert   243
Langland, *Piers Plowman*   56
Lanier, Sidney   250
Launceor   187
Lavayne   15, 226
Layamon   94, 147
Leckie, R. William   57 n. 8
Lena, Pedro Lopez de   30 n. 16
Lewis, C. S.   86, 252
Libeaus Desconus   157 n. 3
Life, Page West   4 n. 4, 241 n. 1
Lionel   215–16
Le Livre de Lancelot du Lac   23
Loathly Damsel   204
Longinus   205
Loomis, Roger Sherman   133 n. 1, 227
Löseth, Eilert   184 n. 2
Lot   142, 144, 150, 158, 185, 198
love   Malory's treatment of 32–4, 43–50,
    51–4, 91, 221, 235, 236–7; in *Tale of Sir
    Gareth* 159–68 passim; in *Tale of Sir
    Lancelot* 16, 32–3, 40, 46, 174–7, 181;
    in *Book of Sir Tristram* 41, 46, 47, 184,
    190–91, 193; in *Book of Sir Launcelot and
    Queen Guinevere* 33–4, 53, 105, 109, 221,
    224–5, 226–8; in the *Morte Arthur* 221,
    235–7; *see also* chivalry
loyalty   20, 27, 34, 166, 224, 233
Lucan   235
Lucius   145–51 passim, 187
Lumiansky, R. M.   5, 78 n. 12
Lydgate, John   97; *A Balade in Commenda-
    tion of Our Lady* 109
Lyle, Lady, of Avalon   39
Lynet   40, 158, 160–68 passim
Lyonesse   159–68 passim, 177

magic   27, 32, 38, 53, 80, 133, 136, 142–3,
    162, 163, 165, 178–9, 187, 196, 198, 217,
    228
Mahoney, Dhira   184 n. 4

Maimed King 204–5, 213, 220
Malory, Elizabeth (*née* Walsh) 115
Malory, John 115
Malory, Nicholas 117
Malory, Robert 115
Malory, Sir Thomas, biography xiv, xv, 115–130
  Le Morte Darthur:
  major divisions: *Tale of the Noble King Arthur* 8, 68, 80, 106, 134–45, 150, 171, 187, 244; *Tale of King Arthur and the Emperor Lucius* 64–5, 83–4, 133, 145–51, 171; *Tale of Sir Lancelot du Lake* 8, 32, 40, 56, 76, 150, 153–4, 163, 169–80; *Tale of Sir Gareth* 30, 40, 76, 108, 150, 153–4, 156–69, 174, 175, 176, 178, 180, 187; *Book of Sir Tristram* 46, 47, 76, 80, 92, 106, 138, 150, 157 n. 3, 183–201, 247; *Tale of the Sankgreall* (Grail Quest) 8, 34–5, 42, 43, 76, 81, 88,139, 141, 149, 150, 203–20, 247; *Book of Sir Lancelot and Queen Guinevere* 8, 14, 33–4, 83, 87, 188, 221–9, 244; *Morte Arthur* 14, 111–12, 229–38
  individual sections: 'Arthur and Accolon' 14, 39, 135, 140; 'Balin' 14, 135, 138–9, 249; 'La Cote Male Tayle' 157; 'The Day of Destiny' 50; 'The Dolorous Death . . . of Sir Launcelot and Queeen Guinevere' 249; 'The Fair Maid of Astolat' 15–16, 50, 73, 83, 88, 224–5, 248; 'Gawain, Ywain, and Marhalt' 14, 39, 135, 142–4; 'The Great Tournament' 31, 225; 'The Healing of Sir Urry' 32, 67, 83, 87, 88, 136, 219–20, 228–9, 248; 'The Knight of the Cart' 16–17, 46, 49, 87–8, 109–10, 225–8; 'The Knight with Two Swords' 39, 43, 135; 'Lancelot and Elaine' 52–4; 'Merlin' 135, 136–8; 'The Poisoned Apple' 45, 50, 88, 222–4; 'Sir Gareth of Orkney' 38; 'Torre and Pellinor' 14, 37, 44, 50, 135, 136; 'The Vengeance of Gawain' 249; 'The War of the Five Kings' 14, 135
  style of xv, 52, 83–4, 95, 97, 100–113 passim, 135, 146, 167–8, 178, 179, 185, 186, 197; unity of xii, 3–17 passim, 78, 83, 84, 133 n. 3, 138, 144, 153–4, 187, 220; *see also* Caxton, edition of; Winchester manuscript
Mann, Jill 139, 186 n. 6, 196 n. 17, 209 n. 17, 234–5
Mannyng, Robert 79
Margaret, of Anjou 68
Marhalt 187, 189, 199
Marie de France 159 n. 7, 165
Mark 27, 46, 47, 51, 63, 186, 187, 188, 189, 190, 195, 198, 200–201

Marshal, William 26
Matarasso, Pauline 207 n. 10, 210 n. 19
Matto 191
McCarthy, Terence 14 n. 37, 48, 52, 83 n. 18, 84 n. 19, 91 n. 28, 106–7, 112 n. 31, 145 n. 15
Meale, Carol 12 n. 29, 13 n. 33, 133 n. 3, 135 n. 7
Meleagant 16, 38, 46, 226
Melyas 212–13
Melyot 178
Ménard, Philippe 184 n. 2
Merlin 37, 38, 39, 44, 75, 85, 135, 137, 138, 140, 141, 142, 143, 144, 187, 195–6, 248, 251
Merlin 63, 101
Mont St Michel, giant of 60, 62, 69, 146, 147–8, 189
Moorman, Charles 207 n. 8
Mordrains 214
Mordred 26, 49, 60, 62, 72, 83, 135, 136, 137, 138, 139, 140, 142, 144, 146, 147, 150, 185, 189, 195, 198, 225, 228, 229, 230, 231, 235, 252
Morgan le Fay 39, 40, 43, 86, 135, 136, 140, 142, 143, 150, 175, 179 n. 33, 193, 194, 196, 198, 200
Morgause 46, 86, 135, 136, 142, 158, 165, 185, 191, 200, 252
Morris, Rosemary 55 n. 1
Morris, William 248, 249
Morse, Charlotte C. 208 n. 16
Morse, Ruth 189 n. 11
La Mort le Roi Artu 65, 76, 87, 91, 146, 147–8, 150 n. 19, 208, 221, 222, 228, 230
Le Morte Arthur (Stanzaic) 63, 65, 77, 87, 150 n. 19, 221, 222, 224 n. 4
Morte Arthure (Alliterative) 63, 65, 79, 81, 84, 92, 94, 106, 145–50
Muir, A. 89 n. 25
Mukai, Tsuyoshi 17 n. 39

Nabon 200
Nacien 216
Needham, Paul 12 n. 31
pseudo-Nennius, *Historia Brittonum* 58, 60–61
Nineve 39, 142–3
Nominale sive Verbale 109
Normandy 67

Oakeshott, Walter 3, 6
Of Arthoure and Merlin 63
Oldcastle, Sir John 67 n. 34
Olefsky, Ellyn 6 n. 12
Olsen, Birger Munk 207 n. 10
Orlando furioso 183 n. 1

Orlando inamorato 183 n. 1
Outlake 140

Padel, Oliver 57 n. 7
Painter, George D. 11 n. 25
Palomides 41, 46, 110, 138, 170, 185, 186, 187, 189, 190, 191–6, 200–201
Parins, Marilynn Jackson 17 n. 39, 241 n. 1
Parker, Patricia 39
Paston Letters 101
Patryse 15, 223
Patterson, Lee 65 n. 29
Pauphilet, Albert 207, 208
Pearl-poet 221
Pearsall, Derek 13 n. 34
Pedevere 180
Pellam (also Pelles) 139, 143
Pelleas 80, 83, 142
Pellinor 135, 137, 138, 141, 142, 144, 150, 198
Perceval 42, 51,138, 201, 203–6, 210, 214–15, 216, 218–20
Perceval's sister 42, 214, 217
Percy Folio manuscript (British Library MS Additional 27879) 244
Peredur 157 n. 3
Peristiany, J. G. 162 n. 12
Perlesvaus 76, 169, 171, 175–7
Peter the Hermit 24
Phelot 179
Philip, of Burgundy 25
Pickford, Cedric E. 12 n. 30
Pius II, Pope 25
Poitiers 29
Priamus 149, 150
prophecy 59, 133, 135, 138, 139, 140–41, 142–3, 144, 145, 149, 187, 193, 195–6
prose, English tradition of 105, 107; Middle English prose romances xiv–xv, 12–13, 27, 105
Putter, Ad 187 n. 7

La Queste del Saint Graal 14, 76, 81–2, 89, 103, 206–8, 209, 216, 217, 219, 220
Questing Beast 137, 138, 186, 191

Read, Herbert 252
recognition scenes 137, 158, 164–6, 168, 173–4, 181, 211, 217–18; *see also* identity
Red Knight of the Red Lands 160, 163
Renaut de Beaujeu *see Le Bel Inconnu*
Richmond, Colin 71
Riddy, Felicity 6, 40, 146 n. 17, 224 n. 5, 227
Rinaldo 183 n. 1
Robert de Boron, *Estoire du Graal* 206

Robert of Gloucester 57 n. 6
Robert, Brinley F. 61 n. 20
Robinson, E. Arlington 251
Roman War 11, 60, 62, 64–5, 68–9, 75–6, 83–4, 133, 136, 137, 145–51 passim
Rossetti, Dante Gabriel 248
Round Table 31, 34, 37, 44, 45, 135, 136, 141; fellowship of 14, 15, 23, 25, 31, 32, 34, 38, 52, 65, 136, 140, 142, 145, 151, 154, 166, 184, 185, 187, 188, 195, 200, 210, 219–20, 221, 222, 223, 230, 231, 233, 234, 236, 237
Royns 137–8

Sagramour 173–4
Saunders, Corinne 186 n. 5
Schroeder, P. 110 n. 30
Scott, Sir Walter, *Marmion* 247
Sedgwick, Eve Kosofsky 45
Segwarides (and wife) 190, 191, 197, 199
Shakespeare 78; *Hamlet* 71; *Henry IV* 244–5; *Henry V* 255; *King Lear* 64; *The Phoenix and the Turtle* 245
Sidney, Sir Philip, *Arcadia* 244
Siege Perilous 210
Sir Gawain and the Green Knight 134, 140, 142
Solomon 214
Sommer, H. O. 163, 164, 243
sorceress *see* magic
sources, Malory's use of xv, 4, 7, 32, 43, 44, 51, 63–6, 75–95 passim, 101, 103, 105, 106, 136, 141, 145–9, 154, 156–9, 161, 163–5, 166–7, 169, 170–78, 180, 183–5, 187, 193, 199, 216–20, 221, 222, 226, 228, 237
Southey, Robert 247–8, 250
Song of Roland 20
Spenser, Edmund *A View of the Present State of Ireland* 244; *Faerie Queene* 244
Stansby, William 242, 245, 247
Stanzaic *Le Morte Arthur see Le Morte Arthur* (Stanzaic)
Steinbeck, John 251–2
Stevens, John 48
Stirling 21
Suerto de Quinones 30
La Suite du Merlin 14, 44, 80, 86, 136
Sully, Maurice 99
supernatural *see* magic
Swinburne, Algernon Charles 248, 249

Tacitus 19
Takamiya, T. 4 n. 4, 11 n. 26
Tanner, Tony 47
Tarquin 46, 176, 177
Tatlock, J. S. P. 60 n.18, 133 n. 1

ARTHURIAN STUDIES

I   ASPECTS OF MALORY, *edited by Toshiyuki Takamiya and Derek Brewer*

II   THE ALLITERATIVE *MORTE ARTHURE*: A Reassessment of the Poem, *edited by Karl Heinz Göller*

III   THE ARTHURIAN BIBLIOGRAPHY, I: Author Listing, *edited by C. E. Pickford and R. W. Last*

IV   THE CHARACTER OF KING ARTHUR IN MEDIEVAL LITERATURE, *Rosemary Morris*

V   PERCEVAL: The Story of the Grail, by Chrétien de Troyes, *translated by Nigel Bryant*

VI   THE ARTHURIAN BIBLIOGRAPHY, II: Subject Index, *edited by C. E. Pickford and R. W. Last*

VII   THE LEGEND OF ARTHUR IN THE MIDDLE AGES, *edited by P. B. Grout, R. A. Lodge, C. E. Pickford and E. K. C. Varty*

VIII   THE ROMANCE OF YDER, *edited and translated by Alison Adams*

IX   THE RETURN OF KING ARTHUR, *Beverly Taylor and Elisabeth Brewer*

X   ARTHUR'S KINGDOM OF ADVENTURE: The World of Malory's *Morte Darthur, Muriel Whitaker*

XI   KNIGHTHOOD IN THE *MORTE DARTHUR, Beverly Kennedy*

XII   LE ROMAN DE TRISTAN EN PROSE, tome I, *edited by Renée L. Curtis*

XIII   LE ROMAN DE TRISTAN EN PROSE, tome II, *edited by Renée L. Curtis*

XIV   LE ROMAN DE TRISTAN EN PROSE, tome III, *edited by Renée L. Curtis*

XV   LOVE'S MASKS: Identity, Intertextuality, and Meaning in the Old French Tristan Poems, *Merritt R. Blakeslee*

XVI   THE CHANGING FACE OF ARTHURIAN ROMANCE: Essays on Arthurian Prose Romances in memory of Cedric E. Pickford, *edited by Alison Adams, Armel H. Diverres, Karen Stern and Kenneth Varty*

XVII   REWARDS AND PUNISHMENTS IN THE ARTHURIAN ROMANCES AND LYRIC POETRY OF MEDIEVAL FRANCE: Essays presented to Kenneth Varty on the occasion of his sixtieth birthday, *edited by Peter V. Davies and Angus J. Kennedy*

XVIII   CEI AND THE ARTHURIAN LEGEND, *Linda Gowans*

XIX   LA3AMON'S *BRUT*: The Poem and its Sources, *Françoise H. M. Le Saux*

XX   READING THE *MORTE DARTHUR, Terence McCarthy*, reprinted as AN INTRODUCTION TO MALORY

XXI   CAMELOT REGAINED: The Arthurian Revival and Tennyson, 1800–1849, *Roger Simpson*

XXII   THE LEGENDS OF KING ARTHUR IN ART, *Muriel Whitaker*

XXIII   GOTTFRIED VON STRASSBURG AND THE MEDIEVAL TRISTAN LEGEND: Papers from an Anglo-North American symposium, *edited with an introduction by Adrian Stevens and Roy Wisbey*

XXIV   ARTHURIAN POETS: CHARLES WILLIAMS, *edited and introduced by David Llewellyn Dodds*

XXV	AN INDEX OF THEMES AND MOTIFS IN TWELFTH-CENTURY FRENCH ARTHURIAN POETRY, *E. H. Ruck*
XXVI	CHRÉTIEN DE TROYES AND THE GERMAN MIDDLE AGES: Papers from an international symposium, *edited with an introduction by Martin H. Jones and Roy Wisbey*
XXVII	SIR GAWAIN AND THE GREEN KNIGHT: Sources and Analogues, *compiled by Elisabeth Brewer*
XXVIII	CLIGÉS by Chrétien de Troyes, *edited by Stewart Gregory and Claude Luttrell*
XXIX	THE LIFE AND TIMES OF SIR THOMAS MALORY, *P. J. C. Field*
XXX	T. H. WHITE'S *THE ONCE AND FUTURE KING*, *Elisabeth Brewer*
XXXI	ARTHURIAN BIBLIOGRAPHY, III: 1978–1992, Author Listing and Subject Index, *compiled by Caroline Palmer*
XXXII	ARTHURIAN POETS: JOHN MASEFIELD, *edited and introduced by David Llewellyn Dodds*
XXXIII	THE TEXT AND TRADITION OF LA3AMON'S *BRUT*, *edited by Françoise Le Saux*
XXXIV	CHIVALRY IN TWELFTH-CENTURY GERMANY: The Works of Hartmann von Aue, *W. H. Jackson*
XXXV	THE TWO VERSIONS OF MALORY'S *MORTE DARTHUR*: Multiple Negation and the Editing of the Text, *Ingrid Tieken-Boon van Ostade*
XXXVI	RECONSTRUCTING CAMELOT: French Romantic Medievalism and the Arthurian Tradition, *Michael Glencross*
XXXVII	A COMPANION TO MALORY, *edited by Elizabeth Archibald and A. S. G. Edwards*
XXXVIII	A COMPANION TO THE *GAWAIN*-POET, *edited by Derek Brewer and Jonathan Gibson*
XXXIX	MALORY'S BOOK OF ARMS: The Narrative of Combat in *Le Morte Darthur*, *Andrew Lynch*
XL	MALORY: TEXT AND SOURCES, *P.J.C. Field*
XLI	KING ARTHUR IN AMERICA, *Alan Lupack and Barbara Tepa Lupack*

Howell, of Britanny 148
Humphrey, Duke of Gloucester 68
Huth Merlin see Suite du Merlin

identity (motif of hidden identity) 135,
    157–8, 161, 164, 165, 168, 172, 173, 174,
    196–7, 211; *see also* disguise, recognition
    scenes
incest 136, 137, 139, 252
interlace 93, 136–8, 144, 150, 154, 185, 186
Ironside 81
Iseult (in Continental versions) 27, 28, 34,
    35, 162
Isolde (La Belle Isolde, wife of Mark, in
    Malory) 38, 40, 41, 43, 46, 47, 189–91,
    193, 199–201, 251
Isolde (le Blaunche Maynes, wife of
    Tristram, in Malory) 40, 43, 189, 190,
    200

Jacques de Lalaing 26
Jameson, Fredric 179 n. 33
Jeste of Sir Gawayne, The 81
John of Salisbury 55, 56 n. 3
Johnson, Lesley 65 n. 29, 146 n. 17
Jones, Gwyn 95 n. 36
Joseph of Arimathea 206, 213, 214
Juan II, of Castile 29

Kato, Tomomi 4 n. 3
Kay 158, 164, 167, 173, 181
Keats, John 248
Keegan, John 67
Keen, Maurice 19 n. 1, 25 n. 10, 56 n. 4
Keiser, George 13 n. 34
Kells, Book of 186
Kendrick, T. D. 133 n. 1, 150 n. 20
Kennedy, Beverly 227 n. 9
Kennedy, E. D. 91–2, 93, 106 n. 20,
    136 n. 9, 145 n. 14, 146 n. 17
Ker, Neil 8, 9
Keyhydyns 41, 46, 190, 191, 193
kin-groups, kinship 48, 54, 185, 189, 193,
    194, 214, 216, 229; *see also* family
Knight, Stephen 133 n. 3, 135 n. 7
knighthood 19–35 passim, 55–6, 93;
    Malory's view of 158, 170, 185, 189, 193,
    194, 195, 196; and church 23–5; *see also*
    chivalry

Lady of the Lake 50, 137, 140, 142
La Farge, Catherine 38, 48, 51, 52,
    104 n. 18
Lambert, Mark 52, 102, 219, 227, 228,
    230 n. 14, 231 n. 15, 232 n. 16, 233,
    237 n. 22
Lambeth Homilies 99

Lamorak 46, 138, 142, 185, 188, 189, 191,
    195, 196 n. 17, 198, 200–201
Lancaster, Henry, Duke of, *The Book of
    Holy Remedies* 28
Lancelot 15–16, 19, 28, 32, 34, 40, 41, 42,
    45, 48, 49, 51, 52, 53, 54, 63, 64, 65, 73,
    75, 77, 79, 83, 86, 87, 88, 93, 94, 95, 101,
    105, 111, 138, 139, 144–5, 146, 147–9,
    151, 153–6, 163, 166–9, 169–81 passim,
    184, 185, 187, 188, 189–98 passim, 200,
    207, 211, 215, 216–17, 220, 222–38
    passim, 251
Lancelot en prose (in the Vulgate Cycle)
    23, 51, 63, 76, 77, 83, 86, 87, 88, 92, 159,
    169, 170, 171, 172–3, 174, 175, 177, 185,
    193, 208, 226
Laneham, Robert 243
Langland, *Piers Plowman* 56
Lanier, Sidney 250
Launceor 187
Lavayne 15, 226
Layamon 94, 147
Leckie, R. William 57 n. 8
Lena, Pedro Lopez de 30 n. 16
Lewis, C. S. 86, 252
Libeaus Desconus 157 n. 3
Life, Page West 4 n. 4, 241 n. 1
Lionel 215–16
Le Livre de Lancelot du Lac 23
Loathly Damsel 204
Longinus 205
Loomis, Roger Sherman 133 n. 1, 227
Löseth, Eilert 184 n. 2
Lot 142, 144, 150, 158, 185, 198
love Malory's treatment of 32–4, 43–50,
    51–4, 91, 221, 235, 236–7; in *Tale of Sir
    Gareth* 159–68 passim; in *Tale of Sir
    Lancelot* 16, 32–3, 40, 46, 174–7, 181;
    in *Book of Sir Tristram* 41, 46, 47, 184,
    190–91, 193; in *Book of Sir Launcelot and
    Queen Guinevere* 33–4, 53, 105, 109, 221,
    224–5, 226–8; in the *Morte Arthur* 221,
    235–7; *see also* chivalry
loyalty 20, 27, 34, 166, 224, 233
Lucan 235
Lucius 145–51 passim, 187
Lumiansky, R. M. 5, 78 n. 12
Lydgate, John 97; *A Balade in Commenda-
    tion of Our Lady* 109
Lyle, Lady, of Avalon 39
Lynet 40, 158, 160–68 passim
Lyonesse 159–68 passim, 177

magic 27, 32, 38, 53, 80, 133, 136, 142–3,
    162, 163, 165, 178–9, 187, 196, 198, 217,
    228
Mahoney, Dhira 184 n. 4

Maimed King   204–5, 213, 220
Malory, Elizabeth (née Walsh)   115
Malory, John   115
Malory, Nicholas   117
Malory, Robert   115
Malory, Sir Thomas, biography   xiv, xv,
   115–130
   Le Morte Darthur:
   major divisions: *Tale of the Noble King
   Arthur* 8, 68, 80, 106, 134–45, 150, 171,
   187, 244; *Tale of King Arthur and the
   Emperor Lucius* 64–5, 83–4, 133, 145–51,
   171; *Tale of Sir Lancelot du Lake* 8, 32, 40,
   56, 76, 150, 153–4, 163, 169–80; *Tale of
   Sir Gareth* 30, 40, 76, 108, 150, 153–4,
   156–69, 174, 175, 176, 178, 180, 187; *Book
   of Sir Tristram* 46, 47, 76, 80, 92, 106, 138,
   150, 157 n. 3, 183–201, 247; *Tale of the
   Sankgreall* (Grail Quest) 8, 34–5, 42, 43,
   76, 81, 88,139, 141, 149, 150, 203–20, 247;
   Book of Sir Lancelot and Queen Guinevere
   8, 14, 33–4, 83, 87, 188, 221–9, 244; *Morte
   Arthur* 14, 111–12, 229–38
   individual sections: 'Arthur and
   Accolon' 14, 39, 135, 140; 'Balin' 14, 135,
   138–9, 249; 'La Cote Male Tayle' 157;
   'The Day of Destiny' 50; 'The Dolorous
   Death . . . of Sir Launcelot and Queeen
   Guinevere' 249; 'The Fair Maid of
   Astolat' 15–16, 50, 73, 83, 88, 224–5, 248;
   'Gawain, Ywain, and Marhalt' 14, 39,
   135, 142–4; 'The Great Tournament' 31,
   225; 'The Healing of Sir Urry' 32, 67, 83,
   87, 88, 136, 219–20, 228–9, 248; 'The
   Knight of the Cart' 16–17, 46, 49, 87–8,
   109–10, 225–8; 'The Knight with Two
   Swords' 39, 43, 135; 'Lancelot and
   Elaine' 52–4; 'Merlin' 135, 136–8; 'The
   Poisoned Apple' 45, 50, 88, 222–4; 'Sir
   Gareth of Orkney' 38; 'Torre and
   Pellinor' 14, 37, 44, 50, 135, 136; 'The
   Vengeance of Gawain' 249; 'The War of
   the Five Kings' 14, 135
   style of xv, 52, 83–4, 95, 97, 100–113
   passim, 135, 146, 167–8, 178, 179, 185,
   186, 197; unity of xii, 3–17 passim, 78,
   83, 84, 133 n. 3, 138, 144, 153–4, 187, 220;
   see also Caxton, edition of; Winchester
   manuscript
Mann, Jill   139, 186 n. 6, 196 n. 17,
   209 n. 17, 234–5
Mannyng, Robert   79
Margaret, of Anjou   68
Marhalt   187, 189, 199
Marie de France   159 n. 7, 165
Mark   27, 46, 47, 51, 63, 186, 187, 188, 189,
   190, 195, 198, 200–201

Marshal, William   26
Matarasso, Pauline   207 n. 10, 210 n. 19
Matto   191
McCarthy, Terence   14 n. 37, 48, 52,
   83 n. 18, 84 n. 19, 91 n. 28, 106–7,
   112 n. 31, 145 n. 15
Meale, Carol   12 n. 29, 13 n. 33, 133 n. 3,
   135 n. 7
Meleagant   16, 38, 46, 226
Melyas   212–13
Melyot   178
Ménard, Philippe   184 n. 2
Merlin   37, 38, 39, 44, 75, 85, 135, 137, 138,
   140, 141, 142, 143, 144, 187, 195–6, 248,
   251
Merlin   63, 101
Mont St Michel, giant of   60, 62, 69, 146,
   147–8, 189
Moorman, Charles   207 n. 8
Mordrains   214
Mordred   26, 49, 60, 62, 72, 83, 135, 136,
   137, 138, 139, 140, 142, 144, 146, 147,
   150, 185, 189, 195, 198, 225, 228, 229,
   230, 231, 235, 252
Morgan le Fay   39, 40, 43, 86, 135, 136,
   140, 142, 143, 150, 175, 179 n. 33, 193,
   194, 196, 198, 200
Morgause   46, 86, 135, 136, 142, 158, 165,
   185, 191, 200, 252
Morris, Rosemary   55 n. 1
Morris, William   248, 249
Morse, Charlotte C.   208 n. 16
Morse, Ruth   189 n. 11
La Mort le Roi Artu   65, 76, 87, 91, 146,
   147–8, 150 n. 19, 208, 221, 222, 228, 230
Le Morte Arthur (Stanzaic)   63, 65, 77, 87,
   150 n. 19, 221, 222, 224 n. 4
Morte Arthure (Alliterative)   63, 65, 79, 81,
   84, 92, 94, 106, 145–50
Muir, A.   89 n. 25
Mukai, Tsuyoshi   17 n. 39

Nabon   200
Nacien   216
Needham, Paul   12 n. 31
pseudo-Nennius, *Historia Brittonum*   58,
   60–61
Nineve   39, 142–3
Nominale sive Verbale   109
Normandy   67

Oakeshott, Walter   3, 6
Of Arthoure and Merlin   63
Oldcastle, Sir John   67 n. 34
Olefsky, Ellyn   6 n. 12
Olsen, Birger Munk   207 n. 10
Orlando furioso   183 n. 1

Orlando inamorato 183 n. 1
Outlake 140

Padel, Oliver 57 n. 7
Painter, George D. 11 n. 25
Palomides 41, 46, 110, 138, 170, 185, 186, 187, 189, 190, 191–6, 200–201
Parins, Marilynn Jackson 17 n. 39, 241 n. 1
Parker, Patricia 39
Paston Letters 101
Patryse 15, 223
Patterson, Lee 65 n. 29
Pauphilet, Albert 207, 208
Pearl-poet 221
Pearsall, Derek 13 n. 34
Pedevere 180
Pellam (also Pelles) 139, 143
Pelleas 80, 83, 142
Pellinor 135, 137, 138, 141, 142, 144, 150, 198
Perceval 42, 51,138, 201, 203–6, 210, 214–15, 216, 218–20
Perceval's sister 42, 214, 217
Percy Folio manuscript (British Library MS Additional 27879) 244
Peredur 157 n. 3
Peristiany, J. G. 162 n. 12
Perlesvaus 76, 169, 171, 175–7
Peter the Hermit 24
Phelot 179
Philip, of Burgundy 25
Pickford, Cedric E. 12 n. 30
Pius II, Pope 25
Poitiers 29
Priamus 149, 150
prophecy 59, 133, 135, 138, 139, 140–41, 142–3, 144, 145, 149, 187, 193, 195–6
prose, English tradition of 105, 107; Middle English prose romances xiv–xv, 12–13, 27, 105
Putter, Ad 187 n. 7

La Queste del Saint Graal 14, 76, 81–2, 89, 103, 206–8, 209, 216, 217, 219, 220
Questing Beast 137, 138, 186, 191

Read, Herbert 252
recognition scenes 137, 158, 164–6, 168, 173–4, 181, 211, 217–18; *see also* identity
Red Knight of the Red Lands 160, 163
Renaut de Beaujeu *see Le Bel Inconnu*
Richmond, Colin 71
Riddy, Felicity 6, 40, 146 n. 17, 224 n. 5, 227
Rinaldo 183 n. 1
Robert de Boron, *Estoire du Graal* 206

Robert of Gloucester 57 n. 6
Robert, Brinley F. 61 n. 20
Robinson, E. Arlington 251
Roman War 11, 60, 62, 64–5, 68–9, 75–6, 83–4, 133, 136, 137, 145–51 passim
Rossetti, Dante Gabriel 248
Round Table 31, 34, 37, 44, 45, 135, 136, 141; fellowship of 14, 15, 23, 25, 31, 32, 34, 38, 52, 65, 136, 140, 142, 145, 151, 154, 166, 184, 185, 187, 188, 195, 200, 210, 219–20, 221, 222, 223, 230, 231, 233, 234, 236, 237
Royns 137–8

Sagramour 173–4
Saunders, Corinne 186 n. 5
Schroeder, P. 110 n. 30
Scott, Sir Walter, *Marmion* 247
Sedgwick, Eve Kosofsky 45
Segwarides (and wife) 190, 191, 197, 199
Shakespeare 78; *Hamlet* 71; *Henry IV* 244–5; *Henry V* 255; *King Lear* 64; *The Phoenix and the Turtle* 245
Sidney, Sir Philip, *Arcadia* 244
Siege Perilous 210
Sir Gawain and the Green Knight 134, 140, 142
Solomon 214
Sommer, H. O. 163, 164, 243
sorceress *see* magic
sources, Malory's use of xv, 4, 7, 32, 43, 44, 51, 63–6, 75–95 passim, 101, 103, 105, 106, 136, 141, 145–9, 154, 156–9, 161, 163–5, 166–7, 169, 170–78, 180, 183–5, 187, 193, 199, 216–20, 221, 222, 226, 228, 237
Southey, Robert 247–8, 250
Song of Roland 20
Spenser, Edmund *A View of the Present State of Ireland* 244; *Faerie Queene* 244
Stansby, William 242, 245, 247
Stanzaic *Le Morte Arthur* *see Le Morte Arthur* (Stanzaic)
Steinbeck, John 251–2
Stevens, John 48
Stirling 21
Suerto de Quinones 30
La Suite du Merlin 14, 44, 80, 86, 136
Sully, Maurice 99
supernatural *see* magic
Swinburne, Algernon Charles 248, 249

Tacitus 19
Takamiya, T. 4 n. 4, 11 n. 26
Tanner, Tony 47
Tarquin 46, 176, 177
Tatlock, J. S. P. 60 n.18, 133 n. 1

Tennyson, Alfred Lord   249
Torre   141–2, 143
tournaments   25–6, 29–32, 33, 150, 162–3,
   165–6, 168, 190, 191, 198, 199–201, 224
treachery, treason   20, 27, 178–80, 184,
   188, 196, 230
Tristan (in Continental versions)   27, 28,
   34, 35, 162, 170, 183, 193
Tristan (Béroul)   159 n. 7
Tristan (French Prose)   63, 76, 86, 92, 157
   n. 3, 183, 185, 193, 194 n. 15
Tristram (in Malory)   38, 40, 41, 42, 43, 46,
   47, 63, 83, 144–5, 183–201, 251
Troy   12
Tucker, P. E.   51, 52
Twain, Mark   251

Ullman, Walter   69 n. 39
Urban II, Pope   24
Uriens   140
Urry   17, 149, 188, 219–20, 228–9
Uther   44, 63, 134

Vale, Juliet   29 n. 15
Valentine, Lucia   8 n. 17
Vayssière, A.   30 n. 17
Vinaver, Eugène   3–17 passim, 34, 37,
   68–9, 75, 85, 87–8, 89, 101 n. 8, 103,
   135 n. 7, 145, 153, 166, 169, 183,
   194 n. 15, 198–201, 221, 243
Vulgate Cycle   63, 76, 95, 136, 154, 155,
   156, 159, 163, 171–5, 185, 188, 208; *see
   also Estoire del Saint Graal; Estoire de
   Merlin*; (*Le Livre de*) *Lancelot* (*du Lac*);
   La Mort le Roi Artu

Wace   147
Waldron, Peter   227 n. 9
Wars of the Roses   xiv, 55, 72, 198
Warton, Thomas   244; *Observations on the
   Faerie Queene* 247
Warwick, Duke of   117
White, T. H.   252
Wigalois   157 n. 3
William I   22
Williams, Charles   252
Wilson, R. H.   77 n. 9, 93 n. 32, 156,
   157 n. 4, 170 n. 16, 179 n. 33, 221 n. 1
Winchester Manuscript (British Library
   MS Additional 59678)   3–17 passim,
   134 n. 4, 154, 166, 199–201, 242
Withrington, John   11 n. 27, 146 n. 16
Wolfram von Eschenbach, *Parzival*   25,
   28–9
Woodville, Anthony, Lord Scales   31
Worcestre, William   71 n. 43
Worde, Wynkyn de   241, 242, 243
Wordsworth, William   248
'worship'   135, 140, 142, 148–9, 154,
   155, 157, 159, 164, 171, 174, 181, 217,
   220, 224, 226, 231–3, 234; *see also*
   honour
Wulfstan   99

Ygrayne   63, 134
Yonge, Charlotte   250
York, Duke of   116, 117
Ywain   140, 173

Zarnecki, George   42 n. 9

ARTHURIAN STUDIES

I   ASPECTS OF MALORY, *edited by Toshiyuki Takamiya and Derek Brewer*

II   THE ALLITERATIVE *MORTE ARTHURE*: A Reassessment of the
           Poem, *edited by Karl Heinz Göller*

III   THE ARTHURIAN BIBLIOGRAPHY, I: Author Listing, *edited by*
           C. E. Pickford and R. W. Last

IV   THE CHARACTER OF KING ARTHUR IN MEDIEVAL
           LITERATURE, *Rosemary Morris*

V   PERCEVAL: The Story of the Grail, by Chrétien de Troyes, *translated*
           by Nigel Bryant

VI   THE ARTHURIAN BIBLIOGRAPHY, II: Subject Index, *edited by*
           C. E. Pickford and R. W. Last

VII   THE LEGEND OF ARTHUR IN THE MIDDLE AGES, *edited by*
           P. B. Grout, R. A. Lodge, C. E. Pickford and E. K. C. Varty

VIII   THE ROMANCE OF YDER, *edited and translated by Alison Adams*

IX   THE RETURN OF KING ARTHUR, *Beverly Taylor and Elisabeth Brewer*

X   ARTHUR'S KINGDOM OF ADVENTURE: The World of Malory's
           Morte Darthur, Muriel Whitaker

XI   KNIGHTHOOD IN THE *MORTE DARTHUR, Beverly Kennedy*

XII   LE ROMAN DE TRISTAN EN PROSE, tome I, *edited by Renée*
           L. Curtis

XIII   LE ROMAN DE TRISTAN EN PROSE, tome II, *edited by Renée*
           L. Curtis

XIV   LE ROMAN DE TRISTAN EN PROSE, tome III, *edited by Renée*
           L. Curtis

XV   LOVE'S MASKS: Identity, Intertextuality, and Meaning in the Old
           French Tristan Poems, *Merritt R. Blakeslee*

XVI   THE CHANGING FACE OF ARTHURIAN ROMANCE: Essays on
           Arthurian Prose Romances in memory of Cedric E. Pickford, *edited*
           by Alison Adams, Armel H. Diverres, Karen Stern and Kenneth Varty

XVII   REWARDS AND PUNISHMENTS IN THE ARTHURIAN
           ROMANCES AND LYRIC POETRY OF MEDIEVAL FRANCE:
           Essays presented to Kenneth Varty on the occasion of his sixtieth
           birthday, *edited by Peter V. Davies and Angus J. Kennedy*

XVIII   CEI AND THE ARTHURIAN LEGEND, *Linda Gowans*

XIX   LA3AMON'S *BRUT*: The Poem and its Sources, *Françoise H. M.*
           Le Saux

XX   READING THE *MORTE DARTHUR, Terence McCarthy*, reprinted as
           AN INTRODUCTION TO MALORY

XXI   CAMELOT REGAINED: The Arthurian Revival and Tennyson,
           1800–1849, *Roger Simpson*

XXII   THE LEGENDS OF KING ARTHUR IN ART, *Muriel Whitaker*

XXIII   GOTTFRIED VON STRASSBURG AND THE MEDIEVAL TRISTAN
           LEGEND: Papers from an Anglo-North American symposium, *edited*
           with an introduction by Adrian Stevens and Roy Wisbey

XXIV   ARTHURIAN POETS: CHARLES WILLIAMS, *edited and introduced*
           by David Llewellyn Dodds

XXV	AN INDEX OF THEMES AND MOTIFS IN TWELFTH-CENTURY FRENCH ARTHURIAN POETRY, *E. H. Ruck*
XXVI	CHRÉTIEN DE TROYES AND THE GERMAN MIDDLE AGES: Papers from an international symposium, *edited with an introduction by Martin H. Jones and Roy Wisbey*
XXVII	SIR GAWAIN AND THE GREEN KNIGHT: Sources and Analogues, *compiled by Elisabeth Brewer*
XXVIII	CLIGÉS by Chrétien de Troyes, *edited by Stewart Gregory and Claude Luttrell*
XXIX	THE LIFE AND TIMES OF SIR THOMAS MALORY, *P. J. C. Field*
XXX	T. H. WHITE'S *THE ONCE AND FUTURE KING*, *Elisabeth Brewer*
XXXI	ARTHURIAN BIBLIOGRAPHY, III: 1978–1992, Author Listing and Subject Index, *compiled by Caroline Palmer*
XXXII	ARTHURIAN POETS: JOHN MASEFIELD, *edited and introduced by David Llewellyn Dodds*
XXXIII	THE TEXT AND TRADITION OF LA3AMON'S *BRUT*, *edited by Françoise Le Saux*
XXXIV	CHIVALRY IN TWELFTH-CENTURY GERMANY: The Works of Hartmann von Aue, *W. H. Jackson*
XXXV	THE TWO VERSIONS OF MALORY'S *MORTE DARTHUR*: Multiple Negation and the Editing of the Text, *Ingrid Tieken-Boon van Ostade*
XXXVI	RECONSTRUCTING CAMELOT: French Romantic Medievalism and the Arthurian Tradition, *Michael Glencross*
XXXVII	A COMPANION TO MALORY, *edited by Elizabeth Archibald and A. S. G. Edwards*
XXXVIII	A COMPANION TO THE *GAWAIN*-POET, *edited by Derek Brewer and Jonathan Gibson*
XXXIX	MALORY'S BOOK OF ARMS: The Narrative of Combat in *Le Morte Darthur*, *Andrew Lynch*
XL	MALORY: TEXT AND SOURCES, *P.J.C. Field*
XLI	KING ARTHUR IN AMERICA, *Alan Lupack and Barbara Tepa Lupack*